Roving Bill Aspinwall

Edited by Owen Clayton

Roving Bill Aspinwall

DISPATCHES FROM A HOBO IN POST-CIVIL WAR AMERICA.

Table of Contents

Editor's Note

"I write Under difficulties, You will please excuse
mistakes and Punctuation"

—William Aspinwall

"Some of these things [Roving Bill's letters] would richly
pay for transcription if there were space. Some ... would
not bear transcription"

—John James McCook

These letters have been selected from the hundreds of pages that William
Aspinwall wrote to John James McCook. Roving Bill wrote his correspondence on whatever he could find: postcards, hotel notepaper, and writing
pads that McCook posted out to him. The original letters, which are held
by the organization Connecticut Landmarks (formerly the Antiquarian &
Landmarks Society), give a sense of someone writing on the move, using
whatever materials he had to hand.

A small number of the letters, mostly those that are very short and
contain little of interest for the general reader, have been left out. If you do
wish to read Aspinwall's complete correspondence, please see the online-
only 'Scholarly Edition.' As well as collecting all of his letters, the online
version has also maintained Aspinwall's original grammar, which in this
version has been amended to aid readability.

I decided to keep Aspinwall's erratic original spellings for this book.
My decision will undoubtedly make the book harder for you to read, but I
thought it was important to balance readability with maintaining as much of

Roving Bill's voice as possible. As will be apparent, he does not always spell the same word in the same way. This means that some readerly indulgence, and some decoding, will be required as you make your way through this book. I have added clarifications and corrections in square brackets throughout. Apart from a few exceptions (such as 'off' being repeatedly spelled 'of'), I have tended to add these brackets for the first instance of a misspelled word only. I have also combined compound words for ease of reading. Aspinwall uses capitalization irregularly, often capitalizing words within but not at the start of sentences. I have capitalized words when adding in full stops but have not removed Aspinwall's eccentric capitalizations.

Sometimes Roving Bill used dashes as pauses, which I have translated into full stops for ease of reading. His use of dashes is inconsistent, however, so not every dash has become a full stop. Ultimately this is a matter of editorial judgement, and I take full responsibility for any inadvertent changes of meaning. Aspinwall uses full stops and commas irregularly, so I have added periods and other punctuation marks, including apostrophes, to aid comprehension. In addition, his paragraphs are difficult to identify because the letters often spill out as one continuous piece of prose. I have put paragraph breaks where he seems to indicate them, even where those breaks are in unusual places. I have generally kept his paragraphing the same, except for adding paragraphs in when he is reporting dialogue. I have not amended his poetry at all, even though no one is going to think that they are great art. Where Aspinwall himself has crossed out words, this has been indicated by a strikethrough. All of the italicizations are my additions.

The majority of Aspinwall's handwriting is abysmal. I must emphasize what a great job the transcriber, Jenny Adamthwaite, has done with extremely challenging material. In some cases she and I have had to make best guesses where words were unclear or where the letters are torn.[1] Inevitably this brings the possibility of small errors, though I am confident that Aspinwall's meaning has been maintained. Occasionally I have relied on McCook's "Leaves From the Diary of a Tramp" for words that are missing in the letters today but which presumably were not when he used them to write up his article series. On rare occasions where sentences were incomplete due to several words being illegible or torn in the original letter, I have either left them out or edited them down. For the complete transcription please refer, once again, to the online 'Scholarly Edition.'

---

1   I have indicated where these guesses appear in the online Scholarly Edition of this book.

Tracking Roving Bill's movements was a pleasure but also a challenge. He admits to getting dates wrong in some of his letters, and so a bit of historical reconstruction was necessary to draw a clear chronology. It is possible that I have on rare occasions made mistakes in reconstructing his location. If so, these mistakes are entirely my responsibility.

Finally, a brief warning. Roving Bill was a man who shared several of the prejudices of his day (and, sadly, of ours). He makes occasional anti-immigrant comments, which is ironic given that his father was one (a clear case of 'last off the boat syndrome'). Worse still, he makes more than one reference to money 'Shylocks,' a phrase meaning East Coast capitalists but having, at the very least, anti-Semitic connotations. While we might forgive his grammar and spelling, such remarks are harder to excuse. There is also homophobia in a number of the letters, a prejudice that both Aspinwall and McCook shared (assuming that Aspinwall was being honest about it, that is[2]). Finally, while his remarks about African-Americans are generally (and thankfully) more enlightened than many of his more well-heeled white contemporaries, he does use outdated racial terminology at times. I felt that it was important not to censor any of this material, uncomfortable though it may be.

---

2   I say this because many hobos had homosexual relationships on the road. Roving Bill mentions different road partners throughout. He never gives a hint of anything sexual occurring between himself and a male road partner, but then it is unlikely he would have admitted it if it had.

Introduction

"I think my Experience in this World is Just Worth as much as Gen. Grant's, Mark Twain's or any other Celebrated Writer I know well that not one of them Can give the Same Kind of Experiance that I Can"

—William "Roving Bill" Aspinwall

Ladies' man. Child soldier. War hero. Egotist. Tramp. Drunkard. Published author. Each of these descriptions captures some part of William Aspinwall's life, and yet none does him justice. Married five times, wounded fighting for the Union in one of the bloodiest battles of the American Civil War, wandering for decades as a penniless and itinerant vagabond, kicked out of numerous jobs and retirement homes for drunkenness, Aspinwall also kept up a twenty-four-year correspondence with Professor John James McCook, and in so doing provided the earliest, fullest and most direct account of life on the road ever written by a hobo.[1] William "Roving Bill" Aspinwall was a complex man who lived an extremely varied life.

---

[1] By 'earliest,' I mean the earliest extant account written by a hobo who was on the road on the time of writing. There are fictional accounts written slightly earlier, while the first of hobo-turned-spy-turned-proto-sociologist Josiah Flynt's articles was also published in 1893. However, Flynt had given up his hobo life (which had only lasted eight months) by this time and was studying for a Ph.D. in Germany. See Josiah Flynt, *Tramping With Tramps: Studies and Sketches of Vagabond Life* (New York: The Century Company, 1899).

He is also a man whose story has, until now, been told by others. When historians have talked about Roving Bill (which isn't often), they have done so by relying on a series of magazine articles that were written about him, called "Leaves From the Diary of a Tramp," which was published between November 1901 and June 1902 by Professor John James McCook.[2] Although they feature heavily in that series, Aspinwall's own letters, which he wrote to McCook between 1893 and 1917, have never been published or even examined directly by anyone. That situation changes with this book, *Roving Bill Aspinwall: Dispatches from a Hobo in Post-Civil War America*, which provides Bill's account of his full life directly for the first time.

This Introduction will outline the contours of Aspinwall's life, as far as we know them, and will then describe his literary encounter with McCook, the article series that McCook wrote about him, and finally say something about the letters themselves. The biography that follows is taken from Roving Bill's letters, as well as from information provided by James Morgans, Aspinwall's great-grandson, for which I am most grateful.[3]

The Life of "Roving Bill"

William Wesley Aspinwall was born on the 25th of May 1845 in Mechanicsburg, Ohio, the son of Dyson Aspinwall (1804–1883) and Sarah Ann Haines (1824–1885). His family was big. He had five half-brothers and two half-sisters from his father's first marriage, along with six full brothers and eight full sisters, making twenty-one siblings in total.[4] Of course, large families were more typical at this time period than they are today, partly because of a lack of birth control and partly because infant mortality was so frequent. Indeed, it seems that at least five of William's full siblings died before they were one year old.

---

2   See Ralph Borgardus, "Reality captured, reality tamed: John James McCook and the uses of documentary photography in Fin-de-Siècle America" in *History of Photography* 10:2 (April-June 1986), pp. 151–167; Tim Cresswell, *The Tramp in America* (London: Reaktion Books, 2001), pp. 181–195; Todd DePastino, *Citizen Hobo: How a Century of Homelessness Shaped America* (Chicago; London, The University of Chicago Press, 2003), pp. 49–58.

3   James and his family have been intrigued by their disreputable ancestor for many years. Although they have not previously read his letters, they have conducted impressive family history research that was utterly invaluable to me. My sincere thanks to all of them.

4   Some members of the family kept Dyson's original surname of Aspinall, for reasons that are unclear.

Dyson Aspinall (note the lack of a 'w') had been born in Huddersfield, England in 1804, before moving to the United States with his family in 1826. He went back to England at some point and was married in 1832 to Francis Wade before returning to New York, this time permanently, in 1841, and changing his name to Aspinwall. Dyson married his second wife Sarah Ann Haines, the Ohio native who would become William's mother, in 1843 in Xenia, Ohio. The 1850 census gives Dyson's profession as the rather general 'manufacturer,' while the 1860 census gives the more specific 'Woolen manufacturer.'[5] In 1850 the family were living in Newberry, Ohio, and by 1860 they had moved to St. Mary's Township, Indiana, which only twenty-eight years earlier had seen the forced removal of its native population. St. Mary's was the site of a woolen mill, which is probably where William first tried his hand at this trade.[6] The adult Aspinwall was, according to an 1884–1885 entry record for the Central Branch of the U.S. National Homes for Disabled Volunteer Soldiers, 5 ft 8 inches tall, with grey eyes, brown hair and a sandy complexion.

On 13th Dec 1861, at the age of sixteen, William signed up to fight for the Union army in the American Civil War, enlisting as an infantry private in Company H, Indiana 47th Infantry Regiment at Bluffton, Indiana. He saw a great deal of action. The 47th Infantry was involved in conflicts at Bardstown, Kentucky, New Madrid and Riddle's Landing, Missouri, and, in Mississippi, at Brown's Plantation, Port Gibson, Champion Hill, Vicksburg, and Jackson. Most significant of all of these for the young William was the Battle of Champion Hill (also known as Baker's Creek), which took place on the 16th of May 1863, just nine days before his eighteenth birthday. Champion Hill was, according to Timothy Smith, the decisive battle of General Ulysses S. Grant's successful Vicksburg campaign.[7] The 47th Indiana saw intense fighting at Champion Hill, charging up the eponymous hill on which the Confederate rebels were situated, facing a brutal counterattack, and then counterattacking themselves. Alvin P. Hovey 12th Division, of which the 47th Indiana was a part, suffered 198 deaths[8] out of a total of approximately 791 people killed on both sides

---

5   This is also the occupation given in the 1870 census. By the 1880 census, when Dyson was seventy-six, his occupation is listed as 'Work In Stave Factory,' suggesting a decline in his financial situation. There was no retirement pension during this time period so working until old age was, unfortunately, common.

6   In the 1860 census, when he was fifteen, William's profession is given simply as 'factory.'

7   See Timothy Smith, *Champion Hill: Decisive Battle for Vicksburg* (Savas Beatie, 2006).

8   Hovey himself claimed the number was 211 killed.

during the battle. This was in addition to almost 5,500 Confederate and Union soldiers who were wounded, one of whom was infantryman Aspinwall. During the rebel counterattack, Bill "Got three Buck shots in Right Shoulder an[d] Struck in Head with minie [Minié] Ball," which knocked him unconscious.[9] His unit having temporarily retreated, the seventeen-year-old private awoke to find himself inside enemy lines, apparently a prisoner of war. During this short time he claims to have been close enough to witness the commanding Confederate General, John C. Pemberton, observing the Union army through field glasses. As the rebels began to give way to the Union's own counterattack, he took the opportunity to slink back to the safety of his own lines, and from there to a field hospital for treatment. He re-enlisted upon his recovery, although in a deeper sense he never truly recovered.

It seems that Aspinwall suffered from what today would be called PTSD as a result of his traumatic experience at Champion Hill, and that this contributed to him becoming an alcoholic and a wanderer in later life. Sadly, McCook's account of Roving Bill's life in "Leaves" fails to acknowledge the trauma suffered by his former comrade-in-arms.[10] More insidious still, Aspinwall points out that when Union army recruiters were searching for volunteers, "they did not Ask them if they Ever Was drunk or Ever drank any Spiritous or Malt liquors. if a Man was only parcially Sound in body no questions asked About the State of a mans Mind or his Habits he was Eligible." Indeed, not only were drinking habits *not* discouraged during the war, Aspinwall writes that they were positively encouraged: "in many instances during the War intemperance Was Encouraged by the Officers And Whiskey issued to the Troops from the Commissary or liquors that Were Captured." This was a common experience for soldiers on both sides. "Drunkenness and alcoholic intoxication suffused every aspect of the military conflict," according to Scott Martin, who argues that "The extent of liquor's influence on military disorder can hardly be exaggerated."[11] Alcohol

---

9   A Minié ball was a hollow bullet invented by Claude-Étienne Minié and used extensively during the American Civil War. While the round bullets that were common in earlier wars tended to dodge around muscles and tendons, Minié balls would go straight through, shattering bones and causing greater damage. Amputations were a frequent result of Minié ball wounds.

10   McCook inquired from acquaintances of Aspinwall whether he had ever shown signs of 'brain disturbance,' to which he was answered 'by an emphatic negative.'

11   Scott C. Martin, "'A Soldier Intoxicated is Far Worse than No Soldier at All': Intoxication and the American Civil War" in *The Social History of Alcohol and Drugs* 25:1–2 (2011), pp. 66–87 (p. 67 & p. 75).

provided a temporary reprieve for the terror and trauma of warfare but at a significant personal cost. Indeed, one year into the war, military doctors added a new disease to their records: chronic alcoholism.[12] Martin asks a question that is pertinent for thinking about Roving Bill: "If Liquor unfitted men for the army, what effects would it have on their ability to function as husbands, fathers, and citizens?"[13] A profound effect, as it turned out. Having given him a deadly combination of trauma and alcoholism, the army left Aspinwall in a poor state to cope with the economic fluctuations of postwar America. Union General Ulysses S. Grant, whose march on Vicksburg Aspinwall had participated in, was also famously an alcoholic. But Grant's rank, status and fame allowed his postwar career to reach the heights of the presidency, while the similarly afflicted Aspinwall had no such advantages. For him would follow years of trying, and often failing, to adjust to civilian life. His experiences foreshadow the better-known stories of veterans from later conflicts such as Vietnam and the Gulf Wars.

Aspinwall mustered out on 23rd Oct 1865. After the war, he traveled across the United States, including a brief and unsuccessful stint as a gold prospector in Leadville, Colorado. According to his letters, he journeyed to Australia, where he stayed for three months. Then he settled into his father's trade, becoming a woolen manufacturer in Ohio.[14] He seems to have become quite successful, since the 1880 Federal Census lists him as 'Proprietor Woolen Factory.' In addition to this he also received a small military pension, which he applied for in 1875, although it seems to have been cut off for a period of time.[15] Despite these apparent safety nets, however, Bill's life collapsed around him, partly due to the economy and partly due to the self-destructive behavior that he exhibited as a result, in all likelihood, of his unresolved trauma.

Something of a charmer and certainly a philanderer, Bill was married five times, although it seems that not all of these marriages were officially registered. He had eight children, which by the standards of his own upbring-ing was quite restrained. His first marriage, to Rebecca Moorman in 1866,

---

12   Martin, p. 83.

13   Martin, p. 84.

14   1870 Federal Census.

15   This detail comes from a letter from Governor Justin H. Chapman of the Marion Soldiers' Home to McCook, dated 29th January 1898. This letter is in the Landmarks Collection. Aspinwall claims that his pension has been cut off in his letter dated 29th June 1896. It seems to have been later reinstated, possibly after legal action.

lasted less than two years, ending in separation. His second marriage took place in 1868 to Amanda J. Dickinson, a relationship that seems to have lasted until 1880–81, at which point Bill met and married (or, possibly, 'married') the twenty-one-year-old Sarah Jane Bond, a woman fourteen years his junior. He moved to Gravois Mills, Morgan Co., Missouri and in all likelihood worked at the woolen mill there, as Sarah Jane had before they met. Along the way he seems to have picked up some German and Dutch, presumably as a result of working in factories with immigrants from those countries. According to a family legend passed down by Sarah Jane and William's daughter, Georgia Lee Aspinwall, Bill's drunkenness grew out of control during this relationship and in 1883, when Georgia Lee was only two years old, Sarah Jane's father, Pressley Bond, told Bill: "Listen to me. Sarah Jane is scared of you when you're drunk, and she don't like you when you're not. So you need to move on from here, and you'd best not ever come back. Ever."[16] Bill left and never saw his wife or daughter again. Ashamed, he wrote to Sarah Jane not long after:

Mrs. S. J. Aspinwall Gravois Mills, Mo.

Dear Wife

I did think I never would write to you again but I cant get you and Georgia out of my mind. I would just give this whole world if I had it to just get to see you and Georgia a few minutes.

Somehow or other I can't believe you will forget me as we have loved so well and used to enjoy ourselves so well together. I don't think true love is so soon forgotten, if ever it is. I know I can't get you out of my mind and I don't believe you have forgotten me. I love you and I can't help it.

I know I done and said a great many things I should not done and said. But you must know I was in great trouble when I was with you. I thought your folks was doing all they could against me and I thought they was trying to get you turned against me. And another thing, I was not able to live the way I wanted to live and that was a great trouble on my mind. All these things went to make me mean and peevish. I can see where I done wrong in a great many places and I hope and pray you will forgive me. Although I don't expect to ever see you again, it would do my very soul good to know that all I done wrong has been forgotten by you and called things of the past by you.

---

16   My thanks to James Morgans, William Aspinwall's great-grandson, for providing this family story and the accompanying letter.

Sarah Jane, I am now trying to live a Christian life. I intend from this on to live [as] a God-fearing man. God helping me, I hope you will pray to God for me that I may hold out faithful.

I found a Methodist church here in Joplin about six weeks ago and I must say it is the happiest six weeks I ever spent in my life. Oh! I realize it is good to lead a Christian life. How much better I feel than I used to. I think my dear old mother's prayers have been answered. They have been holding a glorious revival here and it is going on yet. There have been about four hundred souls that have confessed Christ. The meeting has been going on two months. I hope you are trying to live a Christian [life]. I pray for you often. I do hope that if I never meet you and Georgia on earth any more, I hope we will all die so unspeakable happy [that] we will meet in heaven where parting will be no more.

May God bless you and keep you from all harm.

I am going away from here tomorrow, Monday, to Warrensburg, Mo to take charge of the woolen mills there. I have been working here in the woolen mills and at Springfield but I get better pay at Warrensburg.

I will close by biding you goodby and hope this will find you and Georgia well. I hope you will write to me and tell me how you are getting along.

I am your loving husband

William W. Aspinwall

address Warrensburg

Johnson county

Missouri

May 20 1883

Despite these protestations that he would turn his life around, Bill continued to struggle. By May 1884, rather than working in a woolen mill as he had stated, he had checked himself into a Disabled Veterans' Home at Dayton, Ohio.[17] Though no doubt exacerbated by his drink problems, one of the main factors in being unable to find or maintain work was that the U.S. was in the middle of a three-year recession which, following the 'Panic of 1884,' became a full-scale depression. This was, then, a bad time to strike

---

17   The National Home for Disabled Volunteer Soldiers was a network of home facilities in which disabled former veterans of the Civil War could stay. It was possible to enter and leave the homes at will, a fact of which Aspinwall took advantage. The homes that were run with military trappings, including inspections, drills and a quasi-court marshal system that punished offenses, such as staying away from the home for too long without a pass. Serious and repeat offenses were punished with dishonorable discharge from the home.

out to find new work, which makes Aspinwall's decision to go to the home understandable. He stayed at the home for a number of months before being dishonorably discharged, seemingly for drunkenness. This began a series of stays in a variety of Disabled Soldiers' Homes, stays that often ended the same way and which were interspersed with long stretches of what today we would call homelessness, but which in the nineteenth century was called, variously, 'tramping,' being 'on the bum,' or, in a term that had begun to be used in the 1880s, being a 'hobo.'

During these periods on the road, Bill would wander the country, taking on temporary employment and seeking to do odd jobs for people in the towns and villages through which he passed. Most commonly he offered to fix umbrellas (a job known as 'mush faking,' allegedly because of the resemblance between an upturned umbrella and a mushroom) or, using the skills learned during his work in various factories, repairing sewing machines.[18] Such jobs were often given out of a sense of pity and to avoid accusations of begging, but Bill rightly took pride in his practical abilities. Indeed, according to British journalist Adolphe Smith's 1877 description, mush-faking was a skilled profession:

> The real 'mush-fakers' are men who not only sell, but can mend and make umbrellas. Wandering from street to street, with a bundle of old umbrellas and a few necessary tools under their arm, they inquire for umbrellas to mend from house to house. When their services are accepted, they have two objects in view. First, having obtained an umbrella to mend, they prefer sitting out doing the work in the street, in front of the house. This attracts the attention of the neighbors, and the fact that they have been entrusted with work by the inhabitants of one house generally brings more custom from those who live next door. When the job is terminated, the "mush-faker" looks about him, as he enters the house, in quest of an umbrella which has passed the mending stage; and, in exchange for the same, offers to make a slight reduction in his charge. Thus he gradually obtains a stock of very old umbrellas, and by taking the good bits from one old 'mushroom' and adding it to another, he is able to make, out of two broken and torn umbrellas, a tolerably stout and serviceable gingham.[19]

These jobs would give Bill the money to buy food and (alas) alcohol, and then he would walk to another town. He covered long distances, most often

---

18   The 'fake' in mush-faking meant to temporarily fix up.

19   John Thompson and Adolphe Smith, *Victorian London Street Life* (New York: Dover Publications, 1994, originally serialized in 1877 as "Street Life in London"), p. 100.

traveling by foot but occasionally hopping freight trains, an illegal activity that would fascinate James McCook and others in future decades. Freight train hopping has long been associated with the hobo, though in reality, and until the motor car became affordable, it was the only means of fast transportation over long distances for most working-class people in the United States. It was not, however, an activity that Bill often discussed in his letters, despite James McCook pressing him for more details. Most of the time he simply walked. Often the actual life of the hobo was less dramatic than people wished it to be.

As his letters make clear, Bill's wanderings gave him plenty of opportunity to meet women. He brags about his attractiveness, referring to himself as "quite an Adonis." While there might be a temptation to wonder exactly how desirable a homeless and traumatized drunk might be, there is some evidence that women found Bill appealing. The Landmarks Collection contains several love letters written in different hands, apparently by multiple women, and we also have Bill's own accounts of his flirtations and sexual escapades. And, despite his ongoing problems, in the years 1885 and 1886 he seems to have married (or, again, 'married') two different women, Elizabeth Moores and Mahalia Jane Price. By 1887, if the dates in his letters are accurate, he was on his own again, this time working his way over the North Atlantic to England on a cattle steamer. He also traveled to Calcutta and Bombay.[20] Such extensive travels might seem surprising, but at the time it was not unusual for working-class men to travel around the world as seamen or cattle hands, working extremely hard as they went. In 1889, Bill was hopping trains around the American Midwest in search of work. In Chicago, he was offered ten dollars to vote for the Democratic mayoral candidate, DeWitt Clinton Cregier. A longtime Republican voter but "dead Broke And becoming disgusted and discouraged," he agreed. He got jobs working at mills in Ohio and Pennsylvania but would either fall out with his employer or get dissatisfied and leave.

By 1893, the year he first wrote to McCook, he was alone and back on the road again. Once more, the economy was probably a deciding factor. The economic panic of 1893, which involved the failure of the Reading Railroad

---

20   McCook quotes Aspinwall as describing his journey to England in more detail, visiting relatives in Yorkshire and then traveling to Scotland and Ireland, before getting work as an ordinary seaman to India. I have not seen the letter from which McCook cites this information. In his first letter, Aspinwall claims to have visited Calcutta and Bombay, though he does not give a date.

Company, a run on the U.S. gold supply and the collapse of numerous banks, kicked off a four-year depression that was significantly more severe than the one that had occurred in the previous decade. Until the Great Depression of the 1930s, this was the worst economic crisis to hit the United States, with unemployment as high as 18%. Aspinwall was vulnerable to the market and, more often than not, suffered the direct consequences of these economic fluctuations. As he tells McCook on 30th July 1893, "Buisness is getting very much depressed a Great many mills Shuting down and Hands out of Employ."[21] So he began a journey on the road that would last for years and involve many memorable encounters, stopping and then setting out, appropriately enough for this modern Odysseus, from Troy—albeit Troy in New York State.

In his "Leaves from the Diary of a Tramp" series, which was published in *The Independent* magazine, John James McCook, former deacon and now Professor of Modern Languages at Trinity College in Hartford, Connecticut, explains how Roving Bill came to write to him. Having completed various surveys of tramps in America, McCook interviewed and photographed a white hobo called "Connecticut Fatty" and a black hobo only known by the racist title "Connecticut Fatty's 'Shine.'" "Having heard much of the traveling facilities and rapid flights of the genus [train] jumper Tramp," McCook writes, "I placed in the hands of 'Connecticut Fatty' six postal cards, directed to me, which he faithfully promised to drop in the mail, with suitable memoranda, from time to time, on his way toward the far West."[22] But rather than Fatty writing to McCook with evidence of how far he had traveled, instead McCook unexpectedly received a postcard from Roving Bill, who had met Fatty on the road and got talking about the Professor. At first McCook suspected that Aspinwall was a fake, possibly 'a literary chap' pretending to be a hobo.[23] After checking with various third parties who vouched for Aspinwall, the skeptical Professor was convinced and the pair set about their near quarter-century-long correspondence, about which I will say more towards the end of this Introduction. Despite the length of this correspondence and despite Roving Bill dropping numerous hints that he would like to see McCook in person, the pair never met face to face.

---

21 As this letter is very short and some of it is illegible, I have left it out of the hard copy version of this book. It is, however, available in the online 'Scholarly Edition.'

22 McCook, "Leaves from the Diary of a Tramp I: First Acquaintance" in *The Independent* 53:2764 (21 November 1901), pp. 2731–2767 (p. 2761).

23 McCook, "Leaves I," p. 2761.

Today's homelessness researchers talk about 'pathways' into homelessness, the metaphor indicating that transiency and vagrancy are not straight lines, but rather that they are meandering routes that often involve periods of stability and fixity as well as instability and movement, temporary housing as well as 'rooflessness.' This was certainly true of Aspinwall, who in September 1893 stopped in Pittsburgh, Pennsylvania and, using money saved from his war pension, set up a repair shop. This venture was probably doomed from the start, undertaken as it was during a crushing depression, and by January 1894 he was once more back on the road. He then worked as a canvasman for Sells Brothers' Circus in Ohio, a demanding job in difficult conditions, for perhaps up to two years.

Aspinwall admitted himself into the Marion Branch Home for Disabled Veterans in January 1896. He stayed at the home for almost two years, during which time he was, according to the Governor, "On Offenders Docket three times, for being drunk in quarters, using profane and obscene [language] in quarters and resisting arrest."[24] On 28th November 1897, he showed up drunk for the Sunday morning inspection and was voluntarily discharged on the 1st December before his 'court case' could come up. Aspinwall continued his wanderings throughout the early twentieth century, including a stint living with a wealthy widow in St. Louis. In June 1904, he swore off drink (or claimed to) and set up another repair shop, this time in McLeansboro, Illinois. He did well enough to put adverts in the local paper, though by September 1905 he had left McLeansboro, putting all of his things on a wagon pulled by a tired old horse that promptly died on him, leaving him stuck on the road with no way of moving his possessions.

Aspinwall claimed to have given up drink from about 1906 onward. This does not appear to have been entirely correct, although it seems he did have increasingly lengthy periods of sobriety. His hitherto execrable handwriting also improves, thanks to his study of the Palmer method, much to the relief of this book's transcriber. In his later years, which are not extensively covered in the letters, Bill barreled around a variety of national military homes in Indiana, Virginia, Ohio, Wisconsin, and Tennessee, and he had at least one late period of employment working with one of his sons for the Prairie Oil Company in Oklahoma. Although he stopped being 'on the road' in the sense of being a hobo, his later life was full of wanderings much as his earlier life had been. His final letter to McCook, written in 1917, sees the

---

24   Justin H. Chapman to John James McCook, Connecticut Landmarks Collection.

seventy-two-year-old former solider fantasizing about going to the Western
Front to take on German troops during World War I, and complaining "I
Am not Well, I am Suffering from a Gun Shot Wound in head receivd at
Champion Hill Miss. May 10 1863. Age makes matters Worse." Aspinwall
died on the 14th of November 1921 at the age of seventy-six in Erie County,
Ohio, which was, despite the many thousands of miles that he had covered
in his life, the same state in which he had been born. He had, in a sense,
come home. Bill's legacy has continued amongst his descendants, who even
today have a phrase for when someone in the family does something wild:
"That's the Aspinwall in him."

Looking Like a Hobo: Photographing William Aspinwall (and Roving Bill)

In 1893, a few weeks into their acquaintance, McCook told Aspinwall "to
go to the best [photographic] artist in Bennington and tell him that if he
would take his picture and send me one copy, I would forward my check
for a dollar and a half."[25] The resulting photograph (see Figure 06 on page
30) is the ultimate tramp cliché: Roving Bill stood with pipe in mouth, his
umbrella-mending kit in a box slung over his shoulder and dressed in dirty
clothes, having seemingly come fresh from the road to the photographer's
studio. When they have discussed Roving Bill, historians have concentrated
on this photograph, discussing how it establishes a power dynamic that
sets up McCook as the powerful social investigator and Aspinwall as his
relatively powerless subject.[26] And it is true that McCook does attempt to
dissect Roving Bill's image as if he were a biologist and Roving Bill were
a butterfly on a pin.[27] But no historian has asked what Aspinwall himself

---

25   McCook, "Leaves From the Diary of a Tramp III" in *The Independent* 53:2768 (19 Decem-
     ber 1901), pp. 3009–3013 (p. 3009).

26   In particular, see Borgardus and Cresswell.

27   McCook writes of Roving Bill's photo: "The chin is not strong, nor notably weak." This
     description makes use of nineteenth-century physiognomic theories that a person's char-
     acter was visible on their physical body. McCook also writes that "the trousers are turned
     up, and the shoes, an important item in the diagnosis of these cases, are muddy and worn."
     McCook's medical language ("diagnosis of these cases") is an attempt to assert control over
     Aspinwall. McCook, "Leaves From the Diary of a Tramp III," p. 3010.

thought of the image. You can now read exactly what he thought, in this book, in his letter dated 11th June 1893. In that letter he talks about the pepper box in the photo, which caused him some embarrassment when he would walk through villages, the young boys calling after him "Pepper Sauce!" So we can see that this was probably not an image with which Roving Bill was entirely comfortable.

It is also clear that he did not wish to be seen purely in his tramp outfit, because in the same year he sent McCook a photograph of himself (see Figure 07 on page 96) in smart clothes holding a straw hat, an image which the professor described as "needlessly conspicuous." "The picture as a whole," McCook wrote, "did not please me as well as the one taken just as he came from the road." And no wonder, for in this second image Aspinwall looks respectable and not at all like the stereotypical hobo.[28] Aspinwall forwarded this photograph to McCook at his own expense, which indicates the strength of his desire to be seen in a more rounded way. Indeed, he would continue to send McCook photographs, usually images of himself in uniform. He wanted to be seen not as a type or a social problem but as a person, not just as a tramp but also as a soldier, not just as "Roving Bill" but also as William Aspinwall.

In 1967, popular historian Kenneth Allsop wrote about his disappoint-ment upon seeing a photograph of another hobo, Leon Ray Livingston, who went by the road moniker "A-No.1." Looking at the photo, Allsop commented: "it is difficult to stifle one's disappointment upon finding inside a full-length photograph of a gentleman of ramrod respectability, looking like a retired cavalry colonel, with sensitive cowlick hair-do and a brisk ground moustache."[29] Allsop is disarmingly honest here in admitting that he wants a hobo to look like a hobo: that is, someone who is not respectable, someone who is not part of mainstream bourgeois society, someone who is, perhaps, a rebel. A-No.1 does not look like Jack Kerouac. One can only imagine Allsop's disappointment if he had seen the photographs of Aspinwall in military uniform, which are published here for the very first time, one of which serves as this book's front cover. A similar disappointment can be

---

28   Oddly, some writers have claimed that this image has deteriorated and implied that it cannot be reproduced, which is manifestly not the case. See DePastino, p. 55; Chaseton Remillard, "Visual Representations of Homelessness in the Canadian Public Sphere: An Analysis of Newspaper and Photo Voice Images" (Unpublished Doctoral Thesis, 2012), p. 146.

29   Kenneth Allsop, *Hard Travellin': The Story of the Migrant Worker* (Middlesex, England; Victoria, Australia: Penguin, 1972, first published 1967), p. 191.

Fig. 1

detected in McCook's reaction when Aspinwall sends him a 'respectable' photograph. Considering this history of reception and representation, it is important for us to discard, as much as possible, our own prejudices, to try to meet Aspinwall on his own terms and to consider his life in the round, rather than as it conforms to our assumptions about the American hobo.

"Leaves From the Diary of a Tramp"[30]

In McCook's "Leaves From the Diary of a Tramp" series, Aspinwall's letters are the main attraction.[31] McCook intersperses the articles with his own thoughts about various aspects of the hobo life, as well as accounts and photographs of other tramps (e.g., FIGURE 01). He keeps returning to Roving Bill's letters, drawn and indeed charmed by Aspinwall's adventures and personality. Nevertheless, as Frank Tobias Higbie comments: "Although they were published as Aspinwall's 'diary,' the dominant voice in these

---

30   This image was taken by McCook and his son Philip. Although it may appear naturalistic, the 'feast' was a meal the pair had organized in order to have the photograph taken.

31   McCook originally intended to turn his Aspinwall material into a book but in the end settled upon magazine serialization, which he followed up with a lecture tour.

articles was McCook's."[32] Sadly, no one has tried to correct this imbalance until now. Including McCook's article series at the end of *Roving Bill Aspinwall: Dispatches from a Hobo in Post-Civil War America* allows you, the reader, to compare McCook's version of events with Aspinwall's for the first time. And there are significant differences between the two men's accounts.

Fig. 2

For one thing, McCook censored several aspects of the letters, particularly swearing (including 'damned') and sexual content. Aspinwall's adventures with women, his mentions of homosexuality and pederasty on the road, both of which were common and both of which he deplores, are alluded to but not described by McCook, who was aware of the sensibilities of his middle-class, turn-of-the-century audience. A former church deacon and member of the famous "Fighting McCooks," who had sent seventeen members of their family to fight for the Union during the Civil War, McCook was the epitome of respectability (FIGURE 02).[33] Yet, in other ways, the Professor's representation of tramping is actually more sensationalist than Aspinwall's. While Roving Bill focuses on everyday aspects of his life, such as work or domestic concerns, McCook devotes an entire article to the romantic phenomenon of train-hopping, which he calls "the most characteristic feature of American

---

32 Frank Tobias Higbie, *Indispensable Outcasts: Hobo Workers and Community in the American Midwest, 1880–1930* (Urbana and Chicago, University of Chicago Press, 2003), p. 82.

33 McCook himself did not see much action. According to Charles and Barbara Whalen, "Little Johnny," as he was known, was, at age eighteen, "spoiled," "petulant" and something of a "luxury-loving Beau Brummel." Charles and Barbara Whalen, *The Fighting McCooks: America's Famous Fighting Family* (Maryland: Westmoreland Press, 2006), p. 42, p. 47 & p. 51. Having been involved in one of the first battles of the war, a surprise attack in which the enemy quickly routed, Little Johnny soon fell out of love with the monotony of camp life and, after a few weeks, mustered out to enter Trinity College in 1861, leaving the other sixteen members of his family to earn the 'Fighting' sobriquet. It might not, therefore, be entirely unfair to suggest that John James was the only 'non-fighting' McCook.

tramping."[34] He largely omits Aspinwall's accounts of cooking and washing dishes after settling down to camp for the night. Hobos are not supposed to be domestic. They are, however, supposed to be drunkards, and from reading Aspinwall's letters it can be inferred that McCook repeatedly pressed him on this topic. Also, while there is a fondness in McCook's representation of Roving Bill in "Leaves," allowing his subject to come across as an affable, Whitmanesque wanderer, the series also has a tone of condescension throughout.

Like many of his middle-class contemporaries, McCook had a prejudice against hobos and believed that they were on the road because off their own personal failings, particularly laziness and a love of alcohol.[35] He denied that the state of the wider economy was a factor in creating tramps. He clung on to this prejudice despite the fact that he had conducted one of the earliest ever sociological surveys, the evidence of which had contradicted this conclusion. In 1891 McCook had sent out surveys, entitled "Casual Lodgers or Tramps," to be filled out by city authorities whenever a hobo used their temporary accommodation (see FIGURES 03 and 04). He received 1,349 responses. He followed this up with a survey for police stations upon the arrest of vagrants. Over the following decade, he used the information he received to write several articles in which he argued that men became hobos to avoid work, even though that was not what his survey results actually said. In the same year as the 1893 Panic, and despite the fact that 82.8% of his survey respondents said that they took to the road to find work, McCook nevertheless saw "admirable candor" only in the small number who claimed that they "were 'tired of work' or 'wanted to take life easy.'" His use of the term 'candor' here indicates that he simply does not believe 82.8% of his respondents, allowing him to discount the survey results.[36] Continuing to ignore his own data, in 1895 McCook claimed that "nearly always through mushy, soft hearted kindness, or ill judged, misdirected charity, they [hobos] make the discovery that they can get enough to eat and drink and wear and even to gratify the still grosser animal instincts . . . though [they are] doing nothing, or nothing more serious

---

34 John James McCook, "Leaves from the Diary of a Tramp II: Train jumping—A Digression: Nature: The South" in *The Independent* 53:2766 (5 December 1901), pp. 2880–2888 (p. 2880).

35 McCook was a temperance reformer who lectured extensively on the evils of alcohol. See David T. Courtwright and Shelby Miller, "Progressivism and Drink: The Social and Photographic Investigations of John James McCook" in *Journal of Drug Issues* 15:1 (1985), 93–109.

36 McCook, "A Tramp Census and Its Revelations" in *The Forum* 15:6 (August 1893), pp. 753–766 (p. 755).

Fig. 3

Institution *Police Station* December 15", A.D. 1891
Place, *Cleveland, O.*

[74, SC 44]

CASUAL LODGERS OR TRAMPS.

1. Occupation. .... *Stone Mason*
2. When did you last work at it? *June 191*
   at anything?
3. When did you take to the road? *2 Weeks*
4. Why? *No money*
5. When are you going to work again? *don't know*
6. Have you tried to get work to-day? *no*
7. Health. *Bad*
8. Ever had Syphilis? *no*
   Itch? *no*
9. How often in Hospital? *once*
   At whose charge? *County*
10. When last in Alms House? *no*
11. Married? *no*
    Children. — Number, ... Males, ... Ages ...... Females, ... Ages ......
12. Where are Wife and Children?
13. Where do you generally sleep? *Any place can find*
14. How do you generally secure your food? *Beg it*
15. Age. *73 year old*
16. Color. *White*
17. Nativity. *Ireland*
18. Can you read and write? *yes*
19. When and where did you last vote? *New York State*
20. Temperate, intemperate, or abstainer? *Intemperate*
21. Ever convicted of crime? *no*
    of drunkenness? *no*
22. Religion? *Catholic*
23. Name? *Wm Daugherty*
    Real name?
24. Remarks, including corrections of statements known to be incorrect and impressions as to the person's mental and physical vigor.

Note. — Use a separate blank for each individual.

Particulars, as above, are desired for 150 unselected cases occurring in the month of December. To this please add the total number entertained for one night during the entire month.

Please return by January 1, A.D. 1892, to
PROF. J. J. McCOOK,
Trinity College, HARTFORD, CONN.

xxvii

Fig. 4

Institution, *South Side Police Station* December 1, A.D. 1891. [SC58]

Place, *Milwaukee Wis.*

CASUAL LODGERS OR TRAMPS.

1. Occupation. *Boilermakers helper*
2. When did you last work at it? *about a year ago*
   at anything? *in St Louis 10 days ago*
3. When did you take to the road? *yesterday morning*
4. Why? *cause there was nothing to do in Chicago*
5. When are you going to work again? *soon as can get it*
6. Have you tried to get work to-day? *No I did not*
7. Health. *Fair*
8. Ever had Syphilis? *No*
   Itch? *"*
9. How often in Hospital? *Once*
   At whose charge? *Elkhard Co Ind.*
10. When last in Alms House? *never there*
11. Married? *Single*
    Children. — Number, ... { Males, ... Ages, ...
    { Females, ... Ages, ...
12. Where are Wife and Children? —
13. Where do you generally sleep? *Lodging Houses*
14. How do you generally secure your food? *buy it had have bged*
15. Age. *35*
16. Color. *White*
17. Nativity. *U.S.*
18. Can you read and write? *Yes*
19. When and where did you last vote? *4 years ago in Saginaw Mich*
20. Temperate, intemperate, or abstainer? *Temperate when I got no money*
21. Ever convicted of crime? *No I never was*
    of drunkenness? *Yes about 20 times*
22. Religion? *Catholic*
23. Name? *John Shields*
    Real Name?
24. Remarks, including corrections of statements known to be incorrect
    and impressions as to the person's mental and physical vigor.
    Thinks these are a devil of a lot of questions
    to ask a man for a night's lodging

Note. — Use a separate blank for each individual.

Particulars, as above, are desired for 150 unselected cases occurring in the month of December. To this please add the total number entertained for one night during the entire month.

Please return by January 1, A.D. 1892, to
PROF. J. J. McCOOK,
Trinity College, HARTFORD, CONN.

than odd jobs."[37] He gave several public policy recommendations during these years, including "Don't let people make the fatal discovery . . . that they can live without work."[38] Eventually, however, McCook realized that he was wrong.

This change of mind came around the time that he wrote up Roving Bill's letters for *The Independent.* "My tramp friend, Roving Bill," he writes, "is constantly urging in his letters that the greater proportion of the tramp population are . . . men 'out of work' . . . " And indeed Aspinwall had written to McCook, on the 5th August 1893 from Wolcott, New York, telling him "the mills are all Shutting down" and that "there will be Plenty of H.Bs [hobos] if things don't Change," accurately predicting that the Panic of 1893 would become an economic depression. McCook had not believed Aspinwall, and over the next decade had clung to his theory that men were becoming tramps out of laziness and poor personal habits. By 1902, however, he realized that Roving Bill had been correct. "I must confess," the Professor sheepishly (and to his credit) admits, "my earlier impressions were against the theory of any connection whatsoever between tramping and trade," but by 1902, after examining statistics that showed there were greater numbers of men on the road during periods of economic downturn, he was now "inclined to a different view."[39] Whether McCook's mind had also been influenced by Aspinwall's firsthand account is unclear, but either way the Professor had to admit that Roving Bill had understood the reality on the ground better than he had. There is an infamous story that the twentieth-century hobo "Steamtrain Maury" could predict the near future of the American economy from the length of the cigarette butts he collected from the ground: the shorter the butts, the more people were feeling the pinch and reining in their spending, indicating that an economic contraction was just around the corner. Similarly, Bill claims that "no one is more Able to Judge than my Self" the state of the country, "traveling from place to place as I am." He certainly saw the short-term economic impacts more directly than the comfortably situated McCook, whose information came slowly through official channels like newspapers, journals and statistical analyses.

---

37 McCook, "Vagabondage: What Accounts for it" in *The Trinity Tablet* 28:12 (25 June 1895), pp. 273–278 (p. 277).

38 McCook, "The Tramp Problem," a paper read at the National Conference of Charities and Correction held at New Haven, Conn, May 1895, reprinted in *Lend a Hand* 15:3 (September 1895), pp. 167–183 (p. 177).

39 McCook, "Leaves from the Diary of a Tramp VII: Increase of Tramping: Cause and Cure" in *The Independent* 54:2780 (13 March 1902), pp. 620–624 (p. 620).

The Letters of "Roving Bill"

With only a couple of exceptions, we do not have McCook's letters to Aspinwall, although often their content can be inferred from Roving Bill's replies.[40] Aspinwall talks about alcohol a lot in the letters, probably more than he would have wished, because McCook's letters to him were full of Victorian-era admonitions about the evils of drinking. McCook blamed Roving Bill's problems on his drinking and so Bill, understandably enough, is quite defensive on the issue. Of course, he actually did have a drink problem, which gave McCook confidence that he was on the right track in importuning his friend to put down the bottle. While McCook's letters are largely absent, their presence can be felt in Aspinwall's replies, and modern readers might wish the correspondence had focused less repeatedly on alcohol. Although temperance advocates may disagree, in my view the most interesting letters are those in which McCook's moralizing is least influential.

Yet despite McCook's frequent sermonizing, Aspinwall clearly enjoyed their correspondence. He particularly loved writing down his experiences. On 13th June 1893, he states: "I like to write and tell my Experiances and can Hardly stop when I get fairly at it. I have been through So much and Have so much to write about." He "invested in a Cheap Tablet and a lead Pencil Yesterday and if I Keep on writing at this Rate I will Soon want more." Indeed, if he is to be believed, a day later he "Spent the last three Cents for Postage," meaning that he went hungry that evening. Roving Bill was prepared to make sacrifices in order to get his thoughts on paper. In several letters he expresses hopes that his correspondence might one day be published, which indicates that he suspects he is writing for a wider audience than simply McCook. And when they are published, he is anxious to receive each of the monthly *Independent* editions in which they appear. Aspinwall took pride in his writing, rough-and-ready though it was, and was keen to see the fruits of his literary labors.

Roving Bill's letters are invaluable because of what they tell us about the life, motivations and feelings of a hobo, a member of that much mythologized but rarely heard-from group. When we think of hobos, we may tend to think of the stereotype of a man (always, like Aspinwall, a white man) utterly

---

40   Given that McCook's voice has dominated scholarly accounts of his interactions with Aspinwall, and also because the few letters that do exist are not terribly interesting, I have decided to leave them out of this book.

disconnected from the society around him. We don't tend think about hobos having families, yet Aspinwall did.[41] We don't think of hobos keeping up with the minutiae of party politics, yet Aspinwall did. We don't think of hobos settling down for a period of time before heading back out on the road, yet Aspinwall did. We certainly don't think of a hobo having business cards, and yet Aspinwall did. *Roving Bill Aspinwall: Dispatches from a Hobo in Post-Civil War America* should overturn a number of stereotypes and assumptions about the hobo.

Aspinwall's letters are a slice of American history, providing a personal perspective on historical issues such as the late nineteenth-century 'Silver Question,' as well as accounts of famous places such as Niagara Falls and important events including the 1894 protest march known as 'Coxey's Army.' He kept excellent track of his location and, aside from a few letters in which he gets the week or day confused, of dates. This allows readers to track his movements in time and space with great detail and accuracy. It seems likely that he was encouraged to be so precise by McCook, who was seeking a sociological understanding of hobo movements. But it is also possible that Aspinwall enjoyed recounting his exact movements, extensive as they were.

Another benefit of reading Aspinwall's own words, rather than just McCook's précis of them, is that we get a fuller picture of their exchange. In his final (June 1902) edition of "Leaves," the Professor describes Bill's increasingly militant attitude. In an angry mood, Aspinwall had written to him imagining a working-class army of hobos riding by train to take political power in the USA. McCook replied to Bill, asking what would happen if the government sent a train full of free beer to the hobos. "And I shall hear from him promptly," McCook ends the series by predicting, "I have no doubt and confidently expect to find him once more in his earlier and more cheerful mood," the comment suggesting that Bill was yet to write back. In fact, Bill *had* written back, nearly a year earlier. In a letter dated 1st Sept 1901, Bill penned a retort that made use of his military experience: "The Ho Bos would Steal all of the beer and the Enemy would have the cars With Hobos beating their Way in their back to their Command." The hobos, in other words, would hop the enemy trains back to their HQ where, presumably, they could score a significant military victory, and perhaps even win this hypothetical class war. McCook leaves Aspinwall's witty response out of "Leaves," which gives the

---

41   Despite the persistent stereotype of the lonesome hobo, most transients maintained a
      connection to their families. For more, see Higbie.

impression of the Professor having the final laugh. McCook chose not to cite Roving Bill's reply because he wanted his audience to see Bill as a 'safe' and genial figure, and perhaps also because he did not wish to appear to have lost an exchange of wits with a hobo. With the publication of Aspinwall's letters, we can see for the first time that this was a misrepresentation.

Finally, and most importantly, the letters provide us with a sense of Roving Bill's personality. We understand, from his repeated descriptions (and from love letters that I have also included in this book), that he was a bit of a cad. We understand that he could desert people, especially women, at the drop of a hat or the siren call of a woolen manufacturer. We also understand that he had a sense of humor, including being able to laugh (at times) at his own homeless situation. For example, when describing the fact that he had acquired fleas during his wanderings, he writes that he and his road partner "came to the Conclusion to wash and Boil up our Cloths, for there had got to be more inhabitants in our cloth[e]s besides ourselves." Describing a brothel, he writes of "a House of Ill fame, or of good fame as they Seem to Be in Troy," humorously suggesting that brothels are particularly popular among the inhabitants of Troy. And we also see that, despite lacking a formal education that would have corrected his erratic and inconsistent spelling, he had a nice turn of phrase. Describing picking up wooden planks called railroad sleepers to rest on for the night, he writes that he "waked one of the Sleepers." Later, reflecting on the anonymity of the hobo life, he coins a rhyming phrase using his own spelling of hobo: "Nobody Knows where the Haut Beau goes." But at least, thanks to Roving Bill's own letters, that statement is no longer true, at least in his case. We know precisely where William Aspinwall went, what he did, and much of what he thought. And I for one am glad of it.

William "Roving Bill" Aspinwall was a flawed man who does not seem to have treated the people in his life as well as he ought. Nevertheless, his letters provide an unparalleled insight into the life of that legendary figure, the U.S. American hobo. Rather than imposing our stereotypes onto the hobo from the safety of our reading chairs, as did Professor McCook, we can, for the first time, read Aspinwall's full and uncensored life story in his own words.

I will sign off this Introduction as Roving Bill signs off his own letters, with an apparently mistaken spelling of 'fraternally.'

Fratulently yours,

Owen Clayton.

DISPATCHES FROM A HOBO IN
POST-CIVIL WAR AMERICA.

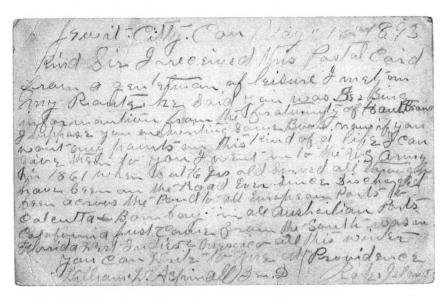

Jewit Citty. Jewett City. Con May 18 1893   Fig. 5

Kind Sir, I received this postal card from a gentleman of leisure[1] I met on my Route, he said you was seeking information from the fraternity Haut Beaux.[2] I suppose you are writing some Book. Now, if you want any points on this kind of a life I can give them to you. I went into U.S. Army in 1861 when [I was] but 16 years old. Served all though, have been on The Road ever since. Discharged, been across the Pond to all European Parts, to Calcutta & Bombay, in all Australian Parts, [and] Calafornia [California]. Just came from the South. Was in Florida, West Indies & Mexico all this winter.

You can write to me at Providence Rode Island.

William. W. Aspinwall Gen[eral] D[elivery]

---

1   This was "Connecticut Fatty," a hobo who had previously been interviewed by McCook. Hobos and tramps adopted road monikers rather than use their birthname. This provided anonymity and some protection from the police, though it also enabled hobos to feel that they had entered a new subculture, which in the early twentieth century would be called 'hobo-hemia.' Adopting a road name like "Connecticut Fatty" or "Roving Bill" could also help a hobo to feel that they had begun their life over again, and that perhaps they might be able to forget whatever difficulties or traumas they had experienced in their previous, settled existence.

2   Aspinwall's original term for hobo. This may have been a simple misspelling or mishearing of the word hobo, or Aspinwall may have been playfully suggesting that the hobo is a "good (or beautiful) man." He spells 'hobo' more conventionally in later letters. The earliest known printed reference to 'hobo' is from Washington's *Ellensburg Capital* newspaper, 28th November 1889, though presumably the term had been used for some time before that date.

Boston, Mass. May 26 1893

Mr John. J. McCook
Hartford Ct
Dear Sir

I received yours [i.e., your letter] of 19 inst[3] at Providence. You must not suppose for a minute that the person [Connecticut Fatty] that gave me the postal with your address is any friend of myne. I do not know him perhaps as well as you do, having just met him on the Road and talked with him a few times. In fact, I make but few friends on the Road.

I was Born of good Parents and Brought up well but have been unfortunate and took to Roaming about, having no Particular Home. I was wounded in the war at the Battle of Champion Hill. This on May 16 1863. Got three Buck shots in Right Shoulder an[d] Struck in Head with minie [Minié] Ball w[h]ich Parcially Disabled me, for wich I get a small Pen[sion] of $6.00 per month. And since the war I was Employed in [a] Woolen mill and got caught on a Revolving shaft and got my Right arm mangled up, so you See my Excuse for taking this kind of a life. I belonged to co[mpany] H 47" Indiana V. Vols, Enlisted in Nov 1861, Dis[charged] in Oct 1865.[4] I will Refer you to Captn S. J. Keller, Bluffton Indiana, Captn of my Com, as to my Record during that time, or to John. E. Sturgis Drugist Bluffton Ind comrade of myne, and I will also Refer you to Mr Thomas Wallace of Lewis Block Pittsburgh PA, who has knowed me for 25 yrs and knows of my Trampin[g] around. Hon E.D. Graff[5] of Worthington Armstrong co Penn knows me well, Having Been in his Employ a Short time and corresponded with him from a number of Points.

---

3   Abbreviation of the Latin *instante mense*, which translates to "of this month."

4   For more about this regiment, see David Williamson, *The 47th Indiana Volunteer Infantry: A Civil War History* (Jefferson, NC: McFarland & Co, 2011).

5   The Graff family were prominent business people in Armstrong County, Pennsylvania.

Also coresponded at intervals with above Mr Wallace.

I think the above Reff should satisfy the most critical mind as they are all undenieded [undeniable] Gentlemen. I would be Pleased if you would address a letter to Each one of them and get their opinion of me.

Now I hope what I have said will satisfy you as to my truth and veracity.

I think I can say without doubt that I have tramped and Roamed about more in my life than any man of my age im awere of. Went throug[h] all the Visisitudes and Hardships it is Possible for a Human to stand and live. At the same time I am Hale & Hardy.

Now, I want you to Distinctly understand me: I am not a Bum.[6] I would Rather be kicked than go into a House and ask for something to eat. I have went Hungry on many a time. Almost starve[d] Before I would ask. I often wished I was more of a Bum when I was good and Hungry but I am consistuted of to[o] much Pride and Manhood.

I traveld all through the south and the West Indies & Mexico last summer in fall and Winter fixing clocks & sewing m.c [machines]. I have taken up mush faking or umbrella mending since I left N.York and am traveling on [i.e., doing] that now. I go Pretty Hungry at times in this country, as there is to[o] many of a kind [i.e., too many transients]. I am going up into N[ew] Hampshire [and] Vermont, and then I will strike west to the world's Fair.[7]

I wish to say that I do but very little Riding on cars on my over land Routes.[8]

I was never arrested for Vagrancy[9] or any crime in my life and there is not a citty of any size or note in the US but what I have been in and spent more or less time in (I will say in the world).

---

6   Transients would often distinguish between hobos, tramps and bums. The latter term was generally used to refer to a transient who did not work. Aspinwall uses it to mean someone who begs.

7   The 1893 World's Columbian Exposition, also known as the World's Fair, was held in Chicago from May to October. An enormously influential event, the Exposition attracted over 27 million visitors.

8   Riding freight trains was (and is) the stereotypical hobo form of transport. Though we do not have McCook's letters to Aspinwall, it is likely that Aspinwall mentions riding freights here in response to a question from the Professor.

9   Vagrancy Acts were common in many U.S. states (as well as in other countries). Under these Acts a person could be arrested for being without "visible means of support"—in other words, being in poverty. Vagrancy laws are status crimes, which means that one does not have to actually *do* anything to be arrested. Instead, it is a person's being that is made illegal. This effectively means that the only victim is the supposed perpetrator. In the twentieth century, vagrancy laws were used to criminalize homosexuals, African-Americans and political leftists, and were eventually declared unconstitutional by the U.S. Supreme Court in 1972.

I think I have said Enough to convince you of my life in the Past - God only Knows what is in store for me in the future. I hope [for] better times than in the past. If the same has to come, [then] let me not live to Experiance many more years of it.

Now if you think any of my Past Experiance or what is to come hereafter will be of any Service to you, I will cheerfully furnish it to the Best of my Realisations and you can Send me sumthing at times to Help me dispose any Expenses. Hoping what I have said will be of service to you, I am

Address

William W. Aspinwall

Lowell. Mass.

Gen[eral] Del[ivery]

Write at once will be there by Monday inst

Fratulently[10] yours,

Roving Bill

---

10   Aspinwall presumably means 'fraternally.'

Lowell Mass. May 29 1893

[WRITTEN ON THE BACK OF A POSTCARD]

Kind Sir, I arrived in Lowell this morn. I did not fare [as] well as Sunday [i.e., the day before]. I had a five cent loaf of Bread and 5 cts worth of Bolona [was] all I had yesterday, and it is 11 am and no Breakfast yet. Slept in Box Car last night. The Haut Beaux you speak about that gave me the Postal I met near New Brittain, Conn. He was going towards New Haven, I towards Hartford. I will try and get you a photo Just as I am as soon as I can Raise the Stuff [money]. I go from here to Nashua & Manchester New Hampshire. Can write to Either. Will write a letter in a few days.

On the Pike[11] between Lowell & Nashua N.H. May 29 1893

Professer Dear Sir I am now on my way to Nashua, will be there tomorrow. I have stoped to Rest alongside of the Pike and I though[t] I would improve the time. I am writing this sitting on the Ground resting on my knees. You wanted to know how I traveled from Jewit Citty to Providence and then to Boston & Lowell. I walked Every step of the way. My preasant Buisniess will not allow of me going by Rail, if [I] went so I would not get much mush fakeing or umbrella mending to do. I have walked Ever since I left new York citty. Came By the way of Bridgeport, New Haven, Hartford and all intermediate towns and then to Wilimantic, Jewit Citty. I have asked no one for any Alms since I left New York. Have made Enough to live by, going Hungry at times. Still, I am Hale and Harty. I have slept most of the time in the Haut Beaus 'Sweet' Home the Friendly Box Car, and nights that are to[o] cold for the Box car I look along the R.R. [railroad] for a Secluded nook and Build a fire out of old R.R. Ties and sleep as comfortable as I would in a King's Pallace. And when it Rains I find a Box Car or some Barn. The day before I arrived at Jewet Citty I stoped one day two nights in a Barn. It Rained all the time. You wanted to know if I ever Rode trains. I have Rode on the Baggage car, just in Rear of the Engine and on the Engine under the Headlight, in Box Cars, Bettween Cars, but never under cars, as that way of getting along always looked to[o] dangerous for me and I preferred to walk. But still there is many a one Rides the Trucks & Rods, I have seen them.[12] I was stealing a Ride [to] Darwin Florida on the J. T. & R.W RR [Jacksonville, Tampa and

---

11   As in turnpike or toll road.

12   For a famous description of riding freight trains, see Jack London's book *The Road* (1907).

Key West Railway] from Enterprise to Titusville. The conductor caught me and wanted to know where I was going. I told him I was going to Titusville.

He says 'are you a glass Blower?'

I told him 'No'.

He says 'you fellows come down here in Winter to Blow Glass and go into up North in summer time to Pick Oranges. Get Off.' I took him at his word.

I found the Southern People in the South very Charitable, More so than the People that has Emigrated there from the Northern States. I Stoped at a Place one day near Lake Citty. Flo[rida]. on the G.S.F R.R. [Georgia, Southern and Florida Railway], a Farm House. He was an old Reble [Rebel, as in Confederate] Soldier. He gave me my Dinner and treated me kindly.

He Said 'there was an Irish H.B. Stoped there one morn and Knocked'. He went to the door.

The Son of Erin[13] 'says Mr. I don't want any thing to Eat but I just want to Borrow your looking Glass. I want to See how an Irishman looks starving to Death.'

He told him to come in and he got his feed.

At another time he said he was sitting in the House Reading, he heard sume one choping out at his wood Pile for all it was worth. He looked out and there was an old Grey Haired H.B. He called him in and gave him his Breakfast and told him he was to[o] old to Chop wood.

I stayed about one week with an old Southern planter about 40 miles north of Savanah GA on the Road Between Savanah and Augusta GA. He was a good whole souled man, Had been a Southern Soldier but is now a good Union man. The Colered [colored, as in Black] People in the South are very good and Hospitible but the most of them are very Poor and have nothing much to give, but they will generally divide with you when asked. I stayed in Collored Peoples' Houses a great many times. Myself would fix their clocks an[d] Sewing Machines for Pay. I have often done fixing for a Meal, the Parties Having no money, Corn Bread, Molasses and fat meat the Fair [fare].

[I am] On the Road between Nashua & Manchester N.H. I arrived at Nasuha last night.[14] Met a fellow H.B. yesterday, he did not know where he

---

13   A slang term for someone from Ireland.

14   Given his later reference to Decoration Day, Aspinwall seems to have written this letter over a few days. The distance between Lowell and Nashua is 13.5 miles, so it is likely that he arrived at Nashua on the 30th May.

was going, Had no Particular Point in View.[15] We took in an Em[p]ty Box Car, the air was chilly. Slept very comfortable, my feet got a little cold towards morning. My Partner got very cold, I could hear him Shivering and Shaking Every time I was awake during the night. He left me this morning, he said he was going to Bum some Priest for a quarter as he wanted to get a shave and something to Eat. I bid him good By[e]. He told me he use[d] to keep Salloon Sumewhere near new Britain, Conn. He told me he had been on the Bum for six weeks this time.

I met and [an] old fisherman last Sunday on the R.R. between Lowell & Boston, he stoped [and] asked me for a match. I accommodated Him. He said 'Be Jasus'.[16] He had worked in Lowell ever since last Christmas and now he was walking out of the town, he said the drink was the cause. Today being Decoration day,[17] I did not do much mush fakeing. I had a part of a loaf of Bread, I done [dined] on that for Breakfast and dinner and then I made fifteen cents fixing an umbrella. I got some crackers and cheese for supper.

You wanted to know if I Ever stoped in an alms House or a Soldiers' Home. I stoped at the Nathional [national] mil[itary] Home at Dayton, Ohio about Eight yrs ago [for] about six weeks, and again last winter one year ago. Over night I stoped in Nath mil Home at Marion for about three days. This Spring one year ago I stoped over night at Soldier House in Bath N.Y. Two years ago I stoped at the Soldiers' Home in Chelsea, Mass near Boston when I came through on last Sunday night. And I stoped overnight at the Confederate Soldiers' Home overnigh[t] at Richmond, Vir[ginia] last winter.

---

15 Hobos would frequently pair up for protection, companionship and, as Aspinwall later describes, for sex. These pairings rarely lasted long and were often broken off without ceremony.

16 This phrase seems to be Roving Bill's way of indicating that the man was Irish.

17 A U.S. Federal holiday to honor military service personnel. Between 1868 and 1970 the holiday took place on the 30th of May; in 1971 it was renamed "Memorial Day" and moved to the final Monday in May.

May 31st 1893

I stoped last night in a Shanty [i.e., a shack] alongside the RR, had a Sleep in it. Built a fire, was Comfortable, was out before sun up. Met a Frenchman that wanted his Umbrella mended. Went with him to his House, done the Job, got my Breakfast and fifteen cents before five A.M. I am now Eight miles from Manchester N.H., will arrive there about 12.[P]M.

Some other time I will give you a History of my travels in the South. I have made two trips through the Southern States. Eight years ago I went all through the Southwest Ill[inois], Missurri, Miss[issippi], Arkansas, Lou[isiana], Texas, Ala[bama]. I Guarded Convicts on a Plantation near Greenwood on the Yazoo River, Miss. I was there three mo[nths]. Was Supt [superintendent] of a Cotton Mill near Carrolton, Miss. Was there the time of the Yellow fever. I Run a first Mill at Cumberland, Mis near West Point. I heard Jeff[erson] Davis[18] make a Speech in a grave near Tupelo, Miss.

I have been in N. Orleans, Mobile a number of times. Been Hunting in the wilds of the Yazoo & Tallahatche [Tallahatchie] & Yellow Bushe swamps. I have been on almost all of the Battle fields East and West of the Civel War. Been on the famous Brandywine & Delaware River of Rev[olutionary][19] times. Seen Bunker Hill, Boston Common, also Washington's Mon[ument] at Wash Citty. Been in all the Capitals of the states of the Union and Seen the White House and Capital at Wash, was in US Pension office, Treasury Building and other places to[o] numerous to mention.

Seen Pulaski's[20] monument at Savanah. Seen also Confederate mon[uments] in Several Citties of the South. I take a great interest and

---

18   Jefferson Davis (1808–1899) was President of the Confederate States from 1861 to 1865.

19   This is a reference to the Battle of Brandywine Creek, the longest single-day battle of the American Revolution, which took place on 11th September 1777.

20   Casimir Pulaski (1745–1779), a Polish nobleman known as the 'Father of American Cavalry' for his service as a General during the American Revolutionary War.

visit all these Places of note in my travels. I made a trip to Leadville, Col[orado] the time of the first Gold Excitement there.[21] Was going to make a fortune but got through in three days, went Back to Denver from there to Salt Lake, thence to Sacramento, San Francisco. Signed as a Sailor, Sailed across to Melburn [Melbourne] Sidney, Aus[tralia] & done the Same Coming Back.

Was over there about three months. Came Back to [San] Fransisco, Beat my way [i.e., hopped a freight train] Back, went down to N. Mexico & Arizona. On my way Back was out in the Indian Teritory amongst the Indians two months, Comanchees & Cherikees. Fixed Clocks and Sewing M all through the South West Missuri that winter. Came out in the Spring Fat & Raged [ragged]. I could tell you many a laughable incident that happened [to] me but time & space will not permit at the Preasant writing.

I went over to London, Eng[land] on a Cattle Steamer near six years ago.

---

21   Gold was first mined at Leadville, Colorado in 1860. It seems unlikely that the fifteen-year-old Aspinwall would have been a prospector at this point, especially given that his description of subsequent travel would have run up against his volunteering in the Union army in December 1861. However, in 1868 lode mining was first attempted in Leadville, leading to the discovery of a large amount of gold; this latter date seems a more likely candidate for a twenty-three-year-old Aspinwall to have tried his hand as a prospector.

May 31st

I forgot to mention when I told you about Guarding Convicts in Miss there was four other Guards besides mySelf and they was all old Reble Soldiers. The Sargent of Guard, Capt Thomas, was an old Capt in [General Robert E] Lee's Army all through the War. I never was treated better in my life than I was by these men, they had Great Confidence in my Guarding qualities. They would in a joking way call me a dam[n]ed Yankee, I would return the compliment and call them Dam[n]ed Johnny Rebs and it would all Pass of[f] with a laugh.

But it was Horrible the way the Poor Convicts were treated. When we was Picking Cotton they had a task of two Hundred, and if they did not get [i.e., work hard enough at] this task they would make them lay down on the Ground fase [face] downward, their Pants down and Shirt Pulled up, their Bare Skin Exposed, and then there was a big Stout Negro Convict that weighed about two hundred [pounds], [he was] Chose[n] for that Purpose for [i.e., because of] his Size. With an inch hemp Rope twisted and looped around his Hand, [he] would Beat these Convicts over the Bear Hide Until the Sargent would say 'Enough.'

The Poor fellows would Scream and Hollow. Sometimes one would say 'Sargent Oh! Sargent I will get [to] my task.'

The sargent would answer, 'A Hell of a time to get [to] it now. Hit him harder or I will have all the men whip you,' speaking to the Convict with the Rope.

I have seen them put in the Stocks until there was no perceivable life in them. It was outrageous the way they was treated. I seen one man fall over Dead in the Field, Sick and Exhausted, Rather die than give up. I have seen them when they was Ploughing take a trace Chain and put it around the Convicts' necks and Chain him to the Round of the Plow I Saw a mule

Running away with a Plow and a Convict Chained to it. That Convict done some late Running and Puling with his hands on the lines and with his head and neck on the Chain, the Sargant and Guards sitting on the Fenc[e] laughing. I went to him afterwards and the Chain had Cut deep Lashes in his neck and many other acts of Cruelty I saw that I have not time to discribe here. Most of the Convicts were colerd men, there was several white Convicts but they was never treated as Cruelly as the Negroes. I seen two Black Convicts shot for Running and trying to get away. They had a Pack of Hounds in charge of a trainer, they would let loose Every time a Convict got away. It was almost impossible for [a] Convict to Escape. Even if he got away from the Guards, we had winChester Rifles and a Colt's manufactured Navy.[22] Some times we would Guard with [our] shot Guns heavily loaded with Buck Shot. I did not Guard Convicts long, I did not like the way they was treated.[23]

After I quit Guarding I and a Professor of Slight of Hand[24] by the name of Jeff Tate went into the Show Business. He performed his Slight of Hand tricks, I was a Professor of Phrenology.[25] We would have our Shows in the School Houses. The Planters would aid us all they could, as the most of them liked fun. I would Feel the Darkies' Heads [and] Give a lecture.

At times we would Gen give the Planters Complimentary tickets. I have had them tell me they never laught so much in their lives as they did at me feeling the Darkie men and womens' Head. It must have been laughable for I did not know but little about it, but Every thing Goes for fun in that Country. I only stayed with the Professor until Spring and then I struck out for New Orleans. I had quite an Experiance in that Citty. But I must be moveing on or I won't get to Manchester today.

I will mail this to you from Manchester.

I am now [in] Sight of the Citty of Manchester, N.H. As I am going to mail this there I won't have time to write much more. I hope you will be able to make out and get the Run of what I have written. If you Read them as they are folded, you may be able to make something out of it, but if you get them mixed up it will be a Chineese Puzel. You will please Excuse all Mistakes Bad

---

22 Probably the Colt 1851 Navy Revolver.

23 Such treatment of black convicts was common in the U.S. South, especially following the failure of Reconstruction and the imposition of Jim Crow racial segregation laws.

24 A showman or magician.

25 The pseudoscience of reading bumps on the head to determine a person's character or personal qualities, often used as entertainment.

Spelling and writing as I have written under a great many inconveniences. The muskeeto is very troublesome today as I sit on the ground, my Back against a Pine tree, my Knee for a Desk, it is not as Comfortable as it is in an Easy Chair in [a] Library or Office. The Country looks Beautiful in its Spring Suit and the Birds sing Sweetly and nature Seems to have taken life Anew. I often in [the] day time [on] nice days get into the woods in some Secluded Spot Day [and] dream in the Shade of some friendly tree and Sleep from two or three Hours, sometimes longer, and Oh Such Sweet Sleep, Such nice dreams. If I were where I dream I was, sumetimes I would be Happy.

I often think god intended man to live as the Indians use[d] to, all the Land Common Property. What Happy times if we was all in the woods together.

I have one more trip of myne to tell you of before I close. Three yrs ago last October I was in Phil[adelphia]. I seen an ad in the Ledger for men to go to Baltimore to go down the Chesapeak Bay catching Oysters. I went to an Employment agent, Hired out [and] was Shiped that Eve. Got to Baltimore, was taken abord the Oyster Schooner. [As well as] Brave Capt Elisha Ward, there was Eight more men abord besides myself: two Englishmen just came over from Liverpool, two Scotchman, and the Rest was Irishmen and Negroes. A motley Crowd we were. None of Us Except our Capt, the mate, a large Negro and the Col Cooks Know what was in Store for us. We left that night for Chrisfield [Crisfield], Maryland the Home of the Capt & Mate, to get Ready to Catch oysters. It was all Right Sailing around in fair we[a]ther and no wants, lots of fun, but when we got down to Buisness then there was Some kicking [complaining] out in the Rain, Sleet and cold all day. Storm came up and then you would hear the Englishmen, Scotchman and the Irish.

First you would Hear 'The Blasted Country.'

'Divel [Devil] take the Country' [and] So on.

It was no Use, they had Signed for three months. I use[d] to tell them, 'Why did you not stay in your Country? No one Sent for you,' and give them the Laugh.

The Capt and Mate were Particular Friends of myne, I think because I was an American. We all had to sleep in the forepeak, a Room about 6 x 8, and you could not stand Streight and Such Seanes [scenes] as transpired in that Fare Peak can't be described, and Body Lice I never saw the like, the army could not compare. Your cloths[26] were full one on top of the other and Such

---

26   This is Aspinwall's repeated misspelling of clothes.

Scratching and Swearing and no Chance to wash, only in Cold salt watter,[27] and no Soap. I tell you, men that goes down the Chesipeak to Catch Oysters deserve pitty, no one knows any thing about it, only those that have been there. Our Bord was Corn Bread & ofal [offal] meat, Coffe once a day in the morning and 13 dol[lars] per month. I was down two months and we Raised a Mutiny and the Capt Run us in to Chrisfield and Payed us of[f]. He was not making any thing or he would not of done it. He had us haul for three months. I was never so Glad to get out of a Place in my life and I fared well to what some of the men did. I went ashore several times with the Capt & mate on Sat[urday] nights but I was the only one of the Crew that was of[f] that Boat in two months and the most of them had no Change of cloths, so you can imagine their Condition. I never went to catch Oysters after that, one time will do mee. And we was treated well [compared] to what some Crews were, they landed sume men on Islands and never Payed them, Some men knocked overbord, all kinds of Cruelties. Some of those Captains and mates are worse than Cannibals. I don't see what this Gov[ernment] means by letting such atrocities transpire Right under the Dome of the Capital. But it is some better now than it was Several years Back.

---

27   This is a phonetic spelling of a regional pronunciation in Ohio and nearby states. Given that Dyson Aspinwall was from Huddersfield in the North of England, it is also possible that Roving Bill's repeated spelling of 'watter' comes from his father's West Yorkshire accent: water is pronounced 'watter' predominantly in Lancashire, which borders West Yorkshire. "Wordsworth's matter/water are full rhymes," as Tony Harrison puts it in his poem "Them and [uz]."

June 5 1893

I just arrived here today. I am going from here to Brattlebourgh Vermont. I came away and forgot the Postals you sent me in P.O [post office] at Manchester. N.H. I have not money to get Photo. Write me at Brattlebourgh, Vt will go from there to Benington. But yours 31" came to Hand today. Rough times in this country But still alive. You must of got my letter by this time,

    Yours William

Bennington — Vermont; June 9 1893

Prof, yours of June 1st Just Rec[eived] this morning. I wrote you a Postal from Keen N.H. I am going from here to Troy New. York. Please send Me some more Postals and Envelopes and Refer to that address as some times I have no money to get them with. What I have writen heretofore and what I shall write you in future is nothing but the truth and I can't well describe on Paper some of the scenes I have Passed through in my travels. I am Hungry now and I have not a cent to get any thing to Eat but may strike something before long. I won't Beg if I Can Help it. I slept last night in a vacant House between here and Wilmington Ver. 5 miles up on the mountains. There was no other hous within a mile of it, I went up stairs got into a little Bed Room that shut the Door, Pulled of[f] my shoes and coat and made a Pillow of my Umbrellas and Slept Sound. Got up at day Break and came Here.

I had quite an Eventful trip since I left Manchester N.H. I walked Every Step of the way. You know the Geography of the country well, it is very mountainous. I had many a Weary step clim[b]ing of those mountains and the muskeetoes, knats and other insects Made Me Miserable. I Slept in Box Cars and once in the woods. It was dark and I was very tiard [tired] and the Muskeetoes were nearly Eating Me up. I filed to the Right up on the side of the mountain and Built a fire, Stumbled around in the Dark and found Some Wood. Pulled of[f] Shoes and Coat and turned in. I left Manchester on June 1st, Slept in a Barn that night. You Know the date I was in Keene. I arived in Brattleboro, Ver on the Eve of the 6 inst, Come through Marlboro, Wilmington & Wood, Croosed [crossed] Hog Back & Hay Stack Mountains and numerous others.

I Came down Hill ten miles yesterday afternoon, most all the way a wagon would haft to have the Brake on or it would Run a way. Every Half Mile or so you would see the wrecks of a wagon or BobSleds where they had got away with a load of logs and of lumber Comeing down Hill. You can imagine the Climbing I had to do to get on top of that gentle raise [rise] in the Earth's Surface. It is down the Mountain Side from them, away I came all the way into Bennington and Part of the way a Surging River Running a long Side of the Road, the watter trying to Pass itself to get down Hill. At first on top of the Mountain there would be little lakes Connected by a little Stream, and father down it turned in to a Surging Roaling tumbling River, Here and there a saw mill and when I arrived at Bennington I found it Propeling numerous Factories. Nature is great to Behold in its Beauties an[d] might.

There is Several clases of tramps or Haut Beaus. I can make about three out of them, four with ocasionaly a woman. There is 1st the Homeles[s] tramp that tramps because he has to no Home, no Friends and Got on the Road from drink, and then No 2 is Fakers and mushfakers, Mechanicks and others on the tramp Hunting work, and Sume of the finest Mechanicks in the Country, comprising all trades, got on the Road by Spending their money to[o] Liberal[ly] and partly from drink and got [too] down and ashamed to ask for a job. And good fellows they are, will divide the last Nic[k]el with you or the last Buiscut. There apperes to be a kind of a Brutherly feeling amongst this class but they have no use for Class No 3, as they are Comprised of Ex Convicts, Jail Birds and Regular Deadb[eats].

There is sume men Haut Beaus that will venture to do any thing, insult Women and [set] fire [to] Barns, Can't be trusted. This makes it Bad for an Honest Man as the Public thinks they are all Chips of[f] the Same Block, but far from [it]. [There] is Just as much Difference in the classes as there is in the classes of Societies in a Citty or a village. It is the last named class [i.e., 'Class No 3'] that has all the Phrazes, Signs, camps and patter.[28] Using the Poor Houses, Jails & they manage to get some money by Stealing or Begging and Buy Alchohall, dilute it in Watter and drink that - they call it Alca or Booze and other names. I have seen several woman on the tramp but Gen very low down Creatures, the Boys Call them Bags, old Bags. A man [who travels] along with a Bag don't stand very High in Haut Beau Society - will write more in time on this Subjects.

---

28   i.e., hobo marks, slang and hobo jungles. It is a matter of dispute as to whether hobos did leave signs in secret code in doorways to alert fellow travelers to the generosity (or otherwise) of individual homeowners. This was a much-discussed topic in contemporary newspapers and some hobos did claim it was true, though most academic historians remain skeptical. If such a system did exist, it does not seem to have been universal.

Farmers are Called Rubers [Rubbers, as in Rubbernecks[29]]. When a Bum goes to a House and gets a lunch they call it Hand out, Lump Soup, Slop. More on this anon.

Mr N E Watson took My Photo. Will Send it to you in a few days. He said he would Run the Risk, I told him I thought there was no Risk to Run.[30] I hope it will Prove Satisfactory. Write to Me at Troy N.Y Gen Del. Send Paper Envallops & Postals. I will try and do the Best I can and Give you Plain Facts, not Polished. I think what you Say Is true in Regard to financial aid, but I have it very Rough at times.[31]

Yours

William W Aspinwall

Don't Delay in writing

29　To rubberneck means to turn the neck to stare foolishly at someone.

30　In his article series "Leaves From the Diary of a Tramp," McCook writes that he had told Aspinwall "to go to the best artist [i.e., photographer] in Bennington and tell him that if he would take his picture and send me one copy, I would forward my check for a dollar and a half." McCook, "Leaves From the Diary of a Tramp III" in *The Independent* 53:2768 (19 December 1901), pp. 3009–3013 (p. 3009).

31　McCook has turned down Aspinwall's previous calls for aid, told him not to ask again, and lectured him on the moral ills of begging.

Bennington Vermont; June 9 1893

I wrote you today in the Photo galery but I have now Started on my way to Troy N.Y and on my way about three miles. I don't know where I will Roost to night yet, but I did not Know where I would get something to Eat today but I got it and all I was Fed. I am a great Believer in a god and nothing will Convince me but that there is a Supreme Ruler, for I have tested his Mercy to[o] often to Believe other wise, but Still I am no fanatic but I Believe if you trust in god he will Help you out as he has done me on numerous occasions. When I was at my wit's Ends, God would Step in and Help me out. I had started to leave the Town when who did I meet but and [an] old friend of myne [who] I was not thinking about, by the name of Sammel Hawks Came Driving by in his Buggie and he Regognized me at once.

'Why Bill,' he Says, 'have you come to this?'

We talked a while over old times. I did not ask him for nothing and he put his Hand in his Pocket and gave me one Dollar. Well you can say that I accepted it Gracefully and went and got a good Dinner and a Shave. He is a well-to-do Business man use[d] to be in Chicago & Marceilles Illinois but [is] now here. His P.O. address S.B. Hawks Bennington, Vermont, you can write him [and] he will tell you something of me. I must move on as it is getting late and I must find some Place to Sleep.

This is a much better Country on the East Side of Bennington than it was on the west Side, the mountains has mellowed down into more graduel Slopes and there is much better Farms. I don't see how some of the Farmers make a living between Bennington and Brattleboro Vt. I noticed that some of them Had no more than a half acre Ploughed up. Some may be two or three, others five or ten but I suppose they live of[f] their Cows and Cutting timber. But Wilmington is quite a Enterprising village. Marlboro is nothing but a tavern and a few Farm Houses, Dry Goods, Drug, Hardware Boots & Shoes comprised the Store. I don't think there was two Hundred dollars worth of goods in the out fit. Those are the only two vilages between Bennington B-boro, Vt is ten miles from Brattlboro West and Wilmington twenty, Just half way to Bennington.

I don't think there Ever was many Haut Beus [who] undertook to Cross those mountains from Lancaster N.H. to Bennington, as it is a Hard Road to travel. You will observe from the maps there is no Rail Roads from Keene N.H through to Bennington, the Country being to[o] Rough to build a Road. It is about one Hundred and twenty mi from Lancaster to Bennington and Mountains all the way. I am Glad to have a Change of Scenery. It is thirty two miles from B to Troy N.Y and no Rail Road Running direct, So I am walking the Pike. I most always travel by myself [for] miles. I can Strike a good civil Partner. I don't take up with Every one. Sometimes I get with a good fellow and we stay together for some time until he wants to go one way and me another or we get lost from Each other. I Had a Partner when I left NY citty but he had to Return to N.Y as his folks wrote for Him. He was a good straight fellow, I was Sorry to Part with Him.

June 10

Well, I came out all Right as far as Sleeping was Concerned. I found a Barn about half full of Nice Hay, I Crawled into it long before dark last night and now it must be 9 a.m. I sleept well, Had a good Rest, the best for some time. It has been a long time Since I have left my lo[d]ging Place as late as I have this Morning, but I am in no Hurry. I don't want to get to Troy before Monday and this is a pleasant Place, Cool and the Smell of the Hay is fragrant and away to itself. I like to be to My Self [with] no one to interrupt my meditations.

I had Some Crackers and dried Herran [herring] of wich I made my Breakfast, Better fare than I had yesterday morning. I am not a Glutton, I am Easily Satisfied as far as my Stomache is Concerned, give me good Plain food. I am particularly fond of Vegetables & Fruit. I have often made a meal of apples alone & oranges alone, a Can of Tomatoes, Can[ned] Peaches & as for getting drunk, I have been intoxicated a number of times but am not an hardened drinker.[32] I go Sumetimes for months and never touch intoxicating drinks. I don't fancy Whiskey much but like good Pure Wines, ale, Beer.

Women has done more to Keep me down in life Financially than any other Evil. Fast and designing woman I have Refference to. I have had numerous Chances to become a good Cittitzen and have been Regarded as Such, and Carry Good Recommendations in my Pocket from Good influential Business men and have Host of Friends amongs Such men. But I get down in the world and am ashamed of my Self and loose [lose] courage, get disheartened and take [to] the Road. I am of a Very Sensitive turn of mind and very independent, to[o] much so for my own good, But I am So Constituted and I can't Help it. The Gaze and Stare and Remarks of People as I Pass along grinds me to the quick. I get quite Ruffled in temper at sume of them. I passed a lot of men walking on the Road over in the Mountains the

---

32   McCook has asked Aspinwall for his dietary habits, including drink.

other day, they all Stoped their work and Scrutinized me. H-B Calls them Ruber necks, others named them goose Necks. I Said to them 'Gentleman this is not a Public Exibition, it is Strictly a Private Enterprise' but it had no Effect an[d] their Ignorance Prevailed. I often am the object of Scrutiny, Especily in the Country [and when] Passing Schools.

Farmers in Fields will Stop their work, Sit on their Plows, Hang on their Hoe and Fork Handles and watch and Ruber neck and goose neck until I would think their necks was actuelly made from the best of Rubber or that may be they was Related to the goose. I often Pass Children and Even Grown People Especily Women and Girls, that will Shy around me, Sometimes Run and then look back to see if I was coming, as if I was some dangerous Beast. I often Say 'Don't be afraid. I will not Harm you.'

I often think to my Self I must be a dangerous-looking Specimen of Humanity and Stop and take out my Pocket Glass and look at my Self but See nothing new, only more wrinkles. Getting older. So I Stop at Some Brook and Wash and Comb my Hair and try to look as Respecttable as Possible. Now you may think I am Exagerating but I am not. All I ask is to try and be Convinced. Pople as a general Rule are not as Hospitable and Kind in these Eastern States as they are in the South and West. They try to be More Aristocratic but not the kind of aristocratic People there is in the South and West. Some may think them Selves away above the Poor Entirely Here in the East but not So in the South and West. I think they Patron[ize] more After the Nobility of the old World Here in the East, more Narrow minded than they are in the South and West. Down South and out West there it seems More like a Republican form of Government. The Tramp Laws[33] of the New England States Shows that a Poor Unfortunate man Has no Chance. South Carrlina Bosts of not Having a Work House or Chain Gang in the limits of the State, but Still she is abused by Some States that would do well to Coppy Her Laws if they wanted to Show justice to Suffering Humanity. I admit there is men on the Road that will do any thing in the way of crime and So you Have in your Citties and Villages as well, and there is lots of Poor unfortunate men on the Road Harmles[s] as far as Crime is Concerned and that deserves Charity and Pitty and Encouragement. You Know there is lots of Crimes Committed by People that are Residents of the community that is layed [laid] at the feet of the unfortunate Tramps. If a Barn is Burnt the

---

33   These are amendments to vagrancy laws that made it illegal to cross state lines without visible means of support.

first theory is Some tramp Set it on fire, when it was Some of the drunken Careles[s] Hoodlums of the Community in the Barn or Building, Gambling, Smokeing and lighting matches, more careless than a Tramp Ever thought of being, that Set it on fire. But the Unfortunate Tramp Has to Bear the Blame. I know the ones that are the most daring and the ones that does the most depredations on the Road are young fellows that Runs away from Home on account of some Crime or depredation down in the Community where they live (Probably Children of well to do and Respectable Parents). I have Seen lots of Boys not out of their teens on the Road and young men of good Sence and learning. I see a boy last winter in Georgia, was with Him and His Partner [for several] days. He was only 17 yrs old and was from the State of Michagan. He told me he Stole his mother's Gold Watch and Run away from Houme, a very Bright Boy and his Father a Rich Farmer of Michigan.

His partner was about twenty yrs old and a Boston Hoodlum & advised the Mich Boy to go Back Home and ask his mother's forgiveness, but he said he was ashamed to. What became of him I don't know. I know he would not Starve, for he Had the Cheek of a mule. I met another young man, a Sun of Welthy Parents of Joliet Illinois, he was in the most Pittiable Condition you can see a Human being placed in. He Had layed by fires until he had burnt nearly all his cloths of[f] and [was] Bare footed and crawling with Vermin.

I met another young man from Atlanta Geo in the middle of Winter with a Straw Hat on, no coat Just a Cotton Shirt and and old Pair of overhauls, no undercloths, no suspenders and you could see the naked Hide Every time he made a Step through the Holes in His overhauls [which he] Burnt in by laying by fire. Still he was in good Spirits. How do you Suppose he Passed the Frosty nights and Cold days? And Seanes of other Cases I could Recall to mind but have not time or Space to mention. I must move on a ways, leave my nest.

June 10 1 p.m

Well, I have just passed through the Village of Hoosic [Hoosick], New York. I have Passed the line of Vermont & N. Y. I done well in Hoosic Considering the way I have been doing, I made 40 cts and it is one of the Cheapest Places to stay in since I Passed Willimantic Con, not accepting [excepting] Boston. You should of seen me coming out of the village with a Paper Sack about the Size of a 15lb flour Sack full of Grub and Bought it all Home, plenty to do me until Monday. I just Eat [ate] dinner, I had nice fresh light Bread, Ham, Cheese, Butter and Cup of Hot Coffee & Sugar but did not care for it until Supper & Breakfast, Haft to use a little Economy you Know. I don't know How it is, it may be in the Watter and in other Element but it is nevertheless a Candid fact there is the greatest difference you can imaging [imagine], as much as white is from Black, in the way People treat you in different localities and the differences in the Price of the necessaries of life. New Hampshire & Vermont are tough States. I guess the inhabitants up there thinks there is no People [who] Should inhabit the Earth but them. It looks that way to a man in my condition.

As I passed through some of their Villages, them tall old Yanks would look at you with a look of disdain and Horror and when you would Speak to them they would Grunt something unintelligible or maybe make no answer at all. I Generally, when I pass a house or through a village, Sing out 'Umbrellas and Parisols to mend', or if I Saw a Lady or Gent in the yard ask them very Respectfully if they Had any Umbrellas to to mend. Some would answer me with a Grunt, Some not at all. Now it is different in this Country. People appear more intelligent and treat you more Respectfully and apear to think you have a right to live. Vermont and New Hampshire are Prohibition States now, as far as I am Concerned. I don't care if there was never any Spirits made of any kind, I can do without them, but the States that allows

Saloons and allows People to use their own Judgement appear to me to be the progressive States. I think if some states would allow of more freedom of thought and not so much of Fanaticism they would be more Prosperous and would know better how to treat Strangers.

People Should Bear in mind it is not the coat or the on-the-outside appearance that makes the man, if it was so we would have had no Christ, no Saviour, for He was Considered in those days what now[a]days is called a Tramp. But I am just illustrating, don't think I am Comparing. Far from it, I am not worthy.

You wanted to know if I knowed or had Seen any H.B. Camps.[34] I have Seen them on numerous occasions. I have Seen them where there was Plenty of Beer and Alcohol, or Alca as it is termed, and Plenty to Eat, Cooked in old tin Cans and any old tin Vessel that could be Picked up. The Grub was Bumed or Begged from Butchers, Bakers and Private Families, and Probably Some of it gotten by the Slight of Hand [i.e., stealing], Such as Chickens, Hams, Potatoes, Cabbage, turnips and other articles to[o] Numerous to mention. Some of the H.B. are good Cooks. You would be Surprised at Some of the Meals Cooked by H.B. How palatable and how Harty a dish they would Eat and nothing but old tin cans to Cook in.[35] It takes a Cook to get up meals in Such a Style and How Patiently they will wait on Each other.

You know from my former writing that I Generly Keep to my Self or with a good Partner and did not go with gangs. Still, I know How they do and have Seen them in camp numerous times. You would laugh your Sides to Acheing to hear them tell their stories and make Remmarks, they are verry witty Some of them and Generally Jovial. I will give you a discription of a Camp my Self and Partner was in near Willimantic. Just My Self and Partner, we Stayed all night the night before in a Steam Saw Mill, it Rained all night and was quite Chilly and we Hugged that Boiler Close to keep warm but the next morning being Clear we came to the Conclusion to wash and Boil up our Cloths, for there had got to be more inhabitants in our cloth[e]s besides ourselves. We got Sume old cans and a good big tin Bucket out of a dump and Cleaned them out and went out in the woods and Built a fire Close to

---

34 Known as hobo 'jungles,' these camps were central to the 'hobohemian' subculture. Hobos would congregate in jungles to rest, eat, and socialize. Contemporary accounts emphasize the importance of storytelling, communal singing and drinking during what were sometimes called 'hobo conventions.'

35 Communal cooking and the free sharing of food were also a significant part of hobo subculture. Given the name 'Mulligan Stew,' the food contained whatever ingredients were at hand.

Watter. Got our Breakfast, Had Bread, Coffe, Sugar and Frankfort Sausages for Breakfast and it was good. Then we took of[f] our Shirts and drawers and Washed them in the Branch with Soap, got them as Clean as we Could and then Boiled them one Shirt at a time in our Bucket, wrung them out and wrenched them and Hung them up to dry and then Came our Preperation for Dinner. We was going to have a Pot Ro[a]st and a Plum and Suet Puding, or Plum Duff, H.Bs call it. I tell you it would have been interesting to see us Preparing our meal. But we Succeeded and a good Meal it was. I never sat down to a table where I Relished a better Meal.

Our Material was Procured the day before in Willimantic, all bought with Cash. We had lemon dressing for our Puding, bought the lemons and made it ourselves. We forgot to byy a white cloth to Boil our Puding in, So we washed out a White Hankerchief and used that. So we Had a good dinner and Supper and a Great many People would of Envied our Feast, thousands did not have as good. We passed the Entire day Sunday Eating, Cooking, Washing and Reading and Sleeping, for we do not forget to get our Paper once a week. Haft to Keep Posted. We put on our Shirts, Drawers, socks and felt like new men. By this time it was dark and we had to find a Box Car to Sleep in. Now this is Just a discription of one feast, we have numerous feasts but not Every day. I could Sit here and describe Until this time next Year of the feasts and Cooking Bees I have been in, but I tell you this to illustrate. Down South we use[d] to make a Meal out of Meal, or Georgia Peas. Most all the Poorer Classes of whites and Negroes cook out of doors in Southern States of Florida & Cuba but they are far better fixed for cooking Utensils than H.Bs, but the H.Bs Get there Just the Same. I and a Partner of myne left Chicago, one night Just after Harrison's Election,[36] for Pittsburgh. We went down to the [train] depot and Jumped a Blind Bagage[37] on the P. F. W & C RR [Pittsburgh, Fort Wayne and Chicago Railroad], and we did not get out of Chicago before two other fellows Jumped on with us and had another Keg of Beer with them. They taped it on the train and I think it was near all drank up by the time we was put of[f] at Valparaiso, Indiana. This is candid fact, I would not of Believed it my Self if I had not of Seen it and of Helped drink the Beer. I suppose they Sneaked [stole] the Beer from some Brewery or some Saloon.

---

36 A reference to Benjamin Harrison (1833–1901), President of the United States between 1889 and 1893.

37 A railway car that does not have a door at one end, which meant that discovery was less likely for train-hoppers.

I asked them no questions as it was none of my Buis [business], Eevery one tends to his own affairs in this Buisness. After we was Put of[f] I did not See the fellows any more after the train left, I suppose they Rode the Rods on trucks. We Stayed Until next morning and Got a Freight Train, went on to Ft. Wayne, Ind [and] we went through to Pittsburgh. In about 5 Days I got in[to] Pittsburgh. I was aquainted and a friend of myne told me where I could Get a job 40 miles up the Allegheny River at Kittaning [Kittanning], PA. I worked there two years for Peter Graff & Co and was very foolish for not staying there, but this Seems to be my lot.

Monday [actually Sunday]
June 11 93; Boytonville NY

I did not rest well last night. I got into a nest of fleas and they tormented me all night. I arose this morn as soon as it was day and made my Exit and Came to this Place. I got Something to Eat and not as well as I fared yesterday morn, but will haft to do. I fixed an Umbrella for a lady and Made twenty Cents and with this and what I had after getting my Breakfast I have twenty Cents in the Treasurey, but will haft to pay some Extra Postage and for this Sheat of paper out of that amount, so you See I do not have much Capital to go on, but I will trust in Providence for the future.

I had quite a comical Experience after I went in to the Barn Yesterday afternoon. I noticed Some Bords [boards] over head with a Considerable amount of Hay on them overhead. I thought to my Self: *that would be a good Place for me to Rest*. So I Climbs up, puling up my Bagage after me, and takes of[f] my Coat and Shoes and Sits my Self down and Prepared for a Pleasant time and Rest. I had not more than got Sit [sat] down and was Eating some Crackers [when] I heard a Busing [buzzing] Singing noise. I begin to look around for the cause. My clothes, during Several Months wear and tear, have warn through on the Posterior and, having disposed of my underwear Some time ago, for Reasons best Known to my Self, you See, I was Close to the Hay. I moved my Self slightly to one side and Behold you, there was [a] Bumblebees' nest under me and they was mad because of my intrusion. I tried to get out of the way but no Use, a few of the Excited Creatures got in there [their] work on my afore Mentioned Exposed Parts. And then there was Some Husling [cursing]. I was mad and Bumbles was mad and I jumped down to the floor below and left my Coat, Baggage and Shoes with the Bees. I afterwards got a Pole and fished them down, but ste[e]red Clear of the

28

Bees. It would have been a laughable Exibition to any Spectator but there was none, so there was not much laughing done.

I mail this to you this morn. Hope what I have written will be of interest. Hope I will Hear from you at Troy NY.

Fratulently yours

William W Aspinwall

Fig. 6

Sunday June 11 1893

Today is the Lord's day and I will not desecrate it any more than circumstances will admit of. I found another Hay Barn last night of[f] in a field by its Self. I went to it at a little after Sun down, found it Partly filled with Hay, ar[r]anged my Bed, took of[f] my Coat, vest and Shoes and retired and Slept soundly. I awoke but once and then I got a little Chilly. I spread my coat over Breast and Shoulders, Spread Some Hay over my lower limbs and soon was again in the land of morpheus, dreaming Sweet dreams of Better days. But awoke this morning to find my Self in and [an] old Barn out in the middle of a meadow, all alone Except [for the] Birds flitting over my Head. They was all the friends I apeared to have. I arose this morning Rather late, old Saul [Sol, i.e., the Sun] being far up in the Horizon, but it being Sunday I was in no Hurry, [so I] aranged my toilet.

Started out where I could find Some Secluded nook, where I could find a place to build a fire to make a can of Coffee and drink it. And a Butiful [Beautiful] Spot it is. About too [two] yds [yards] from the Road along a Babbling Brook, the watter as clear as Chrystal and cool. Most any monarch would Envy my position. But there is always Something to mar your Pleasure, the musketoes were just as thick as they could be without flying agains[t] Each other. But I soon collected together a pile of Sticks, my camp being amongst a Clump of fine Bushes, and built a fire. That Smoke soon thinned out the musketoes with the help of the Smoke from my tobacco pipe, So I could do my cooking. I made a good Strong Can of Coffee, Sweetened it well, Had some Bread, Crackers, Cheese and dried Herran that I procured yesterday and made out a good Breakfast.

My Coffee Pot is a old tomato Can [that] I Cleaned out. And I put on a wire Bail for a cup. I cooked and finished my meal, washed out my dishes and Hung them up to dry and aranged my office and gave [the rest of my time] to writing. It is wonderful at the amount of insects there is in the woods to torment you. Besides Muskitoes there are innumerable ants of all species, Spiders large and Small, and they all appear to be Crawling towards you to see what you are doing and to See what buisnis you Have intruding on there Homestead. They will Crawl over your Paper while you are writing, musketoes and bugs will bite you on the Hands and fingers, Crawl over your face and neck, get into your Eyse [eyes] and Ears and Even try to get into your mouth, the impudent Creatures. Crows will fly over your Head and Squak, a wood Chuck will come galloping out of the Bushes towards you and then look at you as if to ask what Buisness you had on these Premises. Spiders will crawl towards you and Stop and look at you as if Wondering. I have had before now Nice Plumaged Birds to come or fly and sit on my Shoulder – you may think this strange but it is never the case. I am a great lover of Birds and would not Harm one on no Consideration, or any thing of the Kind. I have shoved them out of my Way numerous times Rather than Harm them. When I See any one Harming Such Helples Creatures I think it shows the animal in them and I always chastise them for it. So you See there is always Something to mar your Pleasure, but I think it was So intended or Else your Pleasure would be incomplete.

You will notice in the Photo a Box Hanging on my Shoulder by a Strap and umbrellas, and Handles on the top. This Box contains my Cooking utensils and Camp Equipage. Some old umbrella tops I Spread on the Ground when I lay out or on the floor of a Box Car to Keep my cloths as Clean as Possible. It is a Pepper Sause Box I got in a Store in Wilamantic Conn. You will notice the advertisement in Red letters on one Side. It causes a great deal of mirth as I Pass People, Especialy Boys, you will Hear them Cry out 'Pepper Sauce!' I could not get it of[f], it adheared So Close to the Wood. I had the Photo taken Just as I actualy apeared on the Road. Just came into the Town and got your letter [then] went straight to the Gallery. You notice the Pipe, I Smoke and Chew a great deal of tobacco. Sometimes [when] I have no money to Buy tobacco I haft to go around depots and Public Places and gather[38] up Stumps of Cigars—or Short 'Swipes',[39] H.Bs. call it. When I was in Kokomo Indiana, One year ago this Spring, [I saw a hobo] tell or ask

---

38   The letter is torn here, but in "Leaves" McCook cites Aspinwall as writing 'gather.' I have used McCook's word here in the hopes that the letter was torn after McCook had written "Leaves." It is possible that McCook simply inserted a missing word here, however.

39   The text is missing here. McCook gives this as "Short 'Snipes'" in "Leaves," but 'Swipes' is used elsewhere so seems most likely.

a Couple of lawyers that were Standing talking on the Corner of the Public Square to 'Please Stand a little to one Side', as one of them was Standing on His tobacco. One of the Gents had the toe of his Boot on a good big Stump or Swipe. They Jumped to one Side and the H.B. got a His Swipe. It Created quite a laugh. The H.B. Picked it up an[d] walked of[f] in a unconcerned Buisness Way. Some of the H.Bs has all the Cheek imaginable. As I have stated before there is Several Classes of H.B.[40] Those that make a Profession of Begging, Stealing & won't work, never did work, visit all Charitable institutions[41], Priests, Preachers, Alms houses, 'Pogies'[42] H.Bs name them; Police Stations — not so much the latter as they are gen[erally] leary of the Police. They get their Under wear and shirts of[f] from Some Bodys Cloths line. H.Bs call it 'Picking a Gooseberry Bush'. You will Hear any of them say when his Shirt needs Changeing that he will haft to 'Look out for some one's Gooseberry Patch and go in and Pick Some Berrys'. The next day you will See them with a Clean Rig out and out Probably and other Pr [pair of] Shoes, Coat or Pants that he has Sneaked or Begged. You will hear them talk about Such and Such a town being a good town, or no good as the case may be.

This Class of H.Bs never Walk, or Drill as they call it. They will wait at a watter tank or the end of a division, two or three days, sometimes a week[43] to get a train. Don't Gen[erally] Haft [have] to wait that long but Some of them will go in to a Citty or town and Stay there, Holding down the town H.Bs call it, until the Police, or Bulls as H.Bs call them, get out to them and Either arrests them or Runs them out of town. These are the fellows that you see around Citties and towns loafing in the Parks and other Public Places with a white Shirt Collar, Shoes Blacked, Coat or Pants to[o] Big or to[o] Small, Shoes to[o] large that has been begged or got Some other way, Standing on the Street Car at night, Begging money for a night's loging in Some Cheep Loging House or to buy 'alkca' to get drunk on. These are the fellows[44] that does most of the Riding on trucks and Rods, mostly young

---

40   In "Leaves," McCook states "I had asked him to give his classification of the genus Ho-Bo in order to compare it with other systems." As this comment suggests, classifying hobos into types was extremely popular among the social investigators and proto-sociologists of the day. McCook, "Leaves From the Diary of a Tramp III," p. 3012.

41   'Institutions' has been taken from "Leaves" as the letter is now torn here.

42   Due to the letter being torn, I have taken 'Pogies' from "Leaves."

43   "the end of a division, two or three days, sometimes a week" has also been taken from "Leaves."

44   The end of the previous sentence and the start of this one have been taken from "Leaves."

fellows all the way from ten to thirty years old and [they] are the ones that have most of the Phrazes & Slang Signs & they will tell you of good Houses to Bum, [where you are] Sure to get a Sit down [i.e., a meal], will get a Hand out, only way Such a House is good is for money or Such a Priest, doctor or whoever it may be. [They] will get arrested on Purpose in the Winter in Some locality where there is no Work House to Pass the winter in Jail, [they] Stay in Some Citty and Bum money to stop at Cheap loging Houses.

I will give you a discription at Some future time of Cheap Loging Houses, railroad yards, Missions. In my Experiance You see[45] these fellows' ficticious names in old Houses, depot Watter Closests [water closets, as in toilets], Watter tanks & [meaning etc.], Such As 'Philly Shorty arrived Such a time Bound West or East North or South', as the Case may be, 'New York Slim', 'the Brooklyn Kid', 'Boston Jack' and a thousand other Apelations [appellations]. These are the fellows that Receive most of the charities and Gen never go Hungry because they have that indomitable Cheek: won't Eat Bread, or Punk as they Call it, must have Cake or Pie or dainties, and the ones that are Sassy to Women, won't Saw Wood or do any work of any Kind for Some thing to Eat. This Class is Composed of Jail Birds, Ex convicts and young fellows that have done Some thing in the Place where they lived that they dare not go back.[46] Probably Some of them with Highly Respected families at their Houses, others of them have no Homes, Probably never Had any. Only you Hardly Ever See any Foreigners with this Class, once in a while a London or a Liverpool [i.e., English] Bum. I have Seen these Kind of fellows traveling with the young Boys, the boy doing the Begging. And I am almost ashamed to tell it, not fit to be written that Human Beings will become so low, but I will tell the truth they use these Boys as a man would a Woman, in other Words Practice Sodomy. I have Saw them at it in Box Cars. Disgusting, Lower than Brutes.

I have Seen others [and] have had them try their game on me but it will [not] work. I have never got [in with] that and by God I never will. They take Each other's Person in their mouths, you will only See one in a great while that will do this. To their Credit the H.Bs Call Such fellows 'Fruit' 'Canned goods' and other names [like] 'Prunes!' Now these are the Class of H.B. that get all the Charities and do most of the Bumming where the working man, mechanic and other Profesions that Hapen to be Unfortunate, Bad luck,

---

45   "You see" has been taken from "Leaves."

46   "where they lived that they dare not go back" is taken from "Leaves."

Strong drink or Some other Cause that Brings them down Have not the Cheek to Beg. I have Knowed Poor fellows to be on the verge of Starvation before they they could Rais[e] the courage to go up to a House. I am one of them my Self. So you See the Undeserving gets the Best of People's Charity while the deserving go without. This is from my personal Experiance what I have actually Seen. I did not like to Put on Paper Some that I have writen but a description would be incomplete without it. If you get on the right side of Some Regular H.B, he will without a doubt Substanciate what I have writen, if he will tell the truth. There is Hundreds of instances of different Kinds I have Seen in my travels I can Call to mind. I have not time or Space at this writing to mention, as my Paper is all gone and my letter is already to[o] large for one mailing. I have given you a tolerable fair discription of No1 Class of H.Bs.

Remember this foregoing discription is of the worst or lowest Class of H.Bs. There is Plenty of good intelligent men on the road. The aforesaid Class [i.e., the 'worst' hobos] Gen carry a Revolver or Some Kind of a Weapon and Some of them will Stoop to any Crime almost for a little gain. And amongst them are Smart intelligent fellows, Capable to fill any Position, and [amongst] them you will [also] find ignorance. Some can't Read or write but they are Gen[erally] Well Posted on the topicks of the day. I have never Carried any Weapon Since the War in all my travels larger than a Small Pocket Knife, never any Use for any. I always Shun if Possible any Company where Weapons are Wanted.

Sunday June 11 93

I though[t] I had writen all my Paper up, but in looking over my letters I have found another two Sheets. Then came a Thunder Shower and I had to move my beautiful Camp, where I [had] got my things wet. I got safely Anchored in a friendly Hay Barn. The indications are now that I will haft to make this my Staying Place for tonight, for it is beginning to Rain [again] and at no Moderate rate.

You wanted to know How I Slept in the open air. I remove Coat and Shoes and if I have nothing Else use my Shoes for a Pillow. I Spread my Coat over my Chest and if it is Cool lie under the Coat, also my Breath Helps Keep my Body warm. A Coat will be a Great deal warmer in this way than Keeping it on. Rightly, yes, H.Bs Have signs[47] and Grips and a Kind of a Mongrel language they got up them Selves. But not General, only Amongst a number of the Kind I have writen about this morning. When they Strike a good town to Bum in, they will make a Sign in some Public Place around the Watter tank, Such as a good Character or a good Saloon that will give them a drink, they will make Some Sign on the gate Post, Side of [a] door, or Some Place where their friends may See it. All do not understand these Signs, differen[t] Crowds or numbers Have different Grips and Signs, Probably written on doors, will Get up a Code of their Own. If they Should happen to get parted by Some get[t]ing away on a train and others not, they will write under their ficticious name in Several Conspicuous Places when they were there and wich way Bound. In this way they find Each other.

I am not very well versed in their mysteries but understand the Working of the Order to some Extent. Yes they avoid Citties, I mean certain ones. I

---

47   Though we do not have McCook's letter to Aspinwall, it is clear from this line that the Professor is interested to know if hobos have their own secret language. Many middle-class writers fretted about this possibility, which seemed frightening to them.

don't think New Hamshire and Vermont are troubled much with H.Bs. I have only Saw [seen] one Since I left Manchester. He was going towards Lowell opisite [opposite] from me. He said he Could get no work but Shoveling, and he said he would not Shovel for no man. Stout Built fellow He was.

I have Seen but seldom female Bums, or Bags as the h.bs Call them. I seen Several, in the South Mostly. I Saw one white Woman traveling with Negro Bum and I saw one in a freight Car with four or five Regular H.Bs Profesionals, and Some at different times, man and woman alone. There is a Camp of H.Bs near Philadelphia over in Jersey near Camden where there is Several Women or Bags, but they Gen pass as man and Wifes but then during Berry Picking season they are abandoned. I don't often See them way of[f] on the Road but [usually] Hanging around in the vincinity of Some Citty. I saw Some great times at Hop Picking near Utica N.Y. All the H.Bs and Bags from Citties in Hundreds of Miles of there goes there in Hop Picking time. And Such a drunk & confused Mes[s] of Humanity Can't be described as there at that time. I will give you a discription of that and Grape Picing [picking] at Harvesting, Strawberries Pickin at Some future time.

Prof I have writen [on] all the Paper you Sent me. I hope it may prove interesting to you and others.

I have Endeavored to give you a good Honest discription as far as I have went on my travels and the Subject of Haut- Beaus. I hope it will be apreciated by your Self and [the] Public if it gets that far. I have had a larger Experiance in this life I dou[b]t if there is another man who has seen the Broad Land of America, that has been through what I have and Seen what I have Seen in the way I Have. I am Ashamed of the way I have Passed my life, but it is So. I can't mend the Past but will try and live different at Some future time, if I only Can come acroos an opertunity. I am tirad of this life but what Can I do? Of course, I have not used discretion Heretofore. But that is Passed, can't mend that. All I want is an opertunity for the future. I will mail this letter at the Earliest opertunity. Hope I will Hear from you at Troy N.Y and Receive more Stationary.

I have walked Ever since I left NY citty and from Willimantic alone. Am all alone today, don't want any H.B. company unless it is my Kind; I am about 18 miles from Troy, will Walk Part of it Some time today. Will Read a while.

Yours,

William W Aspinwall

June 13 4 P.M

I Am Just getting in to Troy N.Y - I am now in the out Skirts. I don't know yet or have not Made up my mind wich course I will take from Troy, but think I will go through Schenectady, Utica, Syracruse Rochester, Lockport to Niagara Falls, Thence to Buffalo, Pittsburgh And so on. I was in Troy once before, two years ago, after Hop Picing, will give you a History of that trip at some future time. Will let you Know from Troy where to write to me After I make up my mind as to my course of traveling. This is a Beautiful Country I have Come through today, in fact a nice Country Ever Since I left Bennington, Vt, a wide difference from the Country East of there in the mountains.

It has been verry Hot today and looks now as though there would be a thunder Shower. You will notice I got a day behind in my dates. I have corrected them in this letter, you Can Correct them in What I have [already] Sent You. I mailed you a letter yesterday from Boytonville N.Y, I suppose you will get [it] today or tomorrow.

I got your letter you Sent to Brattleboro but nothing Else forwarded Here.

Will go from here to Utica N.Y.

When I Awoke this morn the Sun was far Advanced in its dayly travels. I Hus[t]led out and found Some Woods along [the] Side of the Road filed Right in to the timber. Found A fine Spring Branch, built a fire, the musketoes disputing my way and progress but I gave them Battle And now I Am the Conquer[or] And Hold the Battle field. My Hands, face and neck are full of little Bumps and Sores where they have Stung me at different times.

I made my tomato Can Coffee Pot full of good Strong Coffee, Had Some Crackers and Herran, Blind Robins[48] H.Bs Call them, and had my Breakfast. That Satisfied me. I took a Wash in the Branch, Combed my Hair, Washed

---

48 Smoked and salted herring.

out My tin Ware, As I am very Cleanly About my Cooking. I Carry a Pocket Comb, a Small Pocket Glass and a Cake of Soap. I wash my neck, face and Hands regularly, Every day once, and more if I have an opertunity. I Some times take of[f] all my Cloths when I have a good opertunity and take a good wash and Bath all over and it makes me feel much better, it Amply pays me for the trouble. And I wash and Boil my Shirts and Under weare once a week if Posible. I am no friend to dirt and filth, there is no [exc]use [for] it – [even] if you are Poor and on the Road, no House, no Home, nature has provided ways and means for Every one to Keep Clean. I have seen H.Bs on the Road that was a Sight Horible and disgusting, So Lousy and filthy they Could not Stand Still, Scratching and Rubing Continually Until their flesh was all torn into Sores. I Can't See how they get any Rest night or day, they must feel miserable. If I was in the Condition that Some Are [who] I have Seen, I would Jump into the first River I came to and Say to my Self, *Here Goes nothing*: it is nothing but Lazyness, no Ambition.

There was and [an] old fellow came up to my camp fire one night last Winter in the State of Tennessee near the Village of Tullahoma. It was after dark. I thought it was Some Kind of an Animal Comeing towards me. Well he was an object of Pitty, inocent as a lamb, he was from Switzerland & Could not talk English, Had no friends in America. Said he had been in this Country three years and had been on the Tramp Ever since he landed at Castle Garden N.Y. I can talk and understand Considerable German Enough to make out what he was telling me. Well he had on nothing but a pair of blue overalls, no drawers, no Shirt of any Kind, no Vest or Under coat, a pair of old Shoes and full of Holes, no Socks. He Had on and [an] old overcoat full of Holes and fastened together with Pegs or sticks in front, careful to have space Enough between fastenings So he Could get his Hands into His Skin so he Could Scratch, for he was Undoutedly the Louseiest man I Ever saw, and I have Saw a good many. He would put his Hand inside of His Coat and pick the lice, or Crumbs as HBs call them, by dozens and throw them in the fire and I could see his flesh all torn by Scratching and dirty. Oh My, Sickening Scales on him like a fish. Well, I Should Say he was the most Miserable man I Ever Saw. I took pains and watched him.

He was not Still I don't think a minute All night. It was A Cold night in November, I was up a great many times ading fuel to the fire. I wanted him to lay on the opesite Side of the fire from me, as I had my Reasons for not Comeing in Contact with Him. He did not Even ofer to get my Wood or fix the fire, to[o] lazy and dilatory I Supose. Would of layed out that Cold night without fire if he had not of Seen myne. No telling the amount of Suffering and tourments that Creature had been through in His time and all His own fault, no Ambition no get up about Him. His beard and Hair Had been growing, I think, Ever Since he left Castle Garden.

It was all matted together. I don't Suppose he Ever Put A Comb to his Hair or Beard Since he Arived in America. And Washing was out of the question with Him: Him and Watter were Strangers as far as out ward applications were Concerned. His face was thick with dirt and Scales, it is almost imposible for me to discribe the man as he Apeared. He told me that He had been Ar[r]ested in some Town in the State of Mississippi because He Had no Shoes and Kept him in Jail 60 days.[49] I Asked him if the Authorities gave him any Shoes or Cloths, he Said 'no'. After he got out of Jail, he went to a Countryman of His that lived in the town And He gave him the Shoes and Coat he Had on. Notice the inconsistency of the Authorities in aresting the man because he Had no Cloths and then discharged him after 60 days in a worse Condition than he was when Arested. Some things work Curiously. I don't Know what became of the man, we parted next morning. He was going South. I made Coffee, divided with him, and gave him part what I had to Eat. He grabed and Eat like a Hungry Hound. I Suppose he had a Hard time geting anything to Eat. He would Scare people when they would See him coming.

Now I describe this One Case in particular and [it] is true Just as I have written, Could Hardly give Him Justice on Paper: this is only one out of Hundreds of others I See on my travels, but ilustrate this Case in Particular to give you an Idea how Some men live on the Road. He was a fairly Educated man in his own language.

Now I am going to give you a discription of a cheap Loging House I Stoped at in Washington Street in the Citty of Boston. The first night I was there, the next night I Stoped at the Soldiers' Home, Sleeping on the Smoking Room floor. I Suppose the Supt thought I was Unfit for a Bed. I have Stoped at numerous Houses before but always got A Bed.

Even at the Confederate Home in Richmond, Vir got a good Bed and the best of treatment. I Probably Seen A great deal more Actuel Service during the War than the Supt of the Soldiers' Home at Chelsea, but I have him to thank for nothing as the People Keep up the Home Well. The first night in Boston I Enquired and found this Cheap Loging House, as it was late and the funds in my treasurer was low and would not admit of any[thing] more

---

49   This arrest would have been for vagrancy.

Costly. I went in upstairs, got into the Sitting Room after the Clerk. Looking through the glass in the door, he pulled the latch String, the latch being Connected by a String to the Rear End of a Counter where the Cleark Presides. No one gets in there Until the Clerk first gets a look at him. I Suppose it is for Keeping out noisy intoxicated Persons, but I noticed a number of such Persons got in. I noticed a great deal of Partiality as the Clerk has his favorites, drunk or Sober. I walked up to the Counter, Payed my fifteen cents. The clerk Registering your name, thinking: *Of course you can't write*, gives you a number of your Bed. My name was put down [as] Jim Jones, I never give my Corect name in Such Places. You give your baggage and cloths to the Clerk, he has a Room, the door being behind this Counter, and the Clerk can Keep his Vigilant Eye on the door and locked besides. Remember, there is All Kinds of thieves Stops at those Places, Will Steal Anything, from a Pin to a Eliphant. But not All are this Kind, some nice fellows but Unfortunate. Well such a Crowd as was there is Hard to describe in detail. Some drunk as lords, Some Curseing, Some Scratching, Some Sewing, Some with Heads tied up, Some with Black Eyse, Been fighting or drunk and the Street flew up and Hit them, Some trying to be dudes in all kinds of imaginable wearing Apparal. A Sight to Behold, a good Place to Study Human nature.

Well I Sit around [a]while [and] took in the Surroundings, Concluded I would go to Bed, took of[f] my Coat Vest, Shoes and Hat, Passed them to the Clerk, he put[t]ing them in the Pigeon Hole allocated to me, and was Shown upstairs in a Room where there was at least 50 Cots, Just Room Enough Between to Stand. The Bed Contained a quilt, Straw-like Sheet and Pillow, and a Spring mattress, good Enough if they Had Been Clean but Reaking with Vermin of all Kinds, and dirt. I Concluded that a man Should be Drunk or insensible to Sleep there. I did not Sleep any. I Soon got in to the same occupation that some of my Neighbors was in, Scratching and Rooling [rolling] Around.

Those that were too drunk to move done good Sleeping and Snoreing. And Such Bedlam. Snoreing, Some loud Enough to almost Shake the building, Some talking, Some Singing. Once in a while you would See a fellow raise up and take out a Bottle of Whiskey, take a drink. Such a Sickening Smell, Whiskey, dirty feet and Bodies that had never been washed probably Since the day they was Born, Some Vomiting on the Beds and floor. A man in your position has no Idea how low and depraved Human beings Can become. What I am telling you is truth and not as bad as it actually is, all I ask is for Some inteligent Person to try a night and See if they don't Substanceate All

41

I have written and more. I did not lay in that Bed long after it Came day. I put in a miserable night and I got away from there as quick as [possible]. A Camp in the Woods, a Bunk on the Hay in a Barn, or a Bed on the floor of a Blue line Sleeping Car Box Car, any of wich is a Pallace to a Cheap Logging House. Now Some dives are better and Some Even Worse than what I have discribed. In a Citty there is no other Chance as you are liable to Arest Sleeping in Box Cars or out any where, and a Cheap Loging House is a necesity. All Clases of H.Bs go there. Citty Bums, Some of these stay there for a year or more. Any Kind of a H.B. is a Credit to a Citty Bum, they are the filthiest Beings on Earth, Some of them. Now the foregoing discription will give you Some Idea. This is only one Place of the Hundreds I have Stoped at in my travels and time. I will in Some future time give you a Complete discription of Some of the Police Stations, Wood Yards and Missions I have visited in different Citties in my travels. I have Writen today more than I intended. It is getting near dinner time and I am Eight Miles from Troy. My fire is gone out and the Musketoes are disrupting my right to remain longer in this Spot, I haft to Keep fighting them away with my Kerchief. So you See I write Under difficulties, You will please excuse mistakes and Punctuation.

I like to write and tell my Experiances and can Hardly stop when I get fairly at it. I have been through So much and Have so much to write about, therefore I use Some more time than I should do. I will mail this to you from Troy. I mailed you a letter yesterday. I invested in a Cheap Tablet [i.e., notepad] and a lead Pencil Yesterday and if I Keep on writing at this Rate I will Soon want more. I only write on one Side of this Paper as it is thin and flimsy. I hope you will be able to make it all out and get Sense out of it and that it will Prove interesting to you and others. I will propse to Move On.

Yours William. W. Aspinwall

Troy N.Y. June 14 1893

I went from Past Albany in Troy down to the Poorer End of [the] Citty yesterday Evening, near a long Iron work, also near the Hudson River. About four miles from P.O I found Some Box Cars on side track, looked them over, found one fairly clean and a little straw in. I went and sit on the River Bank watching the Boats pass and Boys Baithing Until it was good and Dark, and then got into the Car I had Chosen. I have to be a little Careful about Police & Detectives Climbing in to Cars, don't want to be Arested.

I did not Rest well, as there was a Swich Engine Comeing and going past all night and [I] did not Know when they would Couple onto the Car I was in and Haul me of[f] Somewhere I did not want to go. I have had a little Experience of that Kind Heretofore, therefore haft to be a little discreet. Then about 4 o clock, the Iron Works Changed Hands [i.e., workers]. One fellow looked into the door and yeled at me and wanted to Know when the half-past one went down. I told him 'About Seven.' Another fellow look[ed] in and says 'Lost in London?' I was disturbed from that [time] on, Until I got up and Started back for Troy. I layed down Hungry last night. I Spent the last three Cents for Postage.

I did not make a penny yesterday. I done fairly well the day before but got my Shoes Repaired, Clean Socks and some other necasaries and about Busted the Treasury. Expecting to make Something yesterday but I did not. Some times I do fairly for a day or so and then it will be two or three days or [for] a week nothing. I will haft to do without Breakfast Until I make something this morning. I have a little coffee & sugar yet but nothing Else. I have the Promise of a small Job fixing a Parisol. A Butcher Called me as I was passing along and told me to come around in about one Hour and he would give me a Job. I don't know How much there is in it, Enough for a light Breakfast I hope. I have not Begged or Bumed anything.

Since [meaning when] I left New York Citty, a Gentleman Payed my way. About fifteen Miles into Boston, as it was getting dark, I asked him how far to Boston.

He told me. He says, 'Are you going to work?'

I says 'Yes Sir, I am short.'

'You wait', he said, 'and take the train. I will pay your way.'

I waited willingly and thanked Him Kindly; another Man that was with Him put five Pennys in my Hand. This and the Dollar my friend gave me in Bennington is all the Help I have Had, and I did not ask for that. I detest to Bum, it Seems So low and degrading. I must go around and See about my Job as the Hour is about up.

West Troy. New York; June 14 5.P.M

Well, you can Say I have had a great Experiance today. I went down to the 'Helping Hand' Mission this morning after Makeing 25 cts at the Butchers mentioned before, and 10 cts of [i.e., from] a lady [a]cross the street fixing [a] Handle to Her Parisol. While Eating at the 'Helping Hand', any one in Troy Can tell you where it is, I met an Old Soldier Heau Beau. He was Eating the Same as my Self, and full of Rum, of Course, and Adorned with G.A.R[50] Button and V.V.L Badge in Flying Collors. I of course soon made friends with a Comrade.

He says: 'What is the mat[t]er with us traveling together?'

He Had a Silver Polish, would turn Brass Copper or any other metal to Silver, No dout a good Fake. He had Some Counterfeit One Dollar Coins in Cruide [crude] State, Showed Me. He Said we would finish and Pass well. We Started out of course and He Steered Straight for a House of Ill fame [i.e., a brothel], or of good fame as they Seem to Be in Troy.

He was Busted of Course financially and the first thing He asked me was, after we got to the Place, 'Have you got any Stuff?'

'Of Course,' my Nature Says, 'I will treat.' My Partner taking Whiskey, and me Ale.

Well the Girls were not up yet, it Being to[o] Early for them. We Started on a tour, My Partner being well aquainted and we Visited all the Salloons and fancy Houses, He treating Several times, Standing Salloon Keeper. Of [i.e., upon] Being aquainted I fixed an Umbrella for one Salloon Keeper, the Pay going for Drink of course and the old H.B. was an Alcohol fiend, he went into a Drug Store where he was aqainted, got a Pint of Alcohol at two diferent times wich diluted with watter would make [a] half Gal[lon] of Strong Whiskey. So, you See, we was Started in good Shape, or Rather he

---

50   The Grand Army of the Republic, a veterans' organization founded in 1866.

got me Started in good Shape. I never drink any thing Stronger than beer or Ale, but did this day. My Old Sol[dier] friend, a great deal fuller [i.e., more drunk] than I was, He took me into a House of Prostitution in an ally [alley] where he Had been before and [knew] some of the Girls.

Set them up and My friend, having Alcohol, made it known, and the girls drank with us. And we all got full. I was as full as a Goose and the girls was walking around the Alley and ajoining Street with my Kit and my Partner's Hallowing Silver Plating and Umbrellas to mend. One of them [was] in Short cloths showing her lower limbs to her knees. I made love[51] to this one, Of Course, She being good looking and young, and she satisfied my amorous desires, she partaking at intervals of the alcohol. The land lady being out when we would drink the Alca, they would Sing out: 'All the Hores [whores] will be dead when the land lady Comes Home'.

I got out in the kitchen and made love to the young lady [who was] doing the family Washing, as I am quite an Adonias [Adonis] and a favorite with ladies when I get Harnessed up. She being good looking and Reciprocated my advances and drank alca with us, we Soon got to Hugging and [we] was soon Engaged for Better or Worse, Promising to Stick to Each other through thick and thin, I Promising to Return for Her. I got full, that is Enough to navigate. Always keep my Promises But am Sassy. I Even Partake, don't only on the above occasions. I lost my Soldier.[52] I am in West Troy, he's in Troy. I think it best for Various Reasons we Should be two, as His Ways and Myne are different. I met one more Old man. He is at preasant siting talking to Me. A fine looking inteligent and well dressed Man, lives in NY Citty, Been out West But Bums his Way. Him and I will Probably Bunk together tonight. Soon Will haft to Hunt a Box Car as it is getting dark, good night.

---

51 During this time period, 'making love' meant to flirt.

52 Aspinwall means his road partner. He may have still been drunk when he wrote this letter, which is less coherent than others.

West Troy. N.Y. June 15 1893

My Self and a new friend started out together to find a Sleeping place. We did not know where to go, it being dark.

I asked Some Boys on the Corner of the Street, 'Where I Could find Some Box Cars?' They directed Me. I says, 'Now Boys, this is Confidential.'[53]

They answered 'Oh! Yes!'

My Partner did not like it for me to Ask the Boys. He Said they want to follow us and put the Cops on to Us. And he started down a street in the oposite direction from the way the Boys told me to go. I asked him where he was going. He Said to Come on that way. I said 'No.' This was the way he Keeps on his way.

I Said 'You go your way and I will myne.' That is the last I saw of Him.

I kept on the way my Boy friends told me and found all the Box Cars I wanted. Got into one and stoped all night. Boys are my friends, have befriended me on numerous ocasions in My travels. If I want information, I See Some Boys they will give it Me More direct than Some Adults. Boys have fed Me at different times and done a Many a good turn for Me. I like the Boys, they are my friends, they Have at different times had a great deal of fun at my Expence but I take fun.

I did not Rest Well last night. Was Sick from drinking so much different drinks yesterday. I had to get out in the night and go down to the Hudson River and drink, I got so thirsty. I had a taste in my mouth as if I had been drinking Crude Petroleum and feel Sick yet this morn. It is now only about 4 o clock. I am sitting in the Box Car, writing. My H.B. friend I met under the Bridge Sitting on the Bank of the Hudson yesterday Eve told me that he Started from Cleveland, Ohio one Evening about Eight o clock in a Box Car

---

53   i.e., Aspinwall does not want the boys to tell a policeman that he will be illegally sleeping in a boxcar.

and the next morning he was in Denville, just this side of Utica NY. So you See how fast H.B. Can flit over the Country when disposed.

While sitting Under the Bridge last Eve, after I was through writing, a well dressed good-looking young lady Came up to Me and began talking and asking me questions. I invited Her to a seat beside Me on the green. She accepted, My H.B. friend geting up and moveing of[f] from Us Some distance. I had quit[e] a good time with her for near an Hour. She told Me where She lived and invited me up to See Her and Said She would Meet Me at the Same Spot at night. After She went away my H.B. friend asked who She was. I told Him She was one of my Cousins. He thought she was Some Relative and Said She was Mighty good looking.

You notice I make friends with Some of the ladies if I am on the Road. I often make a lady friend at Houses where I stop and do work. I had one in Boytonville N.Y, a well-to-do Widow, She liked of [i.e., could have] talked my Right Arm of[f]! She was an excel[l]ent Conversationalist. One of the Girls[54] yesterday wanted to go along with Me on the Road and no doubt would of went if I had of Said So but I told them any thing for Me but a Woman on the Road. That ended that part of it. My Soldier friend was a great Drinker, the one I was with yesterday, he got dry about Every 10 or 15 Min. He was quite an old Man, I Should think near 60 yrs. He was Bald headed, what Hair He had was grey, a grey mustach a fine-apearing old Gent, and a Smart and intelligent Man, but [he] Could punish the alcohol and Rot-Gut to[o] much for me! He Said he had been onl[y] a drunk in Troy for two weeks. I told Him this Sporting life was a great life to lead. He told Me he Had done ten years' time [in prison], Had traveled all over the world and I have no doubt he Has. I Seen I was getting to[o] much drink abord yesterday, So I watched my opetunity and Sliped away from the old man and Came across the River and layed down Under the Bridge. What Became of Him I don't Know.

I don't want to drink and Make a fool of My self, but when I get started like yesterday [I] get to[o] much and all for friendship. I never drink Whiskey when I am Alone, Some times take a glass of Ale or Beer. I am getting more Temparate the older I get. I See the folly of it. Drinking is a very disgusting habit to See it in the diferent Ways I have Seen it. I am better of[f] Alone than with a drinking Man. I have no money in the Treasurer this morning, I Spent my last ten cents for Tobacco and Envelope & Stamp, two cents to Cross the Bridge, So I am as bad of[f] as I was Yesterday Morn. Don't Know

---

54   One of the prostitutes mentioned in the previous letter.

where my Breakfast is to Come from. I made fifty five Cents Yesterday, Could have had a quarter this Morning if it Had not of been for yesterday's Carousel, but will trust in Providence for the future. What I have written is facts just as the[y] transpired, as near as I can discribe them. Truth is Stranger than fiction, I mention all So you Can get the chain of My life Complete. I was disappointed in not Hearing from you at Troy on account of Envelopes and your opinion. I will Send you a letter as after [i.e., as soon as] I can. I want you to Have a true and full discription of all My doings & travels. As I have Commenced to give it to you, I have got interested.

I Will Endeavour to Give you a list of My Stoping places between Manchester N.H. and Brattleboro Vt. The night of June 1st I Stoped in a Wagon Shed, laying in the Bottom of a Wagon all night. I Eat all the Way, Some times Bread & Bolona, some times Crackers, once in a while Coffee. I went Hungry Some times on that trip as I could not get much Work. June 2 Slept in Box Car. June 3 to June 4" Slept in Woods, Had a fire. I don't just Remember the Balance but Either Sleep in a Car one or two nights in Woods and Several times in Vacant Houses. The Reason I Kept no Memorandum [was that] I lost My Note Paper and my lead Pencil, and Had no money to buy [more].

I made a quarter near Here Helping a Dentist Brake a Colt. He gave Me My Supper.

I will give you in future Some More of My Past Experiance as I have a large Stack in Store with the Preasant. Sent you a letter from Troy, it did not Have Enough Postage but I had no more Money. Hope you will get it as it is a important letter. Also mailed you one a[t] Bennington and one at Boytonville N.Y. [I will] mail this today, [it is] to[o] big for one Stamp now.

Yours W.W.Aspinwall

June 15 / [18]93 4 P.M

I got up this morning to Erie Canal and Started up [the] Toe Path towards Cohoes Falls. Went a little ways and the Capt of a Boat Called Me that was going My Way to mend an Umbrella for him. I got a loaf of Bread, Some Cakes and Some Ale and eat Harty, for I was Hungry. Had no Breakfast but my Treasurer is again Broke and will haft to trust to Providence for the next.

I am now about two mi[les] above Cohoes, Just Past Cohoes Falls, and a Beautiful Sight it is and what a Wonderul Watter. [The] Power [of] Nature and Art combined does Wonders. This is a Beautiful and Romantic looking Country. Today is a very hot day, Every one I meet are Complaining of the Heat. I am resting in the Shade of a friendly Elm. These Canal Boat Captains and Hands are a friendly lot and a Jovial lot, Every one that passes has [a] Jovial Remark. I must move on and try to get a Job or no Supper. Will go to Rest Early tonight, feel tiard and Weary. Will get to Schenectady tomorrow, nothing preventing. Will follow Canal to Utica.

June 19⁵⁵/[18]93

I Passed a Small village Called Creasant, Made 20 cts and made 20 cts at another Store on this Side of there, about two Miles and have 15 cts in Treasurer. After Supper & Breakfast of Coffee, Bread, Ham & new onions, I met another H.B on the Tow Path about dark last Eve. He is a Half-Breed, Indian & French. He only Has one Arm, one arm being of[f] in the Shoulder Joint. He said he Just got out of Troy Jail Yesterday morning after serving 90 days for Stealing. He is a Regular Waddle Bum, Makes his living Bumming Money. From what he tells me he punishes lots of Whiskey. We Stayed together that night, Sleep in a little Shantie out in the middle of a field, Close [to Erie] Canal. Arose Early, Got Breakfast. I finishes every thing but [will] always divide with Any one I meet on the way, I am to[o] free that way But Can't Help it. I will Send you a Postal Card from Schenectady, an[d] this letter.

There is a Petticoat Bum or Bag Just Passed us, Hard looking Case. She is Sitting Under a Bridge near. The Half Breed is after Her. She Wants Whiskey but will fail in my Case. Today is not So Hot as Yesterday.

---

55   This date is incorrect. It was the 16th June, the same day as the next letter (which also has an incorrect date). On this letter Aspinwall has transposed 6 and 9.

June 15 [actually 16th]

I went up to the ol[d] Petticoat Bum And Had a talk with Her. She told me She Stayed all night with an old Farmer and that He was Making indecent proposals to Her and that he was and [an] Old Man of 70 or More years, and that she did not want to Have any thing to do with and [an] Old Man like Him. He followed her in a Buggy this morning. She told me She got in the Buggy with Him. I first Saw her in a Buggy with a very old Man and She was Cussing Him in good Shape but I thought at first She was his Wife, as her face Showed age and Her Hair Silver grey but much Much younger than her Escort.

She Says, 'He told Me that he had Some Boiled Eggs in his Pocket and Some Bread and Butter,' and would give it to her but wanted something for it.

But she told Him he was not going to get it and that She was not that Kind of a Woman, and got out of the Buggy.

I asked her wich way she was going. She Said She did not Know. I See her Comeing along this way, I think She has been on [the] Same Boat as [the] Cook[56] and they have put her of[f]. My Half Breed friend [is] still with Me, He is laying on the Grass Sleeping while I am writing. He told Me he could not Read or Write as the Indians did not learn him. He Says he is a good Indian Doctor and a good Horse Doctor and that Some times he sold Indian Medicines. I will investigate his Abilities if he is in my Company long. He is a great fellow for a Woman, but the one we met this morning won't talk to Him. He may of made some Remark to Her that she did not like. May be the old lady Has no Use for one armed men, the Same as Old Men. We are now in about three Miles of Shenectady. I have made no Money today yet. I am Sitting in the Shade of a tree between the Canal and the Butiful Mohawk.

---

56   It is not clear who Aspinwall is referring to here.

June 16 5 PM.

Some way or other I have got behind one day in my dates, this is the 16" instead of 15" of June. You will Haft to, if you Please, Remedy this when you are Reading it over. I have made nothing today So far. My one-Armed, Half-Breed friend is not with me now, I parted with him in the little village I just passed through. He said He was going up in the Town to Bum Some fruit and Some money. I May See him again and may not. He helped Me Eat up all I had and now I only have one Cent in the Treasury. I don't think he amounts to much. Ninty five out of one hundred H.Bs will work you for what they can and then try and work Some one Else, but [this] is the Reason why I make very few friends among them, I mean regular H.Bs. I just Met one more old Tramp, quite an old man, a German. He was all Broke up, Sore feet and Rheumatism. He told me he was a Brewer by Profession and Said he would get a Stake in Schenectady as there was a Brewery there and he thought they would help Him. Said he had no regular Home and did not know where he was going, Might be to the World's fair. I told him it might be possible he would take a Premium. I left him behind Sitting in the Shade. As I was Comeing along I Saw four More H.Bs, one had a tree to him Self and three Under another Tree fast asleep. I took a look at them and passed on. I saw that one of them Had not Pants Enough to cover His nakednes[s]. I am getting in a Country where they hang out more. A Justice of a Peace told me yesterday, that I Mended an Umbrella for, that they were numerous in this Country and that Some of the Towns and Villages were quite severe on them, but Said if they were brought before Him and they had not Committed no Crime he discharged them and give them so many hours to get out of the Country. I asked Him if there was any danger of Me getting Arested in any buisness, he Said 'no', that I was following a legitimate Buisness.

I was in this Country two yrs ago, around Ft Plains, Utica and Richfield Springs, Springfield Center and East Springfield during Hop Picking. A great many H.Bs come here from all Parts to Pick Hops, and also all the Town Bums from Surrounding Citties and Some from New York Citty. Philadelphia and all this Country an[d] the Hop Country is full of Bums & H.Bs of all description, two and three weeks before Hop Picking Begins, Camping, Sleeping Barns and all Conceivable Ways. Peticoat Bums an Bags are numerous as they can pick Hops as well as any body, Some of them being Experts. And the Farmers' Potato Patches, Corn fields, orchards Suffer as all Class of H.Bs Carry Cans and Kettles and Cook out of doors. The Potatoes, Apples, Corn and other tuck is in good Condition for plucking, as Hop picking takes place in Sept. And lots of Prostitutes [come] fro[m] Surrounding Citties. And Every one that is Idle. When Hop Picking begins the Farmers take their teams and Haul them out to their Farms by wagon loads and Pay their way out on the Cars. When Hop Picking begins they haft to be Harvested as quick as Possible for Some Reason, and the more Hands the better. And a great Many operatives in Mills in surrounding Towns & Citties go out there for a holiday or Recreation, in other words a Spree, during Hop Picking and Every body Has a good time, Whiskey being one of the Principle ingredients and there is lots of it Punished during this time. Hop Dances are all the go Every night, Some times Sunday included. Some dances Are Respectable, others are free and Easy. One of the main Passtimes on Sunday is drinking, as the numerous Surrounding villages ar[e] full of Saloons. I have Seen all [people] over the fields, along Roads [and] in fence corners. Fighting is a Pastime, Black Eyse are numerous in both Sexes.

Hop Picking generally lasts about three or four Weeks and a great many leave Broke and get Arested on their way out. In Some of the Farms, the Farmers pay so much a Box for Picking. Some can Pick a great deal more than others. Farmers feed the Hands and furnish a Sleeping Place while at work for them in their Barns, out Houses, wherever they Can put up a bed. A great many Sleep in the Hay. I went from Hop Picking to Albany, there got rid of all the Money made in Hop Country, then Made my way to Hammond past N.Y. and Picked Grapes. This is Simply a repitition of Hop Picking. Also Berry Picking in Jersey and Southern Illinois, all the H.Bs flock to these Parts both Male and Fiymale, Have a good time, all the Money Earned goes for Bug Juice or Whiskey: Alca. There is lots of H.Bs follow these Pickings up Every year and Has done for Years, Both Sexes. A great Many H.Bs gets a Wife very Sudenly about these times and build[s] a Shantie in [the] Woods,

Keep House at times. The Union Breaks up in a row, all HouseHold goods are destroyed, Black Eyse, Sore Heads and may be an Arest of both, three months in Jail or Work House. A number of these Clandestine Unions End in this way. After their Pickings are over, all H.Bs disappear. Nobody Knows where the Haut Beau goes.

Sat June 7 1893

I came through [to] Schenectady N.Y. last Eve. Did not get a Job there and tried Hard to get some Mending, but no use. Passed three More H.Bs, two of them Professionals, dressed like Dudes. They Bumed Me for Money to buy Beer but I had none. They Had a Coat and Vest they wanted to Sell, Begged them or Stole them. I saw them ask Several for Money and one Man gave them fifteen Cents. They at once Rushed the gin ce[l]lar! The other H.B. Had got a Job, working man, but got down Some way. He told me he Could not get [into a] Bording House and was laying Out and Begging what he Eat Until he got a Pay, and Said he Worked Sometimes Very Hungry. Bording House will not Bord any one Unles[s] the Money Comes in Advance, Especily Strangers if they Look a little Seedy. They Have been Worked So much by Professionals who get Bord and Stay a day a Week, beat the House Rob the House and Borders, and Skip [out]. So the deserving Man Suffers. And the Cheeky Professional and Undeserving gets the Charity and does the dirt. H.Bs are quite numerous in this Part of Country. This is a great Highway, numerous Rail Ways and Public Roads and Canal Between East and West. I found a Shed along Side of Canal, went into it and layed down but soon got out as it was full of Fleeas.

Went up the Canal about two Miles farther and found a Shed with a Wagon in it, layed down in Bottom of the Wagon Box, Sleept Until after day light, it Being near one o clock when I got in there and Hungry. I am now near Rotterdam N.Y[57] in a Box Car and it is Raining and about 2.P.M, done nothing today Yet, Had nothing to Eat. A Boatman told Me there was two mush Fakers just ahead of me and Said he had met a number of them on the way from Buffalo, all of them going West. This acounts for Me not

---

57 From contextual clues, it seems likely that Aspinwall means Amsterdam, New York, although Rotterdam, New York is also in the vicinity.

geting any Jobs. Will Haft to ask for Something to Eat before long, Can't Stand going Hungry Much longer. But [I] Hate to ask and will not ask if I Can Posibly avoid it. Providence May bring Me out All right Yet, I will trust.

Sunday June 18/93

I Came through [to] Amsterdam N.Y. last nigh[t] Just before Sundown. I did not make any thing and was Hungry. Did not want to Ask for any thing. Just on the West Side of the Town and West Shore R.R. track, I Met two Italians. One of them could talk English, the other one could not. The one that Could Speak English Ask[ed] me how far I was going to night. I Said I did not Know, I was going Until I found a Sleeping Place. He asked Me if I felt Hungry. I told him I did.

He Said 'Come with Me and I Will get you Something to Eat, We feel Sorry for you.'

They took Me to an Italian Bording House and gave Me a loaf of Bread, Some Potatoes and onions Cooked, and one of them Brought Me A Schooner of Beer and I Made out a good Supper and by this time it was dark. They also gave Me another loaf of Bread to take along with me, and some new onions and some Cooked Potatoes, also some tobacco, all they had cooked. And then told Me I Could Sleep in the Stable belonging to the House. I got in on Some Straw and got a night's good rest. It Must have been 7.A.M. when I got out. I walked up along RR track about two Miles, Until I found a Grove of trees & Eat Some lunch and am now writing. They told me if I got Hungry to Come back and get Some More to Eat if I Stayed around, So I got favors from where I did not Expect. In fact I did not Expect anything to Eat last night, Had my mind made up to that Effect last night before Meeting the Italians. But Asked god to Provide for Me and he always does in Some way and has done for me a great Many times in my travels. When I get low Spirits and discouraged I pray to God to Help me And He always does in Some way I least Expect, and I See How Ungrateful I am to Him, How I will forget Him in prosperous times Just when I Should Keep Him in mind and be thankful. I believe God brings punishment on us for our negligence of Him, and to bring to our Memory there is a God that Knows our wants and faults and we Are prone to forget His goodness and Mercies. I think the nearer we can live to Him the better. In fact, I Know from My own Experiance I am Blessed with good Health, that is More than a great Many Can say that are Blessed with plenty of this world's goods. I have no doubt A great Many would give me all their Worldly Wealth for My Health, but I would not Exchange. The Mohawk Valley is not More than one Half Mile Wide at this point and the N.Y.C.H R.R [New York, Central and Hudson railroad] 4 tracks run on the North Side West Shore, two tracks and Erie Canal on the South Side. Trains and Canal Boats are Constantly Passing East and West. It brings to My mind what a great Country this is, and yet there [they] are only a part of the Highways to transfer Freight and Passengers from the East to West. It Makes Me feel Proud of My Native Country and Flag and that I was one Amongst the Hundreds of thousands that Soldiered and fought to Make this Land what it is today and Save it from destruction [during the Civil War] and that our Grand old flag, the Stars & Stripes, Can Wave Untarnished all over this broad land and all over the World, all thanks to the Brave Men who Stood up as targets when our Flag was in danger.

I Will give you Some of the H.B. Apelations I took from the door of a Haul [train] Car House Just this Side of Amsterdam.[58] [They] Have had signs or Marks under their names, Such as a Maltise Cross or a Star, Some a figure or a letter:

Yonkers & Slim & Boots
1-5.92 B.W.
Troy Whitey
Tunnel 4-2-69
Whisling Joe. Brooklyn
Yankee Slim
Whiskey Pete Yonkers Pete
Jack the Ripper London. Eng

---

58   Hobos would leave their road monikers on train cars and on watertanks, where they would often wait for hours for a train to stop to take on water. Watertanks became a particularly popular transient communication network, as hobos would also write the date and their direction of travel, in case their friends and acquaintances wanted to journey in the same direction in order to meet up. Extant examples of hobo markings are rare, but some have survived. For more information, see Susan Phillips, Thomas Chambers, and Javier Abarca, *Tramp Directories, Noms-de-Road and Unwritten Codes: A Souvenir of Hobo Graffiti* (Madrid: Urbanario, 2017).

Montana Bill May 24/91
Missauri [Missouri] Kid B.W. 10-90
Allentown White B.W. 10-91

I See thousands of these names of all Kinds on all Buildings along RR.

Monday June 19 1893

I travled from Amsterdam to Galway[59] N.Y. Yesterday, Sunday, about Eleven Miles. It was very Hot and I took it Easy. I Stayed in Galway Until daylight Came through the place. This Morning [I] Stoped all night Under West Shore Freight Depot on a plank. The Stench and Smell was imence [immense] and [there were a lot of] Fleeas, I did not sleep much. There was a Rooster in about five feet of Me and his Musical Voice let me Know when it was daylight. I Came out in Woods and lay down Under a Pine and took a good Sleep.

No Jobs yet, that Means nothing for Breakfast. Will Start in a few Minutes and Hustle. I Met but one H.B. yesterday. He was an old Man and was traveling towards Troy. Said he was Aquainted there, he [was] foot sore and Weary and Hungry, and I think from his apearance deserved Help. He Said He had been Well-to-do at one time but went West, and out there fate Was Against Him and [he] was Comeing back to His former Eastern Home in the aforesaid Condition. Alas, How Sad to Contemplate the feelings of the Old Man going back, Half naked and Half Starved, to the land he left with plenty of this World's goods. Imagine his feelings the Closer he gets to His former Home.

---

59 This is hard to read in the original letter, so there is some uncertainty as to whether this is the correct location. Galway is about eleven miles from Amsterdam, New York.

Ft Plains N. Y. June 20 93

I arrived in this village last night. Slept in a Box Car, got up Early [and] Made 40 cts before Most People was up. Got a good Breakfast and felt much better. There was a H.B. Came and got in the Car I was in Some time after I got in. He was one of these damt Shylocks,[60] a Profesional. He Said he Bumed a good Supper in this near town. He Said he was going East. I asked him if he was Hunting work.

He Said 'Naw, I don't want Work, nobody but Fools Work,' with an oath. I did not have much to Say to him, as I have no Use for His Kind. Will try and Make Some More in this town and then for Utica.

I will try and Send you another letter when I get to Utica. I will try and Keep the dates Straight and Chained together hereafter. Hope what I have written will prove of interest. Sent you a Postal yesterday. I will give you More of my Past Experiance as I get the time and opportunity. I have a great deal to tell yet, it will take a great deal of Writing to tell My Experiance during My life and travels and I should think [it will be] interesting. You Can Rely on what I Write to be nothing but the truth Just as I have Seen and passed through.

Gratefully Yours

William W Aspinwall

60　This is (presumably) an anti-Semitic reference to a person of Jewish heritage. Later in the letters, he uses the term more generically to mean East Coast bankers, stockbrokers and money men.

Fort Plain N.Y. June 20 1893

I Am here yet and it is 12 o clock. I mended an umbrella for a Hotel Keeper and He is the Chief of Police of the Citty and [a] Mighty nice man. I am all right here. He has another Umbrella for me to Mend. I have had plenty to Eat and drink today but I only drink Beer. I won't make very Much, only about 75 Cts but better than nothing. I have got aqainted with Several of the Cittizens here, a Mr James Carpenter and a Mr Winslow and a Soldier, Mr Carpenter, and Myself has Had a long talk about the Hop Picking. He has been out there.

I have left Ft Plain. I am again on my way to Utica N.Y, wich is thirty Seven Miles. It will take me all of three days. This Hot Wether, I can't do much walking today, it is to[o] Hot – I am Sitting Under the Shade of a tree on the Road Side.

I Will now give you a discription of the Philadelphia Wood Yards and other Hang outs for H.Bs. The wood Yards in Phillie I think are Run by the Associated Charities. There is two: one on Lombard St, the other father north East, near the River. If you go to a Police Station in the Center of Phillie for Loging they Will Send you to a Wood Yard. When you Stay in one of them three nights, your time is up and then you can Stay three nights more in Wood Yard no 2, and then your time is up and you Haft to look Else where for your Loging.

I was in the two of them. When you go in there is a gruff Duchman [who] Says to you if he admits you that you must work Until 11 P.M [the] next day. That means Saw Wood. And [he] tells you to go down in[to] the Cellar. You go down in Cellar and there Sits the gang. And Such a Gang: damned mes[s] of Humanity. Old Men Middle Aged Men & Boys, and it is interesting to Sit by and hear them tell their different tales to Each other of Woe and Hard Ships and good times. In the Center of the Cellar is Four common Bath Tubb[s], around the Walls are Benches where the gang Sits.

But at about Eight o clock the Foreman Comes down, or Some of His Corporals, and Yells Out 'Get Ready for Bed.'

Every Man takes of all of His cloths to the Skin and Hangs them on a Spike down in the Side of the wall, one for Each man, and Puts His Shoes Under the Bench as near His Cloths as Posible. And then all Must take a Bath. It Makes no difference if you are clean or dirty, all must Bath[e], that is one of the Rules. And ten or fifteen Bathers in the Same Watter and Sometimes more. They only fill the tubs once and then Probably only one or two of them. Watter Must be Scarce or it is to[o] much trouble to Change it. Just think of a man that tries to Keep Clean Bathing in Watter that Eight or ten Men has Bathed in that has not Bathed for one year, or maybe in their lives before. Yet it is one of the Rules and if you disobey one of the Rules You will be turned out on the Street, it don't make any differance if the thermometer registers below Zero, to Carry the Banner all night.[61] And there is a man Stands near Some Shelves and is[s]ues out night gowns, White Muslin, that Comes down to their feet. The Gang in a little While are transformed from mortal to immortal Beings, that is in appearance. Talk about your Ghosts, now is the time to See them, All Kinds of H.B G[h]osts. You can't tell the difference in them Unless it is Some that have Black Eyse or Sore Heads. And then Comes the Solem Procession up Stairs. All the first ones go up three flight of Stairs until that floor is full and then to the floor below and So on. The Ghosts all Retire on a cot Covered with Cloth and two Grey Blankets, Some of them worn Very thin and full of Holes. They aim to Heat the Room with Steam but the Steam gets Very Weak Economy; I suppose I like to of Froze [i.e., came close to freezing] when I Stoped there. I layed and Shook all night. And then in the Morning at Half Past five or Six you Must get up, return to the Cellar, doff your Gostly attire, don your Wearing apparel, wash your face and Hands and get Ready for Breakfast, wich consists of a Kind of Stew, very little Meat and a great deal of Salt Watter and flour and Some Bread (but Still it is better than going Hungry) and Some thing they Call Coffee, but Coffee is one of the least ingredients of the Compound. After Breakfast all go over the Street to the Wood Shed and then the fun Comences. Each one is Given a Buck Saw or two, takes a Cross Cut Saw, Some axes, and Splits [wood]. After it is Stowed and of all the wry faces and shirking trying to get Soft chores, Such as Small Sticks or leaving the work or Some Excuse or other and 'asking what time is it', 'How long are we going

---

61   To 'carry the banner' means to walk the streets all night without a place to sleep.

to be Keept in' & Some of them never Seen a Saw before and look at it as a Curiosity and any amount of Bosses besides the Right ones and so on, Until 11 A.M then All Can go. I never got any Supper there, never was in time. I was told all that got in by 6 PM got Supper. I never was in by that time. It makes no difference, Supper or no Supper, you got to graft the Same as those that got it. On Sundays they can't come out, Must Stay in and Sing and Hear the Preaching. The dining Room being turned into a Mission Room, wich is all Right if the Congregation would take Heed, listen and Hear and Proffit thereby, you would think Some of them were Saints to See them Sing and the atention they give, but look out for those.

There is a Mission on North twelfth St in Phila Called by the name of the 'Sunday Breakfast Association', Mr. Bean, President, a noble Man. I think this Mission is doing more good and [is] Conducted better than any Mission I know of. They Hold Services three times on Sunday Morning, Sunday School two P.M, and Evening Services. In the Morning Each one gets a good Sandwich and about three Cups of good Coffee. And the Building Holds about three thousand Bums. I think on the two floors they get the Same to Eat. Sunday night and Services Every night through the winter Months, and on Some weekday nights they Serve Supper. And it is a great Sight to See all of these Unfortunates Eating, drinking, Singing and the Atention.

A great many Has been Soundly Converted at this Mission and thousands have Signed the Temperance Plege there. And a great Many have Keept their Plege and thousands have been furnished with tic[k]ets for loging that would have had to Carry the Banner otherwise. I have heard Some able Preaching there. I heard Several nights H.O.Wills, the Ex Convict Evangelist from Detroit, Mich. And then there is Soup Houses in Every Ward in Philla. You Can get a quart of Soup and Some Bread about Noon on weekdays and it is a Sight to See the lines of Men awaiting their turn to get in to the Soup House. A Gentlemanly Policeman Keeps them Straight and Sees that Every one gets His Rights on Eighth and Vine St. It is a good Mission, I have Spent Many a Pleasant Hour there.

On Catherine St Phila is the 'Home of Industry', wich is an Exelent Place, far ahead of the Wood Yards. Every thing is neat and a Bath to Your Self, a Chance to Wash your Cloths and a good Clean Bed and fair Meals. But you Haft to get ticets from the Societies Such as St. George G.A.R. [Grand Army of the Republic] to get in there. I was Sent there by the G.A.R. and Stayed over Sunday. And Some of the Buissness Men Have Ticets to give out to Worthy ones, and How quick the H.Bs find out who Has them. And it is Wonderful how many would-be-Englishmen that goes to St George's Hall but are generally detected.[62] Some times they take Men in without ticets if they Have Room. They also Have Gospel Meetings nights and Sundays. In days through the week, industrial School for Children.

---

62   Presumably Aspinwall was allowed entry due to his English father.

Mindenville N. Y June 21st/93

I Passed through the Village of St. Johnsville, N.Y last night Just before dark. Walked on up to the Village. Stoped in a Box Car last night, Had a good rest. Arose with the Sun and am now on my way. Will be in Little Falls NY this forenoon Sometime. The funds in my Treasurey are again getting low, it Seems that my Wants are to[o] many. When I do get a little money, before my wants are Satisfied the Bank is Broke. I See three More H.Bs last Eve, they was waiting to Catch a Freight going West but did not Know where to. One of them told Me that he Had Rode on the inside of the Pilot of the Locomotive,[63] there is Iron Stays on Braces in there to Hold the Pilot. He Said He got a Suitable Bo[a]rd and placed it across the Braces and got in while the Engine was Still in the Round House, as He Could not get in there when She was out on the Road, and the R.R. Men Could not get Him out Until the Locomotive again Run in to Some Round House or over Some Pit. But Said He did not want to Ride there again, as He was near dead from thirst and being Cramped up in there by the time he got to the End of the Division. Said it was a Cool day and that he got Very cold and numb. I think he told Me the truth as he appeared like a very Venturesome fellow and would Undertake anything. Said it was a fast Mail Limited.[64]

---

63   The pilot car, where the train driver would typically sit.

64   An express train that makes limited stops.

June 21

Today a Very Hot day. I haft to walk very Moderately and do Some mending. I Stoped at a 5 Cent Loging House one night in Philadelphia. I think it was about the filthiest and nastiest place I Ever was in. It was Keep [kept] by a Colored Man. You Payed your nicel, went up stairs, [if] there was no Beds you took the floor and if you Could not find room to lay down you probably Could Stand [against] the Walls. And [the] floor was Alive with all Kinds of Vermin. I would rather Stand than Sit or lay down in Such a Hale.[65] There was a Stove in the Room, Well fired up, that Made the Stink Much louder and the Vermin much livelier. And the inmates were having any amount of Scratching to do. Some of them were Strip[p]ed naked as their Cloths was So alive with Crumbs [lice], it was impossible for them to Stand the punishment with their Cloths on. It was Very Cold out or [else] I would much rather of Car[r]ied the Banner in the Streets all night. The Musketoes are numerous here and I haft to Keep fighting them away, they appear to be very Hungry. I [have] Stoped in numerous Police Stations in Citties and Villages [that] I have passed through, Some of them are very filthy. In the Tramp department in the Citties they Have a Room Especialy for Logers, and in the Center is a Platform about two feet high. The Logers lay on this until all the Room is occupied, then Some Crawl Under the Platform and lay down, and Some take the floor. Some Stations are Keep as Clean as the nature of the Buisness will allow of, the Logers Haveing to do the work in the Morning. Other Stations are very filthy. Some Stations in Smaller Towns [put] Logers in Cells, and if the Cells are full you Bunk on the Stone floor, Some times Cold and Chiley [chilly].

    I was in Town Called Ad[d]ington in Virginia this Spring. It was a Bitter Cold night. It [be]Came night and I had no place to Stay. I Enquired for the Chief of Police but he Had gone Home. I found his House [and] told him what I wanted. He said they had Just built a new lock up and there was no Stove

---

65   This is an unusual use of the word 'hale,' which Aspinwall seems to use to mean 'pile' or possibly 'mess.'

in it, but if I thought I Could Stand it He would take Me over and Lock Me up. I told Him Know [no], I Would Rather go out in the Woods and build a fire. He Called me back and told Me that he could build a fire in the Mayers [Mayor's] office and he would leave the Lock up Door open, but I would Haft to be Locked up in a Cell, as it was the Mayor's orders to Lock Every one up. I thought that would do. He told Me where to go and that he would be there in a little while. He Came, I Searched around in the Dark, found Some Kindling and Coal [and] built a fire in the Office. There was a door from the office into the Lock up. Every thing was new in the Office, Had Just Been newly Carpeted and furnished. The Chief brough[t] Me a fine Lunch, he was one of those good fellows, and told Me to Stay in the office Until he Came back. I Suppose He went and Had a talk with His Honor. Any way he Came in about an Hour and told Me I Could Stay in the Mayor's Office. I took a Bench and Planted My Self in front of the fire and Had a good night's Rest. He Came in the Morning and brought Some Breakfast for Me and asked Me to bring up a Bucket of Coal to Keep the fire going. I done So, thanked him for His Kindness. He Said he wished Me good luck and I went on My Way, thinking *those Virginians [are] good fellows*, and they are as a Rule Whole-Souled People [i.e., good Christians]. I tested them on Several occasions. I traveled with a Collered [colored] Lad about one Hundred Miles in Virginia. He was a Comical Genious. He told Me he was a Hotel Porter. He was a Short, Stout-built fellow and all of his Cloths were to[o] large. His Hat had lost all the rim but about two inches and he had a Pair of Gun Boots on that were at least four Sizes to[o] large for him. All his Make up went to make a laughable Picture. I Most allways laughed when I looked at him and he was good nature its Self, always Singing, and he Could Sing in His way. And He would Saw Wood and do any Work to get Something to Eat and Bum also. He was not Slow at that. Very Gentle when he went to a House. I always had plenty to Eat when he was with Me. He would Say, 'Billy, Ise got my Pockets full of Grub, you Eat when Ever you want to.' He would Cary my Tools.[66] He Stoped in Richmond, belonging there. Him and I build Camp fires Several nights and Stoped in Brick yards and in two Blast Furnices. I would always get Him in w[h]ere I Stoped. He was a typical Colered Lad.

---

66   Some African-American hobos would engage in this kind of deferential behavior in order to keep themselves safe. Jim Crow followed them onto the rails and so they were at even greater risk of violence, whether state-sanctioned or otherwise, than their white counterparts. Black hobos were often given the racist sobriquet 'Shine' as, for example, at the start of McCook's "Leaves" series.

June 21 5 P.M.

Today is Very Hot, More So than any day this Summer. I have Suffered a great deal from Heat today, this Prickly Heat has Broke out all over my Body, it Makes Me feel Miserable. I Walk a Mile or so and then Sit or lay down in the Shade and Cool of[f]. Crops of all Kinds are looking Well through this Country but is wanting Rain very bad. I Met two HBs today going East. The first one I Met Wanted Me to turn around and go Back to a Saloon about two Miles [away] and take a Bowl With him. I told him no, I was not wanting any that bad. He Said Little Falls was a Hostile town, that the Police gave Him one half hour to get out of the Town and that all the Towns above were Hostile to H.Bs. The other one I met was a Young Irish Man. He was laying in the Shade of a Bridge, Had a Scotch Cap on and dressed Very Seedy. He also Said the Towns above here were all Hostile, that they gave Him the Run in all of them and Came near taking Him [to jail] but [he] lied [his way] out of it, told them he was Working on Canal or Some thing Else. Don't think from His talk he Had done a day's Work in Years. Was going East in to Mass and Connecticut, Said he Would not travel these Hot days, only to get His Chewing.

Utica N. Y. Jun 23/93

I passed through the Villages Herkimer, Illion & Frankfort Yesterday. I done Well, have 50 Cts in Treasurey this morn after getting all I wanted to Eat and Enough for Breakfast. I Met Some good People yesterday. It Rained Considerable Yesterday. I Stoped in a Brick Yard, it was 12 noon, the Boys gave Me all I Wanted to Eat. Without asking, a lady in Frankfort and two daughters I Mended a Parisol for Was Very Kind to Me, gave Me a good Supper besides paying Me for my Work, and the best of all wished Me Health and luck in my travels. God Bless them.

I Met three H.Bs this morning. They were English Weavers, good Honest fellows looking for Work. They Was taking a Wash in Cannal when I Saw them. I am Just in out Skirts of Utica. It is Early, about five. I Slept in an old Shed last night on top of a Threshing Machine. It Rained all night but I was dry. Will Mail this today and Will Send You a Postal where to write to Me next. I have not made up my mind fully.

June 23 1893

Well, Professor John J McCook, I have Just Eat my Dinner and Supper together. Excuse me for being so impertinent but I feel good and Rather Sassy. I got five Cents worth of good Warm Biscuits and five Cents worth of fresh Bologna Sassauge and the Same Amount of new onions and Some good Java Coffee and I have Just Eat Meal fit for President Cleveland out here on the River Bank near N.Y.C.H.R.R.R. [New York Central and Hudson River Railroad]. I have not yet Washed up My dinner dish as I thought I would Write Some. I Made a fire, Made a quart of good Strong Coffee all by My Self. I See Some H.Bs Sitting Under a tree a Short distance up the R.R. track, but I though[t] I would prefer being by My Self as I have poor luck in feeding H Bs, they always go back on Me. I have feed [fed] a good Many and never get the Compliment Returned in a Majority of instances. But Some times I run a cross a good fellow or good fellows. I am Smoking Some of the Tobacco You Sent Me and Enjoy it. I am about Six Miles west of Utica. I passed through the Village of Whitesboro since I left Utica. I Made 15 cts in Utica and Went into the town With 50 cts, but Had to buy Some Stock Wine and Grub and a few glasses of Ale. And I Made 31 cts Since in Whitesboro I Mended a Umbrella for a man in a Wagon and Black Smith Shop for 15 cts, Worth 50. And he gave Me an old Broken Umbrella, I mended that up and one of His Mechanicks gave Me 16 cts for it, all the Money he Had about Him. I told Him to take it, a Bird in Hand was worth two in the Bush. It was Worth 50 or 75 cts but it might be a week or longer before I Could Sell it and I don't want to[o] Much Money invested in Stock, Especily when the Treasury is Bankrupt. I got a Shave and have Enough in the larder to do Me at least two days. When I went into the Barber Shop to get Shaved, I See the Barber Smile. I had not been Shaved Since I left Bennington and was looking Shaggy but I was Unconcerned and Had to take a Hint.

Picked up a Paper and began to Read as though I owned Millions. I guess the Barber thought 'I will Urn [earn] My 10 cts on that fellow!' I want them to Earn their Money (I do Myne) and work a great deal longer for 10 cts than the Barber does Some times; I lost My lead pencil and am writing with a Short Piece I happened to Have and have left my Pen Knife. I Sharpen with an old Case Knife I have in my Tool Box. I had two Pen Knifes Back in Vermont. I Made a trade with a fellow in Keene but now I have none. I must move on and find a Place to Hang up to night as it is now about Six P.M. I am walking, Have not Rode [on a freight train] but a few Miles Since Writing to You.

June 24 1893

I passed a Village by the name of Oriskany last night Just before Sun down. They told me at the Village that Rome N.Y was Eight Miles from there. I walked along Canal Until dark, Saw an old Barn a Short distance to right of Canal. Long ago the raging Winds Had torn the great doors asunder. I went in but there was no floor, but I waked one of the Sleepers[67] and found Some Planks that had not been torn up with a Mixture of Broken Hay dirt and Seeds, and afterwards found out there was Fleas Contained in the Mixture, but I Stayed there and worried the night through. And I found out that my domicil was inhabited by innumerable Rats and they was Brave fellows, they were Skirmishing around and over Me all night. You Should of Seen Me with an old Umbrella Strikeing right and left at them but never touched one of them. I was not well last night. I was feverish and my Shoes have worn Sores around My Ancles [ankles]. About 1.0.clock in the night a Boat Stoped Just oposite to Change drivers and Mules and they made a terrible racket. It Sound[ed] to Me as though all Hands, Mules and all had fell [fallen] of[f] the Bri[d]ge into the Canal from the amount of Curseing there was going on. May be that one of the Mules throwed his Heels and got them tangled up in the driver's Whiskers, I don't Know. I layed and let them have it out amongst themselves. I arose from my drowsy Couch at Sun Rise and Resumed my Journey after partaking of a lunch of Bread, Butter, Some Sausage and New Onions. I have plenty of Coffee & Sugar but Saw no Chance to Make a fire. About one Mile before I turned in to the Rats' den last night, I Saw a fine Monument Just South of Canal. I am always Curious to Know to Whom Monument is Erected in honor of. There was a Boat Just passing, I asked the driver for information. He said he dident Know, he had passed it Several times and never Knowed What it was for, So when the Boat Came

---

67   i.e., picked up a railroad sleeper.

up I asked the Captain. He was at the Helm Piloting His Craft through the Raging Billows and foaming Canal, and His lovely wife was Sitting beside Him, apparently proud of her Husband's acomplishments in manipulating the Rudder. At their feet was their innocent child playing on the Snow White Deck. What a responsibility that Captain had on his mind, for fear his Craft Should Strike Some Unseen Rock or Stick in the Mud in the bottom of the di[t]ch. And nothing lost but time to wait for the thickend Watter in the dich to Raise and Set his Craft afloat. But the Captain did not Know what the Monument was for. He Said he had passed it a Hundred times or More and looked at it but had no idea what it meant – what intelligence.

I Should of Crossed over Loch Isle and of Examined the inscription on that monument if there Had of been a Boat or a Bridge, but there was none in Sight. I Just Asked a Farm Hand Whose Monument that was but did not [k]now and [him] living almost in Sight of it. I will find out for what that Pile was built for if I haft to go ask Every Man and Woman I meet, or go to the Mayor of the Citty of Rome. This is Rome N.Y not Rome of old, that former thing of Beauty an[d] her five hills that Ruled the World in her time. Not Rienzies [Rienzi's[68]] Rome that he was so anxious to Recapture from the tyrant Urcini [Martin Ursini], but Rome in this great free State of NY in Great North America that was never Knowed by the old Romans. The Romans of NY are Working men and Mechanicks in their numerous Shops and Factorys, not Warriors by profession. But let our glorious Banner the Stars and Stripes be insulted, and How Soon Rome NY will be turned in to a Military Camp and its Shops turned to the manufacture of the implements of War.

I was thinking Yesterday, as I was walking along the Canal and the new York Central Rail Road, [which is] near[ly], I Suppose, the Busiest R.R. in the World, with its four tracks [and] trains Passing almost Constantly on one or the other of its Tracks, Butiful Vestibuled Express trains near Half-Mile long, and the Engineer leaning out of the Cab Window of His Hansome Locomotive watching Her Every Revolution and the Wind gently Blowing through His matted Whiskers! What Pride he has in that Machine, the work

---

68   Nicola Gabrini (1313–1354), known as Cola di Rienzo or Rienzi, was a medieval Italian politician who framed himself as a 'tribune of the people.' He clashed with the powerful Ursini family and led a successful popular revolt, attempting to restore the Roman Republic. He is the hero of Petrarch's poem "Spirito gentil" ("Noble Spirit") and in the nineteenth century came to be seen as a romantic figure who had prefigured Italian unification (the *Risorgimento*), featuring in Edward Bulwer-Lytton's novel *Rienzi* (1835) and Richard Wagner's opera *Rienzi, der letzte der Tribunen* (*Rienzi, the last of the tribunes*, 1842).

of the Brains of Some of our inventors, and the long lines of Freight Trains. What a Contrast between thos[e] and the Canal & Canal Boat. The Canal was built before Rail Ro[a]ds was though[t] of, but whats the difference in Speed? A Boat travels at the Rate of from one mile to two Miles Per hour while the Locomotives Pull the trains from 30 to one Hundred Miles per hour. The men that Engineered the Building of the Canal done Wonders in their day but it is one of the Has Beens. If Passengers Had to go to the World's Fair Via Canal and Lake or Stage[coach], they would haft to Start the Year in advance to get there in time to see it. But it is my Opinion if there was no other Mode of travel but Canal & Stage there would be no Columbian Exposition in Chicago or no Chicago or other great Citties in the West. I Must Move on. I have a great deal to write about, Especily my Past life. It will take a long time to tell you all my Experience. I think I will Swich of[f] at Rome and take R.W.D.R.R [actually the RW&O, or Rome, Watertown and Ogdensburg Railroad] to Oswego [and] from thence to Niagara Falls. There is to[o] Many Umbrella Men on this Route. I may have better luck by the Change.

Near Westernvill[e] N.Y June 25 Sunday/93

I passed a little Village called Delta[69] last night about Sun down. I found a Barn near the Road, no Dwel[l]ing near. I went in to it. Almost dark and it was partly ful[l] of Clean Hay. I pulled [my] Coat and Vest and Shoes, Spread my Coat and Some Hay over Me as it was quite Cool, and Slept well. Had a good Rest, the best for Some time. It is now about 10 A.M and I have only Just arose. And while writing Can hear the Village Church Bells. I walked about twenty Miles Yesterday and did not feel Well. It is tiresome to Carry my load of about 25 lbs, Some times More, Even 40 when I have a Sup[p]ly of Grub. And do this Sick and Feverish and Sore feet, Sometimes Hungry. I tell you this sporting life is a great life, Especily to go through it as I haft to. I am going to Hunt up Some Vessel large Enough to Boil My Shirts in, if I Can find any, and Wash and Boil up My cloths for it is near[ly] two weeks Since I changed, if I don't, as the Irishman Says, I will Soon be full of Wari Bugs. It is Very Easy to get Crumby or Grey Backs [lice] on, for one is apt to lay in Box Car, Barn, or Some other place where Some Lousey Bum Has been laying and Some times get in Company with Such Crumby H.B. It is always Easy to get the Stait in the Breed! And it is a ter[r]ible Misery to Me to have them on My Cloths and Body. I Soon Boil up and get Some Blue Ointment and dose My Cloths and get Rid of the Pest.

---

69   During the first decade of the twentieth century, this village would be flooded to create the Delta Lake Reservoir.

Sunday June 25 1.P.M

I have walked about 4 Miles from where I Stoped last night and there Came up a Heavy Rain. I made for a Barn along Side of the road and am now Safely domiciled in the Barn and Some Hay. Have Eat[en] nothing today and My Stomach begins to feel a little Weak. I will give you a little of my Experiance. About four years ago I was in Joplin, Missouri near Indian Ter[ritory]. I wanted to go to Pleasant Hill Mo about one hundred miles north. Joplin is the End of a Division of the South West Borough of the Mo Pacific R.R. There was a Passenger Train left Joplin for Pleasant Hill about 3 o clock in the Morning. I went down in the Yard where the Cars were that was going on that Train, A RR Man gave me the information. I got on top of one of the Coaches about half hour before the Train left and got near a Stove Pipe So as I Could Hold on. By this time the Engine Came out and Coupled on and Away She went. I thought I never Saw a Train go faster. The Roof of the Coach was Rounding or Oval and you Can Bet I Hung on to that Stove Pipe with a Vengence. My Hair would raise on My Head Some times as I would Come near Rauling [rolling] of[f] but I Hung on to it Until I got to a Station within about ten miles of Pleasant Hill. Then it was day ligh[t] and Every one Could See me on the Station Platform and they began to laugh and make Remarks.

The Conductor got on to Me and Climbed up on Break Wheel and Asked me what I was doing up there.

I told Him 'Riding, of Course.'

He Said 'Come down.' And I Came down and the People and Passengers Began to laugh and ask me questions. I was one of the dirtiest Smoked up Mortals you Ever Saw. I would of Passed for a Colered Man. I did not Blame the People for laughing.

The Train Started and the People on Platform yelled 'Catch Her!'

I did So and Rode five Miles farther on Her and She Stoped again. I got off[f] and Walked in to Pleasant Hill. I Hung around there Until night. And there was a fast Express Bound for St. Louis on Main line No. Pac[ific] RR. I Jumped the Blind Baggage of Her in Rear of Engine and when we got Under good Headway, the Engine[er] and Fireman Saw me and took the Hose and began throwing Watter on Me. I had to take it, As I Could not get off[f] the Train going at the rate of 60 Miles an Hour. I was Soaking wet and it was Tolerable Cool and I was Shivering.

I got off[f] [at] the first Stop and went and got on the next Car in Rear where they Could not get at Me with their watter. My Self and a Partner United from Pittsburg Pa for Philadelphia. At one time Some years ago we Walked out to East Liberty, a Suburb of Pittsburg. All Trains Stop there on Penn RR. We Jumped the White mail Train and Her next Stop was Johnstown Pa, 70 Miles, and there were four other H.Bs on Same Car. And when we Came near Johnstown, My Self and Partner Concluded we would climb on top, as we was Sure to get Bounced at Johnstown and on top likely they would not See us. But we was Mistaken. The Electric Lights at Depot gave us away and the train Hands at depot and people Could See us. The Conductor was told and He Made us Come down. In a few min there was another train. We made for Baggage Car but Just as I Step[p]ed on, a big Policeman grabed me. I remonstrated with Him [but it was] of no Use, He took me over to the Depot. My Partner was not Caught but Stuck right with me.

The People and Train Hands all Said to Police man 'Let Him go! He done nothing, only took a Ride'. And the Policeman got Ashamed and let me go. We awaited for a Freight and Rode in to Alatoona [Altoona] Pa and in 48 hours was in Philadelphia. I can get there when I take A notion.

Monday June 26/93

I passed through the Villages Westernvill & North Westernvill. I got of[f] my Road, traveling not Much. North East for Oswego, Will Change my Course. I Stoped in a Vacant House along Side of Road, layed one of the doors down and layed on that. Got quite Cool in the night. I had a Partner last night, a Swiszerland [Switzerland] Gentleman. He Came into the House Shortly after I did. I thought it was Some formen belonging here. He Could not Speaking English but Said he Could Speak Swis French & Diche [Dutch], So I made out to talk With Him in Du[t]ch and he was Very talkative. He was a good-looking fine-built Man and neatly dressed. Said he was going to Canada, the French Part. Said U.S. was no good to many Italians and Polacks. He Said he was on the Bum. He said he Asked a Man yesterday for Some thing to Eat and he told Him to 'Go to the Poor Master'.[70] He did not Know what that meant. He was a Civel and Sensible fellow. He has gone on. I had nothing to Eat Yesterday and nothing Yet this Morning. Will Mail this today. Expecting to get a letter from you at Oswego N.Y.

    W.W.Aspinwall

---

70   The poor master being "a parish or county officer who superintends the relief and support of the poor." *Oxford English Dictionary* online (hereafter *OED*), *poor* [adjective and noun]

Monday June 19ᵗ [actually 26th] 1893

Sent a letter this Morning. Walked all day. Made fifteen Cents in Morning, Bought Some Cheese & Crackers. Done all day on fifteen Cents. Passed through the Villages of Abin[72] & Point Rock NY. Stoped in a Barn about one Mile West of Point Rock. Had a good night's Rest. Got out in the morning and Asked first Farm House for Umbrella Mending, got a Job and 25 cts for it.

Went on west a Mile and asked Lady if She had any Umbrellas or Parisols to Mend. She Said, 'No.'

I asked her if She would Sell Me a Lunch. 'Yes Sir'.

She Brought Me a nice Lunch Cake, Pie, Bread and Butter. 'How Much is it?' Says I.

'Nothing at all,' Replies the Lady.

I put a nicle into her Hand and Says 'Take that, I don't want it for nothing.'

Came on towards Tabergh [Taberg] N.Y, asking for Work at Every Farm House. Just after Dinner got a Job, Made 25 cts and sharpened two Pr Shears for Lady, got a nice Lunch for that. Went on farther, found another Lady that had a Umbrella to mend, but Said She Had no Money. I told Her She was like My Self, but told her I would fix her Umbrella if She would get me Some Dinner. 'Alright,' She Says and [g]ot the Umbrella. I went and done Her a good Job and she got Me [a] good Dinner and then I came into the Village of Tabergh and done Several Jobs. Good People in this Country. I give for a Reason that there is not So Many Farms and Tinkers Passing through the Country. Every Boby [body] is friendly and apears to want to See you

---

71 This date appears to be a mistake given the contextual clues about Aspinwall's location. He seems to have got the day correct but been a week out in this letter and in several letters from Taberg and Camden.

72 The writing here is unclear and may say 'Obin.' I have not been able to find a reference to either village. Point Rock is now a part of the town of Lee, New York.

get along. I Made about one Dollar and fifty cts Yesterday and lived well. I went out of the Town last Evening, found a Barn, Crawled in on the Straw and Slept Well. Came down into the Town, Bought a Can Tomatoes, Can Salmon, Some Coffee, Some Crackers and am now on My Way to Camden.

I Stoped along side a River and Made a quart of good Strong Coffee and Have Eat[en] Up all my Tomatoes and Half Can Salmon and but have Some Coffee to drink Yet. Will try to get away with it.

Now last Sunday, as I have writen, I done without any thing to Eat all day, and you See How the Lord provides for Me. I think He punishes me Some times for my Extravagance. I have Plenty for the preasant, thanks be to God.

There is not many H.Bs Comes through this way, it is of[f] Main lines. It Will take Me Some time to get to Oswego the way I am going at Preasant, but when I begin to get good and Hungry I will Soon Shorten the distance.

Weds June 21 [actually 28th] 1. PM.

Made 35 cts Since I left Taberg. Had quite a Set to with one old Farmer. I Saw him in his yard, asked Politely if he Had any Umbrellas to mend. He said no, but he Had Corn that wanted Hoeing Bad. I told Him He should be at it. He infered as much as though I had better be Hoeing His Corn than traveling around fixing Umbrellas. I told Him if all Men were of His Mind they would all be Farmers and May be not Very good ones, and I told Him this was a Free Country if a Man wanted to Farm he Could Farm, and if a Man wanted to Mend Umbrellas or do any other Kind of Mechanical work it was His privilege to do So if he Had Brains to do it. He finaly agreed with Me and Said he Had Some Umbrellas that Wanted fixing but would Rather buy new ones. 'Alright', Says I, 'diferent Men Have different Opinions'. I gave Him to Understand he was not the only Man on Earth. He was one of these Self opinionated fellows, probably Had been Justice of the Peace. H.Bs Call the Farmers Rubes. He was one of the Rubes. They do a good bit of Ruber necking, Goose Necking through this Country, they don't often See a fellow like Me.

Back the Road a few Miles there was five Country Girls, 18 to 20 yrs, old Picking Straw Berrys in a field. They Seen me Coming, they all came to the Fence to See mee.

When I got near them I Says, 'How do you do Ladies? Pleasant day.' they all began to look at Each other and titter and laugh. Stood there and Eyed them close and Says 'Girls what do you think of Me? Any way don't you think I am a good looking fellow?' I Says 'I am looking for a Wife.'

One of them Says 'I don't Believe any of us want to Marry.'

'Alrigh[t],' Says I, 'no Harm done. Buisness is Business, Have you any Parisols or Umbrellas to mend?'

They guessed not. They gave me about a pint of Strawberries.

I took a Seat in the Shade and got away with them and Had quite a friendly Chat with them. They Said they Picked Strawberries and Sold them at the Village. They got 8 cts per quart and that they Had nothing Else to do and had Just as well Pick Berries. I got very well aquainted and aparently interested them, and I bid them good by and resumed my Journey. I find the ladies in Houses as I Pass Watching through doors and Windows, Especily in Country and Small Villages. I always Sing out [in] Passing, 'Umbrellas and Parisols to Mend', so they Can Hear my Gentle Voice in the Most Remote Corners.

Camden. New York. June 22 [actually 29th]/[18]93

I Came in to this Butiful little Citty Yesterday Evening. I Earned Yesterday Eighty Cents and Walked about twelve Miles. I think I will do pretty Well Here today. I have the promise of Several Jobs and Have not Canvassed the Town any. I done one Job after Coming into the Citty about dark, had a good Crowd of good natured fellows around Me. I had a big Job back five Miles at last Station an old fellow and His Son, the Station agent, Had about Eight old Umbrellas. I Made them three good umbrellas out of the lot and they gave me all the rest and thirty Cents. They was good Jovial fellows, Sat and Joked me all the time I was there. And it was about train time and there was Several Passengers in the Depot, So I had quite an Audience Back at Tabergh. I Sat on the Steps of a Store in the Heart of the Village late in the Evening, Mending. I had near all the people in the Town Around me, Men, women and Children, quite a Sight for a Tinker to Come to Town. This is getting to be a great deal better Country for My buissness. There Has not been any Umbrella Men through this way for Some time. I will not get to Oswego before [for] Some time. I will Spend about all day in this Town. And there is Several good Villages between here and Oswego, and I want to get all I can out of them. I was getting discouraged back [i.e., recently], Could get nothing to do, but am getting More Courage now. I am getting where I Can Make a little. I Can't Beg, it Seems to[o] Humiliating to Me. I prefer going Hungry, as you will See by My former letters. I Just write down My Mind and the way I feel the plain facts.

I got into an Empty Box Car last night and passed the night. Was up this Morning at Break of Day, Came out on the Out Skirts of the Town on the Bank of Fish River[73] and Built a small Fire and Made a Can of good Strong Coffee, Cooked Some Frankfort Sausages. Some Crackers and Onions

---

73   Actually Fish Creek.

Constituted my Breakfast and I Eat Harty and feel Much better. And the Sun is Just Comeing up.

I Will Soon go down into the Town and they will Hear My Baritone Voice in all the Streets and in Every nook and Corner in their quite [quiet] little Citty 'Umbrellas! and Parisols! To mend! To Mend!'

I have got one Dollar in the Treasurey this Morning after Paying all Expences. Gaining! I want to get the Treasurey Sollid Financially and Surplus Capital. You will notice I am in much better Condition now than last Sunday. I have Seen no H.Bs Since last Sunday Eve, not many on this Route. Will Mail this today.

Fratulently Yours

William.W.Aspinwall

Near Mexico. N. Y.; Jully 2 Sunday 1893

Much Estemed Friend John J McCook

I Stoped last night Under a Tree in a Butiful Grove along Side of RR Track. I left Pulaski late in the Eve and Walked until late and I Saw this Grove, went over and Examined and though[t] this would be a Butiful place to Spend one night. I Spread and [an] old Umbrella Cover on the Ground, or Should of Said on the downey Grass, and placed my Bundle of Umbrella Handles and Ribs for a Pillow doubled up, Some more old Covers and laid on Bundles to Make my Pillow More Soft. Took of[f] my Coat and Shoes, tied my Shoes [in]to [a] Bundle for fear a H.B. Might Come along and want them. If he did he would haft to wake me before he got them and then it would be a question of Manhood, My Combativeness would Come to the Front. I layed down and Such a nice Sleep I had, nothing disturbed me. I Spread my Coat over my face and Breast and Slept and dreamed of good old days long ago and those good times that Should Come in the Future, I hope they will Come. I awoke at the dawn of day, aranged my toilet and Kit and Made for RR track and resumed my Journey. I walked about five miles and passed the Village of Mexico. Just as I was passing I hear the Clock in Church Tower tolling five O Clock. I Came past the Village about one mile, found an Elegant Grove Along a Creek, Switched to the left into the Grove and Oh! What a lovely Spot, Beach Cedar and Poplar. I Would rather Sit in it Close to this Butiful Sheet of Watter and write than to be in the most luxurious drawing Room in this land. Everything So quite [quiet], Except the Rus[t]ling of the Breeze through the Butiful foliage and the Sweet Singing and the warbling of Birds. Not a Bug or a Musketo to interupt me. How well I Enjoy this lovely Sabath Morning and how Happy I feel with nature adorned in her lovely Summer Robes all around me. All alone, not in Sight from where I sit of the Habitation of Man and all alone. What a Grand Place for Meditation, I must

Say I Enjoy it. I built A small fire, made a quart of good Strong Coffee, Had Bre[a]d, Cheese and Some Cooked Beef Onions And Sit here on the Grass with an Umbrella Cover for a Table Cloth, My Blue Hankerchief for a napkin, a lard can for a Coffee Pot, a Small Potted Ham Can serves for both Cup and Saucer. And I Eat a harty Breakfast and I Enjoyed it. I filled my Pipe with tobacco and Set it on fire and am now Enjoying a Smoke and writing. I have Yesterday's Papers and after I get through writing will Spend Some time in Reading, as I like to Keep posted on what is transpiring in the world. Surely God has Blessed me the last week for I have had a very prosperous week.

I have new Shoes I was Very much in need of, and a new Hat, Pants, Under clothing and top Shirt and Hair Cut and Shave. I am a different-looking Specimen of Humanity altogether to what I was one week ago today. Several Gentlemen, and Ladies to[o], Remark that I was the best dressed & Cleanest and Best-looking Umbrella Mender they Ever Saw on the Road. I don't See why a Gentleman Can't Just as Well fix Umbrellas and Tinker as to Keep Store, Blacksmith, or Practice Law, or any other trade or Profession. It is not the Buisness or the Cloths that makes the man. I am Just as good in old Ragged Cloths as I am in a fine Tailor-made Suit, and I have worn them both a number of times Since I Came to the years of maturity. But these Umbrella Menders & traveling Tinkers are 99 out of 100 tough Cases, Hard-drinking Men. Some of them will make a quarter or Half Dol[lar], get a Pint of Alcohol, go to the Woods, get drunk, or maybe get drunk in the Citty or Village they Happen to be in, Make fools of them Selves, get arested or driven out of the Town. Some of them dirty, Unkempt Specimens. It is the man, not the Buisness, that gets arested and drunk or driven away.

I am going to Show the Public that there is one man that is a first Class Tinker and Mechanic that Can go through their Citties, Villages and Country, that is Honest and decent and Can Keep Sober and does, and treat People with politeness and be Respected by the Public as a Gentleman. All I Ask is for any Person to Corespond With, any Cittizen, Chief Police, Marchall [Marshall] in any Citty or Village I have traveld through, and asertain if what I Say ain't the truth Untarnished. In a great many Places, Depots, Stores, Banks, Black Smith Shops, Dweling Houses are at my disposal for Work Shops. I Carry in my Pocet Several first Class Recommendations from Responsible Men that have tried me and Know my disposition and Character. I Make friends with all intelligent Men and women. When aquainted I state the foregoing so that you may more fully Understand who I am.

I met the Chief of Police of Troy while there on one of the Buisness Throughfares. 'Why,' he Says 'you ain't full.' [i.e., drunk]

'No Sir', I Says, 'I Hardly Ever allow myself to get in that Condition.'

'That is good,' He Says. He Said that he Hardly Ever Saw a Tinker that was not Drunk or in a fair way to get that way. 'We lock them up Everyday.' He told me to go a head and 'Yell out Umbrellas to mend' all I wanted to and make All the money I Could, 'and if any Officer Says any thing to you, refer them to me or come to me. I will stand by You.'

And I have Had a Number of Mayors and Marchalls & Policeman [policemen] to tell me to go ahead and make all I could. I Sometimes ask Permishion of them to work the Town, I have never been refused. I came through one Village and a lot of Young men and Hoodlums got to following me and insulting me and Pelting Stones at me. Some Cittizen Saw it and informed the Marchall. He Came after them and told them to 'Stay away from that man and let Him alone' or He would Lock the last one of them up. They took a Sneak like a lot of whipped Dogs. It is a Shame and a disgrace to this Free Land of Schools and Colleges that Such Hoodlums are alowed to grow up in their Ignorance, a disgrace and a Curse to the Community they live in. If their Parents and Guardians will not learn them Some decency and manners they Should be Compelled to Know Some thing by Law. I went on and was not Molested any more. While there this is one instance, I have had many more but always Have Friends.

This Morning As I was Comeing along I Came across a fine Patch of Strawberries. As the Farmer was Still in Bed I Climb[ed] the Fence and Had a fine Bail of luscius Berries fresh from the Vines. I don't think it is much Harm in taking a few Berries to Eat, as a great many of them will go to waste any way before they are Picked. How Ever, I Would Cast and [an] Eye over towards the Farmer's House to asertain if the Cost was Clear and that the old Rube, as HBs Call them, was not Comeing With Bull Dog and Gun to disturb my pleasure.

I Stoped at a Small Station Called Sand Hill last Evening, only one Store besides Depot. I went in to Store to buy Some Provisions for today, while in there a fine looking young ladie approached me and wandted to Know if I Repaired Parisols. 'Yes Mam', I Replied. She Said She Had a fine Silk one out at Her House that Had the Staff broken and wanted to Know if I would go out With Her.

I replied, 'Most assuardly [i.e., assuredly], I will.'

She Said that She Had brought a Lady friend of hers down in the Buggy that was going of[f] on the Train and that She would be there in a few Minutes and take Me out where She lived.

I replied, with the Greatest of pleasure, 'I will wait.'

She Came in a few minutes with a fine Horse and Buggy. She turned the Wheels So that I would not get my Cloths Soiled and I placed my Box and Kit in front at our feet and away we went. And I tell you She Could drive and talk and She Had a fine Horse to drive and the Tinker was in the heighth of His Glory. But the distance was Soon Covered between the Store and where She lived. She Drove up to a fine Country House, nicely Painted in the midst of a Butiful Grove intersperced with lovely Flowers. I Vacated the Vehicle with a Bound, as I felt like a Young Man, in the position I was. [I] Helped the Young Lady to alight, the Hired man taking the Rig to the Necasary Shelter.

I felt like adressing the man as the College-Bred Adonis did the Hostler at [the] Hotel Just after His Graduation. He drove up in front of Hotel, the Hostler Came and Seized Hold of the Reigns and the Adonis adressed him in this Style: 'Hostler, Extricate the quadruped from the Vehicle, Stimulate and Staminulate[74] Him with the necasary functions of life and [in the] Eve[ning] [when] old Saul Apears in the Morning Horizon, I will fully Repay You for Your Hospitality.'

The Hostler Called the Land Lord and Says 'Come out here. There is a Frenchman Here, I can't Understand Him!'

I went With the Young Lady in to Veranda And She Asked me to take a Seat, placing a Chair near me, and went in and brought out Her Parisol. And it was a Hansome Silk affair, I Suppose Had Cost Eight or ten Dollars and Had been Used but Very little, Until [the] Handle had got Broken by Sitting down on it or in Some other way. And it was Handsome. Gold-Plated Handle, it was Broken in a Place I Could not Make a good Job to Stand the test and told Her So. But I had a Hansome Handle and Staff that would Just fit her Parisol With an Elegant Ivory Hand holt that a lady in Camden had given me. I Showed it to Her and She was well pleased with it and told me to put it in. About this time the Hired Girl Came and told the Young lady that Her Supper was Ready. She asked me if I had been to Supper.

I replied, 'Not Yet today,' but Said I would wait Until I went back to the Village.

---

74 Aspinwall seems to mean 'staminate,' an obscure word that means "to imbue with 'stamina' or vital force." See *OED, staminate* (verb).

But She Said, if I would accept, that I Could take Supper with them and [she] insisted on me taking Supper. I went in through Hall with Her to Dining Room and the Parlor and Sitting Room Doors was Standing open and it was a Superbly Furnished House. The Young Lady and Her Mother and My Self were all that were Seated at the table. Every thing was first Class, they were not Proud but [had] Just Enough Pride Enough to have Every thing in good order and in its place and [to] Use good Manners. I don't want a better Supper than I Eat and Enjoyed with those two Ladies. I Know How to act and Use Manners when in Such Company, I have been there before and those Ladies Soon became aware of this fact. I learned from their Conversation that the Young Ladies [lady's] Ma was a Widow, and She was not over 35 Summers and [a] fine-looking, Buxom, Refined Lady, and I Supposed from appearances that She was welthy. I found out afterwards from the Store Keeper that She was worth near on to one Hundred thousand Dollars[75] in real Estate and Stocks and Money. The Store man Said that they were the best of People, the Cream of Society, and Said She was a noble woman and Very Charitable with her money.

After Supper I went out on the Verandah and finnished Puting in the Handle. I took particular Pains and done a nice neat piece of work, and after it was done the Young Ladie took it and Examined it and pronounced it Elegant and Called Her ma to inspect the Work. The Mother Said it was well done and the Young Ladie, Mis[s] Carrie, I had learned her given name by this time, asked my price for the work. I told Her '73 cts, but as I took Supper I would make it 50 cts.'

She Said 'Please don't mention about Supper,' and took 75 cts out of Her Purse And gave it to me.

I thanked Her very Kindly and gave them to Understand that I apreciated their Kindness. The Young Ladie in a Jokeing way Said when Ever She Carried that Parisol She would think of me and wonder where I was. I told Her I would Always Rem[em]ber their Kindness and Her Self and Ma's Pleasing ways.

She Said 'Please don't flatter Us.'

I replied it was not flattery but Just meant what I Said. And then I asked Her if they had any old worn-out Umbrellas or Parisols. If they Had, I would buy the Handles. They Started the Hired Girl and Hired man to Searching Barn, out Houses and Closets, and they found a Half doz[en] Umbrellas

---

75   In 2020s terms, this is approximately $3,000,000.

and Parisols with Cloth warn-out but Butiful Handles, the acumulation of Years. I offered 60 cts for them but they Said no, if they was of any Use to Me I was welcome to them. And they was good ones, as those Kind of People always buy the best. It Made me a fine Assortment of Handles and a Very important thing in my Buisness. They Even Asked me to Stay allnight but I declined, thinking I was not Clean Enough to occupy and [an] Elegant Room, as I had been Sleeping in all Kinds of Places And no telling what is liable to get on your Cloths. I made an Excuse that I had to be in Mexico Village that night on Certain Buisness and Came about two Miles from there and Slept Under a Tree as before Stated. I Bid them a Harty Good-By and again thanked them for their Kindness and they were Aware by this time that I did apreciate their Kindness and it done them More good than all the money I Could offer. They invited And insisted if I Ever Come Around this way I must Call and See them. Fine People, How I apreciate those Kind.

And then Again you will meet People Just the opesite from these Ladies I have Just told you about. Slam the Door in your face and I have no doubt would Shoot you if they were not in fear of Justice, And answer You As insulting as they possibly Can. And Some of them pretend to be Refined people but I think to My Self that they are ignorant And Brutish, Selfish. Even if they have got lots of this world's Goods, wealth don't make the true refined man And Woman. They don't Know no better. Even if they are Educated, that gentle Kind nature Ain't in them, So they Can't Help their mean treatment to their fellow man.

A Man by the name of Williams Called me in His Store to fix an Umbrella. The Job was worth 25 cts or more but I told him I would do it for 15 cts, though[t] I would put it low Enough. He Said that was to[o] much and wanted to Know if I was a mechanic and Put a dozen other questions to me Until he raised the resenting Blood in my Veins. He Said he would give me 5 cts if I done a good Job. I told him 'No,' I did not want his Work, that I was not going to furnish material and Carry that pack around and work for Him for 5 cts an hour. He Said I had to[o] much money, that there would be around a man Shortly that would be glad to do it for that Price. I told Him to let Him Have it. And then I told him my Opinion of Him in Short order. As there was Some men Came in that I had got aquainted with and found them to be Gentlemen, they gave me the wink, as much as to Say, *give it to Him.* I Supposed He was the Kind of a man to take Advantage of Some Poor Unfortunate's Poverty And Get Him to do Work for nothing or nearly so, and Keep Him down, not let Him Have a Chance.

92

I Says 'the Devel has got the Masons at work Building the Walls of Hell higher' for fear Some men of His Kind would Jump out.

These men began to laugh and the old man Got Hot, but I Just went out of His Store and let Him Heat and meditate on what I Said to Him. I learned afterwards from good Business men that he was not very highly Respected in that Town, Even if he did make a loud Profession in his Church and Was the possessor of Considerable Welth. And His Friends did not increase any by his talk with me. This was in Camden. And I have Hosts of Friends there. So it is I find all Kinds of People, but more Clever People than any other Kind. But I don't Know them Until I find them out. The People on this line are more Respectful to Strangers than they are over on the Erie Canal and N.Y.C.H.R.R.R because they are not troubled so much by Haut Beaus and Tinkers. They don't travel So much [on] this Rout[e] as it is to[o] Cold in Winter and out of the way in Summer. In going from one large Citty to another I have not Seen but one H.B. Since I left Camden, and I did not get to Speak to Him as there was two Young men Farmers Sitting talking to me when he passed. There was a nice old Gent Came by where I Am. Well dressed, Plug Hat and Cane, He looked like a man of leasure and means and was Educated and inteligent. I was Just Eating my Breakfast and drinking my Coffee. He Sit down on the Roots of a Beach near me and Remarked what a Pleasnt Spot I had Selected for to partake of My Morning meal. I offered to divide but he Said His Breakfast would be no doubt waiting for Him by the time He got Back to His House. He told me that All this land belonged to Him as far as I Could See. He Said he thought I was Enjoying My Self. I told Him I Relished a meal in the open Air in a Place like this. He Said that he believed it was Helthy. I related Some of my Experiance to Him and He got very deeply interested and Spent some time with me.

I was Reading your Comments on Corrupt Practice in Voting and think it an able Article and to the point.[76] Also Have Read the Edition's Congratulations and thanks. I think My Self there is to[o] much illegal voting, that money and Whiskey have to[o] much influance over important Elections. In a number of States now the Laws are Such, and the Polls So Closely Watched by officers, it is all most imposible for Repeaters[77] to get in their work. They

---

76   McCook was Chairman of the Volunteer Citizens' Committee on Venal Voting, published several articles on the topic of buying votes, and drafted the 'Corrupt Practices Act,' which aimed to eliminate the practice. Tramps would often be a target for politicians seeking to buy votes, either with money or with free alcohol.

77   i.e., people who return to the same voting booth to vote repeatedly in a single election.

haft to Register a number of days before Election. But a man Can Barter His Vote but that is dangerous if found out, as it is a Penatentiary offence for Either buyer or the one that Sells out [i.e., sells their vote].

I never Sold my Vote but once, and that was in the Citty of Chicago when Mayor Krieger[78] was Elected. There was a great deal of money and Fraud Used to Elect Him by the Rum Sellers. I was a legal Registered Voter and would have Voted for the Republican Candidate, Mayor Roach,[79] if I had not of Sold out. Some of the Politicians Got around me, Knowing I was not going to Vote for their Candidate, and they oferd me ten dollars to Vote for Krieger. Now, I did not Care who was the Mayor of Chicago, it was of no importance to Me and the ten Dollars was. I accepted the Money and Voted with them. And thousands of others done the Same in Chicago on that day. I Knowed of men Selling their Vote for a drink of Whiskey on that day. Money was deposited with Every Saloon in the Citty to treat men and buy their Votes & Black Eyse and Broken noses was in demand. I would not Sell my Vote at the Polls of a Presidential Election, I think to[o] much of the Principles Fought four [for] long years [be]for[e] and Spilt Some of my Blood on Southern Battle Fields. I have Voted in Mississippi at the Polls when my Ballot was the only Republican Ballot in the Box and never was Molested in the least.[80] And they Knowed My ticet for I told them I Could not Vote with them, I Respected them as men but Could not Vote their way. I have often Heard H.Bs talking about their illegal Voting and How much they Had made and How many Drinks they Had got and How Drunk they was in Certain Citties on a Certain Election day. A great many of them make for Some Free and Easy large Citty on Election day to make a Stake and get Boosed [Boozed] up, free of Cost. But this Austrailian Systam of Voting Catches the Boys.

Well I have written more than I Expected to. I have not Moved from where I Eat My Breakfast and it is getting late in the afternoon, and I am 14 M[iles] from Oswego and want to get there before dinner to morrow and must go Part way this Eve. On the nights of June 29" and 30" inst, Slept in Hotel and took my Meals. Also Hope what I have writen will prove of interest

---

78 DeWitt Clinton Cregier (1829–1898), Democrat Mayor of Chicago from 1889 to 1891.

79 John A. Roche (1844–1904), the incumbent Republican Mayor who lost to Cregier in 1889.

80 During the nineteenth century, the Republican Party was dominant in the North and the Democratic Party in the South of the U.S., the former Party being more liberal and the latter more conservative. These demographic and political positions would swap during the course of the twentieth century.

to you. Will Mail this to you at Oswego and inform you where you Can write to me next. If Ever any of my Experience Comes out in Print, Should like a Copy. The [writing] Paper you Sent was very Accepable.

W.W.A

Fig. 7

Oswego, N.Y, July 1893

[WRITTEN ON 'WAGNER HOUSE' HEADED NOTEPAPER]

Profs Jon J McCook
Niantic Con[necticut]

Dear Sir, I mailed you two of the Daily Papers Printed Here and will Mail you todays "4", Sir, that you May peruse and have Some Idea of the doings of this Butiful and Patriotic little Citty of about 22 thousand inhabitants. Excursions are Comeing in Here from all lake points, Canada Citties as Well the Steamers and Schooners dressed in Flags and Bunting, the Stars and Stripes Proudly Waving from Most Head and Flag poles. Yesterday's Pirade [parade] was grand in Uniformed Millitia and Secret Societies, the od[d]fellows[81] taking a Most prominent part. And Such Splendid Bands, and Martial Music. The Rochester Martial Band was Splendid, Reminded me of old Soldier days. And Every Brass Band here was giving the people Elegant Music, Particularly a Buffalo Band. And Such Perfect Marching and Manouvers as was Executed by all. And I don't think there is a Window or a door in this Cittie but what displays a flag, sometimes a half doz or the Nathional Collors in Some way. And almost all Young Ladies, Gents, Boys and Girls, Old Men and Women wear a Small Flag pined on to them in Some place where it can be best Seen. And large Flags, the Starry Banner Floating from the Flag Pole and Tower of Every Prominent Building and over all Main Streets. I never Saw Such Patriotism and how Proud it made me feel that I was an American and Served my Country over four long and Bloody Years, that our Grand old Stars and Stripes Should Proudly wave as She does in Oswego N.Y. A Soldier and His deeds done for liberty all honered [honored],

---

81   A fraternal society founded in England in the eighteenth century. An independent U.S. American branch was founded in 1819.

Much More So than they are in Some of Your Bo[a]sted Eastern Citties.[82] I have been in all of them and have heard Gilmore, Damrosh & Wagner and All great Mucitions [musicians] but they are only Greater in name not in Execution than the different Band Masters in Oswego on 3" & 4 July 93.

Some of these Western Citties and Villages Can give Some Eastern Citties [and] Villages lessons in Respect for the Men that Saved this Country, And Also in Enthusiasm and Patriotism and love of Country, I notice. In New England on Decoration day, You Know where I was, Shops in ful[l] blast, Farmers at work in their Fields, Bicicle Races and all other Sports Carried on, on that Should-be-Solemn day. And Probably a Handful of old Grey Crip[p]led Vetterons [Veterans] and Friends decorating their Comrades' Graves. Shame, I Say! Come West: And take lessons in Patriotism and Respect for those that deserve Respecting. I Am Saying Just what I know to be facts, for I have been there. If You want to See true Patriotism, go to the Citty of Pittsburgh on Washington's Birth Day; or any other Nathional Holiday, or any other Western Citty, And they Observe Decoration day in its true Senses. Why two thirds of our Population Are drilled Soldiers, take All Uniformed Societies, Mollitia [militia] and fine Specimans of Physical Men. And the Ardor and Patriotism that are in them, impossible to Conquer them. And Every Citty and Village are full of them. And the Ladies, God Bless them, are Ready to Stand to their Backs.

I had two tin types[83] taken Yesterday but it does not do Me Justice, it is a Poor Excuse of a Picture. I Shall Send You one So as to give You Some Idea of My Apearance when in private life. I Am doing a good Buisness here and have Made many friends. I Am Stoping at this Hotel and payed from Yesterday noon to today at noon. An Old Soldier is Landlord and all His Clerks the Same So I am at Home.

Good day Respectfully Yours

William W Aspinwall

---

82 It is unclear why Aspinwall does not consider Oswego, New York an Eastern city. (EDITOR'S NOTE: Taking U.S. history into account, at the time and of the habit, land west of the Catskills and the Poconos and Adirondack and Appalachian Mountains was considered the "West.")

83 A type of photography that created a direct positive image on a tin surface. By the 1890s, tintypes had been superseded by newer photographic technologies and survived largely as a novelty.

Oswego July 4; 5 PM

At Preasant I am Sitting in my Room, Can Hear Bands of Music but lend a deaf Ear As it Has become to[o] familiar in the last few days. You can adress Your Next letter to Wallington, New York and if you think I will get there to[o] soon to get it, You can adress Charlotte. New. York. Be Sure and let me Hear from you at one of these Places. I want to Know from time to time How you appreciate what I write, and if it amounts to Nothing tell Me So. And if you Ever Have any of it Printed Send me a Coppy. And I will be in Suspension Bridge N.Y and also Niagara Falls, New York, adress me at Your will, Useing your Judgment.

I met a Reporter of the *Pittsburgh Dispatch*. Simply got to talking to Him as one man would to another. I Related Some of my Experience to Him in my travels and He Said 'I would like to take a Memorandum of Your travels' and then he told me His Position, but I told Him 'not at Preasant.'

He gave me His card and told me to adress His Paper at my leasure. I said nothing about Writing letters to You, but anyone that will Compensate me Gets my writing. I am willing to do a great deal for Charity but I must live, you Understand. I am traveling through and am Comeing in Contact with all Kinds of Hardships and giving the truth Just as it is, and I think my Experiance in this World is Just Worth as much as Gen[eral] Grant's, Mark Twain's, or any other Celebrated Writer. I know well that not one of them Can give the Same Kind of Experiance that I Can and tell the truth. And am Satisfied that You, as an intelligent and Educated Man, as I Know you are, will Agree with Me. Will Close for the Preasant.

Yours

William W. Aspinwall

Stearling [Sterling] Valley. Caugu [Cayuga] County New. York. July Sunday July 9/93

Profs Jon J McCook,

I Sent you a Postal last Wendsday Evening from this P.O. I Came out here on the Evening of the 4" inst. I met this Young Man at Oswego at the Hotel And got in to Conversation with Him, and He insisted on me Comeing out Home with Him. And He Said I Could do what I Could on the Farm and He would alow Me one Dollar per day and my Bord. I came out with him And, as He had a good Horse and Buggy, he Covered the distance in About two hours, leaving Oswego About Eight P.M. We got out to His Butiful Home, all were in bed. He Showed me to a Room And I reclined into a Comfortable Bed And Slept well And Had a good night's Rest. They called me at about 6 am in the Morning And partook of a good Substancial Breakfast. And I got Aqainted [with] Old Mr Calvert and Old Lady Calvert. They only Have the one Child at Home with them, the young man that brought me out, Mr. Fred Calvert. And they have a Hired Girl but She was not at Home, Had not got back from the 4" July, [they] Expected her there to get Dinner. The old Lady, Mrs Calvert, is 75 yrs old And is Cripled up with the Rehumatism [Rheumatism] So that She Has to Hold on to the back of a Chair to Stand and push the Chair Along in fr[o]nt of Her when She walks. And a fine intelligent old lady She is, Very Kind and Motherly. And I feel Sorry when I See Her trying to get Around, trying to Attend to Her House Hold duties, As I have no doubt She Has been a good Manager in her Younger days.

She is an Aunt to our preasant Secretary of War, Daniel Lamont.[84] Her Maiden name was Lamont and of Scotch Ancestors. The Old Gent, Mr

---

84   Daniel Scott Lamont (1851–1905), Secretary of War during President Grover Cleveland's

Calvert, is 78 yrs old and His Hair and Beard is a Redish White. In His Young days I Suppose His Hair And Beard were Red. And He is Very Slim and Some what Stooped. And a Very Religious man, Askes Grace at Every meal and Holds family Worship, And I think H[e] Means Just as He does. Always Have Respect for A man that Practices daily the duties of His Religious Faith, Vice-Versa for a Hypocrite. The old Gent is an Irishman from the north of Ireland And a Prusbyterian [Presbyterian], And the family Are members of that Denomanation. Him and His Son Have gone to Church today and Gave me a Very pressing invitation to go with them, but I declined as I Wanted to Read and Write Some. Quite a Picture to See this old Couple Sitting at the table with their Specks [spectacles] reared up on the top of their Heads, and the old Gent as Attentive to Her as He was in His Young days, And the old Lady takes a great deal of pains in His Comfort. It looks like Comfort in old Age with a Good Home and plenty. What a Happy life this old Couple must Have Spent together. The Old Gent Milks three Cows, Attends to His Pigs And takes Great Comfort in doing So. And delights in Showing You His Stock, wich is as fine As I Ever Saw. And the old Gent Works out in the Field, Hoes Potatoes, Helps Make Hay And Can do as much of any Kind of work on the Farm as Some of the Young men, And [is] as Steady as a Clock.

The Hired Girl was at Home when we Came into dinner. She is Rather good looking And of Irish decent. I noticed Her Sizing me up when I came into the House and while I was Eating dinner. I would look up ocasionaly and Catch her with her lamps [eyes] Glareing At me. And She was Shy at first but Her and I have got to be good friends. And She is quite talkative and quite good Company, drives away Some of the Monotonous moments when Around the House. I have Cultivated Potatoes with and [an] old mare they Have Had on the Farm for fifteen years. And She Knowed more about Plowing than I did, I Soon found that out. For I would forget My Self And Hallow 'Haw' when I wanted Her to go 'Gee' And Vice-Versa. So I would let the old nag Have Her own way and She learned me, and She went Slow and we got Along Admireably well for the first day. The next day they Set me to Hoeing Corn and Potatoes in the forenoon. The old Gent was with me part of the time and it was all I Could do to Keep up with Him, as old and feeble as He is. I felt rather ashamed of My Self but He Said I was doing remarkably well. After Dinner, My Self and the Son Fred went to putting Paris Green[85]

second term (1893–1897).

85   An arsenic compound powder used as an insecticide, so called because it had been used to

onto the Potato Vines as they were alive with thes[e] Colorado Bugs, young and old, and Eggs. And Some of the Vines were Striped of leaves. We took a large Tin Pail and filled it with watter and then took of Paris Green one Heaping tablespoon ful[l] and a Half, and Stired in this watter and then took one of these common Whisk Brooms And Sprinkled the Vines of Every Hill of Potatoes in that four acre field. And I was Just about as tiard as I wanted to be when night Came, but we done the Buggs great damage and the Potatoes a great deal of good. I looked on the Vines the next Morning and the Bugs Had disappeared. And the next day, Friday "7 inst, done Some Hoeing and Helped Make Some Hay. And on Sat "8" I Hoed Potatoes All day, the old Gent being out with me the most of the time. I have got So I Can Get a long much faster now than He Can. They Have A fine Bed of Strawberries and I Spend a Great deal of my leasure time in that and one or the other of the numerous Cherry Trees and it is a Caution[86] the amount of Fruit I get away with besides what I Eat at the Table in the Evening. At times We go down to the Village, Stearling Valley, Always Riding down in the Buggy, as Fred is not much of a Hand to walk. All the Farmers or Rubes Congregate there at the Stone and talk over what they Have done that day, And what they dident do and what Should of been done, and About Crops, Hired Hands, wich is good ones, And How much they (diferent ones) Can do, and the Price of Hay, and the different Kinds of Farm Machinery, and the Best brand of Tobacco. And the different Hired Girls, Ministers, and all Classes Comes in for a Share of the Gossip at the Village Store. It is quite interesting to Sit by and listen and take Items. I Suppose I Come in for a Share of the Gossip when they meet. Amongs[t] Women and men as I am a Stranger in the Neighborhood, but I Stand in with these People And they give me a good Name.

Today is Sunday and I am Sitting in My Room on the Side of my Bed with my best Cloths on, White Shirt and Collar and dressed neat and Clean from top to toe. I went down to the Creek last Eve After Supper and washed out a Suit of Undercloths, took a Bath and felt much better. I left my Umbrella Kit in Oswego at the Hotel So that I Can get it when I go Back. I was doing Very well mending Umbrellas Since I Struck Camden, but I thought I would Come out Here and Stay A while to rest and [for] a change, and get Some good living for a while.

---

kill rats in the sewers of Paris. It was superseded in the 1930s by cobalt green, which was a less toxic alternative.

86   A nineteenth-century slang term meaning something astonishing.

I may not Stay any longer than another week, which is about as long as I can Content My Self, and then I Shall go Back to Oswego and get my Kit and proceed on my Journey to Naiagara [Niagara] Falls, making the Streets in Towns on my way resound [to] the Echo of 'Umbrellas to mend! to mend!'

I have Just been down Stairs and Enjoyed a good Country dinner of a Ro[a]st, Home made Bread, milk Coffee or Buttermilk, Baked Beans, Vegetables, and for desert Strawberries & Cream, Cake, Rice Puding. Good Enough for the Infanta Eulalla.[87]

I have from time to time been realating to you Sketches of My Hard Times and travels, of wich I have only begun to tell you of the incidents, and Marvelous times I have Had during my life. You will Understand that Since I was 16 yrs old, the time of my Enlistment, and Ever Since has been Almost Constant Travels, at no time Staying more than one Year at a Place, Constantly Moveing about. And I have a great deal to write about of my past life. I have had good times And Enjoyed myself. And at other times the World Seemed to be against me And, do what I would, fate was against me, as you no doubt have noticed by Some of my former Writing. I am going to give you today a brief discription of about one year's [worth] of Experiance of Some of my good times, when I became a member of the best Society And Respected by the Welthiest and best Cittizens in the Community where I lived. The Spring after Harrison and Morton was Elected[88] I was in Chicago, dead Broke And becomeing disgusted and discouraged. I Started out one night And Jumped [i.e., illegally hopped] a[n] Express Train, went to Ft. Wayne Ind[iana]. Tried Hard to get work but without Success, went to the depot and again mounted a Train.

Made my way to Canton Ohio, looked around that Citty for Employment, Succeeded in getting Some at gardening & with different parties. Amongst others I worked about two weeks for Mr. Miller, Cashier of the 1st nathional Bank, made Garden, mowed his Lawn, and Cleaned up His Cellar. Had worked myself in to the good graces of Mr Miller but became dissatisfied And Said nothing to no one. Went down to the R.R. Jumped a Freight Train and Rode in to Pittsburgh. Had a little money but it was all gone before I left that Citty. Was told there that I possibly might get work in a woollen mill

---

87 María Eulalia Francisca de Asís Margarita Roberta Isabel Francisca de Paula Cristina María de la Piedad, otherwise known as Infanta Eulalia of Spain (1864–1958), Duchess of Galliera.

88 In March 1889, Republicans Benjamin Harrison (1833–1901) and Levi Parsons Morton (1824–1920) took office as U.S. President and Vice President respectively.

in Worthington, in Armstrong County PA, near Kittaning. I Made my Way
to Kittaning on RR, 40 miles up the Allegheney River. From there Slept in
the Train Grounds all night. The next Morning Walked out to Worthington,
six Miles West. Got there Hungry and fatigued. Went in the Buffalo Woolen
Mills Just before dinner. Enquired for the Supt, found him and got a Job at
one dollar per day, And He Sent me to a Bording House. I worked my Self in
a little time into the Good Graces of all members of the firm, Especily the
Hon Ed Graff, formerly a member of the Legislature of Penn[sylvania]. He
is Welthy and was a fast friend, and they Promoted me to Overseer of the
Carding department with wages at $2.50 per day. And I took a great interest
and attended Stricly to my Buisness, And won the Confidence of the Firm
and all the Community. And I wore the best of Tailor-made Cloths, Sported
a Gold Watch. My Credit was good for all I wanted, as Mr Ed. Graff would
Back me. After I was there a while they got up a Lodge of the Junior Order
of American Mechanicks. I was a Charter Member And they Elected me
Financial Sec; And also marcial or Commanding Officer in all Parades. We
went to Kittaning on 22" Feb 1889 to take Part in Parade. I was in Command
and made a fine Showing with my men and Came back Home with Honors
to My Self and the Village we represented, the Press Giving me great Credit.
And on decoration day folowing I was again in Command in our own Village.
And the People in that Vincinity never Saw the day Keept in Such Style
and our dead Heroes Honerd in the way they was on that day. And Such
Grand marching, I had 100 fine men Uniformed a good Drum Corps and I
was in full Commander's Uniform. And we made A fine Showing. I was the
Hero of the day. Afterwards, in June, we Concluded to get up Some Kind
of an Entertainment but it fell through in Some way, So My Self and Mr
Alexander, the overseer of Spinning in the mill, Concluded we would Send
and get Miss Jillian Berkhart, a Star Elocutionist of Pittsburgh. We procured
the Presbyterian Church and Miss Burkhart's Services for one night, Her
Price being thirty Dollars and Expences. I also Engaged the Services of the
Kittanning Brass Band. And when the night Came it was Raining. I Got a fine
Rig and went to Kittanning, met miss Burkhart at [the] depot and Brought
Her out to our Village and the Band Came and, well, to Sum it all up we Had
a good time, My Self in particular as I was Miss Burkhart's Escort. But the
Entertainment was a Financial Failure. All the best people, Ministers, all
tried hard to make a Succes but no Use, the Elements were against us. My
Part of the Expensce Amounted to $60 and I Stood the most of it, Mr Ed
Graff Helped me.

My Best Girl in the Vilage got jelous of my driving Miss Burkhart around and would not Come to the Entertainment. The Kittaning Band Came out in the Rain and when they got there the Show was going on. And they was all feeling good, haveing brought Several flasks of Paddy's Eye Watter [i.e., alcohol] and Had took Some of it inwardly. And they Could Blow like Good fellows. But Every one Had different Music and they though[t] they was doing Wonders. I did not intend the Band Should Play in the Church as we Had a Elagant Choir and other Music more Suitable, but the Band Boys Got at it and they made that Church Ring and it Shocked the more Sanctimonious of the Members, [who were] thinking it a most Horrible Catastrophe to Have a Band Play in their Church. And the Consequence was that Church was Closed to all Exibitions of that Kind. And Such a time as we Had at the Hotel Afterwards, Music by the Band Until you Couldent rest. And after we was all in bed and quite [quiet], Some fellow would Slip around and Hit the Drum and Cymbals a Belt. And all would quite [quieten] down again. Some one would Blow a Cornet or Trombone Until your Hair would Stand, and it was Kept up all night. The Landlord Came to the foot of the Stairs at one time to quite [quiet] the Boys, but Some one Poured a Pitcher of Watter on to His Head and he immediately disapeered.

Miss Burkhart Came to Her door and implored the Boys to Keep quite [quiet] As She wanted Rest Very bad, and Some fellow would Say, Probably the worst one, 'Yes Boys do Keep quite [quiet], it is a Shame to Keep People awake All night'.

The Band Boys Started for Home next Morning And wanted to Play me a tune before they Started, but as it was Sunday I told them not as the People in this berg were not Use to music on Sunday of that Kind. So they peacefully departed. They were all fine young men, Clerks, Book keepers and Some Printers. And the Editors of two of the County Papers was in the Crowd, they Came out for a good time and they Had it.

One time after this there was a magic Lantern Show[89] Came there. No Good of Course And the Boys all Knew it. He Held forth in a School House. About the time it was to Commence there was no Ladies in the Crowd. The lights were put out, nothing Showing light but His Lantern. Some one threw a Bench and Struck his Lantern and it went to pi[e]ces. Simultaneously a Revolver was fired of[f]. The Showmen immediately disappeared through a Window & Absconded.

---

89   An image projector used for entertainment since the seventeenth century.

He Came Around Again in a few days. The Boys Payed Him for His Lantern but he never Showed in Worthington again. At another time there was a Man and Woman Came there to give a Kind of a Variety Show, but it did not Suit the taste of the Worthingtonites and Buffaloites and they got Rotten Eggs [thrown at them]. I never Enjoyed My Self better in any place I Ever was in than I did in that Community, but got dissatisfied and quit my Position against the will of my Employers. Went to another Mill as overseer in Emlenton Pa but Could not Agree and left that. And Have not done much Since, only Roam around. So you See I Sometimes Have Some good times. This is only one instance, I have many more to tell you at Some future time. I have Writen Enough for this time. Direct to

   Stearling Valley
   Cayuga County
   New York

Sterling Valley NY; Sunday 7 PM

I wanted to tell you that I have a first Class letter of Introduction from the Buffalo Woolen Mills Peter Graff and Co

Worthington

Armstrong. Co

Penn[sylvani]a

As to being Honest, Industrious and attentive to duties and looking to the interest of the Firm and Competency, I use[d] to be the Village Corespondent to the Armstrong County *Republican* [newspaper].

Mrs Calvert Just asked me if I would like to Have Some Bread and milk for my Supper. I told her it would be Very acceptable as I was Particularly fond of the Combination. Fred Has Gone to See His best Girl. The Hired Girl Ella Has Gone to Her Home on a Visit, So I am all Alone with the old People. Mrs Calvert wanted to Know who I was writing So much to. I told Her I Had a Friend in Niantic Con, And He was fond of reading long letters. Will Write a Postal Sometime, the middle of the Week. Will Send another letter in about one week.

Oswego, N.Y, July 16 1893

[WRITTEN ON 'RINGLAND HOUSE' HEADED NOTEPAPER]

Profs Jon J McCook
Hartford Ct

Kind Friend, As I have throug[h] writing or Coresponding become a friend to You, there is allways Some Magnetism in the way a man Writes that Speaks and Explains the disposition of the one Writing. I can tell Anyone's Ways through Corespondences As well as I can through Actuel Conversation, that is to a Certain Extent. You Certainly are a man of a wide Mind and Extraordinary inquisitiveness, and of a nobel disposition to be interested in the Subjects and Modes of living of Your fellow Man. Not Many in Your position in life Stop to think! Their minds generally goes forward with Civilization, they don't Stop to think of Unfortunate Brothers that are living in Ways at the preasant day that would put to Shame the Modes of living of the Wild Men of Africa and the Wild Red Men of America. I fully apreciate and admire the interest you take in this way and the Public Should be informed and be familiar with the ways and Modes of living of Every Human Creature, let them be Savages or brought up and Educated in the Schools and Colleges of our Bo[a]sted Civilized America. I only wish that Every true intelligent Man and Woman Could See and Understand As you no doubt do by this time the ways of H.B.s. I think they would Conclude that more Mission Work Should be done in the U.S. and not So Many Missionaries Sent to India & Africa.

Yes, Professor, Your Apelation [i.e., title] is Correct. You are a true Professor. You Have a Brain Capable of teaching the Youth of any part of the World. This is my Opinion. You are not narrow Minded but want to be informed of Your Surroundings and apreciate true Knowledge.

I left Mr Calvert's [place] out at Stearling Valley Yesterday afternoon, Sat. I was there 10 days and lived well and a good Bed to Sleep in Every night and a 10 dollar bill when I Came Away. And I won the Respect and Esteem of the whole family and neighbors as far as I Got aquainted. You would of thought it was Some near and dear relative leaving to Hear the old Lady talking. She Said there was no Use of me going to Oswego for I was perfectly Welcome there. And the old Gent was of the Same opinion and the Son Fred Had to interfeare in my behalf. Oh! How I apreciate Such People, [they are] Noble. I am going back there next Week, tomorrow, Monday Morning,[90] and Stay with them one more week. Oswego is a fine little Citty, I am Captivated by the Surroundings and the Kindness of the people to Strangers. Certainly there is other Citties in this U.S. that Could learn lessons of Courtacy [courtesy] from this little Citty in Lake Ontario. Yes Sir, Your Conjectures were Correct to a Certain Extent, I was Exceedingly prosperous on the 3" and 4" inst. I met and made many good friends through my Patriotism and devotion to My Native Land and in other ways. I no doubt partook to[o] freely of the flowing bowl Yet at the Same time Keeping My Equalibriam. You will notice in my Corespondences I always make Friends with Police Officers. I have had them when I got a little to[o] much [i.e., drunk] to take me to my Hottel and in Some instances to their own Homes or Bording Houses. I am Very quite [quiet] and Gentlemanly in Such a State. I Made a good Friend last Evening, the Chief Engineer of a large manft [manufacturing] Plant here, and my friendship May result in my getting a good Position at Some future time with the Standard Oil Co[mpany]. One Cause of my Misfortune and poverty at times is my liberality and Big Heart. I will give to an Unfortunate [person] and Suffer afterwards my Self. I leave here in the Morning for Stearling Valley, Please write to me at that Office. I hope you are Enjoying Your Vacation. I will not write much of a letter at this writing as I want to go out on the Beach. Have Some interesting incidents to relate that Hapend out on the Farm at Some future time. You would not take me for the tinker and Tramp to See me Here in this Hotel. Yours Wm.W. Aspinwall

---

90   The 16th July 1893 was a Sunday.

Wolcott N. Y Aug 5 1893

Jno. J.McCook
Niantic,
Cn.

Profs I left Oswego on last Tuesday "3 inst. I am going to Niagara Falls. I am again Fixing Umbrellas. I have made $1.00 Since I left Oswego. The mills are all Shutting down. I Worked one week for Oswego heft Co and they Payed All Hands off. There will be Plenty of H.Bs if things don't Change. Address Charlotte N.Y. Will Send a letter Soon. Yours, William

Wallington N.Y. Sunday Aug 6 1893

I Stoped last night at Rose Station, Seven miles East of Here, in a Box Car. The first night after I left Oswego [3rd August] I Stoped at Wheeler Station in a Vacant Building that was at one time Used for a Station. The next night, the night of the 4" inst, Stoped in a Box Car at Red Creek Station. I have walked Since leaveing Oswego. I met in Red Creek a Baptist Minister, Pastor of the Baptist Church at that Place, the Rev. J. M. Shotwell D.D. I Sat in his yard in front of his Residence and Conversed with him near two hours. He asked me numerous questions, Wanted to Know my Pedigree and Where I had been in my life. I told him I did not think he would have the Patience to Sit there Until I related to him where I had been in my life and my Experience that was Connected. And then he wanted to put me on to an Easier and more Speedy way of making Money than fixing Umbrellas. It was Sel[l]ing Soder [soda] and Polish. He Gave me Receips How to make [them and] I wrote them down in my Day Book. Also took his address. He Said he had made Some money Pedling those Articles in time gone by. And then he Said, when I got Able, he Had a Buggy that he payed $20.00 fir[for] but he would Sell it to me for $18.00, and when I got new tires, new Shafts and Some other things new, it would be a good Buggy. I Acquiesed in all of His talk and then he gave me Some Religious Advice, and I went on my way feeling for my Right Arm.[91] I Called at Stearling Valley as I Came by and got the Papers you Sent me. I Peruised them at intervals when I would Stop to Rest. I have them yet. I put them in my Valice and have Expressed [mailed] it on ahead of me to Charlotte N.Y, as I found it to[o] Cumbersome to Carry.

I Car[e]fully Read Your prop[o]sed Law for the Punishment of Tramps and others found Sleeping out or Begging, and the Proposed new Reforma-

---

91   i.e., the Minister has talked his arm off.

tory[92] of the State of Con[necticut]. I will Just Express my Opinion, meaning no Offence. It is all Plausible Enough on Paper and will do for the Legislation to pass away time on, and the State to Spend Some of its Surplus Cash in Erecting the necasary Buildings & a renumerative institution for Officers, As they are about the only ones that will be Benefited.

I don't talk this way because I am a traveler and Sleep out nights, but from Experience. I have been in numerous States where they Have Laws Enough to Almost Hang a Poor Tramp or Vagrant. Look up the Laws of New York, Ohio and most of the Eastern States on that particular Point, and numerous other States but [I] Just mention these for an Example. None of them Enforce these Laws. For why? [i.e., why not?] Because it is inpracticable. And [these laws are] Just to Some [people], while they are Unjust to others.

Take the Cittys of N.York [and] Chicago. If the Police would Enforce the Laws, the Tax Payers would haft to build a Citty one fourth the Size of the Original to Accommodate the Ar[r]ests.

When I was last in Chicago there was near fifty thousand Men out of Emplaw [employ]. That means 50,000 Tramps or Vagrants and the Mayor at that time Isued an Order to the Police not to Arest any one for trivial Offences Such as Sleeping out [and] Drunks [drunken] Brawls, as there was no room in the Citty Prisons. Take Chicago at the preasant time. I Supose there is twice or three times as many of the Same Kind as at that time and the Mayor of New York and other large Citties has at times issued the Same Orders. I think Your Reformatory in Connecicut would in time Assume Huge dimentions And be more densely Populated than any of your Citties of your State, laying as the State does between the large Cities of New York and Boston and Surrounded by the fairly large Citties of Your own State and Border States. It is my Candid Opinion you would Have all the Reforming that you would want if you Undertook to Reform all the So called Tramps and Vagrants and others that Should belong to your State and that would pass through. People that have Homes and Good Saliries and that have never

---

92   In 1893, McCook drafted a bill aimed at ending of the practice of jailing men under vagrancy and tramp laws in Connecticut. The bill called for the establishment of a state reformatory for the rehabilitation of transients (we might call it a 'Roving Bill' bill). While more
compassionate than the vagrancy laws it sought to replace, this bill was still written under
the assumption that hobos were on the road because they were lazy. McCook wrote that
the reformatory would be a place where a tramp "may both learn to work and overcome
the habit of idleness." McCook, "A Tramp Census and Its Revelations" in *The Forum* 15:6
(August 1893), pp. 753–766 (p. 766).

Experianced any of the Hardships of this Cruel World don't apear to have Much Sympathy for their Unfortunate Brothers. We are not all Constituted Alike any More than we are all fit for Professors or Doctors, our dispositions are different and it Can't be Helped. It is So and always will be So. I think Kindness and a disposition to Show Unfortunates that Christian People and all other well-meaning People are interested in their Wellfare I think will do more to Reform Some than Laws or Reformatories. There is thousands of HBs And others that try to get in to the Jails and other Places to Spend the Winters, Even go So far as to Commit Some trivial Crime in, and so to be Sent up for Six or three months in the Winter.

This I Know to be a fact. So Prisons Has no Horrors for Some. Well, it is better to be locked up in Some Jail if you do haft to go a little Hungry than to be out[side] without any House or Friends or Money in the Cold Blasts of Winter. I have never went to Jail in my life but think it more preferable than Some of my Experiance in Winter. And then it is Hard to tell the deserving from the Undeserving on that Acount, all Hast to be Used alike Until Acts and deeds distinguishes them.

I am of the disposition my Self that a little persuasion and Kindness goes a good ways (but not all the way). Any Kind of Punishment will Ussage [usually] makes me obstinate and I will do any thing to be Contrary to the one Misusing me, and I think there is many others of near the Same disposition. I have quite a Spirit of resentment. I don't think Confineing Such dispositions as my own in Prisons or Refrormatories would do much good. Confinement in Such Places might Posibly Reform the ignorant but not a Man of any intelligence. How many Comes out of States Prisons Worse Criminals than they went in, their dispositions Hardend and the Schooling they Receive from fellow Convicts.

This question of Reforming People is a very Grave one indeed. All Smart men have their Ideas. Christ our Savior Endeaveord to Reform the World And was Crusified. I think the only way is to Keep Actuel Criminals Seperated from the rest of the People but not Abuse them. Be Human and others Use Persuasive Powers, Kindness and then if it won't take, apply Something a little more Severe. I will Close as it is geting dark.

Sodus N. Y. Monday Aug 7 1893

Prof, I Stoped last night in a Box Car at Wallington. I walked 4 miles to this Village and got my Breakfast at a Restaurant. It is now after 1P.M and I have Earned one Dollar today. Taking out my Breakfast and dinner leaved me 50 cts. My next Stop will be Williamson about 6 mi west, will get there this Evening and will Probably mail this letter to you from there. As I was Comeing along the R.R. this Morning, I met a Well-dressed man but his Countainaince [Countenance] and Cloths Showed that he had been laying out in the Rain. He told me that he had been working for a Farmer near Han[n]ibal N.Y and that he went down to Rochester N.Y to buy a Suit of Cloths and he drawad thirty Dollars of his Wages. And when he got to Rochester he went in to a Saloon in Some Rough Part of the Citty and he woked up Sunday morn and did not have a Cent. And had walked Sunday afternoon and most of the night last night in the Rain to get back. When I met him he had about 40 mi East to go yet to Get to Hannibal. All I could do for Him was to Sympathize. I suppose He got Amongst the demimonde[93] Society and Had to Pay the fiddler as thousands [of] others have done before Him. I don't think from his talk he will Visit a large Citty Soon again. I think he is reformed for the time being.

I did not get through my Comments last night, it Came dark on me.

Now there is a great deal of Reforming that Should be done out Side of Tramps and Vagrants. Take Society, it is Rotten to the Core. But you take a Society man or Woman, Especily of Welth and influence and they Can perpetrate Almost any Crime, Some times murder and they Can get out of it with their money and influence. Is their feelings any better or their Blood any better than their more Unfortunate Brother Human Beings? I

---

93 Meaning "women of doubtful reputation and social standing," most likely here referring to prostitutes. *OED, demi-monde* (noun).

Should Say not. Why do Judges and Jurors discriminate in favor of Money and influence? I can tell you [about] money and Popularity, when a Welthy man becomes a Tramp or a Vagrant he Stands no more Shaw [sure] than any other Tramp. Why was the Cincunatti [Cincinnati] Court House Burnt by a mob a few Years Back?[94] Unjust decisions and discrimination. Now all Churches and Society will Cry out against the Poor and Unfortunate, 'they must be reformed in Some way' when if they Would Stop and Consider and look out of their own Back windows they Probably might find Subjects to Commence on, for I don't think there is any family Rich or Poor but what Some one Connected with that Family in Some way Has Violated the Laws of their Country and their God in different ways.

Please Understand me that I am a great Respector of Christians and those that Sincerely try to live Christian lives, but How many Wolves in Sheep's Clothing [there are] in the different Churches of today.

How long would Some of these High Saliried Pastors Preach if there was nothing but a Poor living in it? Not long, they would Soon turn their talents in Some other direction more renumerative. Not many would do as Christ done or John the Baptist. I am Saying what I Say and don't mean any offence to any one, Just to ilustrate The World is Sadly in want of Reforming. But Altogether, not the Unfortunate Tramp or Vagrant Alone, but All. Take for instance these Bank failures,[95] beating Poor Men & Women out of their Hard-Earned Money, Manufactureing Tramps, Vagrants and Subjects for Asylums, and Convicts. There is a great deal to do before this World becomes Perfect.

I believe Capital Punishment is wrong and the more I Study the more I become Convinced. For instance, the Case of Carlyle Harris[96] that was Electrocuted a few months Since Here in N.Y. I have my doubts, and a great many others Have their doubts, of His Guilt. Amongst them the Hon. Danl. Vaorhees[97] of Indiana, one of our greatest Criminal Lawyers. Evidence is Easily manft [manufactured], Especily Circumstancial. I think life imprisonment Should be the Extent of the Law. What a Horrible thing for the Law

---

94 A reference to the 1884 Cincinnati Courthouse riots, which followed on from an unpopular verdict in a murder trial.

95 A reference to the economic panic of 1893, which involved several large bank collapses and led to years of economic depression. The Panic was caused in part by overinvestment in some railroads in the 1880s and their subsequent collapse in the 1890s.

96 A medical student executed in 1893 for the murder of his wife.

97 Daniel Wolsey Voorhees (1827–1897), lawyer and U.S. Senator.

[of] the People to put an innocent man to death. And I will Cite you again to the Pardoning by the Gov of Illinois [John Peter Altgeld] of those anarchist.[98] Now if those Pardoned were innocent and as not tried fairly, August Spies and Albert E Parsons and others that were Hung Surely must [also] have been innocent, or not farly tried by Law for they Was all in the Same Box, All Arested for the Same Crime. I Can't See the Consistancy in Such ways of Administering Justice. There is a great Wrong and it Should draw the Attention of Men of Brains and Judgement, there is a Reform wanted here most Certainly. And I Could go on and Ennumerate Hundreds of other Cases but you are no doubt a great deal better Posted than I am on the foregoing Subjects, So I will leave them with you to Meditate over. If I have Said any thing that will do any one any good I am thankful and Hope no one will take offence, for I Just Simply give my Opinion. Reading over your Proposed Law brought these thoughts to my mind. I do think that the Poor Unfortunates are discriminated against Unfairly, not but they Should be punished in for Certain Offences but I think there is a better Way to Reform at least Some than Jails, Penetentiarys & Reformatorys. And All Should be treated alike, Rich and Poor, High or in low life, no discrimination. I have Said all for this time. I must be moveing on, for I have Several miles to Tramp before I lay me down to Rest.

Good Rains here last night and night before, wich was wanted as Every Kind of Vegitation was drying up. The wether is quite Cool today.

Yours

Fratulently

---

98   A reference to the anarchist 'Haymarket Martyrs' George Engel (1836–1887), Adolph Fischer (1858–1887), Albert Parsons (1848–1887), and August Spies (1855–1887), who were executed in Chicago, as well as Louis Lingg (1864–1887), who killed himself before his scheduled execution, for the 1886 bombing of a policeman in Haymarket Square. These sentences were handed down despite several of the men not being present at the Square and the bomb-thrower never having been identified. A famous miscarriage of justice, to many on the left these events symbolized the willingness of the capitalist state to execute political radicals with little justification. The surviving prisoners were pardoned on 26th June 1893.

Near Ontario. N. Y; Aug the 8" 1893

I had Company last night [of] a Genuine H.B. He Said he had not done any work for Several Years And that he did not intend to if he Knowed it. We Stoped in a Box Car at Williamson Station. He Said he was Just puting in the time Until Hop Picking Commenced. I told him there was no money in Hop Pic[k]ing, A fellow Spent it as fast as he made it. He Said there was not much work about it but lots of fun, and a fellow got a month's good living, wich took the wrinkles out of his Belley. I talked to Him [about] where he Had Stayed last Winter and he Said he put in the winter in the New England States in the different Stops and H.B. Camps. I asked him if he Had Ever Sold his Vote and he Said he Had Several times and would again if any man put up the Stuff [money], that he did not Know as it made any differance to Him who Held Office, one Party Helped Him as much as another.

I Says, 'Don't you Some times Vote for Principles?'

He Said Every Body was of the Opinion that a Bum had no principles and he might Just as well Have the game as the name. He Said he Seen no other way but that he Had to be a Bumm all of His life, for he Said it was Either Bum or work and he was not going to Punish Himself with Hard Work. And if he had to be a Bum he was a going to be a good one, and if a man oferd him any thing for His Vote he would Sell it Just as often as he Could.

I asked Him if He Ever done any Repeating [i.e., repeat voting]. He Said he Had. But I did not find out where, As he might think I was get[t]ing to[o] inquisitive. He apeared to me to be a inofensive Kind of a Chap, was fairly well dressed, he gave me Considerable of information about Hostile towns and Citties. The last I Saw of Him he Started to Hunt His Breakfast. He was going East. I Bought my Breakfast. I have done no werk today Yet. Made no money, may Strike luck before night.

Ontario. Beach. Near Rochester NY; Aug the 14"/93

I have been here and in the Vincinity Since thursday morn, "10" inst. On the night of 9" inst Slept in a Box car near Winsor Beach. Done Some Work fixing Umbrellas. I have made about two Dollars Since I Came Enough to live on. On the night of 10" 11" 12" & 13" inst I Slept in a Barn partly filled with Hay. The night of the 10" inst I was all Alone in the Barn. On the night of the 11" inst there was about twelve H.Bs in the Barn, when I got there the Hay was Covered. I was Greeted with the Remark from all I approached when I Climb up in to the maw 'Say don't Step on me', 'Be careful', 'You'r[e] over here' and 'is that you?' and So on. It was near twelve Midnight when I went in. I had been out to the free Theater in the Paviliun. And the nights of the 12" & 13" were Repititions of the night of the 11" inst. I did not talk a great deal with the H.Bs in the Barn but last night they go in to quite a Political Argument. Some of them Some were Democrats and Som were Republicans, but the Demicrats Seemed to out number the Republicans. I Keept my mouth Shut through the Argument, would do me More good Just to take items of their different Ideas. One H.B Advanced the Idea that the Moneyed men and Manufactures of the Country were all Republicans, And he Emphasized With an oath they were So mad that Cleaveland was Elected And a Democratic Congress that they, the Republicans, Shut down all the mills and Closed all the Banks and took the Money out of Circulation to Spite Working men that Voted the Dem ticket. And the Argument got warm at times. None of them Advanced Any Good theorie for the Preasant money and tariff questions. Some of them are very ignorant and it makes me tiard to hear them talk. Others again are fairly well informed on these Subjects.

My Ideas about the Silver question[99] are the Same as Congressmans Blands of Mo.[100] He Spoke to the point last week in Congress. The West must not be ignored. They are geting to[o] powerful an Element at this day and age of this Republic. And my Views on the Tarriff question is to let the Tarriff alone as it is. If it must be Changed at all they Should do so gradually, not to throw the Country into a Panic By Suden Changes of the Tarriff Laws. Of Course the Democrats have made no Laws as Yet but it is their threats and what their Platform purports to do that Has Caused this preasant Stringincy and Hard times. Buisness men and Manft [manufacturers] have no Confidences in the Wild Cat theories of the Democratic Party. Manft will not manft a large Stock of Goods and [will make] Congress go to work and make or Change the tariff Laws, Making the Raw Material Cheaper and Cheapening the Manft Product. It is all as plain as the Nose on a man's face, all Can See the result if they look out of their Buisness Eye. It Should not take much Argument to Convince intelligent men. I think if there was a Presidential Election this fall there would be a wide Spread Revolution in Politicks. The Common People Have Come to their Senses by High priced Experiance and will not be So Easy influanced as they was last fall by Democrats.

---

99   The Panic of 1893 led to an oversupply of silver and public debate about how much, if any, silver ought to be minted as coins. The populist 'Free Silver' movement, led by farmers and agrarians, argued for the unlimited coining of silver to combat deflation. This would be the main plank of the Populist Party's platform and, later, of that of the Democratic Party under William Jennings Bryan (1860–1925).

100 Richard Parks Bland (1835–1899), Democratic Representative 1873–1895 and 1897–1899, who was known as 'Silver Dick' for his promotion of bi-metallism (the minting of both gold and silver coins) and silver currency.

Near Watterport [Waterport] NY; Aug 15 1893; 4 P.M

I Stoped last night at East Kendell in a Box Car. This is Something like Some of the Country I have described to you before, no Umbrellas to mend. I have done nothing in the way of making any money today and don't Expect any thing. There is a great difference in the People in different localities. Some places I Strike, the People are very pernicious and Superstitious and think You are around to Rob them. Other localities the People are more liberal and want to let you live as well as themselves. You will notice this in my Writing Heretofore. I notice when I get into a neiborhood where the People are fanatical and don't allow any Saloons or will Hardly allow their Children to play Crochea [croquet] that they are the Most pernicious And mean, and I think that Self Esteem [i.e., arrogance] is very prominent on their Craneums [Craniums]. Farming Vilages as a general rule are no good for my Buisness. Once in a while I Strike a liberal farming Community. Give me the Manft Towns where Every thing Goes free, those are the people to Patronize my Buisness or any other Buisness, not the narrow-minded fanatics. I don't Care any thing about Saloons but I notice where they are you will find the Best and most liberal People.

Now about Creating H.Bs or Tramps: I think the Laws of the Country has a great deal to do (and the Buisness of the Country) in making Tramps. Now, this preasant Shrinking down of Buisness[101] will make thousands of Tramps because Every one is a Tramp when once on the Road. People make no discrepancies whether you are on the Road a week or a year. A majority of the mechanicks and laboring men have nothing layed up and no Houses and when they are throwed out of Work there is no other Alternative but to take

---

101 Meaning the depression.

the Road. My Opinion [is that] the government Should be Managed So as to have good times Always and plenty of work, and it Could be if it was not for these money Shylocks influencing the Administration of this Government And the Emigration [immigration] that is daily arriveing on our Shores. You Can Expect no better as long as the preasant State of Affairs Exist but You Can Expect Even worse. Make Good Wholesome laws and Enforce them Against all Clases Rich and Poor Alike. And make all obey and Start up all the Manft Plants. Bring our Money on a Sound Basis, one dollar worth Just as much as another. Break up these Combines [i.e., large monopolies] and trusts. I will Just mention the combine last winter on Pork making, the Poor People of the South pay 20 Cts per lb for Pork. Outrageous, and this is only one of the many Combines that are Robing the People and making Tramps. Do away with all of this and Bring Good times and plenty of work at fair Wages, So that the poor man will not be a Slave. And then make laws that Every able-bodied man Shall go to work or be made [to] work. And then make it a Crime to be a H.B. or a Tramp and then the nuisance of tramps Can be done away with. There would be no Excuse then for tramping.

My Opinion is that this would be the only remedy. You may build all the Reformatories that is to be Possible to build and they will all be filled, as are all the Prisons in the U.S, and will be as long as the preasant State of affairs Exist. Men are not to Blame. One man Has Just as much right to live as Another. Cloths and Education and influence don't make the man. I believe Every man's disposition is Born in Him. Rich or Poor Education Sometimes Smo[o]ths over the Surface, Some men have better opertunities than others have, [it is] not as [i.e., that] they are any better men than their Poor Brothers. Take the late Senator Ingalls of Kansus,[102] him and Jay Gould[103] went to the Same College. In the Senator's own wards [words] Jay Gould Carried the Pocket Book while he, Ingalls, Carried the Sheep Skin. This Tramp question is

---

102 John James Ingalls (1833–1900), Republican Senator for Kansas 1887–1891.

103 Jay Gould (1836–1892) was a ruthless U.S. railroad magnate and railroad speculator, one of the Gilded Age's so-called 'robber barons.' An old hobo song, "Jay Gould" (circa 1907), parodied Gould's attitude towards people who took illegal rides on his freight trains:

Ole Jay Goul' said, before he died,
He'd fix a way fer hobos to ride.
Said, "Ride on the bumpers, en' ride on the rods,
En' trust your life in the han's uv God!"

Collected in E.C. Perrow, "Songs and Rhymes from the South" in *The Journal of American Folklore* 26: 100 (Apr-Jun 1913), pp. 123–173 (p.168).

a great question and no doubt a great nuisance to Some, and Probably a great nuisance to a great number of Tramps them Selves. But the question Can be Solved if taken in the right way, but not by force. This Country is Supposed to be free to Rich and Poor Alike. I Could write [for] a week on this Subject, the Causes and the Effects and on the Absurdities of Some People, but will let this I have Said Suffice for the preasant and [LETTER ENDS ABRUPTLY]

THE RAIL ROAD SUSPENSION BRIDGE.
NEAR NIAGARA FALLS.

Fig. 8

Niagara Falls NY; Aug 20 Sunday

I am Camped about two Miles Above Niagara Falls. I Slept in a Box Car
between here and the Falls last night. I bought my Sup[p]ly of Grub last night
in town. And I have a nice Pot Ro[a]st today, Onions Potatoes, Coffee, Sugar
and I am living w[e]ll today, all by my Self. I made Yesterday about two dollars
in Supension Bridge[104] and about one dollar on Friday at Lewiston N.Y but
Some way I can't Save any. I made a quarter this Morning as I came along,
fixed a Parisol for an Italian lady or Else I would only have 4 Cents in my
Pocket. I will haft to let up, I am drinking to[o] much Beer. I don't drink any
thing Else but I can Spend a great deal of money on Beer. As I was Comeing
Along last night on the Side walk I Run into (a Bull)[105] A Policeman. I had
my arms full of Bundles, A tin Bucket, my tool Box, Bundle of Umberellas.

---

104 The village of Bellevue was known colloquially as "Suspension Bridge," named for the Ni-
      agara Falls Suspension Bridge which, from 1855 to 1897, stood 2.5 miles downstream from
      the famous Falls.

105 These parentheses are Aspinwall's, suggesting that he knew that McCook may not be
      aware that 'bull' was hobo slang for a policeman.

I Could not Carry any more and I had about all the Beer I Could well Carry. I Run my Bundle of Umbrellas in to the Bull's Abdomen.

He Jumped to one Side and Says 'What? Are you moveing [house]?'

I told him, 'Yes, I was going out in the Suberbs to Rent a House'.

He laughed And Said I would do to travel [i.e., get out of town before he is arrested].[106]

I helped put out a fire at a Hotel in Supension Brige yesterday. The Clerk noticed me Carrying Watter and working like a major, and he took me in and gave me a good dinner and all the Beer I could drink, and told me whenever I Got Hungry to come back. I come in Useful Sometimes. I always make friends Wherever I go and don't get into any trouble. On the Weds the 16" inst, I Stoped in a Box Car at Lundonvill [Lyndonville] N.Y. Made nothing, foraged Some Potatoes and Corn to live on. On the 17" inst [I] Stoped in a Box Car at Hess Road N.Y, made 25 Cts. On the 18" inst Stoped in a B.C. at Ransomville, made nothing. Have Walked Ever Since I left Oswego N.Y. I am going back to the Citty of Niagara Falls tomorrow, I think I Can make Some money there. May Stay there a few days. I Called at the Post Office last night but I was to[o] late, will Call again tomorrow. There is quite an influx of Visitors here to See the Mighty Falls of Niagara and the wonders of Nature that is to be Seen here. I have been here before, two years ago, Stayed here about two weeks. Will go from here to Tonawanda and Buffalo, and I think from there to Pittsburg.

I met at Ransomville, NY a H.B. fixing Sewing Machines. He Had been all over America. I think he Could talk a arm off a Sewing Machine. He was one of the wardens. I met Several H.Bs, all of them was going East. All Said times was Very dull out west. What do you think of the Rumors in the Papers of the west and South Secedeing from the East? But it is my opinion Congress will Remonetize Silver and make Every Satisfactory Law for all Parts of U.S. The money Barrons work to[o] much to the intterest of Europe. I don't Blame the South and West, they are bound to have their Fights. The day has gone by that [i.e., for] these two great Powers, the South and west, to be Governed financially by the East. There is any Amount of Idle men through this Country, not more than one out of ten working.

---

106 Almost one year later, on 28th June 1894, a young Jack London would be arrested at Niag-ara Falls for vagrancy and sentenced to thirty days in prison, a story which he recounts in his book *The Road* (1907). Roving Bill's business of fixing umbrellas and other mechanical devices seems to have saved him from the same fate here.

Sunday Aug 20 4 P.M

I am here where I went in to Camp this Morning. I have put in the day Cooking and Repairing up my Cloths and washing and fixing up my Umbrella Kit for Buisness tomorrow. I had a good dinner and have Enough and more for Supper and Breakfast. I procured a Ro[a]st last night and I Cooked Potatoes and onions with it, and the gravy was fine to Eat with my Bread. And I have a good Supply of tobacco and a pipe. So I put in the day to good Advantage to My Self. I think if you would have been here you would of relished Some of my dinner. There is Some High-toned Gents in Camp in tents, a Short distance from where I am, on the bank of the River fishing. One of them Came over to See me while I was Cooking dinner.

He Said I apeared to be Enjoying My Self. 'Good for you', He Said, 'that's what we are in the world for.'

I Also Had a H.B. Visitor, Had quite a talk with Him. He told me He traveled all over the South and West with a Umberella Mender. He Said he Carried a Pot and done Sodening. He was Going East.

Now You will not mistake me in my writing heretofore that I don't Champion All the H.Bs' causes, Only a Certain Class. You will Understand what Class by my former Corespondence. I know there is men on the Road mean and low Enough to Commit any Crime, and again there is a good number of different dispositions. I Simply Give you my Candid thoughts Just as I See and feel at the time of Writing. I will mail this tomorrow. I am out of Stationary, I have one more Postal Card. You Can write me at Buffalo N.Y. I will be there Some time the Coming week.

Niagara, Falls, August 21 1893

Profs J J McCook

Dear Sir, Just Rec yours of the 7" inst. I had quite an Experiance last night after Comeing in from my Camp. I droped in to a Saloon on the Out Skirts. It Proved to be an Italian Joint. And it is Close to where they were working on the great Niagara Tunnel.[107] And there was a Conglomerated Mass of Human beings from all nations. The Negro was very prominent. All drunk and geting drunker. I Just took a Seat and took in the Show, it beat any Variety [show] I Ever Saw. Polacks, Italians and Negroes Kissing and Hug[g]ing, fighting, Shooting Crap.[108] You can Judge the Sights for Sunday.

I may Start for Buffalo today. I have made 40 cts this morning, doing a very good Buisness here. I May go to the World's Fair Yet, Have not made up my Mind. Write as Soon as Posible to Buffalo, Gen Del. Will let you Know there my future Course. Thank you for Compliments.

Yours

W.W. Aspinwall

---

107 In 1890, the Niagara Falls Power Company began the construction of an ambitious tunnel, 2.5 miles beneath the village of Niagara, that would divert water into a shaft capped with a turbine. This was the first large-scale attempt to generate electricity at the Falls.

108 A game in which players bet on the outcome of dice rolls.

Bradford Pennsylvania, Sunday Aug 27 1893

I arrived here last night, Came in on a Train over the B.R. & P.R.R [Buffalo, Rochester and Pittsburgh railroad]. Got permission to ride from train Hands. I walked out from Buffalo to Springdale N Y, About 30 Miles but got disgsusted at not doing any buisness so Jumped here. I left Niagara Falls [ab]out last wedsday. Slept that night under Tree between Tonawanda and Buffalo. Walked into Buffalo on the 24 inst and out to Buffalo Creek Junct[ion]. Stoped in a Freight Car All night and walked out 20 miles. On the 25" inst Stoped in a Box Car all night. Walked 10 miles on 26 and got here about 7 P.M last night. Made 60 Cts yesterday. Will Stay here over Monday and then Resume my Journey to Pittsburgh. I have Had an very hard Sunday, I got drove out by the Rain and took Shelter Under Some Lumber Sheds. Made the Aquaintance of two Scotch Coal Miners Just Come over [and] was waiting for a train for Dubois, Pa. And they are nice Clever fellows. They Had a Bottle they Brough[t] from N.Y. Citty, of Course I imbibed with them. About a dozen of the town H Bs Came around And Had a Great Chat with them.

I went to Yel[l]ing out 'Umberellas to mend!' this morning. Did not Know it was Sunday Until a Gentleman told me.

This Citty Use[d] to be one of the great oil counties, but has lost all of its former grandure. I have met hosts of H.Bs at Niagra Falls and Since. A Great many out of work owing to Hard times. I met the Half-Breed one-armed French man I wrote to you about Some time ago at Niagara Falls. He was a total wreck. He wanted to go with me again but I Got Shot of him the Easiest way posible, and I thought my own Company was the best and took self advice. I am going to Stay in Bradford over tomorrow, Monday. I think I Can make two or three Dollars to Help me Along. I am glad once more to See the old Oil Derricks and Mountains of Pennsylvania, it looks like Home. I

Was out in the Bush this Morning and got my Breakfast and made Coffee. I Borrowed [i.e., stole] Some Potatoes and Green Corn and made a Splendid Stew and Eat of it Until I was in misery [i.e., full]. It was very Palitable. Every thing Smells of Petroleum here in this Citty of Derricks. Been very Dry in all the Country. I have traveling through Since I left Oswego but Got a glambing[109] Rain today.

---

109 I have been unable to find a definition of this word, which Aspinwall seems to use to mean 'very heavy.'

Bradford Pa Monday Aug 29/93

I Stoped in the Same Box Car I did on Sunday night. There is one thing. I never was in better Health in my life than I am at the preasant time, this Kind of a life appears to agree with me. I got my Breakfast this Morning near a Creek. Had the Usual Rite of fare: Corn, Potatoes, Coffee, Bread, onions, a Steak done very well. I had to Push the Oil back of the watter on Creek in order to get Clean watter. There is so much oil floating on the Surface My Coffee tasted of Petroleum.

I am going to Canvass this town today. Have Read the Horrors of the Elmira N.Y Reformatory,[110] Just about the way they are all managed by Some Brute with a Plug [i.e., Top] Hat. Think I will go to Titusville, thence to Oil Citty, from there thence to my old Home Pittsburgh. I have no Relatives there but Hosts of friends. The Air is well impregnated with Oders of Coal Oil in this Country. Will Send this today. I will also Send you A [news]Paper [so] you can See that All the toughs are not on the Road.

---

110   A reformatory run along military lines. Known colloquially as "The Hill," the facility was renamed Elmira Correctional Facility in 1970.

Bradford Monday Aug 29 1893 11 P.M.

I am in the Citty, have Canvassed part of the town but nothing to Compensate. Every thing Very dull, Men all out of work and no money. This Panic has got to a terible State of affairs. No one is more Able to Judge than my Self, traveling from place to place as I am and meet and talk to all Classes. I think a good many Democrats will haft to go to Cooking the Roosters they Was Carrying around And that was Crowing last Fall.[111]

I will Send you today a Pittsburgh Paper Containing est[eemed] Speaker [name unclear in original letter]'s Speech, wich Suits my fancy. And he portrays the Cause and Effect Just as they are and the Remidies to my notion. The Republican Eagle is to[o] Proud a Bird to be cooked Just yet a while, Always on top, in the Pot or out. I also Send you a *Chicago Sun*, wich Contains Some desirable information from Some other Papers. So You can See that I am thoroughly posted on the topick of the day in all parts of this broad land, [there is] not many that can Argue with me when they come down to Buisness.

I will go from here to Titusville and Oil Citty, Pa. You Can write to me at oil Citty, Penn, Gen Del. Will be there in a few days. I will write a Postal to Corry, Pa to forward my mail After to Buffalo N.Y. I met a Poor fellow this Morning, a married man and [with] Children. He was Tramping, Hunting work and wanted to Know if I Knowed where he Could get a Job, as his family was in want. I Says to Him 'Are you a Democrat?' He Said 'Yes', but Said if God would forgive Him he never would Vote that way again. This is only an instance, I could mention many more. This Use[d] to be the once prosperous Oil Country, Many Fortunes made but no more, is fast declining from her former Grandure. And no Farming-Country Financial Kite-Flying; many noiseless Derricks that Use[d] to be full of life and a Conglomerated

---

111   i.e., after the 1892 Presidential election, which the Democrats won.

mass of Human Beings of all Nathionalities. No ballpin, no foundation. You will perceive what I mean. Oil no Price, overproduction, don't pay to drill more wells or to Pump old ones with only a limited amount of the desired ilumination. Petroleum once to bo[a]st of Penn. Will Close writing to hear from you at Oil Citty.

Fratulently W.W.A

Pittsburgh Pennsylvania; Sept 8 1893

Profs Jon J McCook

Niantic Ct

Profs, Kind Sir, I Arived in Pittsburgh on Weds the 6" inst. Received Your Postal and Tablet of [writing] paper. You Said in your Postal you had Writen A letter but I have not received any as yet. I think if you have Writen a letter it must of got lost, or it Surely would have been here by this time. I wrote you Post at Mt Jewit. I had quite a trying Experience in that Country as I could make no money, Every body was out of work and had no money. I would manage to make a quarter Every day or So and Kept Soul and body together Until I arrived in Pittsburgh. I had to Cook Potatoes and Green Corn Several times to fill up on and to drive Hunger from the door. I procured the Corn and Potatoes in Fields as I passed by, borrowed them you Know. After I left Mt Jewit, I passed through the Reynoldsville Coal district and through all the Principle Towns & Vilages. Found times Very dull and the Principle portion of the People all out of work and giving it to the preasant Democratic Administration. I found this Universal where I have been, the People invariably lay the blame on the preasant administration. I Came down through Brookville, New Bethlahem Pa and Struck the Alegheney River At Mahoneing [Mahoning] Pa and the A.V.R.R [Allegheny Valley railroad].

About 60 Miles from Pittsburgh, Came down through the Valley past Kittaning [Kittanning] Pa, Ford Citty and Tarantum [Tarentum] Rolling Mill and Pottery was Shut down, at Kittaning Men all loafing around the Streets. Came down the River to Ford Citty where the large Plate Glass works are located, the largest in the U.S, wich Employ from 12 to 1500 men. All Idle, Had done nothing Since the 15" of last June. It looked discourageing to See all these men loafing around and no Prospects. And at Tarantum another large Glass Mft Plant all Shut down. Kensington, another Mft Town, all

Shut down. And the R.R. on both Sides of the River lined with men going both ways, the Picture of despair on their Countainances and asking how the times was where I had been, but it was no Encouragement I Could give them, wich I would Gladly of done if I Could of give them an Encourageing word. How Sad it made me feel to See these Strong Helthy Men Use[d] to Manuel Labor and willing to work And Earn their Bread and Some of them to[o] Proud to beg or to make their wants Known, despair and trouble plainly visable on their faces but no work to be found in this land of plenty. It is a Shame and Shows Groas [gross] Mismanagement in the Law makers of this Republic and Surely Something Rotten. This Citty, Pittsburgh, is very dull, thousands in and around the Citty Seeking work.

I don't think the preasant Administration Altogether to blame for this trouble. It is my Humble opinion it has been brewing for Some time past. And it reminds me of a Spent Ball, Had to drop and Hapend to drop on the preasant Administration. Of Course tariff Agitation done its part, but as I have Said before there has been to[o] Much financial Kite-flying, Men and Corporations trying to make fortunes out of nothing. I don't think we have [had] what I call prosperous times Since 1873.[112] Hard to get Employment, Something Rotten about our financial System. I Hope the Preasant Congress will make Some good wholesome laws to Govern the finances of this Country and Make Some laws to Govern the Emigration to this Country, Stop it, at least for a while. Of Course these times don't make much difference to the regular H.Bs. I don't Know but what it is better for them, as they depend on their indomitable Cheek for a living and the Public is not able to distinguish, and the HBs, Having more Cheek than the Working Men, of course live better. I have Got a Room and Bord here, Expect to pay for it out of my Pension. My Friends here was all glad to See me, it has been near two years Since I left here without Any Money. And I have traveld About twenty thousand Miles And Come back with my Health.

Where I have been I have already Stated to you. I intend Staying Here this winter if I can get Employment, but if I can't will haft to move on. I am Geting tiard of Roaming Around And I would be Happy indeed if I only had a permanent Home. I am Satisfied I could apreciate a Regular Home but will haft to do what God intends for me to do. I have Seen about all of this World I care about, I am Satisfied. But don't want any Soldiers' Homes or Alms Houses, they don't come up to my Idea of a Home, would Rather live

---

112 The 1873 Panic had caused a financial depression that lasted for four years.

on the Road by far. I have a great deal to write to you Yet of my travels and will give it to you from time-to-time as opertunity offers. I was out of money and paper Since I left Mt Jewit and had all I Could do to live. I Slept in Box Cars Some times and Some times in Barns, old Houses and once or twice in the open Air. I made 75 Cts today Cleaning a Colored man's Watch. This is the third day for me in Pittsburgh and have made one Dollar.

Please write as Soon as Convenient And Address William. W. Aspinwall
Lewis Block
Pittsburgh. Penn
Care. Thomas Wallace

P.S: Understand you Use to be in Stubenville Ohio and Relatives of the noted Gen & Cols McCooks.[113] Excelent Material.

---

113 James McCook was a member of the famous "Fighting McCooks," a family that sent seventeen members to fight for the Union side. McCook himself saw relatively little action before mustering out to join Trinity College.

Pittsburgh. Pa Sat Sept 9 1893

I am feeling good this morn. Employed a good night's Rest. Don't you think I have done Exceedingly well in all my travels to never be Arested or Molested by Police Officers, or have never Got into any fights [or] Brawls in all the different Kinds of Society and Communities I have been in? I never Carried a Revolver or any Kind of a Murderous Weapon. Some times I had a Small Pocet Knife And [was] often without [even] that. And in all my Experience I have never had any Use for any Weapons in the least. And I have been, or necesity Has forced me amongst the toughest of the toughs; but I Always at[t]end Strictly to my Own Buisness and Counsil My Self and let Every body Manage their own fights and Brawls; I was not Concerned; and if I got into bad Company got my Clearance papers as Soon as posible. I will be pleased if you Send me Some more Papers and Reading mater for I like to Keep posted in your part of the Country, and any of your Writing that Should be Printed will be of interest to me. I hope you may have passed a pleasant and Profitable Summer. And may you live a long and Happy life, And your teachings and Experience be the means of Advancing mankind to higher and nobler Spheres. Yours,

William

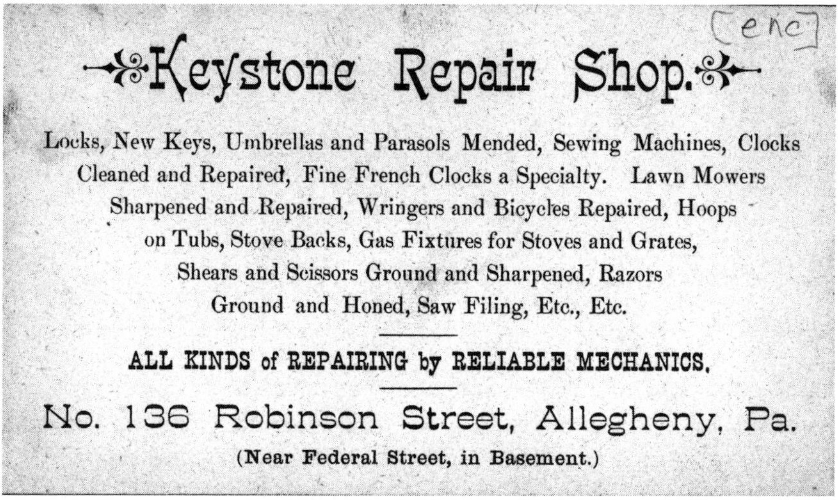

→❖Keystone Repair Shop.❖←

[enc]

Locks, New Keys, Umbrellas and Parasols Mended, Sewing Machines, Clocks
Cleaned and Repaired, Fine French Clocks a Specialty. Lawn Mowers
Sharpened and Repaired, Wringers and Bicycles Repaired, Hoops
on Tubs, Stove Backs, Gas Fixtures for Stoves and Grates,
Shears and Scissors Ground and Sharpened, Razors
Ground and Honed, Saw Filing, Etc., Etc.

ALL KINDS of REPAIRING by RELIABLE MECHANICS.

No. 136 Robinson Street, Allegheny, Pa.

(Near Federal Street, in Basement.)

Fig. 9

Allegheney. Citty. Penn; Weds Sept 20 1893

Pros Jon J McCook
Hartford Ct

Dear Sir, Yours of the 18" inst Came today. I have Started in Buisness
for My Self, A Repair Shop. I took my Pension Money And [with] the Help of
Some of my friends I have a fine Shop and am beginning to get Considerable
work. I Also take Orders for Coal for one of the best firms in the two Citties.
I am going to make a bold Stand to Hold out as I am tiard of the Road. I am
Shure Intemperance Will not Hold me back. Buisness is very dull Here, many
out of Employ, as You Say All that are Hard up now. Have been intemperate
or to[o] Lavish in Some way. There is no doubt but that a Great deal of the
preasant Distress Could have been Avoided if People had of been more
Economical. But Such is Human nature and it is Hard to remedy. I have not
time to Say more at preasant. Wishing to Hear from you frequently.

Respectfully Yours
William W Aspinwall
136 Robisan St
Allegheney Citty
Penn

Allegheney. Citty. Penn; Sept 26 1893

Profs J.J. McCook

Dear Sir. I Just Rec yours of Aug "3" forwarded from Oswego, N.Y and from Place to Place Until it Arived in Pittsburgh. Buisness is Very dull here, Scarcely anything doing. I feel very much discouraged. I took what little Pension Money I got and Rented a Place for Buisness and Bought Some Stock, and now if it was not for a friend of Mine Could not Subsist. And that is Something I don't like to do, depend on Friends, it is not my Disposition. I like to be independent not dependent and Consequently I am very much Worried and dissatisfied.

There is many good Honest Mechanicks out of Employ Here and Actually Suffering for Necasaries. And families also. And a Mfts Starting, are Cuting Wages. The outlook for Working Men is not Bright. And there is intense Suffering Amongst those You Would think from their outward apearance that was not in want but are to[o] dignified to let it be Known. This is the State our Country is in at Preasant and don't look as though it was going to get Any better Soon. It is All very well for Reformer[114] to Cry out 'Intemperance does it all'. In a great many Cases intemperance in its different Modes Has and does Cause a great deal of Suffering, and in other Cases it does not or is not the Cause of the preasant distress. Any Way, When Men and families are Starveing they Want imediate Relief, it is no time to Call [i.e., have] an Argument. It is So; what Has been done Can't be Helped. Or teling a Man what he Has done don't Satisfy his preasant Hunger, Death might result before the Argument was through. Give Him Work and Satisfy his Hunger first, and then Reformation.

I was Reading an Abstract of one of Your letters in Yesterday's Press. You give the northern States the Credit for all the tramps. Now you Just take a trip

---

114 i.e., McCook.

throug[h] the South Dec & Jan and you will find thousands of Negroes and a great many Southern Whites Tramping, And Also numbers of Northern Bums. I don't think there is any denigration[115] to be made in the parts of the United States. As far as furnishing Bums, I think the Eastern States deserve the Credit of furnishing the greatest number and the meanest Class. I mean the States north of Virginia. This is my Experience.

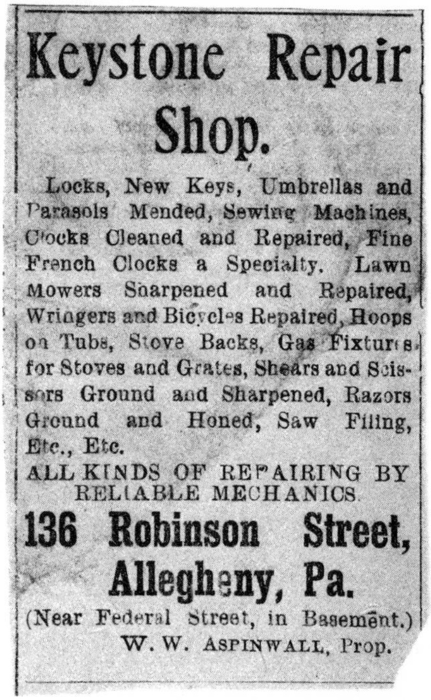

I Would like to See Every Man, Woman and Child that is in want of it Reformed and made Reputable Cittizens and Christians, but it does Seem to me that a great many of these would-be Reformers get the Cart before the Horse and rely to[o] Much on their own Migh[t], regardless of the Suffering and feelings of their would-be Clients. This Country is Sadly in want of a Reformation but they want to Commence at the top Round [rung] of the Lad[d]er in all Society and Politicks, and Come down to the Bottom Round, to Poor Starveing Humanity. Now I am Just giving You Some of My Ideas. I mean no offence to any one. Reformation must Come in this Country, in these Monopalies & Trusts and in a great many other ways, or I fear the worst is to Come. Tramp on a Worm and he will Squirm for his life.

Frat Yours

Wm. W. Aspinwall

136 Robison St

Allegheney Citty

Keystone Repair Shop.

Locks, New Keys, Umbrellas and Parasols Mended, Sewing Machines, Clocks Cleaned and Repaired, Fine French Clocks a Specialty. Lawn Mowers Snarpened and Repaired, Wringers and Bicycles Repaired, Hoops on Tubs, Stove Backs, Gas Fixtures for Stoves and Grates, Shears and Scissors Ground and Sharpened, Razors Ground and Honed, Saw Filing, Etc., Etc.

ALL KINDS OF REPAIRING BY RELIABLE MECHANICS.

136 Robinson Street, Allegheny, Pa.

(Near Federal Street, in Basement.)

W. W. ASPINWALL, Prop.

Fig. 10

---

115   Aspinwall seems to mean 'differentiation.'

Allegheney. Citty. Oct 15/93

Profs Jon J McCook
Hartford Ct

Yours of the 11" inst Came to hand Yesterday, and [was] read with interest. I am Still Carrying on my Repair Shop but Have not much to do in [it]. No one in Pittsburgh and Vincinity is doing much while thousands are Seeking work and Beging for Something to Eat after all. The Bosts of the Press, that Suports Money Shylocks and Trusts, of 'the improvement'.[116] I fail to See it and I look at the Situation the Same as thousands of intelligent men. So I am not in the Boat alone but I have plenty of Company. I am Sorry to Say You do me an injustice when you Say that my long habit of Wandering or Excess in drink may interfere with My Success in Buisness: You do not fully Understand my disposition and Will Power or you would have no doub[t]s from that Source: all I want is a fair Showing and Encouragement and I will Show You what I am Capable of doing. I have went through and am now going through Hardships in Pittsburgh Since my recent arrival here. I fared much better at times on the Road but I am Weary of Wandering and Want to Settle down, therefore I am determined to Stop here if Posible. I will pull through if I Can.

It is a Great task to Perform in Such times as these when there is So many People in want and the Rich Have no Mercy. I have about lost all Confidence in Both great Political Parties: they apear to be bough[t] up by the Combines and Trusts and the money Shylocks of the East. And Poor People have no buisness on Earth in their Estimation, but they may find out their Error when it is Everlastingly to[o] late. A Worm will Squirm when tramped upon, and most all living Creatures will Show their Combatativness

---

116 i.e., the newspapers are claiming that that the economy is improving, claims that would prove to be wildly inaccurate as the depression would continue for four years.

[combativeness] when imposed Upon, Espesily when they want to Starve them in this land of plenty. The Preasure [pressure] will become to[o] great at Some time and the Safety Valve will be Stuck as Glued, and then the Explosion and the result I am not qualified to foretell. It All Sounds very well to those that live in Gilded Mansions and Holding Saleried Positions[117] to Hear the oratory and Press reports of the improvements in times and buisness, but the Working man Knows better. And well Housed People look through their Plate Glass Windows at the Poor and destitute and they pass along the Street and Say 'there goes a drunken Loafer', 'there goes a Tramp', And pile upon the poor and needy all Kinds of Vile Epithets Simply because they are not So fortunate as themselves. I Say Shame on Such Civilization. They do not Realize the fact that a Raged Coat Covers at times a more noble disposition and an open Heart. Probably the Cause of him Having to wear the raged Coat and Probably the Contents of the Raged Coat is more Acceptable in the Sight of a Wise Creator than Some of those looking through their Plate Glas Windows with the Eye of Suspition and Making Sarcastic Remarks about Unfortunates.

I do and always will Hold Sympathy for the fair and Worthy Poor and Claim we all Came in this World Equal dust, no different grades of raw Material, but Some develope after Birth into different Grades of Humanity and the different Clases are to[o] numerous to Mention but all return to dust the Same!

I will be be pleased to have a Coppy of my letters after You get the Extracts into Print. I hope You are Well & Enjoying life. I Send you Some Cuttings from Pitts Papers to Sustanciate my Arguments. Will be pleased to hear from You Soon.

William W Aspinwall
136 Robison St
Allegeney Citty Pa

---

117   In other words, people like McCook.

Allegheney Citty Pa; Dec 10 1893

Profs J J McCook
Hartford Ct

Dear Sir, I received your letter of a few days Since. I will Send you one Containing Clip[p]ings of News Papers Containing information that it would take me weeks to Write You and get you to Understand. This fellow has had the Same Experiance I have had my Self but not so Extensive. But my Experiance is Just the Same. As you well Know there is a great deal of difference in Ho. Bos, Just as much difference as there is in the difference in Society. In naturel life I am a H.B. but I don't Rob or Burglarize or Murder. I am a Gentleman when it is Necasary and Can Make Just as good as apearance in Society As any one, and a great deal better than Some. I think it a Great Wrong Some of the Laws Some of the Towns and Cittys and States Even has Passed on Vagrantcy. You Know to[o] well what I mean; they are an outrage on Humanity, Worse than Barberborus, and if you had of had Some of my Experience You would Coinside [coincide, here meaning agree] with me. And the truth will Come Home to you all in time and prove all what I have Writen to you to be facts. Theory will do but Practice makes perfect. I have had the Practical Knowledge but I Know You have had nothing [but] theoratical Knowlege. Of Course we differ. Can't Help it.

I Refer you to the Gov of Kansas, once a H.B, and don't deny the fact I am Proud of what I have been through because I Know there is Know [no] ordinary man Could Endure what I have. Our Refformation is Coming Slowly and will Come. I want the Wilson Tarriff Bill[118] Passed, I think it the best for the H.Bs to get them Something to Eat and get Some body to work. And

---

118 The Revenue Act or Wilson-Gorman Tariff, which would become law in 1894, reducing tariff rates and imposing a 2% tax on income over $4,000. This was the first peacetime income tax in the United States.

down the Syndycates and Monopolies, they are Worse than the H.Bs, and [are] what make[s] them.

There is no Use in a man of my Capacity Writing and Arguing with an intelligent and Educated and Briliant a man [such] as Your Self. You Know to[o] well what I Say is true and to[o] true, but I have no Doubt there is an affect in You to Argue otherwise. You Know my position, I am not Radical. I want all to have their Just dues, Rich, Poor and Ho Bos of all denominations. There is none [i.e., no one] Perfect, not one Says Paribl [parable, meaning the New Testament]. Let Us all live and we must live at all Hazards. I am going to bust up my Shop. Can't Stand the times. My Landlord is a Presbyterian Preacher and his terms don't Suit me [during] these times. Write Soon Profs to Gen. Del

    Pittsburgh

    And Send Some Stationary

    Yours

    Wm. W. Aspinwall

Findlay Ohio; Feb 2 1894

J.J. McCook,

Dear Sir, I have neglected Writing to You. I had a good letter Writen And all incidents and dates from the time I left Pittsburgh, I am positive it would have been interesting to you. However, I will try and give you Stoping Places and fare and about the number of H.Bs met on my trip from Pittsburgh to Findlay. I forgot to tell you what became of the first letter. I wrote you the day before I arrived here. It rained all day and I walked through the Rain from Tiffin to Corry, twenty Miles, and about Half way from Corry to Findlay through the Rain. And my Manucript got wet and Completely Spoiled.

I left Allegheney Citty on Jan "10" Walked down the P.F.W & C.R.W RL [Pittsburgh, Fort Wayne and Chicago, west rail line] tracks to or near Economy. Stopped at a fire near track, where there was ten H.Bs Camped. Stayed there with them Until near dark and then we made our way up to Economy. Found the Marchall. They have a Place for Bums, Clean and neat and Give all that Comes a good Substancial Breakfast. And the next morning drill the boys out of the Corporation line. On Jan 11" I Jumped a Freight and made Mansfield Ohio, about 150 M[iles]. Got there about 8 P.M. Very Cold. Found the Police Station, Got loging that night. There was 32 Bums in that Station and one night's Stay was the limit. I Stayed in Mansfield all day the 12 of Jan, as it was a Cold Blustering day. The Bums was all Just out Side of Corporation line, had Several big fires. And Stayed Around the fires all day. There was at least 150 bums that I Seen at Mansfield. I Stoped in an Office at a Brick Yard by a hot Stove that night. I had a little Money and bought Something to Eat but I learned from the H.Bs that Most Every House gave them Something. The People are Very Charitable but I found the regular Graduated H.Bs was reaping the benefits, and deserving men Going Hungry: the Cause [was that they were] to[o] timid to Ask [for food] or in Some Cases to[o] Proud. On the 13" Jan Jumped a train went to Gallion [Galion] & Stoped in Police Station All night. And Stoped in two Stations between there and Tiffin, have forgotten the names of Towns.[119] 14 & 15 Jan Arrived in Tiffin. On 16" Stoped in Station. The Boys all Have to Bre[a]k Rock[120] two Hours in morning in this Citty, and then they take them to a Hotel and give them a Good Breakfast. I mended an Umbrella for a Policeman and got relieved of my task, but got my Breakfast Just the Same. I made about one Dollar in Tiffin on the Morning [of] "17" and Started for Findlay. Had to walk as all Trains had gone, the RR being a link Road. And I Got Soaking wet with the afares [affairs] and Results. I walked to within about 10 miles of Findlay and I Spyed a Vacant House Along Side of track. Went over, it then being about ten o clock at night, gathered Some wood and made a fire in the Smoke House. And got a Plank and layed down beside the fire and to my Rest as best I Could. Got out Early and finished my trip to Findlay. Have a Brother Married Here, also a Sister Married and liveing here also, a[nd] nice[ly] Married and liveing here. So You will See I am at Home Here. My dear Mother lies buried here in Maple Grove Cemetary. I don't Know how long I will Stay here. I have Reparied Several Umberellas, Clocks and Sewing Machines. I have Quite a Reputation with my Relatives as a Mechanic, Consequently Get all their work and Bord. I don't think I will Remain here more than one month more.

This Citty Findlay was Boomed at one time but the Boom has died out, with the nat[ural] Gas and all the Factories are moveing to other Places I Suppose more desireable. I Should Judge at least one third of the dweling Houses here are Em[p]ty. And the Small Boy is geting in his work on the Window Glass of the Emty Houses with his Sling Shots and Stones. Real Estate is very Cheap and Rents low and this is [a] Butiful little Citty. But how Helples a Citty is when there is no work for the mechanic & laboring man. This town is a good lesson for Capital to Study.

I have the Pipe you Sent me yet, but it is burnt through. Write me as Soon as you get this to Findlay. I Sent you two Postals on the way. There is a great number of men of the Road but they [are] Honest men that wants to work. Are Staying Around large Citties. The Reg[ular] Bums Know their Buis

---

119 The likely candidates are Bucyrus and Melmore, Ohio.

120 Breaking rock was a form of hard labor often given as punishment for vagrancy and other offenses. Though he does not say so explicitly, this would seem to suggest that Aspinwall had been picked up for vagrancy, or perhaps that hard labor was simply the 'price' for a night in the warmth of a police station.

and take in all the Country towns and Stops. I heard Some of them Singing a H.B Song, it went to the tune of 'After the Ball' but Could not Catch the words.[121] No more at Preasant.

Respectfully

Wm. W. Aspinwall

---

121 "After the Ball" was a popular sentimental Tin Pan Alley song written in 1891 by Charles K. Harris. There were many parody versions. One included the verse:

> After the ball was over,
> Bonnie took out her glass eye,
> Put her false teeth in water,
> Hung up her wig to dry
> Put her peg leg in the corner
> Hung her tin ear on the wall
> And then what was left
> Crawled into bed,
> After the ball.

In the early twentieth century, the radical hobo writer and musician T-Bone Slim (Matti Valentinpoika Huhta) wrote a more politicized version, entitled "After the Bawl," which imagined life after a successful working-class revolution:

> After the Bawl is over,
> Nation may cease to mourn,
> Rid of its erstwhile Jonah,
> Some of its fear now flown,
> After the debts quit crowding,
> Wages no longer fall,
> Then follows the sunshine,
> After the Bawl.

Maumee. Lucas. Co Ohio; April 29 1894

Profs Jon J McCook

I left Findlay Ohio about the 10" of March, have been Roaming around here in Ohio Ever Since. Have been in Every Town and Village in the Northern part of the State, fixing Umberells & Clocks and Sewing Machines. Have Managed to make a liveing but Sometimes it was tough. I met at times Several Squads of Ho boos Claiming to belong to Coxey's Army.[122] The H.Bs are liveing fat this Winter Under the Garb of Working Men. The People Generally have been Very Generous this Winter And the Regular H.Bs have taken Advantage of the Same all Hard-Working Men. I think this Country is Comeing Swiftly to a Crisis of Some Kind from what I have Seen and heard in my travels. What is Your Opinion? Soon one third of the male population of this Country will be liveing a nomadic life And liveing of[f] those that Work. Soon America will go back to the Uncivilized State, worse than the Savage Indians before Columbus discovered this Country, a tribal State of afairs. I think the Gen Government Should Enact Some laws to furnish all Idl[e] men work of Some Kind And Compel all to work or leave the Country, transport them to Some portion of Africa. I have Seen Enough in my travels to disgust Any Sensible Man of the Ho Boo himself. Write as Soon as You Receive this As I am going to Stay here for a while. Send me Some Stationary & and if you have had any of my writing Printed Send it. Resp Yours,

William. W. Aspinwall

Address as above Gen. Del.

---

122 Coxey's Army (also known as the "Army of the Commonwealth in Christ") was an 1894 protest march of unemployed men to Washington, D.C., led by Ohio politician Jacob Coxey (1854–1951), to call for government intervention and public works programs to combat the worst effects of the depression. Constituting up to 20,000 participants, the march was termed a "petition in boots." It was the first significant protest march on Washington, D.C., and provided a model for later marches in the twentieth and twenty-first centuries. Jack London participated in the march, which he recounts in his book *The Road* (1907). The demands were not met and the U.S. government would resist intervening in the economy until the Great Depression of the 1930s.

Zanesville Ohio 3/14 1895

Dear Sir

Your letter of 11" inst Came to hand today, was glad to hear from you. I am Still in the land of the living but I am not Very well. I have had a very bad Cough the most of the winter. I have done no tramping Around Since I left the Circus in last June. I worked in a Woolen Mill in Piqua, Ohio Until "11 of last month, Feb, and then I Came here to Work in Woolen Mills here as overseer of Carding, but they have been Stoped all but a few days. Since I have been here their Boilers gave out and they are putting in a new Battery. And it will be two weeks more before we will get to work.

I am Bording, have a good place with a fair Widow and her daughter. And they are neat, Clean house Keepers And good Cooks, And they do all in their power to make me feel at home & Comfortable. But the price is $4.00 per week, I will be in debt Some by the time I get to Work Again. I am negotiating with a Company in Chattanooga. Tenn. to Supt [superintend] a new Woolen Mill that is to be Erected there the Comeing Summer. I Asked them [for] $1,200 per year[123] to Supt their plant for them. I think I have About Come to the Conclusion to Stop tramping and running Around the World. I think I have Seen and had Enough Experiance of that Kind And Know About As much about this World And its Vices As any one of my age. I am fifty yrs old the 25" of next May, And think it is About time for me to Settle down Some Where. Don't you think it will be a Wise Conclusion?

A great Many people of meanes travel All Around the World And Visit Every place of any importance and a great many places of no importance, And all they Can tell you when they get back is about how much Money they have Spent. There is but few that have traveld as I have done And has Seen as much of the World as I have Seen it And in its true light And made my own way And done it Honestly. I Would Suffer before I would Steal. And in all my travels I would not Keep Company with thieves & Cutthroats and of low

---

123   This is about $39,500 in 2021 terms.

down Charactors. I preferred to be by My Self. The Consequence was [that] I never was Arrested or Molested by any officers of the Law. And [what's] More, I never Carried A Shooting iron of any Kind. And A great part of the time [I was] Without a pocet Knife. I have Come up with Some dangerous gangs in my travels but Managed through Strategy to give them the Slip.

I think there has been more Hoboes on the Road this Winter than Ever before on Acount of the Hard times and the Scarcity of Employment, that is of the Kind that Would possibly Work if they Could get their Kind of Work. There is a great many men that have Certain trades of profesions. And before they will work At Any thing but their Kind of work, they will go on the Hobo. Cigar makers, Printers, Stone Masons, Brick Masons & Weavers are very numerous at times on the Road. As a general Case there is not many Profesional Hobos on the Road in the Winter, Especily Such a hard Winter as this has been, they are to[o] wily for that. You don't Catch them Suffering with the Cold. A great many of them manages to get Arested and locked up in Some Work House or Jail for a few months, While others go South to Florida and to Mexico and Even to South America. You would be Surprised if you would go South at this time and investigate the matter Closely at the Amount of Profesionals [i.e., hobos] you would See traveling. A Common Cittizen Would not See the half of them Even if he made it his buisness and Scrutinized Each and Every man Closely. He would take a great many of them for Buisness men and Proffessors of Some Kind. Detectives as a rule Are not smart Enough for them. The Professionals I have met, Some very Smart Men Amongst them Equal to any Emergency.

As I have Writen to you before, Hobos Can be placed in a great many different Clases. Some are i[n]nocent and harmless. Some are Cut throuts & theives. Some are Murderers, Would take a presous [precious] life for any thing of any Value. No Crime is low Enough for Some of them to perpetrate. Some will work if they Can get it to do.

I think Hobos As a Class generally Speaking Are a Curse to our fair land, but I can't See how You are going to remidy the Evil as long as the preasant State of af[f]airs Exist in our Country. When the day Comes that there is a demand for labor of all Kinds, then I think the General Government Should have laws to prosecute And make Idlers and Hobos go to work or take the Whiping Post or Some Severe punishment.

I have never Seen Any persons in the Acts of Sodomy[124] but have often met parties that I Knew were practicing it, for I have had them tell me So. And I have Seen Small Boys with Parties frequently that were used by the brutes As Subjects.[125]

I have had Brutes aproach me and want to take my person in their mouth. Two or three different times I had to Knock one fellow down to Keep him away from me. The Hobos Call Such fellows 'tasters' or 'lopers'. There is a great Many Women that follow the Same buisness. Some Call them 'Fruit'. I did not Know of any Sodomy being practiced on the Cattle Ship I crossed on, Still it may of been done And no doubt it was. Self Polution [i.e., masturbation] is practiced to Some Extent on Such Ships, And Among[t]s Hobos. I have frequently Caught them in the Act.

I Started With Sell Brothers Circus And Menagerie[126] on the 19" of May 94 from Toledo Ohio. I [was] hired as Canvasman [i.e., setting up the big tent and equipment]. And I can tell You there is no Brutes that have a life Equal to a Canvasman's life With a Circus, Especily Sell Bro[thers]. Rain or Shine, Snow or Hail, Half Enough men or not, that Canvass must Come down And go up, the Heavy Material must be Unloaded And loaded on their Wagons. And we was up Every night Until 1 and two o clock and often the trains were loaded. We had to hunt up a Place to Sleep, Sometimes Under a Wagon, on the floor of the flat Car, Some times in a Canvas Wagon if one Could find room. And Exposed to all Kinds of Wether, the train running, the Wind Blowing and generaly by daylight we would be at our next destination or Show Town. Then the Wagons must Come of[f] the Train Unloaded, Canvass put up and Seats [and] Rings made, Hypodrome stand leveld up. By this time it was dinner time. After dinner, Guy out the Canvas And then

---

124 McCook has asked Aspinwall about adult homosexuality on the road, which was a frequent and oft commented-upon phenomenon.

125 Some hobos (who, among other names, were known as 'jockers') would entice young boys (known as 'punks') onto the road with tales of adventure. In the late nineteenth century; these tales were called 'Rock-Candy Mountain' stories, and gave the title to the well-known folk song of that name. One early version of the song "Big Rock Candy Mountain" is a frame narrative, in which a jocker tells a punk about the easy life to be found on the road. In the final verse, which has never been recorded, the boy breaks from the hobo:

> I've hiked and hiked till my feet are sore
> And I'll be damned if I hike any more
> To be buggered sore like a hobo's whore
> In the Big Rock Candy Mountains.

126 An Ohio-based circus show.

all deploy out and go on watch Around the Canvas Until the Show was over, then Place all those Heavy Wagons by hand ready to be loaded after the Show at night. By this time it was Sup[p]er time. After Supper, Go on Watch again Until time to tear down. I tell you it is an Excitable time, tearing down at night, Curseing And Every one on the run, All Excitement, and more So if it is Raining. And Every day & night this is repeated. And About as tough a Crowd As can be got together, from Propiertors down to the Hundred Canvasmen, all nationalitys and Collors, Indians not Exempt.

I was with them in all the principle Citties and Towns in Ohio, Indiana and Michigan, Illinois & Wisconsin. By this time I got Enough of the Circus buisness. I was About as Welthy when I quit as when I commenced. Minus Cloths our Wages was 15 dollars[127] per month And Bord, Such as it was. Wishing to hear from you Soon. Very truly Yours,

William. W. Aspinwall

118 South St

Zanesville

Ohio

---

127   About $500 in 2021 terms.

Indianapolis, Indiana; Sept 8 1895

Profs John J McCook
Hartford. Conn

Dear Sir, I wrote you last at Zanesville, Ohio, but did not receive any awnswer. I Am Stoping here in Indianapolis at preasant And may Stay here all Winter.

I have had Some what of a diversified Experiances Since I last Wrote you. I Walked all the Way from Zanesville to this Citty, mush-Faking and fixing Clocks and Sewing Machines. Camping out all night And Every night. Came in to this Citty healthy. I think this nomadic life is a healthy life.

I think if Some of you Professors [and] Students would live more of a nomadic life And feel the Enjoyment of the fresh Air more And take More Good Wholesome out door Exercise And live More of a rough and tough life, You would Enjoy better health And live longer. If Such was the Case there Would not be So many of our great Smart men die in the prime of life and mankind would Enjoy their Usefulness a much longer period of time. I was fifty years old the 25" of last May and I feel as well as I did at 20 yrs of age, With the Exception of my Wounds recived during the late War and my Eye Sight is failing me Some. Otherwise I am Stronger today than I was at twenty yrs of Age. When I was a boy I was a weak-lunged Philhisicay [phthisicky, meaning asthmatic, tubercular or wheezy] Morsel of humanity. Now I can lay me down on the green under a tree, or take the Soft Side of a plank And Sleep as Sound as the beasts in the field, And Arise in the Morning feeling as fresh and Vigorous As a Colt Just turned out in the field. I have traveld a great deal in my time Since I left home to go to War. I doubt if there is a Man liveing that has Seen as Much of this World And traveld as Much as I have, and put up with the hardships I have and went through what I have. It takes an iron Condition and indomitable pluck and Grit.

What do you think About it Profeser? You Know a great deal of My Experience, but not all. Have you had any of my Writing Printed Yet? If So I would be pleased to peruse the Same.

What do you think of the preasant times And the future outlook for A large number of People in this Country? I think And am of the Opinion (I may be Mistaken, I hope I am, but barely possible) that this Country, [be] loved America, is nearing a Crisis in her History. If All the Manufacturing Plants in America and the mines and all improvements were Run[n]ing full blast Still, there would be thousand of Idle people that Could not Get work.

You Say 'What is the Cause?'

One Cause is machinery taking the place of Mechanicks and laborers. Another Cause is immigration into this Country. The Cause of immigration Can be remidied by Stoping it. If we Can get Enough Law Makirs [makers] in Washington that Can See any Law that is to the benefit of their fellow Country men. I believe in the doctrine America for Americans.

But our improved Machinery has Come here to Stay And we will Still have more. Machinery is Still in its infancy, I believe.

Of Course, we have thousands of Worthless Characters of men and Women in America that Won't Work And [who] live from Begging or Some Criminal Act. This I am fully Aware of and have Come acroos And had to Asociate With numbers of this Class in my travels and Experience. But at the Same time I Know there are thousand[s] that would work and lead a honerable life if they had the opertunity to do so, but there is not Employment for all. And as our population increases the Evil will increase. I Know this from my own Experience going to these Factories, Seeking Employment and my Association with numbers of others that I became Aquainted with in going to these Shops. Here's where I think the Crisis of our beloved America will Come in. How are you going to make Laws to punish these people because they can't find Employment? How are you a going to Seperate the honerable Unemployed from the dishonerable Unemployed, Unles[s] the Strong hand of the law takes hold of the last named for their numerous Crimes? From what information I Can gather from reading the daily Papers, there is now in America about two Millions of Unemployed Men (Saying nothing About Women). Would be a grand Army if organized, Wouldent they? A terible State of afairs ain'tit? And yet the Press of the Country Says that we Are having good times.

This is a Problem in the Second Century of this U.S. Existence for our Philosiphers to Study. And they Can fence in a half dozen Tramp Farms in Every State in this Union and it will all Avail nothing. Of Course there is numbers that won't work and deserve Such treatment, but numbers of inocent will Suffer with the Guilty and Holy Writ says that ninty nine Guilty Should go free where one inocent man Should be Punished. I think the Holy Scriptures is the true foundation for all Laws of man. My opinion is the only way to Solve the Problem is to Create a demand for Mechanicks and labor in this Country And the Problem will Solve its Self. And then all men found Beging and out of work, the Athorities Can find them a Job And the Great Tramp & Hobo nusance of the U.S. will be Settled. At the Preasant a large portion of America's Population is drifting back to a nomadic life far worse than the native Red men of our Country, for the Indian had a home of Some Kind, but our preasant nomads has no place they Call Home, only a Friendly Box Car or the Shade of a tree, And in Winter Jails, Calibooses [Calabooses], and Camp Fires.

Write Soon
Gen. Del.
William W. Aspinwall
Indianapolis
Indiana

Indianapolis Indiana; Sept 29 1895

Prof. J. J McCook

Hartford. Ct

Dear Sir, I received Your letter a few days Since. Perused it Carefully. Also Your Pamphlet.[128] I Consider it an Able Document And facts that Can't be denied. I My Self Am not Much of a Whisky drinker, my favorite drink is Ale or Beer. I don't partake So much of any Kind of drink as I use to in former years, the older I get the more I See the folly of Such buisness. I Sometimes go for one Month or more and never touch Any Alcoholic drink. It would be no trouble or discomode me in the least to Abstain Entirely. I Sometimes think I will make up My Mind to let it alone Entirely because there is no Good in it, And it has, in My life and Experiances, Caused me a Great deal of trouble and bitter Experiances. I don't want it when Alone but the trouble is with me when I get with drinking Company or Comrades. My first Experience in drinking Was after My Enlistment in the Army. My Mother was a Great Temperance Advocate And Said Manny A time She Would rather follow one of her boys to his Grave than to See him Come Home drunk. But She saw it before She died and it nearly broke her Heart. I often think of Her and her teachings in my lonely Hours. I am Working in a Caning House here at $1.25[129] per day, but I am going to Work on a new building tomorrow, Monday Morning, helping to put up the Iron Work. I think I will get better Wages, if I Can do the Work. I don't think I will Go South this Winter if I Can make a living here. I Am getting tiard of romeing around. I Have Seen About all the Country it is posible to See and it would only be a repetition of Scenery to go over the Ground again. But if I Should Get out of Work and Hard up I may go South.

---

128 McCook had sent Aspinwall a pamphlet on "Pauperism and Whisky."

129 As of 2021, about $40.

When I get out of Work and financially busted I think there is no other Alternative only to take to the Road. I will as Soon as I Can gather you up Some Hobo Songs.[130] I have heard Some beautiful Songs and Some good Singers on the Hobo, but Can't Remember the Words or the Music.

I Will Close for the Preasant Wishing to hear from You Soon.

Fratulently Yours

William. W. Aspinwall

95. S. West St

Indiannapolis

Indiana

---

130 Hobos were (and are) famous for their songs. Many hobos' songs were published by the Industrial Workers of the World in their *Little Red Songbook* while others were compiled into book collections. See, for example, George Milburn's *The Hobo's Hornbook: A Repertory for a Gutter Jongleur* (New York: Ives Washburn, 1930).

Nathional. Soldiers. Home. Marion. Ind. Barracks. 6; June 29 1896

Profs J. J. McCook
Hartford. Ct

Dear Sir, I received yours of "26" inst today. I Am not Well, I am Suffering from the Reaumatism And have been for Some time. I am pleased to hear from you again. I Will Endeaver to interest you the best I Can, Ac[c]ording to Abilities. I Will not promise you a lengthy letter today. But will promise you a more detailed Acount of my Journeys and doings at Some future time.

I Came to this Home about the 10" of last January. Have been away on 60 days Furlough and on one ten days Pass Since my Admittance. I Came here from Indianapolis, Ind. Got out of Employment and Money there, So I made my Way to this Home. I think this is one of the best-managed institutions of this Kind in this Country, if not in the World. The Officers Are Gentlemanly and Sociable. I don't See how they Could behave better towards the inmates. Still, there are Some Complaints against the Officers, but that is a foregone conclusion. Amongst So many different Characters no Man, Even So perfect, Can please all. And You give Some men the Earth And they Will Want Some of the Planets throwed in. If an inmate here obeys the rules of the Home he Will have no trouble and All the priveliges Consistant, he wants in fact more than members have in Private Life. But the Punishment for disobedience I think is light. But if they become Chronic they get it a little more Severe, wich I think is Proper. I have never been punished in the least Since my Sojourn here. I have A Standing Pass to go and Come When I Want, and all other Priveleges Acording. What more Could I ask?

Some here have taken the Keely Cure,[131] there is here What is Called the Gold Club. It May of been A benefit to Some and to others an injury.

---

131 A popular but dangerous treatment for alcoholism offered by the Keeley Institute. The treatment involved injections of bichloride of gold and other, unknown compounds. For

I don't Know much about the Workings of the Gold Cure, only as I get it from others. I have no faith in it My Self and think it only a S[c]heme to Extort Money. I think the Gold Cure of no avail Unless the Patient has the Disposition and the nerve and the Will to Abstain Within him Self, and if he has these requirements he Can Abstain as Well without the Gold Cure As with it. Some tell me that have taken it that it is injurious to helth, And there is often Cases of [people who] return to the liquor Habit after taking the Cure, and death has Ensued by So doing. There was a Recent Case in this Camp.

I feel Proud of the Republican Platform Adopted Recently at St Louis And the Nomination of [William] McKinley for President. I think the leaders of that Convention Showed Great StatesmanShip and Patriotism, but I fear they are going to have a hard Battle to fight With the Free Silver Element in this Country. The Common People are fast Comeing to the Conclusion that the money mongers and Welthy are oppressing them beyond Reason. There are a great many 16 to 1 men[132] Amongst the old Soldiers, but I Can't See the Advantage it Would be to them if Adopted. Some go Wild on the Subject but I am Slow of Conviction. But We are all Aware that this Country, Especily the Producing Element,[133] is in Very precarious Condition. But the next thing is: What is a good Remedy for Existing Evils?

I had my little Pension Cut of[f] by the Existing Regime. And I have a hard time to get Enough tobacco. And I am often Short of Stationary & Stamps, Hence my delay in Writing to you. I Will Answer your questions in Some future letter. I did not get in to Coxey's Command but have talked With numbers of them. I do not believe all Coxey Says [but] at the Same time Some of his talk is logical, if it Was Practicable.

Our Bed Bug Man has Come in And is annoying me. I will haft to Come to a close. I may go South this Winter in to Florida and Probably to Cuba.

Write Soon. I Will close by Wishing you a long and happy life.

Fratulently Yours

William. W. Aspinwall

Barracks 6

---

this reason, it was also known as the 'Gold Cure.'

132 16-to-1 was the slogan of the Free Silver Movement and represented the key demand of the 'silverites': the coinage of silver at a ratio of 16-to-1, meaning that silver would have one-sixteenth the value of gold.

133 i.e., the working class.

Nathional. Military. Home. Grant. County. Indiana
July 5 1896

Profs J. J. McCook,

I Concluded to Write You [about] the Proceedings in Side of our Grounds Yesterday And Send you a Program of dinner.[134]

In the afternoon at 3 o clock, We assembled in our best Uniforms, Flags and Banners flying And all the Buildings Gayly Decorated, Band Playing, Cannon Booming. Amidst thousands of Spectators We Paraded and then formed a Square of 15,00 Vetterans Around our Flag Pole. The Band in Center And a Platform with the Gov and Officers of the Home and a Galaxy of Butiful Ladies Seated upon it. Old Glory was lowered and a Beautiful Young lady, the daughter of the Captain, Attached another Star for the State of Utah, Admited Since last H[oliday].[135] When finished, old Glory Was again run up. Amidst the deafening Cheers of the old Vets, Cannon Booming, Band playing 'Hail Columbia' and then We had a Short but Patriotic Address from our Excelent Governor. It Was a Very imposing Ceremony and it done my Patriotic Soul Good.

On last Friday the 3" inst, Buffalo Bill's Wild West Show[136] Was in Marion. I Was there And Knowed a great many of the Cow Boys, Especily

134 Aspinwall includes a program that took place at the Marion Soldiers' Home, which included dinner and a 'Home Band.'

135 Utah had been granted statehood on 6th January 1896.

136 *Buffalo Bill's Wild West* was a touring theatre show organized by William Frederick "Buffalo Bill" Cody (1846–1917) that portrayed the conquest of the West and battles between 'cowboys' and 'Indians.' Running from 1883 to 1906, the show was famed for featuring 'real Indians,' who had often personally fought against the dispossession of their people by the U.S. government and white settlers. The show depicted them as savagely attacking innocent settlers, setting the standard frame for the Hollywood western films of the following century. The show featured famous figures such as the Hunkpapa Lakota leader Sitting Bull (circa 1831–1890) and the sharpshooter Annie Oakley (1860–1926).

haveing Seen them and became Aquainted in my travels. I was treated very Heroicaly by them. I Was introduced to Col Cody. He gave me four Complimentary tickets And Said I Could take my Self and lady in, but I would of got in anyWay if he had not of give me tickets. I Was introduced to the Soldiers of Different nations,[137] tried on their Helmets And talked With them. Went in to the Indians' Wigwams, Sat down and talked With them by invitation from them. I don't think there was a man in Marion Seen the Show as I did. I Enjoyed the Sociability And Kindness of the men in their quarters better than I did the Performance. There Was multitudes of People to See the Parade and the Seating Capacity of the Canvas was packed day and night. It is a Wonderful Show And is Worth Seeing.

I will Close, as it is geting near dinner. We Always have a good dinner on Sunday. We Always have good meals but Sunday and halow days [hallow days, as in holidays] is Extra good.

Respectfully Yours,

William. W. Aspinwall

Barracks. 6.

Nat. Mil. House

Grant. County

Indiana

Write Soon

[WRITTEN UPSIDE DOWN AT THE TOP OF THE LETTER]

There was 10,00 People in these Grounds last night to Wittness the Fire Works and to hear the Band. 500 Carriages and Vehicles, the Grounds Were Packed.

---

137 By 1896, Cody had renamed his show *Buffalo Bill's Wild West and Congress of Rough Riders of the World* and introduced performers from all over the world, largely focused on horse cultures.

Nathional. Military. Home. Grant. County Indiana July 16 1896

Profs J.J. McCook
Niantic. Ct

Dear Sir, Your Esteemed letter of the 10 inst Came to hand yesterday. I Enjoy Coresponding With you, for I believe you apreciate my letters to you.

There is no Canteen Connected with this home. I Understand there was a Vote of the members of this Home taken at one time in regard to establishing a canteen here but it was Voted down. But they Sell Cider at the Home Store, wich I think is Worse in its Effects than Beer for I realy believe three Glasses of it Would Set a Hog Crazy. But I think a Canteen on the Grounds managed by the Home Authorties would be a Credit [compared] to the low-down Saloons Just out Side of the main Entrance to the Home Where the Bum Elements in the Home Congregate, Get Drunk, Sweare, Curse And disgrace the Home before the Gaze of the numerous Visitors passing in and out of the main Entrance. And they frequently have free-for-all fights. I don't Mind to See a Man drink Some and Enjoy him Self but I do Abhor to See a Man With the Nathional Uniform of his Republic on Making a Hog of Himself And playing Bear in plain View of the Hordes of Visitors Comeing and going from this or any other institution. If they want to do so they Should Adorn them Selves With the Garbs of Bums, not the Blue. I Would like to See a law passed not Allowing A Saloon or a house of ill fame Withing five miles of any Soldiers' Home that is out Side of the Gate or Grounds, but have a Canteen run with Strict Rules Allowing no one to get drunk or use fighting or abusive or facetious[138] language, for a great many

---

138 This word is a best guess as Aspinwall's handwriting here is difficult to read. Another possibility is 'fastuous,' meaning arrogant or prideful.

Are determined to to Spend a great part of their money for drink. And Why not Spend it in the Home Where the money and proffits will be used for benefit And Amusement of the Home? And drive of[f] the low down dives and Sharks out Side the Grounds that have no love for the old Soldier, only to get him drunk or drug him And fleece And Rob him. And there appears to be no laws. Or they are powerless to Stop it.

Of Course When they[139] Wanted Volunteers, they did not Ask them if they Ever Was drunk or Ever drank any Spiritous or Malt liquors. If a Man was only parcially Sound in body, no questions [were] asked About the State of a man's Mind or his Habits. He was Eligible As a Volunteer. And in many instances during the War intemperance Was Encouraged by the Officers And Whiskey issued to the Troops from the Comissary or liquors that Were Captured.[140] I Know one Battle We Was in Every dedd [dead] Rebel's Canteen Was from half to two-thirds full of Whiskey and Gun Powder. I Was an Orderly at a General's Head quarters And I had a Standing Order for two Canteens of Comissary Whiskey Every day for the Use of the General. But the General did not get to use it All, I Used Some My Self. And gave many a poor fellow a drink that I found laying by the road Side played out, wich gave them renewed Animation And no doubt Saved them from Capture. So the Soldier is not So Much to Blame After All for his Drinking Habits, if it is fairly discussed And all points brought Out. But I blame them for Making fools of them Selves And think they Should have better Judgment than to make Asses of themselves With the true Blue on their Backs before a Critisizing public. But not all Old Soldiers Are Such. This Home will Compare better in Morals than [meaning to] the Same number of Cittizens Out Side. There is men in this Home as Well Educated and Smart and intelligent as any in the land, And others Vice-Versa.

I Understand the Governor of this Home made a Statement that there was 1,600 members here and out of that number there Was 1,200 that has never been up before him on any Charges Whatever. So you Can Judge from these figures the percentage that behaves them Selves. In the language I heard the late and lamented Gen. John A. Logan[141] Use in one of his

---

139 Meaning Union Army recruiters during the American Civil War.

140 Aspinwall's assertions here are all too believable. Excessive drinking was part of the military culture of both the Union and Confederate armies. For more information, see Scott C. Martin "'A Soldier Intoxicated is Far Worse than No Soldier at All': Intoxication and the American Civil War" in *The Social History of Alcohol and Drugs* 25:1–2 (2011), pp. 66–87.

141 John Alexander Logan (1826–1886), Union General and politician.

Addresses to the Soldiers, he Said 'How Proud I am of this Government for furnishing You Boys with Such beautiful Homes'. He Said it was no disgrace to be An Unfortunate Soldier of this Republic and Said 'I Know to[o] Well where you have been and What you went through for this Government.' When John A Logan died the Saviors of this Republic lost one of their best friends, And we mourn his loss.

The Governor of this Home, Justin. H. Chapman,[142] is from Connecticut, I think from New Haven. He formaly was Ad[j]utant of the Dayton Ohio Home. I Understand, but this is only hear Say, that When he Arived at the Above-named Home he came With a Cleaveland[143] badge on the Seat of his trousers And that his first Job was Guarding the Pears on the trees. But nevertheless he is a fine Afable Gentleman And Aproachable by the most Humble. And [he is] Just as a Magistrate And Very lenient in his Rules. More So than Any other one of the Homes. Infact there is no Guards, Members are allowed to Come and go at Will, As long as they Keep out of the Guard House. He lost a leg in the War, for Which he no doubt receives a good Pension And his Salery here as Governor and a fine Residence [for] free, makes a good thing for him. I Suppose you are aware of the remark droped by the late Gen B. F. Butler[144] that these national Homes 'Would be a Paridise for the officers And A Hell for the Privates'? While this is So in some respects, they Appear to be Well Provided for and their Wants and Health looked after.

While this is Called a home And Well Provided for, All I want to Eat, Good Clothing, A good bed to Sleep on, and the Barracks all fitted up with all the latest appliances in Plumbing, as to Watter Closets, Bath Rooms, Hot And Cold Watter, it does not Suit my taste as a home. Whenever You Seperate the Sexes, part men and Woman And Children, it is Unnatural and Contrary to the laws of nature. I had a Woman down in the Citty of Marion of rather loose Ways tell me that there was an old Soldier Came to See her that drawed 34 dollars Every three months and that he was about 75 Years old. Every time he got his money he came and gave her 30 dollars And that She recompenced him by by Allowing him to Come once in a While and feel around her and play with her. He was not Physicaly Able to do any Manly

---

142   Justin H. Chapman (1839–1904) was Governor of the Marion Home from 1891 to 1904.

143   Stephen Grover Cleveland (1837–1908), Democratic President of the United States from 1885 to 1889 and from 1893 to 1897. It is important to remember how Aspinwall felt about the Democratic Party at this point in his life.

144   Benjamin Franklin Butler (1818–1893), Union General and, from 1866 to 1879, President of the National Home for Disabled Volunteer Soldiers.

duties. This is one illustration, I Suppose there is hundreds of others if they was only Known in their different modes. It is nature for Man to be With Woman And the Pasions for Woman Are more fierse in Some men than others, Any Price Will be Payed to Gratify it.

You Wanted to Know my opinion of the Chicago Platform.[145] I think it An Experiment, A Wild goose Chase. We have had Enough of Such And Should now Come down to buisness And Prosperity. And in my opinion the Only Cause to persue is to Elect McKinley.[146] I am a Republican heart And Soul And Will do all I Can for the Election of McKinley. There is Some Free Silver Men Amongst the old Vets but I Can't See Where they Could be benefitted if [William Jennings] Bryan Should be Elected.

I overheard some Argument in the Grove Yesterday. A Son of old Ireland was in the Argument. And he Says 'What is the good of Yees[147] Paupers Arguing this financial question when ys have nothing but a little Pension Comeing to yees, And Some of yees not that?' I thought the Son of Erin About right.

I received a letter of Congratulation from Wm McKinley in Answer to one I Sent to him. I Will Send you a Copy as Printed in the Marion news.[148]

I have my trials and tribulations. I had a fight With a Kansas man right here in the Barracks. We call him 'the dude'. He is a Considerable Younger Man than I am And Served I think About three Months, And Probably then not out of his State. But I Gave him a good drub[b]ing And made him Say 'Enough!' twice. He made Some insulting remark About Indiana Soldiers And I objected with a Will and a determination. The officers Said nothing

---

145 A reference to the Democratic Party Platform, unveiled in Chicago at the Democratic National Convention 7th–11th July. The Democratic Party's presidential candidate was William Jennings Bryan, a charismatic proponent of the Free Silver Movement whose nomination was secured by his famous 'Cross of Gold' speech on the 9th July, which concluded: "You shall not press down upon the brow of labor this crown of thorns, you shall not crucify mankind upon a cross of gold." Bryan would go on to lose the election.

146 William McKinley would win the election and become President in 1897. He won re-election four years later but was assassinated in 1901.

147 Aspinwall is here representing the Irish brogue for 'your.'

148 Aspinwall includes a clipping from the *Marion News*, dated 16th July 1896, containing a letter in which future President McKinley (or, more likely, one of his aides), has written:

> Mr William Aspinwall, National Military Home, Marion, Ind.
> My dear Sir,
> Please accept on your own behalf and convey to your comrades, my most grateful appreciation of their greetings sent through you.
> Yours, very truly, W. McKinley.'

About it. I Expected trouble, As the Rules are Strict on fighting but I Under-stood the Captain Said I did not give him Any more than he deserved. I am not quarlsome but will resent An insult quick if in the President's Mansion.

It is dinner time And I Will Close Wishing to hear from you Soon And hopeing what I have writen Will interest you. I have A bad Pen, Excuse [the handwriting].

I am, Very truly, Yours

William. W. Aspinwall

Nathional Military Home; Marion Indiana; Sept 2 1896

Dear Profs J.J.Mc.Cook

I received Yours of Aug "13" Some time Since. I Am Still in the Soldiers' Home but have removed from my former Home Co. 9 on Barrack 6 Where I had made numerous Friends, Amongst them the Capt and Officers of the company. I have removed [to] Co.A. on Barrack 1 Ward 1, the Post of Honor, I Am now Waiting on Tables in the Officers' And Clerks' mess. They have a Seperate Mess from the Main dining Hall. And they pay two dollars per month a Head And buy Extras for their Tables besides their regular Rations. They Also have a Kitchen And Cook of their own, independent of the General Mess. And out liveing is immence. We have all vedgtetables, fruits & delicacys in their Season. We live as Well as any three dollar-a-day Hotel in the land. I Am Head Waiter, Have Charge of the dining Room and Help. And My Borders Say that I am a Success at the Buisness. I Keep Every

tractors for the new barracks, are here and will commence work immediately.

An Ode to Soldiers' Beer.

Tell me not, ye empty tumblers,
 Life last night was all a dream!
That the beer was drank—in slumbers,
 And things are not what they seem.

Whiskey's real, sugar ditto!
 Lemons do unite the whole;
Dost thou dare or dost thou dare not
 Pitch into the full beer bowl?

Not in haste, and not in sorrow,
 Should we send it on its way;
But so drink it, that tomorrow
 Finds us "straighter" than today.

Beer is going, beer is fleeting,
 And our heads, though stout and brave,
Still like muffled drums are beating,
 Funeral marches o'er its grave.

In that glorious field of battle,
 In the brewery of life,
Drink, but not like thirsty cattle,
 Quarrel nor create a strife.

Trust no whiskey howe'er pleasant—
 French or German, or "Home made!"—
Drink—drink all the beer that s present,
 Think not of an aching head!

Lives of topers all remind us,
 That they had a "jolly time,"
And departing, thus defined us
 Their position in the hyme.

Drink brave soldier, lest another
 Eager comrade all may drain;
Drink! or else some thirsty brother
 Will take heart and drink again!

Let us then be up and doing,
 Doing, drinking, soon and late;
And while someone beer is brewing
 Learn to drink it, not to wait!

—William W. Aspinwall,
National Military Home, Marion, Ind.

Real Estate Transfers.

Instruments filed for record in the recorder's office of Grant county, Aug. 31, as furnish

Fig. 11 [149]

---

149 This poem is modeled on Henry Wadsworth Longellow's "Psalm of Life," though whether as a parody or an attempt at plagiarism is not wholly clear.

thing neat and Clean and Attractable. I Wish You Could drop in Some time and See and Partake of one of our Meals, I Am Positive You Would relish it.

I am of the opinion that Comrade McKinley Will be Elected by the largest Majority that Ever a President of this U.S. received. We have had Experiments Enough. What All thinking and loyal People Want now for the next four Years is Confidence And Prosperity, And to get the money we have in Circulation, open up our Factorys and Work Generily [generally]. Give the People Employment at good Wages And We Will find that our Financial System is all right. I think we Have this Assurance in McKinley And the Republican Platform. Give us a Booming Majority in Grand old Connecticut. There Will not be So much Strife When the People become Educated up to the is[s]ues of this Campaign. How about Vermont? 25,000 reported Here.

Yes, there is a great many of the old Boys, I Should Say one Half, that have been on the Road And numbers [who] have traveld Extensively, both in this and Foreign lands. And it is Very interesting to listen to their Stories of Pleasure & Woe.

I Will Send You Some of my Poetry of My own Composing, wich pleased the People Here Generaly.

I Was Congratulated Generaly, a great many Said they did not think there was one amongst them up to Snuff as I was. You Know that I have Seen Some of this World And I think I have profited Some by it. And if my Experiance is of any benefit to the People they Can have it. I am Poor but a Gentleman. Still Write Soon Yours, Fratulently

William. W. Aspinwall

Address Barrack 1 Ward 1

Nathional. Military. Home.

Marion Indiana

The Tramps Soliliquy[150]

And Men are housed, and in their place
In Snug and happy rest
Save the tramp who walks with weary pace
The highways frozen breast

His limbs, that tremble with the Cold,
Shrink from the Comeing Storm;
But Underneath his ragged fold,
His heart beats quick and warm.

He hears the laugh of those who Sit
In homes Contented Air;
He Sees the buisy Shadows flit
Acroos the Windows Glare.

His heart is full of love Unspent,
His Eyes are Wet and dim;
For in those Circles of Content
There is no room for him.

He Clasps his hands and looks above;
He Makes the bitter Cry:
"All are happy in their love –
All are beloved but I!"

Acroos the threshold Streams the light.
Expectant o'er his track;

---

150   Part of this poem has been reworked without attribution from Bayard Taylor's "The
Mariners" (1856). McCook had suspected plagiarism but had not been able to trace the
source, which was pointed out to him following the publication of "Leaves." Aspinwall then
claimed that he had not said the poem was entirely his own composition, although in fact
he had.

No door is opened in the night,
To bid him Welcome back.

There is other tramps Abroad,
In all this Wintry Gale,
And lower upon their lonely road
The darkness and the Vale.

Our frames Are Worn And little Worth,
And hard Our rugged hands;
We Struggle for our hold on Earth
With the Storms of many lands.

Say that We Curse if You Will,
That the tavern and harlot possess our gains
On the Surface floats What we do of of ill
At the bottom the Manhood remains,

I wash my hands; I bathe my brow;
I See the Sun on hill and plain.
The old Allegiance Claims me now,
The old Content returns again.

W.W. Aspinwall.
Nath. Mil. Home. Indiana.

Nathional. Mil. Home Indiana; Sept 20 1896

Profs Jon J McCook
Hartford Conn

My dear friend, I received your Ever Welcome letter of "14" inst. I Am Still at the Home but must Say I don't like it. It is a Home and Yet it Ain't the Home I had in my boyhood days. It ain't a home Where you have Your Wife and darling Children Around you. Very different. You have the orders of half doz Upstarts of officers to obey that have more cloths than Brains. They have what they call a Guard House Here and another institution they Call the light House. I See old Men, Cripled up With the reaumatism, pulled out of bed And taken to this Guard House and there they are Kept Some times four days, laying on the hard floor Amongst the Vermen and probably they are Suffering from reaumatism or Some other disease. And While in there their Companion is a Maniac or Some one with the delirium tremens.[151] And then they are taken before His Honor the Govenor, Who Probably drinks as Much Whiskey As they do but has a better Chance to Conceal it and its Effects. And they are given from 30 to 90 days in the light House. They are penned up 30 and 40 together in a Place not as good As Some farmers have for their Chickens, and Marched out to their meals Under Guard like So many Convicts. This is the Way these Poor old Men are treated, Men that Maintained this Government in its hour of Perril, And better men than the men that had them put there. I believe in discipline but I do not believe in giveing a lot of Upstarts the right to Punish these Poor old fellows for Crimes they are Guilty of themselves, And to Show partiality and to have their favorites. One man Should Just be as good as another in a place like this. Ben Butler's Words are Comeing true, 'A Paradise for Upstarts and a Hell for the Men who fought the Battles'. There is none Perfect, no not one,

---

151 The most severe form of alcohol withdrawal.

So Says [Saint] Paul. Then Why Punish these Poor old men for habits they had long before Comeing Here? And the Government Encouraged those Habbits [i.e., during the Civil War].

I have not time to Write more at preasant. I Am Well and hope you are the Same. I Send you Some Verses, Hope you Will appreciate them. I am Still of the opinion that McKinley will Carry the Country With An Enormous Majority. How is Vermont & Maine, Allright Arnt they?

Yours truly Wm. W. Aspinwall

Write Soon

Nathional. Military. Home.
Marion Indiana; Oct 19 1896

Profs JonJ McCook
Hartford Ct

My dear Sir, I wrote you a month or Six Weeks ago but have received no Awnswer, So I have concluded to Write Again. I do not Know your reasons for your Seamingly [i.e., seeming] neglect. You may have been overdone with Your daily ro[u]tine of buisness. I have become to look for a letter from you regularly, I have been Coresponding with you So long. Especily in my preasant Situation here, a member of a Soldiers' Home, this terible Monotonous life. The Government May [have] intended Allright for the Comfort of the Vetterans of its Wars, but I am of the Opinion they have put more men in Misery than has been benefited by these Homes. I think if they, the Gov, had of given the money they give to Support these homes [directly] to the Worthy Men who fought the Battles of this nation and let them Carry on a home of their own, Acording to their own notions, the Gov would of Confered a greater blessing on mankind And the Vetterans. And there Would of not been So many high-Salleried Officers liveing in their fine Mansions furnished by the Gov, Swindling Common Soldiers out of what the Government intended for the men, these laws, Creating thes[e] homes to benefit. I think the only Solution of this Soldier Home question (and it is the opinion of the majority of the members of the Homes) is to give them into the hands of the War department and then we will get our Just dues the Same as the Regular Army. And get rid of these Blood-Sucking Officers that are Enriching themselves at the Worthy Volunteer Soldiers' Expence.

'These homes Would be a fine place for the young generation of Cittizens to Visit And have Picknicks and hear the Band music and Waltz and dance, if it was not for the Horible Old Soldiers Around the Homes.' So Says Some of our Visitors.

I think Major McKinley is going to be Elected with the largest majority Ever a President of this U.S. was Elected. The American People are this time going to Se[a]l their fate on Anarchism, disloyalty and reputiation As never was done before. I Am of the opinion this State, Indiana, will go Republican by an Enormous majority, probably fifty thousand or more. We had a great day here in Marion on last Wendsday when the Generals was here. Forty thousand People in the town And Bryan's name not Mentioned. A day long to be remembered by Marion for Patriotic Enthusiasm. I was in line And done my Share of Marching and Cheering. Gen Alger[152] Said he could talk to farms of People and probably to a township but it was out of the question to Address a County of People. He wanted to Know where they all Came from And who was left at Home.

I have worked like a Beaver in this Campaign for McKinly, with good results. I had a letter from him A few days Since. I want to hear from you. I am lonesome when I don't hear from You. Wm W Aspinwall

---

152 Russell Alexander Alger (1836–1907), who would become Secretary of War under President McKinley.

[THIS POEM AND THE NEXT WERE ENCLOSED WITH ASPINWALL'S
LETTER DATED 16th NOVEMBER 1896]

Hovey's Division at Champion Hill

I think of the gallant boy's Who died,
Amidst our foe's Shot And Yell's So Shrill.
And Sorrow for our Slain Subdued the pride
Of our Cheers at Champion Hill.

Our brave foes in Grey With their Stearn Sullen brows,
As they in numbers did Us Surround,
And the battle fog its phosphor radiance throws,
On the faces of our downed

So Many a nobel hero is Cold in Earth,
That Shared battles and duties there,
I have looked full oft in the face of death,
But he came to no better men.

Death Will Come to all in its Chosen time it's true,
But Indiana And nation in Ages Will,
Remember brave Hovey and boy's in blue,
For Victory Won At Champion Hill.

William. W. Aspinwall
Co H 47" Indiana
Hovey's division

Profs, these Verses apeared in the *Morning Chronical* Just as I have
written them her[e], Oct "28" 1896. The battle of Champion Hill was fought
on May "16" 1863 in the rear of Vicksburg, Miss. It was one of the most bloody
battles of the War, our division looseing [loosing] about 1600 men in Killed
And Wounded. Your Humble Servant Was Shot four times. I got three buck
Shot in right Shoulder, Wich I am Carrying Around in my Shoulder Yet As
a reminder of that battle. I was Also Struck in the top of the head With a

Minie ball tearing the hair, Scalp, And Chiping up my Skull. This Knocked me insensible And my Comrades, thinking I was dead, Carried me back And layed me in the bed of a Small brook. When I came to I was inside the Confederate lines, they having driven our division back. A Rebble Captain Came and talked to me And gave me Watter out of his Canteen.

Gen Pemberton[153] And Staff Came Within touching distance of me, Viewing our lines through field Glasses. All this time Shell and bullets [were] Striking All around me like hail. The Rebles gave away. I got up and got Away from them, all Covered With blood. Got into our lines, found my Command. My Captain got me in an Ambulance, Sent me to the Hospital. Stayed in the Hospital on bush Shed only two days. Caught the blood and Matter runing from my Woulnds And my Head Swealed [swelled]. I was only 17 yrs old at this time. Hence I write these Verses. I refer you to Gen Grant's Memoirs for the Achievements of Hovey's 3 div 13" Army Corps. W.W.A

---

153 General John Clifford Pemberton (1814–1881), the commanding Confederate officer at the Battle of Champion Hill.

Charmian Jones found the Paint.

You pay it for Your Grocers tea's,
Or View it through a lawyers bill: -
Put on what Eye Glass you please,
Your dollar is a dollar Still.

Say's Jones to Bryan[154] We can no longer doubt,
They ran and leaped in to the flood,
There they Stuck And Could not Get out,
All Coverd o'er with bryan And Mud.

We must now Keep our blow horns Still,
As We have often been told before,
For We Will no doubt meet Save Hill: -
Up on that beautiful Shore.

Salt river Was raging high,
In places out of her bank,
As Allgeld[155] & Gilman[156] came by
On their Anarchist plank

Tom Watson[157] With the Wart on his nose,
And all the free Silver Crank's - :
When they get up and Change Cloths
They will Sink the free trade plank.

---

154 William Jennings Bryan. It is unclear whether 'Jones' refers to a particular individual or is
     a generic name to represent the everyday American citizen.

155 John Peter Altgeld (1847–1902), a progressive Democratic Governor who in 1893 had
     pardoned the surviving Haymarket anarchists. Partly because of this act, Altgeld lost his
     reelection campaign in 1896. Aspinwall's view on the Haymarket Martyrs seems to have
     changed between 1893 and 1896.

156 Possibly a reference to Theodore Gilman (1841–1930), a former railroad financier who in
     1894 had been arrested for fraud.

157 Thomas Edward Watson (1856–1922), free silverite and leader of the Populist Party.

These Verses were published in the *Morning Chronical* Marion, Ind on Nov "7" inst. I Wrote them after Knowing of Bryan's defeat [in the election]. Of Course they are Subject to Correction. Would be pleased if you Can make any improvements for you to do So.

Wm. W. Aspinwall

Soldiers' Home Marion Indiana Nov 16 1896

Profs. J. J. McCook My Kind friend, I received Yours of the 9" inst a few days
Since. I Am pleased that you like my Attempt at writing Poems, And thank
You and Your Profs. of Eng[lish] Literature for your Compliment. I Send
you Some more Verses, hope you may Appreciate them, And Wish when
you read them over With your Critical and Educated Eye, if you observe
Where there can be Any improvement made in them You will do so and
your Kindness will be Apreciated by me. I think Your State, Connecticut,
done nobly in the last Election. I think the people [who are] in favour of
good Government and Honesty And prosperity gained a Great Victory
(Equal to Apomattox[158]). But I was not Surprised, it turned out Just as I had
Expected. I have Confidence in the Wisdom And intelligence of the Mass
of the American People.

I do not Know or Cannot Acertain of one instance Around this Home
or in this County Where money Was Used to influence Votes.[159] This Home
was Sollid for McKinley With but a few Exceptions. And Us Soldiers had
no Use for a Man that Ever Wore the blue that would Vote the Papecrat
[democrat] ticet. And what few did Vote that Way here Are branded, and
Some have Jumped the fence and Vanished, the helthiest thing they Could
do. No, I am not Stewart in the Officers' and Clerks' Mess Any more. They
Wanted to[o] much for the Amoount of pay there was in it. I am Sollid with
the cook And when I want Some nicnax I go and Visit him. I Will try and
Worry out this Winter here and I think by that time buisness will improve

158   The 1865 Battle of Appomattox Courthouse, at which Robert E. Lee's Army of Northern
     Virginia surrendered to General Grant's Union Army of the Potomac.

159   Presumably McCook has asked about whether Aspinwall saw any votes being bought at the
     Soldiers' Home. Most of McCook's letters to Aspinwall have not survived.

So that I Can find Employment. I Am Very Short of Stationary. I haft to Skirmish Considerably to make Ends Meet.

Wishing to hear from you Soon Respt Yours

Wm. W. Aspinwall

Nathional. Military. Home, Marion Indiana; 1–8 1897

Profs Jon J McCook
Hartford. Ct.

My Dear Sir, I fear that you have been Seriously Sick, or you no doubt Would of Awnswerd [answered] my last long before this. I have been Uneasy about you, fearing about your health. I do hope You may have your health and Continue your noble life of Usefulness to the people of this Great Government. I have writen for the Marion daily *Chronical*, they are Contained in the folowing dates Oct "28. November 17" 7" 3" and Dec 18" 15. They Will no doubt Send you the Above dates of their isues if You Should desire them. I got great Honers [honors] as a Hero in the papers a few days a go by Saveing A man and Woman that broke through the ice on the River from drowning.[160] Nothing new here at the Home, the Same old ro[u]tine. We are haveing Winter now. I Want Spring to Come, I Want to get Away from here. I think President-Elect McKinley Will Apoint me to Some position, he Writes Very favorable to Me. By the Way Could you not help me Some With him? I think I am Worthy of Something, I done Considerable in the last Campaign and have done my part to maintain this Government, don't you think? So I Send you Some Clipings on the tramp issue. The towns out here are all overrun with Hobos. It is a deplorable State of Affairs, and is a bad Showing for this Enlightend Country. A portion of the poor fellows are to be pittied, for they are the Underdogs in the fight for Existance.

I Shall Close by Wishing an Early Awnswer from you in regard to your health.

Very Respectfully Yours
William. W. Aspinwall

---

160 From letters that Aspinwall later sent to McCook, it seems that he saved a woman called Belle Whitson and a man called "Mr. Houff," both of whom had fallen through the ice of a frozen lake.

Nath. Military. Home; Marion Indiana; 3 2 97

Profs John J McCook
Hartford Ct
Dear Proffesser

Yours of the 26" of last month came to hand last Evening. I Was Somewhat Surprised, though[t] you had Given up writing but was pleased to hear from You. Yes, You are right there is a many a good man tramping the Country that have got on the road through Strong drink, Some as good Artisans and tradesmen as there is. And men with as good brains And as fine qualities as there is in the Country but have got down and fell again, and have got discouraged and lost Courage and think they have no friends.

And again there is the professional Hobo. They are quite numerous and are the ones that have the indomitable Cheek, and also the ones that Commit All the low dastardly Crimes Such as Sodomy, Rape & if they Could be Seperated from the others they Should be banished from the Country. A reformatory is to[o] good for them. But it is hard to distinguish. Some of this Kind dress well. Or better than the working Class that are on the Road. It takes a mine of Experience. I my Self was a long time before I got on to them but know them now on Sight. And this Class of Hobos Are the recipients of the Charities from well meaning people, and will live well and dress well while the men with honor and pride left in them Will Suffer for their timidity.

There is Another Class of Hobos that are geting Very numerous in this Country in wich a reformatory would be Very Useful, but they are like Black Birds, You Could fill a reformatory and you would not miss the number. These are the boys from ten to twenty yrs old and Some of them are from respectable families. All Such Should most Emphaticaly be kept of[f] the road and discouraged from such Work, they drift into Criminals of different

Kinds and professional Hobos. I think your reformatory[161] located at a good point to enlist numbers of these fellows [would be a good idea]. And it is no doubt but that it is this Class that it is your intentions to reform, as it wuld be a great Undertaking to try to learn old Dogs new tricks, don't you think So?

I think I have Awnswerd your questions quite Correctly. I Could of went more into the details but You will Understand What I mean. I don't think I will remain long here in this Home. I am geting Very tiard of the life here and by the time You get this I may be gone. So you will not Write Until you hear from me again.

I don't build any hopes on getting any appointment Under McKinley, but if I Should be so fortunate I will try my luck. I notice by the papers that Col J. J. McCook of New. York will receive a Cabinet position and Still another dispatch Says he has declined. He must be a Cousin of yours, is he not?[162] I Will Write you again in a few days and let you Know my intentions.

Very Respectfully

William. W. Aspinwall

---

161 See letter dated 6th August 1893 for McCook's proposals for a reformatory for tramps.

162 Captain John James McCook (1845–1911) was indeed a cousin of his namesake, Professor McCook, and another of the famous "Fighting McCooks." A prominent lawyer after the war, Capt. McCook did turn down an offer to serve in President McKinley's cabinet.

Nathional. Military. Home. Marion. Indiana; March 12 1897

Profs. Jon. J. McCook
Hartford. Ct.
My dear Sir

I mailed you a letter a few days Since Stating to you that I would go away from this Penitentiary in a few days. But I have Concluded to Stay until Sometime in the far part of April next. I have Carefully and in an Unpredudiced Way taken items And investigated the management of these Would-be Nathional Military Homes. And my Conclusions and opinion Candidly and I Express my Sentiments without fear and to Justice to my Worthy Comrades I Say, And it is the Candid truth, that these Nathional Homes Are the Greatest frauds Ever perpetrated on this Gov and the people And the Worthy men who defended this Gov in the hour of her peril.

In the first place, the officers manageing these Homes do not have the interests of the Worthy Soldiers at heart but only their own pecunary gain and Self Agrandizement. Men are throwed in to this Vermin-infested Guard House for trivial offences and Keept there 4 days before they are Allowed a trial, and then no Chance for defence. And then throwed in to a Pig Pen Seting in a Swamp Called a light House for from 50 to 100 days. And denied medical Attention. I Know of men throwed into the Guard House And denied medical attention, and afterwards taken to Hospital And died in a few hours, a bigoted young Doctor refuseing to Attend on them.

And I have Known of Worthy Soldiers of four Years' Service to Come here for Admision, And [having] Endured All Kinds of hardships to get here, to be turned away without a night's loging or a bite to Eat, And [been] refused Even a Second-hand Pair of Shoes as they Was nearly bare foot. And this done to men that Served this gov [for] Years where these Bigoted officers

Served months. I tell You Such proceedings makes the blood boil and will not be tolerated, if the old Soldiers haft to again resort to Arms [they will].

The officers of these Homes are fast becoming Welthy men and millionairs of the funds intended by the Gov and the People to make the old Soldier Comfortable.

Contractors Come here and make Contracts here for Supplies, And then they will Send to these Officers A rebate. And they build fine houses And take Stock in Mft [manufacturing] Enterprises. If an inspector General Comes here and Wishes to ask any of the Soldiers questions relative to their treatment, they trot out Some Pimp that will tell the inspector what they want told, while the abused men are Afraid to Say anything for fear of geting the gate [i.e., being kicked out]. The Gov[ernor] of this Home only Saw about 30 days' Active Service And then lost a leg. Some of the boys Say if he had of had His head Shot of[f] instead of a leg it would have been a great deal better for a great many of the Survivors.

Another Great dissatisfaction is Created by Apointing Eastern Officers over these Western Homes. They was not liked by the Western Soldiers during the War, And time has not increased our love for them. A Great many of Us Know of Such Men as Gen Banks and Gen Franklin, having partook of the Red River Campaign And its disastrious results Through the Mismanagement of Such men.[163] As Gen. W. B. Franklin has made himself A Milionair of these Homes by his Rascality, And the humblest Vetteran Knows it. We Knows he Uses his Money Stolen from Us to lobby in Congress.

These Homes Should be thoroughly And impartially investigated in Justice to the Worthy Soldier and the People and the Government. And we will never Cease our agitation Until Justice is obtained. Officers Should be Changed in these Homes once a Year And then Elected by the Members. If not, they become tyrannical Despots and bigoted at that. You go to Stinson Hall dedicated for the benefit of the members of this Home, one third of the total Seating Capacity is reserved for the Officers and their Pimps. And the Governor And his Cabinet are Seated in the Center of the Hall in draped and Cushioned boxes, puting You in mind of a King on his throne.

I Could Write page after page for a Week in discription and then not tell half of the injustice perpetrated by these Bigoted insignificant Officers And their Pimps. I think I have given you an idea of What is going on. And

---

163   In 1864, General Nathaniel P. Banks (1816–1894), with support from William B. Franklin (1823–1903), commanded the failed Red River campaign to capture Shreveport, Louisiana and to occupy East Texas.

it is the truth and hundreds will Sweare to it. And it will be Agitated Until the Soldier Gets Justice And their dues and what the People of this U.S. thinks we are given and intend we Should have, but [is] Stole[n] by inhuman Officers and Apropriated to their Use. And the men Starved Abused and mistreated by a Set of thieves.

I will Close for this time. If you write to me before I leave here, do so as Soon as posible So I will get it before taking my departure from this place. I think now that I will go to Nashville Tenn this Summer And atend the Exposition, if Mr McKinley don't appoint me as Counsul to Some point in Mexico. Should like another letter from you if posible before leaveing here. I will take my discharge and my papers from these Homes and will not return to any of them Under Existing management. There is hundreds of worthy Soldiers taking discharges both Honerable And dishonerable, but I think I will get a Hon one if nothing Unusual turns up. But it is no disgrace to be Sent out of this Roten place dishonerable.

Very Resp
William W Aspinwall

Nath Military. House. Indiana; April 25 1897

Profs J J McCook.

Hartford. Ct.

Dear Sir, I received Yours of 17" inst a few days Since. I have Concluded to Stay here until my Pension Claim is Ajusted. I have our Congressman And a Lawyer in Washington Working on my Claim. I Will have my Just dues from this Government or I will Know the reason Why. I am Well Enoug Satisfied with these Homes but I do abhor to See my Comrades Mistreated, that I Know were good and brave Soldiers, by men that Are far their inferiors in Army Record And [who] hold office in these Homes through patronage, but for no brave act done during the War. And I Abhor to Know of the funds that is Apropriated for these Homes Used to Enrich Such men. But these Officers are desperate, more So than any Monarch in the old World. What they Say goes, and the humble Private has no redress Under Existing laws. They Even go so far as to interfere with the religious rights of the men. But I think there will be a Change in Some things, as I believe the majority Should rule in this Gov. We that were up Red River in 1864 have no Use for Gen. W. B. Franklin, not Even the men from his own State. I have talked with many of them. Otherwise, if there Was Just and fair men in Office, the Homes Would be all right. I Am one of the Home Guides now and have a Chance to make A little Change When Visitors are liberal. Wishing to hear from you Soon.

William. W. Aspinwall

Fig. 12

Nathional. Mil. Home. Indiana; June 6, 1897

Profs Jon J McCook
Hartford
Ct
Dear Sir,
    I received Yours of May 22 Was glad to hear from you And your acknolwedgement of the receipt of papers Sent You. I have Sent You Some papers Since. I Enclose You today A Copy of Morning News, You Will find Marked of a finding of a Court Martial in this Home. If it had of been Some Worthy Soldier instead of an After-the-War non-Commishioned Officer they would of turned him out of the Home. There is no Justice When it is left to these after the War Officers. They Endeavor to Screen one another but A Common member can Walk the Scratch. I Enclose you One of my Photographs recently taken.
    Yours Respectfully
    William. W. Aspinwall

Marion Indiana; Nat. Mil. Hom. June 24. 97

Dear Profs

Yours received Containing 50 cts,[164] wich I am Grateful to you for. I am Kept busy now[a]days with the Guide buisness. Besides I am the regular reporter in the Home for the Marion *Evening Chronical* also I Write Anonymous Articles for other papers. You Spoke about retaining a portion of the Vetterans Pensions to Support the homes. That Would be an Outrage and inconsistent and would be powerfully resisted by Old Soldiers And their friends. The Old Soldier And friends Was a powerful factor in the last Campaign And will be in the next, and it is best for the Party in power to treat them Just and Consistent or it might be posible they would lose their Jobs. There has been to[o] much bickering with Pensioners

I Can't Say When I will go to Nashville, May be later on in the Season and posibly not at all.

We have been haveing Some Great Storms and Wet Wether here. Buisness Seems to be good here in the Gass Belt,[165] All factories Are running and Constructing more of them. We have a good Governor here in Indiana,[166] he is bringing the high-Saleried blood-Suckers to time. He is a Governor for the interest of the people and Will be Suported by the people in his policy of reform and retrenchment.

Yours truly

William. W. Aspinwall

---

164 Presumably this was payment for the photograph Aspinwall had recently sent to McCook.

165 A reference to the Trenton Gas Field, which covered Indiana and the northwest part of Ohio and which boomed from the late nineteenth to the early twentieth century.

166 Republican James A. Mount (1843–1901), Governor of Indiana from 1897 to 1901. He introduced antitrust laws, improved regulations for worker health and safety, and lobbied President McKinley to allow African-American soldiers to serve as officers in the U.S. Army.

Nat Mil Home Marion Indiana; August 17 1897

Profs Jon J McCook

Hartford. Ct.

My Dear Friend, I received Your letter a few days Since And was pleased to hear from You. I am Still here at the home, and a guide and reporter for the Marion *Evening Chronical*, and have a free pass On the Marion Citty Street Car lines for One Year, presented to Me by the Company. I am getting Considerable noteriety as a Writer and humanist. I Will Send You Some of the papers in a few days. I may Stay here this Winter.

What has become of Your reformatory school.[167] Do you think it Will Work All right? I am Sure you Could do A good buisness in the Condition the Country is and has been in. Don't You think So? My Way of of a reformatory Would be to furnish Employment to all (at good wages) that Will Work And reform the residue [i.e., the rest].

I will Close for the preasant as I am buisy. When You publish What You was telling me in your letter You will please Send me a Copy, Will you not?

Fratulentlly Yours

Wm. W. Aspinwall.

---

167 Though McCook's Reformatory Bill had been approved in 1895, support for the project waned and the Bill was repealed in 1897. The Reformatory was never built.

Minster, Ohio, Jan 19 1898

[WRITTEN ON 'CENTRAL HOUSE' HEADED NOTEPAPER]

Profs J J McCook

Dear Sir, I have left the Soldiers' home last Nov. I Am foreman in theis place in a Woolen Mill. Could not Stand the preasure of Oficers that Was never Soldiers And that had no More to do With putting down the rebel[l]ion than Jeff Davis had. The Soldiers' Homes Are a Gigantic Steal And a Snap for Officers.

Write to Me here

Respt Yours

Wm. W. Aspinwall

Nathional Mil Home. Feb 4 98; Hampton Virginia

Profs, I arived here last Sat in hard luck. I Am Admitted here temporally. Write Me here at once. And Send me postage and I Will Give You an out line of my travels. Will be here a few days. Respt Yours,

Wm. W. Aspinwall

Soldiers' Home Hampton Virginia

Minster, Auglaize County, Ohio.; February 16 1898

Profs Jon J McCook
Hartford. Ct.

Dear Sir I received Yours of Jan 29" Some time ago but have not had time to Awnswer Sooner. I Am Still foreman here in this Mill. Probably you are not Aware that I am an Expert at the Woolen and Shoddy[168] buisness.[169] I have had over 40 yrs Experience of[f] And on. I Worked at one time in Your old Home, Stubenville, for the Wallaces and Also for the McDermits. Probably You Know of them.

These Men Are Just Starting this mill on Shoddy Casimeres [cashmere wool]. When I Came here they was Completely Stuck. I have helped them Out in All departments of the mill After Some of your Eastern back leg Mechanicks failed And Condemed the Machinery. And the firm is on a fair way to Success. I am bording at a private house, have a nice room to My Self, and living like a fighting Cock. This is a German Catholic town, the Entire population being teutonic. I am popular with them. Numbers of Saloons And a brewery. A great Masquerade ball in progress tonight, have a pre[s]sing invitation but will not go. I was [i.e., went] to a ball last Sat Eve one Week Ago, Got to be Very popular and familiar with the German band. Got up on the Stage and made a Speech, was Cheered Vociferously by the Germans. Blowed in about five dollars. Got up the next morning with a big head [a hangover], and Concluded to rest with my honors.

Yes, Marion is the only home where beer is not Sold, but the Cider they Sell gets the men Crafty. Ten times Worse than beer And more intoxicating, And Creates more trouble and discord And fills up the Guard House. There

---

168 Shoddy is inferior fiber, and has given its name to anything of poor quality.

169 McCook's father, Dr. John McCook, had built a woolen mill in New Lisbon, Ohio, so the Professor was not entirely unfamiliar with this industry himself.

is no Use of talking Experimenting on temperance reforms Ammongst Old Soldiers, is out of the question And won't work, let them have What they want And treat them decent Until the[y] die of[f]. They have generally to[o] much independence And will Suffer no indignities from Assumeing And important Officers, if they was Soldiers Ever. (My Opinion)

After I left the home I Visited Amongs friends, Walking and riding And no Money Until I Struck this Job. I would not Stay at the home And be A Slave to men I Knew were never Soldiers, And Any man that has any Vim or pluck will not put up with them if they Can posibly help themselves.

Write Soon

Yours Very Respectfully

Wm W Aspinwall

Late. Co.H HY. 11 Indiana Who Manfully Served over four Years to Maintain this Government.

Tecumsie [Tecumseh]. Trail. Park; Lafayette Indiana

[POSTMARK DATED 1ST JULY 1898]

Prof John. J. McCook
Hartford. Ct.

Dear friend, As I have not heard or received a letter from You for Some time I thought I would drop You a Short Epistle. I Am now at the Indiana State Soldiers' Home, Close to this Park. I Came here About Six Weeks ago from Minster Ohio, the Mill there having Shut down And throwing me Out of a position.

I Am Attending to the Hireing out of Boats here in this Park on the Wabash River. I Some times make from 50 cts to $1.50 per day as My Commision. It beats doing nothing. I like Some things about this home better than I do the national Homes. One thing is we are not Crowded together So much. But in Some other things the National Homes are far better managed. If a Man has a Wife he can bring them here And live With her, providing they Was Married prior to 1890 and the Woman is over 45 yrs old.

The Wether is Very Warm here now, the thermometer rangeing from 70 to 90. There has been an Unusual Amount of rain here So far this Spring and Summer. I Am now Sitting on the banks of the great Wabash And near the famous Trail of old Tecumsie And his tribe, and about three Miles South (down the River) from the renowned battle Ground of Tippecanoe,[170] And immediately on the old Indian Camp Grounds And Hunting And fishing Grounds, Just four Miles up the River North from the Citty of Lafayette.

---

170 The U.S. Army defeated Shawnee chief Tecumseh's forces on 7th November 1811 at the Battle of Tippecanoe. Tecumseh (circa 1768–1813) himself was not present at the battle, which dealt a fatal blow to his tribal confederacy.

I Am in hopes Your health Still remaines good And that Your Self and family are Enjoying life. My health is Unusuly good this year, wich I am Very thankful for. I Should like to of gone to Cuba with our boys.[171] I Am Shure I Could of Endured the hard Ships As Well as any of them, And took as many or More of Spanish Scalps. I Wrote to Sec. Alger for a Chance to go. I wanted to go as a Scout or Orderly or Some General's Staff. And Wanted to go to the immediate front where there is a Chance to do Some buisness. I have not received any reply as Yet. I believe I would make a good Acquisition in Extending the Shade of Old Glory.

What is Your Opinion?

Write Soon. Your Friend And an Admirer of Your Self and illustrious family,

William W Aspinwall

Indiana State. Soldiers. Home.

Lafayette, Indiana.

---

171 A reference to the Spanish-American War, which took place between 21st April and 13th August 1898. The war was a victory for the U.S. It led to Cuban independence and, until the 1959 Cuban Revolution, American political and economic dominance of the country.

Bridgeman [Bridgman] Michigan; July 30 1898

Profs Jno J McCook.

Dear Sir, I wrote You a letter from Ind. S.S.H at Lafayette but have [not] received Any awnswer, probably [it] has been returned to You. I left there on July "5" inst, went out in the Country near Lafayette And worked on a farm making Hay att one Dollar per day And bord. Worked one week And Started leisurely Away on foot, not Knowing my destination. Finally brought up near Wanatah Laport [LaPorte] Co, Indiana, Employed to Work on a farm for a German Widow Woman.

Worked three days at 50 cts per day from day light until dark. Got My Money, $1.50, And proceeded on My Journey on foot north on the Monon R.R tracts[172] as far as Westville, Where I indulgeded in a few Glasses of Lager And procured a ticket for Michigan Citty, Indiana. Arrived in the above Citty About 5 P.M, partook of a few more beers, took in the interesting Scenery Around in the Evening. Walked out and Viewed the Ind State Penn [penitentiary]. And rendvoused [rendezvoused, here used to mean slept] in a lumber Yard on a pile of lumber. Next Morning returned to the Citty, partook of a few more beers And lunch.

Visited the butiful Lake Side Park. Wittnessed a Steamer With a Excursion leave her Dock for over Lake Mich for Chicago. Started leisurely north on the Mich. Cen. R.R. tracts on foot, not Knowing my destination. Walked out to New Buffalo. At the Croosing of Chicago and W[est] Mich R.R, floped My Self on the floor of a Box Car And Sleept Good. Arose at Early dawn, took a due north Course on the C.W.M.R.R. Got My breakfast and dinner in a Raspberry and Blackberry patch, Arriveing on foot at this Place about Sundown last Thursday Eve.

---

172   Also known as the Chicago, Indianapolis, and Louisville Railway.

Comeing upon about 40 Ho Bos Along Side R.R Cooking Supper, Who Kindly donated me my Supper, wich was relished by my Self, Especily the Strong black Coffee as it had been my first that day. These Ho.bos are Affectionate And liberal to Each other in distress when they have any thing. These fellows are Picking berries here and they informed me where I Could get a Job Picking. I picked Yesterday And made 50 cts And have plenty of Grub of my Own now. I invested in Coffee, bread, Meat and Potatoes, Eggs. And Sleep in a Box Car. Last night I Sleept in a farm in the Hay Among the Goats.

We do not Pick berries on Sat as there is no Market in Chi on Sunday. Therefore the Pickers lay of[f] on Sat And Work Sunday. I think I Will Spend this next Week here Picking and then I Will go to St. Joseph, Mich, 10 miles north And take A Steamer to Chicago. I have not made up my mind where I will go from that Citty, all depends on Circumstances. I may go Sout[h] this winter. I Am tiard of Staying at the Homes. It is to[o] monotonous And Stale And to[o] Much Red tape.

I would rather brieathe the free Air [even] if it ain't So Comfortable. A Man is lost to the World in one of those Homes. It is Simply a place to go to die. And a place for Upstarts to Use Authority that was never Soldiers. Still, it is all right for those that Can't help them Selves. I like a nomadic life to[o] Well. Write me At St. Joseph, Mich, Gen Delivery. Send me Writing Material and I will inform You of my Where abouts and Circumstances [and] Experience.

Write as Soon as You receive this So that I will receive it when I Get there. Respt Yours,

Wm W Aspinwall

Near Bangor, Van Buren Co.; Michigan.

Profs Jon J McCook
Niantic. Ct.

Dear Professor, I received Your Ever Wellcome letter at St Joseph on last Friday "5" inst [August 1898]. I left Bridgeman Mich the Same day, Walking to Stevensville five miles distant. There taking a train to St. Joe[seph], paying my fare at the town of St Joe. I Engaged loging at a Hotel And Also meals. Stayed Until Sunday Afternoon the 7" inst, going then over to Benton Harbour. Floped in a Box Car all night. On Monday "8" inst LaPearl's Great Shows[173] was at Benton Harbor. You Know from my former letters I am familiar with Circus life, having been with Sells Brothers near two Years. So I was at Home when geting With the boys. I Spent the day Very pleasantly With the boys, haveing free access to Circus, Menagerie, and Side Shows and Cooking and dining tent, which Came in Very Useful to me throughout the day. I Stayed around until Very late in the night, went and again flopped in a Box Car. I Could of got a position with the Show but having partook of Circus life I do not fancy A repetition, therefore will run Chances other Ways. On the Morning of the 9", I Walked back to St. Joe. Got My Baggage at the Hotel And Was on my way to return to Benton Harbor, having in my mind to go farther up in to the State into Allegan County to pick Peaches. Just as I was Crossing the bridge over the St Joe River between the two Citties, A Man in a [horse-drawn] buggy overtook me. He asked me where I was going.

I told him, 'to Benton Harbor.'

He Says, 'Jump in And ride.'

I accepted his invitation, as it was Very Kind in him. We got into Conversation And he told me that had been at one time (recently) deputy County Clerk of Berian [Berrien] County, Mich, And that he was A Stenographer And

---

173 A circus show.

had been Employed with Some larg[e] firms in that Citty. I found from My Conversation with him that he was Unusuasally bright in intellect, And he Accertaining that I was well posted We opened up a familiar Conversation on a number of Subjects. He told me that he had Just returned that morning from Chicago on a Steamer and that he had been on a big drink. He was in a bad Shape from the Effects of bad Whiskey and other drinks. He Said he was Just driving out to wear of[f] the Effects of it. He was going up to Wattervaliet [Watervliet] twelve Miles distant, And As I Was going in that direction I was welcome to ride with him. On the Way he told me that he had taken the Keely or Gold Cure twice And related to me how [he] Came to return to drink. He Said it was the Company And the associates he had formed, And that they was more difficult to break away from than the drink. The Keely Cure he Said had Completely relinquished his desire for drink, and that he was a going to again take the Cure And get out of the rut he was now in. He Claimed that he was always prosperous when he left drink alone and had good positions. I advised him to give up drink and its Associates, again take the Cure and Make a Man of him Self. He told Me he was 38 yrs old, had a Wife and two Children but She had left him. He Came from a good family, having two Bros prominent Lawyers in St. Joes (and others told Me the Same), but him Self a total Wreck of a Mis-Spent life. He got to Wattervaliet, drove out to Paw Paw Lake, A Summer resort for Chicagans. Drove Around Amongst the Cottages, it was a beautiful place. Returned to Wattervaliet. My friend had a friend there that was formerly County Clerk, And Was Keeping [a] Drug Store in this Village. My friend had been his deputy for him. He went in to See him, borrowed five dollars from him. We drove to Coloma two miles distant where there was Saloons, as he Said he was Slowly dying for a drink. We got What he Wanted And Some lunch. He Wanted me to return With him to Benton Harbor but I declined and bid him good by, thanking him Kindly, and Walked on to Hartford 7 miles distant. I Write You this discription illustrating my Varied Experience. He told me he had frequently got down on the tramp but Would telegraph to his friends to Send him money to Come home on. His address is B.E.O.Hara. St. Joe, Michigan. I Arrived in Hartford about 10 P.M, Again overtaking the Circus. Sleped in a Box Car. Am now Setting Under a tree near Bangor, haveing Walked here Since Morning.

Pearl, Allegan County, Michigan.

Since My last I have went to work for Congressman Todd of Kalamizoo, Mich,[174] on his Peppermint farm of 1,400 Acres.[175] He is here himself. He has built him Self a Summer residence here. He is making Money, he has three Stills and gets out daily 1,500 lbs of Peppermint Oil. There is from 75 to 100 men Employed at $1.10 per day and $2.50 per week for bord. The men Employed Are as a General rule Hobos: And they are Comeing and going all the time: as the boys Says it is a bum Job, and only last[s] Until frost. And frost Comes Early here in this Swamp land. This land has all been reclaimed from Swamps and thickets, and origonally bought Cheep. Judge Severn[176] of the U.S. Supreme Court has a large mint farm adjoining this.

Two Hobos Came With me from the Station but they only Worked 4 hours a pi[e]ce and got their Supper And Called for their time and quit. Mr Todd gave them their few Cents and they went their Way. But Such Circumstances Are transpiring daily. This is a great place to Study Human nature. I stand in amazement And Wonder at the different freaks of Hummanity. I Suppose Some of them do the Same When Watching the moves at Mint farming, but Candidly I wonder to My Self, when I Rubber Neck this Motly Gang of Americans, 'Why it is that Uncle Sam Hesitates to annex Cuba or the

---

174 Albert May Todd (1850–1931), who was Congressman for the 3rd Michigan Congressional District between 1896 and 1898, having been nominated by the Democratic, Prohibition, and People's Parties. A silverite, Todd was also in favor of the public ownership of utilities, breaking up monopolies and regulating the railroads. Also a successful and flamboyant businessman, Todd's A.M. Todd Company supplied the majority of the world's peppermint, earning him the nickname "The Peppermint King of Kalamazoo."

175 This is Todd's "Campania" farm in central Allegan County, Michigan.

176 This was Judge Henry Franklin Severens (1835–1923).

Phillippine Islands?'[177] I believe Your Self Would be Amazed. The Old Hay Seed[178] farmers Are more of a Study than the Hobos. I Candidly am of the opinion that the bos are the Most inteligeent and Independent Monstrosities of the two. The Hobos don't like the HaySeeds. They Say the Hay Seeds Keep the Wages down, and if it was not for them they Would be Compelled to pay $1.50 per day for this Work. The farmers around here are poor, that is the Small farmers, and they haft to Work at any Price to Keep their families. And the big Guns take advantage of their poverty. And the Hobos haft to Come to time also or not work. The last named are great boys for high prices And are very indignant at any Set of Men that are the Cause of process being Cut down. Some of them made as much as $4.00 per day picking berries. There is Several big bed rooms, With from twenty five to 40 beds in Each room, and You Can Judge the rest. There is Several Gang foremans And they are about as full of Knowledg[e] As the Average fat Porker.

I May Stay here the Comeing Week and I may not. I am going to Pick Peaches as Soon As they are ready. Will haft to travel from Six to ten Miles from here And then I Shall go to Grand Rappids. I have not mapped out My Course from there. You Can Address Your next to

Fennvill,

Allegama County

Michigan

Very Respectfully Yours

William. W. Aspinwall

You made a Mistake when you Said in your last [letter] that I had been bumming Around [i.e., begging] for over thirty Years. I am a poor bum. I would about as Soon Starve as beg. I generally pay for my Eating. When I Can't, I will go in to onions Corn or Potatoes[179] before I will go to a Man's House and Ask for any thing.

---

177 The Philippine-American War, which lasted from 1899 to 1902, took place between the U.S. and the First Philippine Republic. At the end of the war the U.S. had annexed the Philippines. The war was noted for numerous atrocities: estimates for Filipino civilian deaths range between 200,000 and 1 million people. The American Anti-Imperialist League, formed in 1898, attempted to shift public opinion to oppose American domination of the Philippines, having prominent members, including the author Mark Twain.

178 'Hayseed' is a derogatory term for people from the countryside, connoting a lack of intelligence and sophistication.

179 Aspinwall means that he will steal vegetables from a field before asking for money, though quite why this is morally superior is unclear! (EDITOR'S NOTE: Hungry people taking from a farmer's field was considered acceptable. You only take what you can eat and never more than that.)

Near Grand. Rapids. Mich.;
Sunday August 28 1898

Profs J.J. McCook

My Dear friend, You Said in Your last, Received at Fennville Mich, that You had received My last Without date. I am not Certain About the day of the Month today. I often forget And Unless I have a late [news]paper, wich I Always have When I Can forget one. I have lost My pencil with An Eraser on one End and if mistakes are not rectified You will Know the reason Why! I have a tablet of this paper, [which] is Why I don't Use what You Sent. I will inform you that my buisness is So Urgent and important and Must be Attended to promptly, that it is no Wonder I Make Mistakes in Writing and dates. I left the Peppermint farm one Week ago Yesterday, I had three dollars Comeing. After Shaveing my time Check, and getting Some Clothing I Went to Fennville and got Some Beer and bought a Shirt, Some Socks and a Valice, wich I have With me now, & Slept all night on the floor of A box Car.

Sunday Morning I went north on a drille (We Call Walking drilling.) And Met another Old Soldier. He was laying Along Side of the R.R. in the Shade in full Uniform. He Said he had belonged to the 3" U.S. Cav[alry] but had got S[h]ot and disabled and Was now drawing 12 per Month pension. He an My Self Struck up a friendship And Enterd in to a Solemn Agreement to go to gether And work from hensforth for the partnership's Mutual benefits. There being no Money in the treasury, We repaired to a nearby hamlet and foraged Some Corn and Potatoes. I had the nesasary Coffee & Salt in my Knap Sack and we Got up a fair Meal, wich my Comrade partook of Very lavishingly, As Well as my Self, as he Said he had been on a big drink And had not partook of any of the necasarys of life for a few days. After Eating We took the first Cross roads and Started for the Peach belt, intending to get Work together and lay by funds and go South.

We Stoped together one night, the next night I lost him.[180] He was a little to[o] Slow for me. He had been Staying at the Michigan State Soldiers' Home at Grand Rappids, but Said he was dissatisfied there And would rather tramp and[181] to Stay there. There is a great deal of dissatisfaction in All these Homes, both State and U.S [i.e., Federal], wich is Caused by to[o] Much Red Tape and the Want of proper Judgement in Officers. As Gen. Ben Butlers of Mass remarked, these Homes would be a 'paradise for the Officers but a Hell for the Privates', wich is true. I Know Some thing About these Homes. Not one in ten in number of the total numbers of the inmates of these homes are Satisfied. It is a mere matter of Compulsion for a Man of refinement or intelligence to Stay in them. Oh, in the Case of Some ignorant or half Witted Officer's succor [sycophant], he May Say he is Satisfied in order to Stand in With the Officers.

I tell you Profs McCook, When I have An Officer Over We hose.[182] Especily Millitary, give me an intelligent And Educated man, Educated to his buisness, one who has passed through the Schooling under his Superiors and has had a taste of Red tape and Worthless Orders. And if he is a man of intellect You have a good Offcier, Such as Gen Sherman Was, or Gen McCooks; are included in the list Gen Miles of today and Col. Rosevelt. of the Rough Riders[183] And a Score of Others in this Spanish War are good ones. I have no Use for Gen Shafter,[184] he is a brute And no good, A good bigfoot monkey on a Horse Would Make Just as good a General. Shafter reminds me of the important man of Your town, Hartford, Gen W.B. Franklin. Only

---

180 Such short-term temporary partnerships were (and are) a feature of life on the road. The sociologist Jeff Ferrel terms this way of relating to the world and other people as 'drift.' See Jeff Ferrell, *Drift: Illicit Mobility and Uncertain Knowledge* (Oakland, CA: University of California Press, 2018).

181 Aspinwall presumably means 'than.'

182 Aspinwall appears to use this word to mean "talk frankly and honestly."

183 Theodore Roosevelt Jr. (1858–1919), who led the 1st United States Volunteer Cavalry, known as the "Rough Riders" at the Battle of San Juan Hill during the Spanish-American War, earning himself a level of fame that he would later use to become Vice President and, following William McKinley's assassination, President.

184 William Rufus Shafter (1835–1906), who served in both the American Civil War and the Spanish-American War. Shafter oversaw supplying the U.S. Army's expedition to the Philippines. In 1899, he was quoted in the *Chicago News* as stating "It may be necessary to kill half the Filipinos in order that the remaining half of the population may be advanced to a higher plane of life than their present semi-barbarous state affords." William Shafter, cited in Henry Hooker Van Meter, *The Truth about the Philippines: From Official Records and Authentic Sources* (Chicago: Liberty league, 1900), p. 368.

Shafter was with an army that took Something, but an Army never took any thing from an Enemy Under Franklin.

There Seems to be Considerable of Criticism Hurled at Sec. Alger And Gen Shafter on the Management of that Santiago Affair.[185] Now if a line Officer or Private goes to Sleep on his post and imperals the Safety of an Army, they Shoot him. The Same rule Should Work All round. If an Officer, no difference how high in Command, if through his negligence he Causes Suffering, Court Martial him And, if found Guilty, lead him out and Shoot him. You Ask Me in Your last My Oppinion of our going in to Colony buisness and Keeping the Philapines.[186] My Motto is to never take down the Stars and Stripes after once being raised after battle and American blood being Spilt. Never turn those natives over to the brutal Spaniards Again, Give them their liberty. Place Some protectorate over them Until they Can Govern them Selves. Humanity Asks our Gov to do this.

I have no Serious Objections as to being Clasified as a tramp, for a more independent And Joyous mode of life at times than that of a tramp with a Small income, I Cannot imagine. Tramping in Some Countrys is far More feasible than Cycling. We Soon discover what our brother tramp discovered Centuries ago: that the best Way to Carry a budget or bundle is to hang it on a Stick over Your Shoulder. Noon Comes but no sun, and the tramp lunches on Some Crackers or bread and Makes black Coffee in a Cast-away Can. And Makes a Stew for Supper or breakfast in the Same, out of foraged Potatoes, Green Corn or Onions, in fact any Vegetables that Comes in his way. And lunches on fresh fruit out of the nearby Orchards and Mellon Patches throughout the day.

When I pass through Village or hamlet, in passing Groups Either at Work or play, All Such is Suspended for the time being. And a drink and Some Whisperd remarks as the tramp passes by: Such is ignorance in Some Cases and the Want of fore though[t] in other people. The tramp May in his time (that is Just passing) May have forgot More than all Such Groups Ever Knew, or will Ever Know. If Some of the groups thus Congregated to rubber neck could read the tramp's Mind they Would quickly dispearse, or resume their Work or play. I have one more incident in My recent travels to relate to You and then I Shall Close for today. I went from Holland, Mich

---

185 Shafter mishandled the siege of Santiago during the Spanish-American War and was wide-
     ly seen as causing an unnecessarily high number of American casualties.

186 i.e., making the Philippines an American colony.

down to Ottawa beach, A resort on the Lake Side. I Walked down About Six Miles on the R.R. I only Stayed A Short time and When returning took the Wagon Road about one Mile out of the resort. I Came acroos a Young lady, about 18 years old, Sitting Under the friendly Shade of a tree.

I politely Spoke and bowed to her and was passing on my way and She remarked 'Why don't You rest Your Self?'

I quietyly threw my bundles down Under the Shade a Short distance from her. I was Eating Som[e] Cakes I had bought at the beach and offerd to divide With her, She Saying that She Was Hungry. I was Astonished and asked her where She lived. She would not tell me but Said it was a long ways from here. I finally drawed her into Conversation and She related her Exploits to me as her Confidence in me increased. She told me She had run Away from her home to meet her lover but her lover never Came. He had got her into trouble [i.e., pregnant] and instead of doing as he Said he would and protecting the Girl, he had Ab[s]conded and left her in trouble. I got Very Much interested in her. I proposed to her to go to Some more of a Secluded place and Make us Some Coffee, as I had the necasary Utensils and Coffee in My Pack. Before going She requested me to go back to the town and get Some More to Eat as She had plenty of Money, wich I done after She reached in her purse and took out a five dollar note. I went and Came back gave her her Change and I gatherd up Some Wood and She prepared a good meal. I See She was a beautiful Girl When She took of[f] her Sun Bonnet and washed her face and Combed her Hair, but trouble had Already Made lines in her face. And She was intelligent and partially Educated and no doubt Came from a good family. She finally related to me that When She ran away from home She Stole over one Hundred dollars from her Father and a gold Watch from her Mother, and that She had been Keeping away from town[s] and going Around them for fear of capture. She Said I was the first one She had told any of her Secrets to. I got it all out of her. She Said her lover and her Self had been Very intimate, And he had promised to Stay by her through thick and thin but he had proved false. I made a bed out of Some Straw And built a Small fire near the Shore of the Bay and we retired for the nigh[t]. She Said I Was the only one, Save her lover, that had Ever partaken of her forbiden fruit. I told her if She Would of Still of held her Chastity [i.e., if she was still a virgin] I Would of Advised her to Keep it, but as She Already Knew the ways there was no harm in me partaking of the fruit. She Wanted Me to Stay With her, but I told her her predicament Was Such that it was Unsafe for Me to. I Was liable to be Arested and Severely dealth With if found in her Company. I advised her to return to her Home And to implore the forgiveness of her Parents as the best Course for her to pursue. She Commenced Weeping when She found I Would not go With her. I Went with her to near Holland. We Stayed together one more night And I influenced her to take a train for Home. And I Supose She is today Under the Parental Roof.

> Unto my bosom I Caught her
> And Kissed her Upturned lips;
> When lo! She Vanished like a Star
> Into a dark Eclipse.

> But never never Will I find
> My fairy Anywhere;
> Yet, Oh, for that one Moments Kiss.
> How dreamful is Despair.

Affairs Will Soon be quite [quiet] Enough in the Philippines for the transportation Companies to begin to discover Gold there.

Getting back from Cuba is a Joyous Experience, provided You don't get back dead.

August 29 1898

Arrived in Grand Rapids, Mich. Will Stay in this Vincinity A few days. Will try And get a Job for A While, forward Your next letter to this place. Slept in a box Car Just outside of Citty. It is now 9 A.M. Have had no bruakfast As Yet. Lived fairly Well Yesterday. Walked from Holland Mich. [I am] over Trusting in good luck for fortune

    Yours With Respect
    Wm.W.Aspinwall

In Camp near Kendleville [Kendallville]. Ind.; I think About Sept 26 and 27[187] 1898

Profs. Jon J McCook
Hartfort
Ct

My Dear Sir. I have lost the run of the day of the Month but today is Saturday. I received Your letter of Sept 5" inst about the 15" inst, at Plainwell, Mich. I had it forwarded on to me. I have had quite a Varied Experiance Since I last Wrote You. I got a Job in Grand Rapids With A Man by the name of Philips, driving Ice train. I got Enough of it in two days. if I had not of quit I believe it Would of Ended my Career Sudenly, the work was So laborious And disagreeable, And Such long hours from 2 P.M. to about 9. P.M. I looked Around for Another Job two or three days, Walked out into the Country 10 Miles but did not Succeed. I then took My Grip on a Stick over My Shoulder and Started out [on] the G.R. I. R. R. [Grand Rapids and Indiana Railroad] towards Ft. Wayne, Enquireing of All I met for Work. Near Monteith Junction I Succeeded in getting a Job, Cutting up Corn at 50 Cts per Acre and bord. I Cut up Six Acres in Six days. It Went Very hard with me, not being Use[d] to the Work. The farmers tell me that two Acres per day is an Average day's Work for an Expert at the buisness. The farmer furnished his table With bread, butter, potatoes, and Milk. I believe the money I Earnt at the Ice buisness And Cutting Corn in Michigan was As hard-Earnt Money As Ever I Earnt. That is, I layed out more physical Strength. I took the Money And bought My Self a new p[ai]r of Strong Shoes, Socks, Shirts Overalls, and Some feed. I was laying in a box Car at Plainwell,

---

187 If Aspinwall is correct that it was a Saturday, then this letter was written on the 24th September.

Mich during the night. A Hobo opened the door And Came in. He had lost his Hat and had a Hankerchief tied around his Knot. He Said he lost his hat looking out of the Car door. He was a Miserable Specimen. During the night he Wanted to Come over and Spoon up to me. He Said he was Cold, that he had no Undercloths. An[d] I at once certinaly Said 'no'. I am Very Careful in my Asociation with Hobos, not to Get in touching distance Unless I Know them And Know they are Clean. Some of them Are full of Grey backs. I left the Soldiers' Home at Lafayette, Ind on the 5" of last July and I have not had a Grey back on me. I manage to bath and Wash up my Cloths once or twice a Week And Keep away from the Hobos' dens. I am of the opinion this fellow was a thief and I believe he would not hesitate to Shed blood to Accomplish his designs. He Used More Strong phrases than I Ever heard on the Road before. He was Always talking about 'Grafting' And 'Rooting', 'flapping', and 'picking Gose berries'. I am not a Graduate in the Giberage [i.e., slang] And do not Associate with that Class of Hobos Enough to Catch on. I think he belongs to What is Known in this part of the Country as the Lake Shore Gang. They travel the L.S. & M.S. R.R. [Lake Shore and Michigan Southern railroad] between Buffalo & Chicago and are the toughs from All the Citties Along that line of R.R. And they do not hesitate, As I am told by Hobos, to Commit Any Kind of Crime. They Rob And Even murder Hobos that do not belong to their Gang. I was told a Young boy, probably 16 or 18 y[ears] old from Kalamazoo, Mich hapened to Jump into a box Car to beat his Way, And there was A number of the above Gang in the Car. They Striped the Young fellow of Everything but his Pants & Shirt, Committed Sodomy on his person And then threw the fellow out While the train Was running at full Speed. The fellow Was found With his Shoulder broke And otherwise Cut and bruised up, More dead than alive. I tell you this Just as I got it from a Hobo that Made his Home at Victsburgh [Vicksburg] Mich. This fellow Seemed to be in dread of this Lake Shore Gang and he was Warning me of them. He Said they had Committed Sodomy on his Person and that a number of them had Jumped him And beat him. And he was a Strong Healthy Young man. I have not Met Any of the Lake Shore Gang but once, after the young fellow in the Car, and that was at Vicksburgh, Mich. I Seen eight or ten Camped out in Some Woods aways from the town. I talked to one or two of them. They was fairly well dressed, I think they took me for a Rail Road Man. They Asked me at What time trains Went South. I awnswerd them as if I Knew all About it And Came to the Conclusion they was a tough Set and passed on into the town. After leaveing Victsburg I Came on a foot towards

Ft. Wayne to near Lagrange [LaGrange]. I met A farmer drilling Wheat Just over the fence. He Asked me if I wanted Work. I Awswerd him I did. He Said he wanted Me to Shock Corn After a Machine.

I Says 'What is there in it?'

He Says 'one dollar per day and bord'.

It was then about 4 P.M. He Wanted Me to go to Work at once. I went. I Worked that and the next day. And then it began to rain. The first day it rained, I Stayed at his House and helped His Wife make Grape wine. He was a Young married man And had a fine good looking Woman and had been married two yrs and no Children. They had a large amount of Grapes And they did not Know what to do with them, as they Could get no price for them. I proposed making Wine out of them And he told me to help his Wife make Wine. We Sent him to town after Sugar, So we Made the Wine. The woman And My Self got intimate. I asked her how it Came about they had no Children.

She Says: 'You Can rest Assured it is not my fault.'

And then She gave me a history of Her Married life. She Said her Husband was a torment to her. I felt Sorry for her and Sympathised with her. She was awnxous [anxious] for me to make my Home with them permanently, but I left the next morning as it was Still raining. I went up to Lagrange and drawed my Money from the Young Man's father who Kept a Music Store in the town.

On my way up to town I Came Across a Hobo, an old Man, a duchaman [dutchman], who Said he was a black Smith By trade. He Said he was Camped Under a tree, and had a Motto [i.e., a sign] he Had picked up in Some dump pile Hanging on the Side of the tree, wich had incribed thereon: 'God Bless our House'. He went to town with me but he was All for drink and was Soon drunk. I Soon left him. I was interru[p]ted Very Abruptly by a Storm in my Camp. I have Got in a farmer's barn, on the Hay. It is raining Very hard with heavy thunder. I feel Unwell today, I have a nauseating Sickness but am of the opinion it is a bilious Attact [attack]. As a general rule I Am blessed With Excelent health. Exposure don't Seem to Effect me in the least. I never Catch Cold. I Can lay on the wet Ground and Shiver All night And get up in the Morning Hungry. I have been Soaking Wet with a Sleety rain and let my Cloths dry on me And it never injured my health in the least. How is that, Profs, for a Man 55 yrs old? I have About Came to the Conclusion I Am immune and impervious to all Sickness. I don't believe there is another man living of my Age that has went through the hardships I have. And I am Sound and healthy Yet, And Can Stand more than the majority of Young men. Yet I am troubled Some with the rheaumatism. Those Gun Shot Wounds bother me Some, the older I get the more I feel their Effects. Since I Started on this trip on the 5" of July I have not begged one penny or one morsel to Eat, or beat A train. All the riding I have done I payed for, wich was only ten Miles. I have had opportunities to ride but preferred Walking. I was in no hurry. I am about as well of[f] in one locality as another.

As for begging, that Seems to be Very foreign to my nature. I don't like to do it and it is all most [i.e., almost] imposible for me to do. When I Ask a person for anything you Can Just bet I need What I Ask for. You wanted to Know if that young lady I met near Ottawa beach had Ever been in a reformed School.[188] I think not. But am not Certain. I did not get any thing intoxicating with Her Money. I thoug[h]t About it when I went [into town] but I resolved to My Self I would not Encourage her to drink. I don't believe She Ever partook of Any liqors in her life. I did not Mention it to her or She to me, and She did not have the Appearance of that Kind of person [i.e., a drunk]. Her demeanor was to[o] refined and lady like. I hope She Went home as I Advised her. It is well She met me instead of others.[189] I fully Advised her on those facts And told her to make no more male Aquainances, for She Was liable to lose Everything She had And maybe her life. Or Come in Contact with Some loathsome disease. I think She returned Home, for She was Very much Affected when I parted with her And Seemed to take What I Said to her to heart.

Profs, I Some times think it is about time for me to Stop Somewhere and Settle down. I want Your Advise. I Can never be Satisfied at a Soldiers' Home. I think if I was with Some well-to-do family, And look after his place and interests generally, where I Could have All the reading matter I wanted And opertunities of Writing, I would be Satisfied. Maybe You Know of Some family that Would want Such A man?[190] I Can be a Gentleman And Honest And will do Just as I Say. You Can Send Your next letter to Ft. Wayne, Indiana, Gen. Del. And if I leave there before I get it, I will have it forwarded. My Wish is that your Self and family will Enjoy good Health. Has your Sons returned Home? I May go South this Winter, have not fully determined Yet.

Very Respectfully Yours

Wm. W. Aspinwall

---

188 It is typical of McCook's Victorian attitude that he has asked a question that puts implicit blame on the young woman described in Aspinwall's 28th August letter.

189 This is, to say the least, a questionable claim.

190 Aspinwall seems to be hinting that he would like to work for McCook.

Near Charleston. W. Virginia; Nov 3 1898

Profs. Dear Sir. I left Ft. Wayne, Ind five weeks ago. I have got near the Above Citty And have Walked All the way, Sleeping in Emty Houses but principally by Camp fires. Some times we have Stoped over night With families Since we have Struck Virginia. The people in Virginia are generally Very Hospitable. I have never Went hungry on the trip So far. I am mending Umbrells & fixing Clocks and Sewing machines. I have a partner with me, his name is George Rutter. He is a Harness Maker. He mends Harness[es], Horse Rasors [razors], Sharpens Shears and lawn Mowers, and So on. And we manage to get plenty to Eat So far. We take the by-roads and Keep off the Main rodes as Much as posible. I Am Very healthy, I weigh near 180 lbs.

Little Sewell. Greenbrier. Co. Va; Nov 18 1898

Profs Jno J McCook
Hartfort. Ct.

Dear Sir, Since my last Postal from this Office I have Came Very near looseing [losing] my life. I have been Stoping With A typical old Virginian, Well-to-do, for the past few days. He owns an old-time Flouring Mill And Saw Mill, the power is Steam. I have been puting his Mill in repair And My partner [George Rutter] is making them a Side Saddle. I With the old gent was working on the Saw Mill And we Sawed a plank of a log And there was no one there to Catch the plank, So the Saw Caugh[t] the plank under a full head of Steam and hurled it back With A tremendious force. And it Struck me over the heart and Abdomen and on the hand, Knocking me down and over another log And breaking A lead pencil in 5 pi[e]ces that was in my Side pocket, Also grinding the Glass in my Specks almost into powder Against my ribs. So You may Judge I got a good jolt. I got up And Went to Work with my hand bleeding And feeling Sore And turning blind at times, but I Soon had to quit And go to the House and go to bed. And I was a Very Sick man for about two days. But these folks treated me Very Kindly. And done All they Could for me. My trouble Was in My Stomach but I Am much better now And will Soon resume my Journey. The old Gent and his Son made the remark that I was the most nervey [nervy, here meaning brave] man they Ever Saw, and that [is] quite a recommend[ation] for Virginians to Give a Man. His name is Harvey Hendrick, Little Sewell, P.O Greenbrier Co, Va. We are Just at the Eastern foot of Little Sewell Mountain. There was Several Skirmishes took place near here during the War, Along the Muddy and Greenbrier River. I think, if My Memory Serves me right, one of Your Brothers was in Command of the Yankees here at one time.

Since I Wrote you at Ft. Wayne Ind, I have traveld through Paulding, Allen, Puttnain [Putnam County], Auglaze, Logan, Champaign, I have forgotten New London is the County Seat, Ross Jackson Gallia in Ohio, West Va. We Crossed the Ohio River at Point Pleasand, Mason, Puttinum, Kanawah [Kanawha] and Greenbrier Countees And Walked All the Way. I done Some Work fixing Umberells, Sewing Machines, Clocks and So on. Never tasted liquors or beer but once on the trip, And that was at Gal[l]ipolis, Ohio. My partner got beastly drunk. We have Camped out a few times And Stayed in Churches and Knowledge boxes [schools] a few times, but lo[d] ged with families and Eat our regular Meals the most of the time.

Ravens Eye P.O. where I wrote you is on the top of big Sewell Mountain. We are now in about 19 miles of Lewisburgh. Va.

Respt Yours

Wm. W. Aspinwall

P.S. You Can have the Acount of the Saw Mill Accident published. I refer you to Mr Heidrich who is a Staunch old Cittizen here as to the Acuracy of my statement. You will observe I have run a number of narrow Escapes from death in peace As well as in War. I was in A Saw Mill [that was] blow[n] up near Spencerville, Ohio in 1870, where the boiler blew up, passing over me. I Also have Escaped Very narrowly A number of times on R.R. And Around Machinery.

You Can Write to Lewisburgh

Greenbrier County

West. Virginia.

Meadow Bluff P. O.; Nov 21st. 98

West. Virginia.

I left Mr Harvey Hedricks today at noon, or after dinner. It was like leaveing Home, they was Such Kind good Christian People. They made me promise to Write to them and to Come and See them if [I] got in to these [h] ere parts again. I Am going now over the mountains to See a brother-in-law of Harvey Hedricks by the name of Arbough. He has a Woolen Mill.

Yours

W.W A

Goldston. Chatham. Co. N. C.; Dec 23 1898.

Jon J. McCook.
Hartford.
Connecticut

Dear Sir, I am down here in N.C. fixing Clocks, Umberells & doing fairly well. Have traveled a long way over hills and Mountains, have had a good many Ups and downs. Write to me at Fayetteville North Carolina, USA N.C. Will be there in a few days. Yours,

W. W. A

Nathional Soldiers' Home; Hampton. Virginia.
3.9.99

Profs Jno J McCook
Trinity College
Hartford. Ct
My Dear Sir

I wrote you A Postal over one month since, on my Arival here from the South, And fearing You did not receive the Same, or Some thing Serious has hapend to you, I address You Again. I traveld through Ohio, West & Old Virginia And N. Carolina down as far as Wilmington. I had an interesting And Adventurest Journey. I made the trip mostly on foot following the vocation of Umberell repairing, Clock & Watch fixing, and Sewing machine repairing. I made Enough money at times to buy my Eating. Most of the time Sleeping out by Campfires, or in Vacant houses through W.V.A and part of old Va. Stayed over night with the natives, found them hospitable.

My motive in Such trips is the pure love of travel And the Satisfaction that Changes of Scenery And the habits of the people in different parts of the Country Give my mind. Roaming about Seems to be a mania with me Since the War of Rebel[l]ion. I would like Very much to go to the Philipines, if I Could get Some Kind of a position with the Gov. I am Sure I Could Stand a few yrs there better than most of the Younger men. Wishing to hear from you as Soon as Convenient. I remain as Ever Your friend.

William. W. Aspinwall.

Urbana Champaign Co Ohio; July 31 1899

Profs Jno J McCook
Hartford. Ct.
Dear Sir,

I received yours Addressed to New. Bremen, O[hio] Sometime Since but have neglected Awnswering. I am now Employed in the Urbana Woolen Mills. I am doing what we term 'Sorting Wool'. I Select the different qualities of Wool to make the many grades of Casimeres. It is a particular Calling and requires a great deal of Experience. In fact there are but few men that make good Sorters, Some thing like the material for College Professers, wich there is a great deal of but a Very Small Amount of it matures into Usefulness. I mean no reflections on any one However and not Correct. The manager of our Mill died with the Typhoid fever last Friday morning.

His name was George Batchelor Origonaly from Boston Mass. And he was a Very Useful man to the Citty as well as the mill. He Was layed in a Vault Sunday Evening And will be taken to Mass when the weather permits and intered. We Shut down two days, Friday and Sat, but Started again this Monday morn. My Salery is $12 per week.[191] I have purchased A great deal of Clothing And dress now in the latest fashions And Apear as a Gentleman. Bord at a good Hotel and have a fine furnished Room. I do not miss a Working day. I left New Bremen because these men offerd me a better Salery. This is my native County. I was born in this County the 25" day of may 1845, Yet I am A Stranger As I have not resided here Since A boy of 5 yrs. It is getting late And I will Close. Glad to hear from you, Profs.

Respectfully Yours
William. W. Aspinwall
300 East Market. St.

191   Slightly under $400 in 2021 terms.

Fig. 13

Urbana.
Champaign Co.
Ohio;
10/12 [actually
10th December]
1899

Profs Jno J McCook
Hartford Ct
Dear Profs

I received Yours of "Nov "25, Some ten days Since. Was Glad to hear from you. I had begin to think that in your hurry in your Professional buisness You had forgotten me. But I observe that you have not, for wich I am thankful, as I have, in Coresponding with You So long, formed an Attachment for you.

I am Still Working in the Woolen Mills here, Sorting Wool. My Wages are 10 dollars per Week[192] full time, but I Am not making full time now on acount of the Short days, as we Can't Very well Sort Wool by Artificial light.

My Room Costs me, With fire, $1.25 per Week. I Get my meals at a restaurant, wich Costs me $3.00 per Week. I Am Sorry to Say that I Am not a total Abstainer. I only wish I was. But I Am Guarding My Self. I See the folly of it and I no doubt would be a Well-to-do man today if it had not

---

192 It is unclear why this amount differs from his previous letter.

of been for Such habits. My disposition is Such that it is hard for me to be a total Abstainer but I am determined to reform my Self.

No, I do not Aprove of Sending a dear beloved daughter into those obnoxous Countries So far Away from her attachments and home, but probably her Self and Parents and friends believe She is fulfilling Holy Writ And that She Will receive A heavenly reward. I hope She will and I wish her Good health and good results And a Safe return home.[193] I was raised in the Methodist Episcopal Church. My Mother And Father And Some of my Sisters were devoted Christians, but I am near an Unbeliever.[194] I belonged to the Evangelical Lutheran Church at one time and go here Some times, not often.

I believe, in this preasant War between the Boers and English,[195] that both parties have Grievances, but the Boers are a non progressive people & they Should not Stand in the Way of progress. But they have proven So far to be brave men And I believe it will take Some time for the English Army to Subdue them. I will Send you one of my Photos. Please Write So I will get your letter before Christmas, as I may go away there. Don't forget the Photo.

Very Respectfully

Wm. W. Aspinwall

General Delivery

Urbana

Ohio

---

193 This seems to refer to something in one of McCook's letters, but as that letter no longer exists it is uncertain exactly what Aspinwall is discussing here.

194 This is notably different to what he says in early letters.

195 The Second Boer War, often referred to as "The Boer War," was fought between the British Empire and two independent Boer states, the Orange Free State and the South African Republic. Despite Britain having overwhelming military superiority, the war lasted for three years, from 1899 to 1902, and only ended with a victory for the Empire after a brutal scorched-earth campaign.

Urbana, Ohio; May 18 1900

Profs J J McCook

Dear Sir, Yours of 4" inst duly received. I was Very Sorry indeed to hear of Your Sad bereavement of the death And burial of Your Noble Son,[196] taken away from you in the bloom of Manhood, And So far Away from home in a Strange Country, Withering Your Expectations in him for future life. But God's Will be done, We Can't Countermand it. We must All Obey His will in death at Some time.

I am Still in Urbana, Employed in the Woolen Mills. I Am getting along Very nicely, have an Elegant room and good food, Wich Costs me $4.25 per week. I have many good friends here And Enjoy My Self. I have About Giving up the Road buisness, I think I have traveled near Enough And Seen about all there is to See in this World. I Certainly have had a Great Experience. You Know that not Many Men Can bost of a quarter [as much] in that line.

I Keep my Self well posted on the topics of the day. I take an Indianapolis Daily, it Comes in the Evening and I read at nights And [in the] morning. I Always Get a Sunday paper and Some of the popular weeklys. I am of opinion the British has got the Uper hand of the Boers now and will End the war in a few months. I also think McKinley will be our next President.[197]

Good night

W.W. Aspinwall

---

196 This may have been George S. McCook (born 1875) who, like his siblings, appears on the 1880 U.S. Federal Census but, unlike them, does not appear on the 1900 census. From Aspinwall's letter, it seems likely that George McCook was killed fighting in the Philippine-American war.

197 i.e., that McKinley will win re-election, which he did.

Columbus O[hio]; 10-8-1900

[LOVE LETTER TO ASPINWALL, WHICH HE REFERS TO AND ENCLOSES
IN HIS LETTER TO McCOOK DATED 5th SEPTEMBER 1902.]

Mr Wm Aspinwall.

My dear friend:

No doubt you have long since forgotten your correspondent, but am going to write a line anyway and ask for a renewal of correspondence and friendship. Have been in Cincinnati all summer but am at home again to stay. Have not heard from you in a long long time but want to receive from you again those same sweet, loving letters. And, dear one, they will surely be appreciated. Hope you deem this worthy of an early reply and don't forget to tell me all about your self, but dear me don't grieve me by telling me of another sweetheart in my place. And remember I am

Your devoted friend

with love, Ella.

P.S. Address me.

Miss Ella Swingh

C/o General Del.

Columbus

Urbana Ohio Jan 8 1901

[A LETTER FROM A DIFFERENT WOMAN]

Dear friend, I know you will be as much surprised to get a letter from me as I am disappointed in getting none from you.

I did not think that you would go away like you did. Do you know when I went over to the mill and found you were gone I thought I would sink through the floor? You can imagine how I felt. However, I will forgive you and pray for you every day that you may come back again soon and take your old place in the mill. Now please write and let me know how you are getting along. I hope in good he[a]lth. As this leaves me, goodby from your dearest and truest friend

Y. Meintel

When you read this, throw it in the fire and burn it, no-one need know it, only you and I.

Tahlaquah. Indian. Teritory; July 1 1901

Profs. Jno J McCook
Hartford.
Connecticut

You Will no doubt be Surprised [at my location]. This is A good Country, good Crops, plenty of Every thing, fine Spring Watter. I Am going into Oklahoma and the Comanche nation. May Marry and Get Some land, can't tell [yet]. Hope you are well.

Yours William W. Aspinwall

Neosho Newton County Missouri; July 29 1901

Profs JnoJ McCook

My Dear Friend, I Wrote you last at Tahlequah I.T. I have had quite an Extended trip Since that [time]. I went from there to Wagoner I.T. Took the fever there, I think from drinking Excessive quantities of the Aleali [Alkaline] watter they was Selling at 25 cts per fill. I was in Wagoner the 4" of July And the thermometer stood 108 in the Shade. Consequently there was not much Celebrating. On the 5", Mecury went up to 111 in the Shade. And they did not have any rain there for 8 weeks, but Since I left there I Understand they have Copious rains and the Country was Saved from a threat of famine.

The Indian Teritory is one hundred yrs behind the States in improvements And civilization generally. I Could tell you many amusing incidents of my travels through the Teritory, fixing Clocks and Sewing Machines, And my Conversations with Indians, half-breeds And Squaw Men but I have not the time at preasant.

I went up to El Reno and registered, Thinking I Would try and get a Slice from Uncle Sam's domain, but I think the Chances are Slim, as there is only thirteen thousand chances and Some of them verry poor.[198] And there was over 160 000 registered. I am of the opinion that the Chances would of been better if the Money had of been bet on Some Crap game or Country Horse race instead of being invested in Uncle Sam's lottery scheme. The numbers of covered Wagons and tents, Horse men and Crazed humanity was a Sight to behold and one not Soon to be forgotten.[199] I am going to Stop

---

198 In 1901, the U.S. government held a lottery to give away land that had been ceded by (or more accurately stolen from) native peoples in Oklahoma.

199 Thousands of people camped out at El Reno for the land lottery, causing significant sanitation problems for the local area.

here in Neosho for some time. Please Write to me here as soon as you can Conveniently. This is a healthy place And good Spring Watter. I want to Stay here And try and get the fever and malaria out of my System. The drouth [drought] has destroyed all Crops here. There was a good rain last Thursday but to[o] late. Wishing to hear from you soon.

Respectfully Yours

William W Aspinwall

Aug 20 1901; Sunday near Boston Mo

I am on my way to Sedalia, have walked from Carthage. Was at Lakeside one Week at A Soldiers' reunion Jasper County. Had a good time, Ex cons Blue of Kan[sas] Col Cloud of the 2" Kan, Cons Benton of Mo, And an old Confed with one leg Spoke, with many others.

And you wonder why there is Tramps, you Call these 'prosperous times'. You are not Educated up to the Causes of all the Social plagues. You will be in time.

Four hundred thousand men Striking for the preservation of their rights As American Citizens.[200] Eighteen free men at Tampo Flo Kidnapped in the open Streets in defiance of law and decency.[201] The wheels of trade and Commerce in the great Citty of San Francisco Standing on the drag buster.[202]

Ye Gods, What a picture for an inteligent nation to Stand and View with Calumniousness, A nation wich bosts of being the freeest and most democratic of any nation on Earth. All now is a dead Calm, But in the words of McCullough, the tragedian, in his great character Virginia,[203] It is Calmness that Eats the heart out. It is a Calmness born of Sullen determination.

For Years a Steady Undercurrent of Unrest has been flowing through [the country]. All those that are not Millionairs, or hundreds of thousands

---

200 This seems to be a reference to both the 1901 Workers' Strike in Tampa, Florida (known as "La Resistencia"), in which approximately 5,000 immigrant cigar factory workers went on strike, and the 1901 San Francisco Waterfront General Strike. Aspinwall's statement is an exaggeration in terms of the numbers of workers on strike, but captures his sense of strikes proliferating across the country.

201 On 5th August 1901, thirteen Hispanic union leaders were kidnapped by policemen in Tampa, Florida. They were put on a boat to Honduras and told if they came back to the USA they would be murdered. The Tampa strike collapsed in the face of this State violence.

202 Aspinwall seems to be using 'drag buster' to mean "a device for retarding the rotation of the wheels of a vehicle when descending a hill." See *OED*, *drag* (noun).

203 A reference to the famous stage actor John McCullough (1832–1885), who had his own production company. His biggest success was a production of John Sheridan Knowles' play *Virginius: A Tragedy in Five Acts* (1820).

people, through the tyranny of the afore Said Class, Labor and All the Common people Are now So Strong as to be almost Uncontrolable, and threatens to burst forth and Engulf the World in Chaos.

13,000 Government land Claims gambled of[f] in a lottery and Eighty thousand applicants, one half of these applicants at least were poverty Stricken and were Suffering for the necasarys of life. And the Gov took this Money they Should of Kept to Sustain life.

John. W. Bookwalter of Ohio[204] has been traveling all over Europe Studying the people. The other day he was interviewed in London And Said that a World Wide War was Comeing between the Centers of Wealth and the Common people, and that he felt that it was comeing first in the U.S. It is queer that Every person, whoever is the Subject, [and] any [meaning every] study Comes to the same Conclusion, isnt it?

There is a half-million Nomadic healthy tough Ho Bos in America. If I had them organized, Equiped and disciplined, they would make the grandest Army that Ever Shouldered a gun, And would be invincible. I would have no trouble in getting them transportation. They would beat their way and Subsist at the back doors of the towns they passed through.

Already, in Virginia, only property classes Can vote. And the Same law is Comeing in other States.

Read a paper. Travelled from Carthage, Saw paper while I was there:

'There is no other Country in the World where the opertunities for Making not only a living but Saving a Competency is so great as it is in the U.S.'

I will bet that the [newspaper] Editor doesn't half live. I found in that Country [i.e., Carthage] poverty, rags, ignorance, And the worst of hovels. His paper Shows that it is not Equiped for decent printing And that he does not Know any thing about the printing buisness. And if he does not Know his own buis, it is not likely that he Knows much of Social philosophy. But he does Very well to back up the Capitalists. They do not need to Know much.

I will Close, More Anon. Hope you are well.

Address me at Sedalia

Pettis County

Missouri

Truly Yours

William W Aspinwall

---

204   John. W. Bookwalter (1837–1915) was an Ohio-based Democratic politician and author.

Sedalia MO Sept 1 1901

Profs Jhon J McCook
Hartford. Ct.
Dear Sir

Yours of Aug "28' 1901 Came to hand last night, Also A letter you had Written to Tahlequah J.J. I Arived in this Citty on last Friday foot Sore and weary, having Walked from Joplin. MO. Came through the Country fixing Clocks and Sewing Machines, Honeing Razors, Sharpening Shears & I Started Without one Cent and Arived here with $2.00. And lived well on the way, of Course. I Slept out Some nights but I never Went hungry or dry.

I Am working here in the Woolen mills as Engineer. The Manager discharged the Engineer And gave me the Job because I Understood the Woolen buisness.

I will be pleased to have you publish Some of My Writing, it will be of interest to Many. I will Send a picture of my Self in my clothes for buisness as Soon as I Can get Around to it. I refer to my Journey from Joplin to this Citty. I was in better Condition than when in Benington, Vt. I have a number of different Experiances to relate to You about my recent Excursion at Some future time when I have more time and a better opertunity. I love to travel And A nomadic life. I always feel So good And So healthy And the life Appears to Satisfy my desires.

I would not trade my Condition with the Condition of Some of the money Kings [i.e., capitalists]. Of course, money is A nice thing, but it would not improve my health And Some of the pleasures I Enjoy.

The Ho Bos would Steal all of the beer and the Enemy would have the cars With Hobos beating their Way in their back to their Command.[205]

Fratulently Yours

Write Soon to Sedalia MO

William. W. Aspinwall

---

205 Referencing Aspinwall's imagined hobo army in his 20th August letter, McCook had replied facetiously by asking what would happen to that army if it were given free beer, delivered by train. Aspinwall's response was that the hobos would secretly ride the trains back to enemy HQ and thereby score a military victory, a reply that McCook omitted from his June 1902 edition of "Leaves from the Diary of a Tramp."

Sedalia MO 1/8 1902

Profs Jno J Mc.Cook

Kind friend

I received Yours of Oct 19" 1901 A long time Since And I Can offer no Excuse for not awnswering Sooner, only neglect. I Am Still in Sedalia MO. But have no Job. I think I Will Stay here two or three Weeks. I have not made up my mind Where I will go. It is A tough time of Year to Start out. I Am bording here with An Cow Boy Evangelist, he is runing a hotel Called the White House. And a fine Man he is, he is Just what he pretends to be. He is a great friend of Mine. He Says I have got a heart in me As big as An Ox, And A genial gentleman With it, only I will get a little tipsy once in a while, but he Says my good deeds more than Covers up all my faults. His name is Rev George Ayers.

108 South Osage St

Sedalia. MO.

If you Write to him it may be he will give you a little of my history. But will not Say any thing to him About it. I lost my position here by A younger man takeing my place And Working one half Cheaper than I would.

I Am Sorry I Can't Send You any of my photographs, I have no means. I Should like to hear from you before I leave here. If you Write as Soon as You get this, I will get it before I go.

I do hope this will find Your Self and family in good health. I am not Very well, I have got a Severe Cold. I have made many good friends here. And I Actually hate to leave here. We are having beautiful Winter weather, we had About one week of [below] zero wether so far. I have Several lady friends here.

I have one that Worked in the mill with me, A fine looking And I Know A Virtuous Girl of 20 yrs. She loved me And I loved her for her Virtue and true

Fig. 14

A
bes...

GOES TO ST. JOSEPH.

William W. Aspinwall, the accomplished woolen mill workman, will retire from his position in the Sedalia Woolen Mills. His large circle of friends regret to part company with the gentlemanly and sociable Billy. He will go to St. Joseph, Mo., Friday, January 3, and will be employed in the woolen mills there.

CAME NEAR BEING A FIGHT.

William Aspinwall was released from his duties at the woolen mills the other day and his position given to James Hawkins, step-son of Foreman Sanders. Mr. Aspinwall appears to have harbored a feeling over the matter and returned to the mill, Friday afternoon, ostensibly to search for his spectacles. When he met young Hawkins, they came together with a crash. The impact of the collision startled Mr. Sau-

ders, who took a hand in the case and in short order Mr. Aspinwall was given een the short end of the argument. He will leave for St. Joseph today to accept work.

Fig. 15

Womanhood. I disdain to tear My Self away from her, none of the Younger lothairios [Lotharios] Could take my place in her Affections. She is Allright, if I had means I never would part with her. She is a poor Girl but a lady.

I Send You Some Clipings from Sedalia, Papers Showing you what I am though[t] of here

I will Close for the preasant, wishing to see A letter from you by return mail.

Very Respectfully

William. W. Aspinwalll

108 Osage St.

Sedalia.

MO

Sedalia Mo 2/9 1902

Profs Jno J McCook
Hartfort
Ct
My Dear Professor

Your of Jan "20" Came duly to hand. I am Still in Sedalia And I think it is likely I Will Stay here Until warmer weather, anyway a month or So, Unless Some thing Unexpectedly happens.

We have been having Some Extreamly Cold Weather here this Winter, Away down below zero as far as 10 & 12 degrees.

I have Some Warm friends here. Among them is Mr G. H. Ayers the Evangelist, who I am bording with. I give him my last Pension Check in full, wich I received on the 8" inst. He told me to Consider this my Home and I am So Considering for the preasant.

I Also have Some fast friends Amongst the female Sex here. One in particular is a beautiful French Grass Widow.[206] She has become Very much Attached to me And Came to See me Every day. She told me She loved me better than Any man She Ever Saw And that She Studied about [i.e., looked for] me day & night. I am inclined to believe her because She is Very faithful And true. She is a Sweet and lovable brunette, About 30 yrs old and I am inclined to Stick to her. She was informed that I was going away And She Came to me, with tears runing down her Cheeks, Entreating me to Stay. My big heart went out in Sympathy for her.

---

206 A grass widow is "a married woman living apart from her husband, either temporarily or (sometimes) permanently; esp. one whose husband is away often or for a prolonged period." *OED, grass widow* (noun).

I Also have other fair ladies that deeply Sympathize with me. Amongst them is two beautiful maidens that are about 20 yrs old. And I Know they are true blue and Virtuous.

I have the name here of being a favorite with beautiful and lovely women. I don't Know the reason why but I think it oweing to my disposition and Kindness of heart and my good treatment of them. All ladies Seem to have Explicit Confidence in me on Short Aquaintance. And I do admire a true and Virtuous Woman. And would protect them to the Utmost point of my Ability.

Send those Papers here to my Address And as soon as you can, as I am awnsous to read them. I Sincerely hope this may find Your Self and family in good health and Enjoying this life as much as posible.

Profs, will you please inform me Your Age? I am awnxous to Know. I was born in 1845 May 25" In Champaign County Ohio; I have not a gray hair in my head And many tell me I don't look over 35 or 40 yrs old. I am a well preserved man to have went through what I have done, but I owe my good health and my iron Constitution to my love of a nomadic life. I am very healthy.

I don't believe there is one other man on Earth that has traveld as many miles in the Same way as I have And Under the Same Conditions. I don't think there is another human being or beast that has the Endurance And tenacity that I have. I Know a many a Ho bo has played out [i.e., become exhausted and quit traveling] that Started With me And I would get there Alone. I am like a bed bug. I have no wings but I get there Just the Same. And wherever I stop, I make friends. And when I want to ride I generally ride when others are put of[f].

And when I get hungry, I make up my mind to get Something to Eat, I get Something to Stay my hunger. I don't regret what I have went through, it has been a great Experience. I don't believe there is another liveing man that Can relate Just Such an Experience.

I will Close for the preasant. Wishing to hear from you Soon Again.

Fratulently Yours

William. W. Aspinwall

108 South Osage St

Sedalia

MO

Sedalia July. 17–1902

[A LETTER TO ASPINWALL FROM A LOVER, PRESUMABLY THE
FRENCH 'GRASS WIDOW' HE REFERS TO IN HIS 9th FEB LETTER.]

My Own Darling

I got an awful cold un[n]atural letter from you but I know that you know
I love you better than anything on earth. Oh sweetheart, if I could only kiss
you once more and be with you one hour. I sit and see other women out
walking and riding with thier lovers and then think of my own precious
love gone from me. Billie, I sit and look at the moonlight and think of you
until I can see and feel you. Surely there is something [that] tells you when
I am thinking of you – surely your heart answers mine. Oh darling, I love
you and always will. If I was never to see your precious face again I would
love you through all eternity.

Now, dear one, if you love me and want me with you, see if I and Will,
Fred, and Dora[207] can get work in the mill and if you think I can make a living
there. I can't come right now. I am no[t] able to do anything yet, but in a
month or so I will be able to come, if I am ever going to get well. My mouth
and throat is just one solid sore. I haven't eat[en] anything for 2 weeks but
milk. The Dr says it is caused by my stomach. Billie, you would not know
me, I am so thin, I don't look like human. But I believe if I ever get over it I
will have good health again.

Just 16 years ago today was my wedding day. And what have those
16 years brought me? Nothing but trouble and heartache. Will send you
stamped envelope and want you to write me one of Billies' old sweet, loving
letters like his own precious self.

Good By my precious darling sweetheart, love and darling – a thousand
kisses – Nell.

---

207 Possibly her children. Aspinwall seems not to have told Nell that his job had been given to
another man.

St Joseph Mo July 21 1902

Dear Sir, I received your letter of July 21st but have not the magizines, wich Are held in Sedalia for Postage. I Suppose I have had quite a trip. Left Sedalia About June 1st, have been here about one week. I Am Employed in the Woolen Mills here. Respt Yours, Wm. W. Aspinwall

2212 S 10" St

Sedalia Saturday Aug 02 1902

[ANOTHER LOVE LETTER FROM 'NELL']

My Own Sweetheart

I got your letter and card yesterday. I am always glad to get your letters, for next to seeing you is getting a letter from you. I have been trying to do something with my property to get some money. I had a chariot to trade for property in Tipton. I went there day before yesterday to look at it but decided not to trade. The difference was to be paid me in cash. I went down to Tipton on the 5 O' clock train and came back at midnight. I thought of you all the time there and while there, and about you writing me from there. I will try doing something else.

Everything here is dull as a village, both town and country. This is splendid crops of all kinds but yet there is no money anywhere. Now, Billie, size up everything and decide whether it would be best to come to be got.[208] It would not do to come unless we could all get work, and I can't unless o[209] can sell some of my real estate, for I had to borrow money when I was sick and can't borrow any more.

I am going to sell some of it [even] if I have to sell for almost nothing. I have the illness, I am not able to do any work of any kind. I have the awfulest cough and just have no strength. I don't see why I don't feel better. I sleep and eat well, when I don't cough to keep me awake – I was sick abed all day yesterday. Just over a little trip to Tipton, so you see about how strong I am [i.e., not very]. I will rest up and take my next trip to Warsaw.

I got the papers you sent me and wrote you that I did. I think it you that don't get [my] letters, for I have written you once and twice a week ever

---

208 Presumably this is asking whether it would be a good idea for Nell and Roving Bill to live together.

209 It is unclear to whom 'o' refers, but it may be a lawyer with that initial.

since I got well enough to write. While I was so sick I did not write any, for I did not know any thing about letters or anything else.

I will close, for I want to get this off on the morning mail so you will get it by Sunday. For that is always a lonesome day. Write me [as] often as you can. Yours in love – Nell

St. Joseph. Missouri Sept 5 1902

Profs Jno J McCook
Hartford Ct

Dear Friend, I have not heard from you in So long a time I am getting to have the opinion that you Are going back on me, rather letting me down Kind of Easy you Know. Or maybe not, you may be Very buisy and have not the time. I Know your duties in your profesion Are Ardurous And Confineing. But you must not forget that you have in the past Awakened in me a true And fast friendship for your Self, I have the Utmost Confidence in you and respect you As A learned Scholar and A gentleman of integrity and honor. I must Say that I feel proud that I have As one of my, I will say friend, not acquaintance, Such an honorable gentleman as your Self. I Candidly and most Emphaticaly Can Say that I respect you.

You Know from my past Writing my open and contrite heart. I am full of Emotion and patriotism, not only to my Country but to my friends. I am Very Courageous, to[o] much So. I do not fear. Yes, I do at times have a Sensation of fear, but when I Know I am right fear must Stand Aside.

I got those magizines[210] and have perused and analized Profs McCook's writing and opinion of Roveing Bill. Yes, I am a rover. I don't think there is my Equal on Earth acording to my means. Yet there is no harm in me. I would not Step on a worm or an insect to Crush the life out of it because I had the power to do, So I have often Steped over them and Said to My Self 'that Creature has a right to live as well as my Self'. I have had domestic Animals And Even wild birds Show great affection and loyalty to me in my travels. I would much prefer their Company to Some of the Hobos. I had a Valuble

---

210 He has now read McCook's description of him in the "Leaves From the Diary of a Tramp" article series, which concluded in June 1902. He does not seem to have read all of the articles yet.

New Foundland dog take up with me during one of my trips through N.Y. Where he came from I don't Know, or whose he was I don't Know. He was a fine large inteligent Specimen. That faithful Animal would Guard me And watch over me day & night And bum his own liveing. He Seamed to Enjoy A nomadic life. I tried to give him Away Several times And Sold him once or twice, but he was invariably with me the next day.

Finally, I Sold him to A Section foreman on the N.Y. Central for five dollars. I took him and tied him in the Hand Car house. The foreman did not dare to touch him. I told him to Keep him tied for Several days or Else he would follow me. I think he Kept him, for I never Saw my Nobel And fast friend Any more, but he Still is in my memory. I relate this to prove to You that my friends Are not Confined to the human family. I think that the noble Animal got a better master than I posibly Could be.

I Will Enclose you Some Actual Samples of love letters Sent me by inteligent and Worthy Women. You may think I Am devoid of the love of the Gentler Sex but you are mistaken. I am loved. One of these is from a beautiful Well formed Young Woman of Columbus, O[hio],[211] and [she is] Well Educated. The others are from a lovely young French Widow of Sedalia, Mo,[212] And She has Considerable real Estate. I Send you these in Confidence to Show You that I am not Altogether dead and also to Show you that I am not a back number,[213] As many old Soldiers Are.

Please Send me as Soon as posible the other numbers of the *Indepen[d] ent* Containing Your Articles And Extracts of roveing Bill's writings. About one month ago I was weaveing nights for the Beauel Woolen Mills here. They Shut down nights [and] I Could procure no Work in day time [so] I took a flying trip to Omaha, St Paul, Mineapolis And other Citties. I left here after bording with an Irish Widow and Oweing her a bill. After comeing back I Came to my old bording house and was welcomed by the Widow. She Said She was not Uneasy about me, that her opinion of me was that I was honest. I have So proven the Same to her. I am here And in her good graces and also of the Woolen mill Co, for I go to Work for them Again next Monday at better wages. I am so Constituted that I can make friends when I So desire.

---

211 See letter from Ella Swingh, dated 8th October 1900.

212 The woman who writes to him as "Nell."

213 Meaning, as the *OED* puts it, "behind the times, out of date, or useless." *OED, back number* (noun)

Now, Kind friend, be Sure And Write as Soon as posible for I am awnxous to hear from You. Fratulently Yours

William. W. Aspinwall

2212 South 10" St

St Joseph

Mo

Kansas. Citty. Mo; Sept 15 [probably 14th] 1902

Profs J J McCook

I Wrote You a few days ago at St. Joe. MO.

I Am again on the road. I left St Joe last Sunday Eve, one Week ago. I came Via Stewartsville, Cameron and Platsburgh. I Could not get back to Work in the Woolen mill. I was weaveing nights and they Shut down nights and it left me out [of work], So I had no other Alternative but the road again. I got my Kit together and Started out Sharpening Scissors and fixing Clocks. I Walked all the way in order to get buisness.

I notice that there is not So many Hoboes As there Use to be. I only met 4 So far on this trip. I came upon them at Plaltsburg last Weds morn, they was Eating breakfast. I hid my Pack and overcoat in the weeds and went up to them. They politely asked me if I had been to breakfast. I replied in the negative, So I was asked to partake with them, And of Course I done So. They had good Strong black Coffee, Pork Chops, tomatoes, bread and boiled Eggs. I made out my meal. While I was Eating a train Came along on the O & K.C. R.R [probably the Omaha, Kansas City and Eastern Railroad] going to Cameron. Two of them [the hobos] got away [on the train], the other two got left [behind]. One that got left was a young fellow that was a Crip[p]le, one leg of[f] about the Knee. I asked him how he lost his leg, he replied 'in a Saw Mill'. He told me that they had all been drunk the day before and that the Marchall had ordered them out of town. I believed him, for I Counted as many as ten Emty quart bottles and other bottles laying around the fire, good Evidence of a drunk And hilarious carousal.

The Criple Came and Stayed with me Until I left him. He was to[o] tough for me and did not Suit my taste. They were Undoubtedly all of them toughs and Would Steal or do anything. I don't like to be caught in Such Company, for the Minions of the Law Would Say 'birds of a feather flock together'. I don't fear being molested by Officers when by my Self, or with Some one or others I Know are all Straight. Today is Sunday.[214] I am Sitting in a box car Just across the Mo River from K.C, all alone. Sunday is my day of rest. I don't Know what way I will go from here, but think I will go South for the winter.

If you have not written to me at St Joseph Mo, don't do So Until You hear from me again. I am getting Considerably discouraged. I am getting to[o] old to hold a Job with the youngher folks, I Can't Stand it as I Use to.[215] I mean tramping and Work. Still, I am healthy, but I ain't got the Vim I use[d] to have. I don't Know What Will become of Me. I Suppose I will be found dead on the road Some of these times, no friends or any one to care for me. If I had my life to live over I would live a different life. There is nothing like a home and friends. As it is I am an outcast, nobody and no one cares for me.

There is a time for all things and my tramping days are getting Very Monotonous to me. I don't Enjoy it any more. But I Can't help my Self, I have nothing And what Can I do? If you have no money you are nobody. I Slept in box cars and Straw Stacks and Suffered Considerable from the Cold at times.

How did you appreciate my love letters I Sent you in my last [letter]? I Sent them to prove to you that I am not devoid of lady friends. I am going to Enclose in this a letter from the Young lady that I Saved from drowning at Jonesboro, Ind while at the Marion Soldiers' Home. You will find the dates in the letter. I also will Enclose a letter from a Cittizen there. I do this to prove to you that I will risk my life for others, Especily When they Are helpless.

I have lost my right to the Soldiers' Home. I and a Captain of a barracks had a fuss. I Called him Some bad names and they dishonerably discharged me. He was an impudent and overbearing officer and illiterate. But to[o] much drink was my fault. This was at Marion, that is why I left there. Fratulently, Wm. W. Aspinwall

Sept 16 [probably 15th], I am in K.C. May get a Job here. Address me here. If I don't Stay here, will have mail forwarded.

Yours, William

---

214 If so, then the date is the 14th September.

215 Aspinwall was fifty-seven years old when he wrote this letter.

St Louis MO Dec 21 1902

Dear. Profs. I am living with a Welthy Widow, [in a house with a] Brown Stone front. She has five Daughters Grown. I am the only man About the House. Have plenty of the best. Should like to hear from you. Hope you Are well & your family.

Wm.W.Aspinwall

4334 Washington Bolivard [Boulevard]

St Louis. MO.

St Louis Mo Dec 30 1902

My Dear Profs JnoJ McCook

I rec Yours of "24" inst. I Could not imagine What was the trouble [when] you did not awnswer but supposed your time was Employed in Something more important. I rec the two numbers of *Independent*, thank you very much for them. I miss one number, the May.

You Seem Curious to Know how I Came to be here. I may as well tell you how my time has been occupied Since I Wrote you my last in Kansas Citty. I procured a Situation in that Citty as assistant Shiping Clerk for a prominent Chemical Co but only temporary, that was the understanding.

I worked My Self into the good graces of the Secretary, who got Explicit Confidence in me. He Even Entrusted me to do the banking for them and attend to their mails. They finaly though[t] to Cut down Expence [and] I had to go, but this Sec in the name of the Company Gave me a gilt E[d]ge letter as to my honesty, Sobriety and buisness intelligence. The next day, Sunday, I awnswerd an add in the *Kansas Citty Times*. They wanted a man to Sell Sewing machines from a wagon, 'a hustler and a man well Recommended'. I Concluded I Could fill those requirements. On the next Tues I got a letter from a firm in Louisiana MO, the Suda Hardware Co, and they Wanted me to Come at once if I Could bring good letters. I had Some letters from Ohio Woolen Mills And the Sedalia W.M. I Enclosed them in a letter and Sent them to the Suda. H. Co, telling them I did not have the price to pay the R.R. fare. I got a Special Del. letter the next day Containing ten dollars And [was told] to Come at once. I was duty bound to go as the Suda. H. Co was So Considerate as to trust to my honor, and me A Stranger to them. I felt proud And Elated. I took the first train East on the C & A [Chicago & Alton railroad] and got to Louisiana the next Morning. I at Once went to the Store [and] asked for the Manager. I was Escorted to the Office, to Mr Suda.

Fig. 16

I told him who I was. He Shook hands with me & at once Commenced to talk buisness. He had three Wagons & teams, one team was Selling ranges. I Got ready with a Mule team And four Sewing Machines. I had an Elegant outfit, a Splendid team and wagon. I Started out that Evening and Went out, Mr Suda Advancing me Expence money. I went N.W. About 50. M. to New London Centre and through the rough Country Along Salt River. And What times I and that mule team had. My Experiance in two weeks would make an interesting book and no fiction. I have not time to relate it now but I Know it Would interest You. I Worked hard for the Co and Sold two Machines in two Weeks. You Simply Could not Sell them at their prices. Farmers are no fools now[a]days, there is a Mail box at Every Croos Roads.[216] I Stoped all night with a number of Well-to-do farmers And they all became Very much interested in me, in my reminissences & naratives of travels.

& the next morning I would Say, after hitching up, 'Well Sir, What is my bill?'

'Wall [Well] if you had it to pay I would not Charge you any[thing], but as You are working for A rich Company I will charge you $1.50.'

The Co tellagraphed me to Come Home. I drove in on Sunday, and Monday went to the Office and reported.

Mr Suda Says 'Mr Aspinwall, this is Just an Experiment With us. We though[t] we Could do Some buisness in that way, but I am Satisfied now

---

216 Meaning that the farmers are in communication with the outside world, and so know how much the sewing machines should cost, which was apparently less than the Suda Hardware Company charged for them.

We Can't.' He Says, 'I am fully Satisfied you worked hard and to the interest of the Co' (wich I did). I Wrote to them Every day. He Says, 'you done better than the others, you sold two machines in two weeks, the others Sold none.'

He Says, 'I am going to quit that part of the buis.'

So I was out [of work] again. They Settled up with me and gave me five dollars more than was Comeing to me and gave me an Excelent letter of recommendation as to my Honesty & Sobriety. I Came to St Louis, put an add in the *Globe Democrat* [St. Louis *Globe-Democrat* newspaper] & *Post Dispatch* for position as Janitor, detailing my Abilities. I got about twenty Awnsers. The Manager of the Monticello Hotel, A Benton family resort near the World's Fair Grounds, Came After me. I Worked for them two Weeks. The[y] wanted me to Work from 4 in morn till ten at night. I Concluded that was to[o] much. You Know my independence, I am like A hog on ice: if I can't walk, I can lay down and roll. The next place I went was to a Col Inglestraus, who was a Col of a Missouri Millitia Regt. [He] had a wife that was to[o] high toned to Sit down. I formed a dislike for her at once And did not hesitate to let her Know it. The Col begged of me to Stay With him. He Said I was honest & inteligent, but I went one Sunday afternoon.

I told her in these Words: I Says 'Lady, Slavery was Abolished in America in 1863.' I Says, 'you had better Get Some one in my place.'

'When are you going to quit, William?'

I replied, 'At once!' And I went.

And then in A day or two I Came here. They treat me Kindly And don't Consider them Selves above me. They Are Welthey but they have Got Some Common Sense and Judgement with it. There is nothing to[o] good for me, I get the best that is going And they trust my Honor & integrity. We live in the fashionable West End of the Citty and they have a Grand & beautiful home. I Am getting well Known Amongst the Whelthy Class in this Citty and I get a letter Every day or so from Some of them Wanting me to Come & live with them. Honesty goes a long way & Knowing how to do things. I would like for you to See my letters of recommendations. I like 'Leaves from a tramp's diary', it is all right, all true, And no White Washing. You rather praise me at times but you told all truths and the half was not told.

I must Close, for it is late. I hope this letter will interest you. I hope you had A Merry Christmas & will have a happy new Year's. Yours,

Wm W Aspinwall

4334 Washington Ave

St Louis Mo

St. Louis Mo. 5/3 1903

Profs JnoJ McCook
Hartfort Ct
Dear Profs

Today is Sunday, So I have concluded to write you a letter. There is not much that interests me around a citty any-more, my experiance and travels have been so extensive. I don't see much lately that has much interest for me. I do not enjoy loafing around a saloone or card playing or gambleing. I love nature, I can enjoy life in the mountains all alone and along some beautiful stream of watter. I spend a great deal of time meditating on the different problems of life as it exists in different human beings and the brute creation [i.e., animals]. I was out last Thursday, April "30 ultimo,[217] viewing the grand parade and the dedication of the great World's Fair.[218] I was fortunate enough to get to shake hands with Teddy Rossefelt [Roosevelt] and Ex-Pres Grover Cleaveland, of wich I think I was highly honered. I was stoped by a detective before I got to them but Teddy saw me [and that] I had a Grand Army button on the laple of my coat. Teddy says, 'Let that old Soldier come to me, I want to shake hands with him.' And we Shook hands and a hearty Shake it was, and also was Grover Cleavland's shake. Teddy is all right in my estimation. There is no flies [that a]light on him. Grover is a grand old man, he is to America what Gladstone was to England. I also shook hands with a number of the foreighn embassadors and other no-tables [notables]: Cardinal Gibbons, Bishop Potter, Gen[eral]s Miles, Fred, Grant, Gov[ernors] Odel, Gates, Dogharty, Bailey & others to[o] numerous to

---

217 'Ultimo' in this context means 'last month.'

218 The Louisiana Purchase Exposition, or St. Louis World's Fair. The Fair was dedicated on 30th April 1903 but, following delays, not officially opened until 1904. After its official opening, it would be attended by almost 20 million people and would have a significant impact on intellectual history and popular culture.

mention. But after all my trouble in getting to them, of what benefit is it to me? I am only a pebble on the beach of humanity. I have shaken hands with many notables before: Garfield, McKinley, Lincoln, Grant, Sherman, Logan and among others, and I don't observe any stable benefit, only the consolation of haveing Shook hands with them. And they was the World's greatest men. After all they was only human beings like myself, with faults just the same. There is none perfect, no, not one, So says holy writ, and in my opinion it is a candid truth. I am yet making and cul[t]ivating garden, but last Thursday evening's frost killed my grapes & beans, cucumbers, and done other damage. I have some young chickens. So you will observe I have something to occupy my time. I get nervous and uneasy at times and want a change. When I fully make up my mind then I will change but the world is getting old to me. There is nowhere to go to see anything new or strange to me. The World's Fair will have no special attractions for me. I am living now in sight of the grounds.

I have been reading some rather scientific books lately & I have about come to some conclusions. A clam is a clam. So was its ancient ancestor. Ideas influencing other forms of life have been of [no] interest to the clam unles[s] productive of some forcible disturbance, in wich case the clam closed its shell and waited for death or a return of peace. Eternal life as a clam will be the reward of that kind of morality and a clam-bake will never cease to be among the posibilities. I hear and read a great deal about the deploreable habits of our age, of how the use of tobacco, morphine, beer, whiskey, coffee [etc.] are all tending to deteriorate our race. I find that an antelope can eat an unlimited quantity of tobacco and enjoy it. A pigeon may swallow morphine, wich if taken in one tencth the quantity by us would cause our death. And there are many other striking facts.

What do they signify? They are evidence of our lack in functional power. One learned writer says he believes it is in the cause of truth and its advancement to say that those who acquire the ability to drink unlimited amounts of whiskey and to commit all other sorts of excesses and survive them are doing more indirectly to elevate the race than many a worthy person who never committed a physical so-called sin. He says 'I urge the use and performance of verry many things now hurtful, but to do so well within the bonds of endurance. The field for pos[s]ible pleasure enlarges with every added capability, as with the youth who learns to smoke.'

The misery of the people is due to the sins, negligences, and ignorances of those who rob them of their earnings and grow rich upon their moral ruin and physical destruction. Is it true that poverty is the result of idleness of improvidence and of vice?

The inhabitants of this earth is divided into two great masses, one party does the work [and] the other the theoretical part of it. Theory will not do alone but theory and actual practice will assimulate sometimes. I believe from my own personal observation, wich has been extensive, that the poor are much more temperate than many of their critics would have us believe. If mere doing [great deeds] is to get us praise, what laudable and industrious men were Alexander [the Great] and [Napoléon] Bonapart[e], [yet] the seeds they sowed were evil. It is all verry well for the author or member of Congress to abuse us as idle drifters and drunken Bums and hobos. You must remember our vocation is somewhat exciting. But not pleasant, ennobling, nor renumerative. Often I have heard proffessional men say 'what does the hobo know about work?' About as much or more than the proffessional men. At the same time we must acknowledge that there are many professional hobos that never work, but they are only a small per cent of the large and flourishing society of hobos. It is easy to tell a hobo to go to work and be industrious and contented in that walk of life to wich Providence has called him. But it would be neither easy not pleasant to take his place and show him how it should be done, and I tell you frankly I believe that if Providence called a Senator or a Bishop [or] a Profs to do the Hobo act [i.e., live and work as a hobo], Providence would have to use a trumpet or the gentlemen would not hear. The hobo he must have change and relaxation. If you will make hobos do work and drudge [then] you must and shall provide them an antidote to the same, or they must and will provide the antidote themselves.

Wishing to hear your comments soon.

I am Fratulently

William W. Aspinwall

Hoofman [Hoffman], Clinton County, Illinois; May 18 1904

Prof Jno J McCook

My Dear Friend, I have not heard from you for Some time. I Just Came out here from St Louis a few days Since. I came here to pick Straw Berries but I am to[o] Soon for that buisness, they are not ripe yet but will be in a few days. I am Stoping with a farmer by the name of Hadley. He has a fine lot of Berries. I plowed for him Yesterday and hoed potatoes last Monday. I have a Hobo with me by the name of Ed. Kelly. I met him at Bellville, Ill, This Side of St. Louis. He is one of these Cowardly toughs, does all of his Work with his mouth. Except his Sneaking & Stealing from drunks & t[h]rough open doors & Windows. He is what you Call a Sneak thief. He tells me he Just got out of the St Louis Work House last Sunday after doing three Months. The Police Catched him Robing a drunk man in St Louis. He is rather a bright fellow on Som Subjects but dull on others. No doubt Was Well raised. I have got him well Under hand [i.e., in control]. He is afraid of me, what I Say is law. But the fellow likes me & will do any thing for me. He is about 28 or thirty yrs old. I had a Varried Esperiance in St Louis the last winter, but Came through the winter in good Shape. I have Seen all the World's Fair, having Spent Several weeks in and around the Grounds. Was in there opening day. And Several days Since. The Fair is not Completed yet and won't be Until Some time in June. St. Louis is full of Hobos from all quarter[s] of the globe. I am tiard of it And [having] seen all the Exposition I want to, I will go from here to Chicago, thence to Michigan to Pick Berries, thence to Niagara Falls, thence South for the Winter. Please write as soon as you receive this to this Address, as I will be here two or three Weeks. Resp, Roving Bill.

[WRITTEN UPSIDE DOWN AT TOP OF LETTER]

We Sleep in the Barn in the Hay And Cook out Side. I Stand in well with the farmers but they have no Use for my Partner.

Hoffman Ill; Aug 11th 1904

Prof J. J McCook

Dear Sir

Wm Aspinwall come to me last may (him & Kelley) together as hobos without money to pick strawberries for me (Kelley picked last year for me.) I let them have money to buy food with, so they would stay & pick for me. As they come 10 days before they [the strawberries] were ripe, I give them 2 or 3 days work to do.

Wm Aspinwall drew his pension, $18.00, while he was here. He bought Liquor same day. Gave me $15.00 of it for safe keeping. But asked for it next morning & that was the last I seen of him.

Kelley went of[f] with him, owing me $1.50 & I am quite shure I seen Kelley this morning, Beating his way on a freight train going west.

They together beat me is all I know.

Yours Respect,

S. S. Hadley

Mr. Aspinwall has done work for me on sewing machines. He is all right.—Frank J. Chapman.

Take your repairing of any description to Billy Aspinwall, Stelle block, east side of square, one door south of Lunn's Furniture store, and get it done in a mechanical manner.

Fig. 17

McLeansboro Illinois 6/28 1904

My Dear Friend JnoJ McCook
Hartfort Ct

I rec yours of "24" inst Yesterday. I am Well & running A repair Shop here. I Send you Some Clipings from the McLeansboro *Times & Leader* Concerning my buisness. This is a temperance Citty, not a Saloon within ten Miles of it. I am Strictly Prohibition now. I have not touched a drop of Spirtitous or Malt Liquors in two months. I intend, God Helping Me, to forever Abstain from its Use as a beverage. I am fully Concious of the fact of the injury I have Sustained from the to[o] Copious Use of intoxicants throughout my Care[e]r, both financially & Mind & body. I Selcted this Citty on Acount of its being less [i.e., having fewer] inducements to indulge.

There is a number [of people] here that order Beer by the Keg, and other Stimulances [stimulants] by the quantity. I was asked once Since I have been here if I did not want to go in on a Keg of Beer, but I replied I had no Use for it. So I have not been troubled Since. I Am determined to let the Stuff alone. It flashes on my mind Verry brilliantly the trouble it has caused me in bygone years: the Excel[l]ent positions I have lost, the hard times it has caused me, Struck with Poverty, Vagrancy, all through its Use. I Know I am competent to go in good Society and have lots of Good friends if I let it alone. I do not Want for the Stuff And feel better. So I Can Conceive no reason Why I can't let it alon[e]. I have Some good friends here amongs the better Class of People. I Went to Church last Sunday Eve through the Solicitation of Some of My friends. What do you think My dear friend, do you not think that I have got the Staminy [stamina] to do as I have made up my mind to do?

I have not received the letter you Sent to Hoofaman [Hoffman]. I will write the P.M a Postal today.

I think the Japanese Are manageing their Side of the War Admireably. I believe they will Eventually drive the Russians out of Manchuria and win the War, Unless some Unforseen disaster happens [to] them. I Wish the Japs Victory, for I think the Russians Are tresspassers & Should be driven out.[219]

The Japs have Out Generald [generaled] the Russians in Every Engagement so far by their Celerity[220] of Movements & secretiveness. What is your opinion?

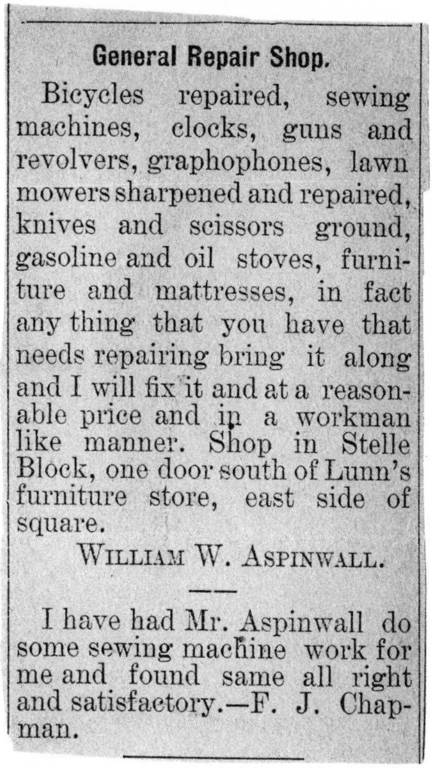

Wishing to hear from you soon. I remain, as Ever, Sincerely your Friend. I think my Hoboing days are about over.

Very Respectfully Yours
William. W. Aspinwall

General Repair Shop.

Bicycles repaired, sewing machines, clocks, guns and revolvers, graphophones, lawn mowers sharpened and repaired, knives and scissors ground, gasoline and oil stoves, furniture and mattresses, in fact any thing that you have that needs repairing bring it along and I will fix it and at a reasonable price and in a workman like manner. Shop in Stelle Block, one door south of Lunn's furniture store, east side of square.

WILLIAM W. ASPINWALL.

———

I have had Mr. Aspinwall do some sewing machine work for me and found same all right and satisfactory.—F. J. Chapman.

Fig. 18

---

219 Aspinwall refers to the Russo-Japanese war of 1904–1905. The Russians were indeed driven out, leading to political upheaval and the first Russian Revolution in 1905. Racial epithet aside, Aspinwall's favoring of the Japanese here is notable because many U.S. newspapers saw the conflict as a race war and were demonizing the Japanese as "the yellow peril."

220 Meaning speed or swiftness.

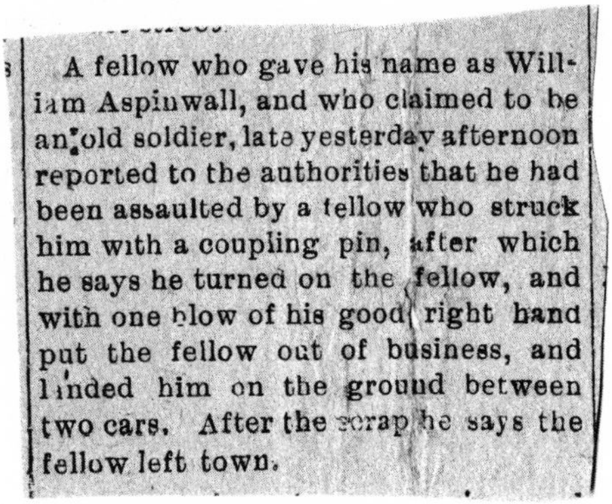

A fellow who gave his name as William Aspinwall, and who claimed to be an old soldier, late yesterday afternoon reported to the authorities that he had been assaulted by a fellow who struck him with a coupling pin, after which he says he turned on the fellow, and with one blow of his good right hand put the fellow out of business, and landed him on the ground between two cars. After the scrap he says the fellow left town.

Fig. 19

Answer Soon Please; McLeansboro. Illinois. Aug 11 1904

Profs JJ McCook

My dear friend, Yours of August 5" inst received Yesterday. You are quite Excuseable for not awnswering Sooner, for there is none of us perfect in all things. Paul Says there is none perfect, no, not one. I am proud to inform you that I have not touched, tasted or handled any intoxicating drinks Since I formed my resolution three months ago. And I want to inform you, my dear friend, that I am more determined than Ever to Abstain Absolutely. I have no inclination Whatever or hankering After the Stuff. I have been invited & tried to be persuaded to partake by Would-be friends, but I have at all times Absolutely refused, So now they have quit me and don't trouble me any more. I Am now beginning to See and desire the benefits. I have A nice Shop and a good Stock of repairs & Sundries for Bicicles, Sewing Machines & Guns & Revolvers and [am] doing a good profitable buisness. And Excellent Credit. The largest Hardware Company in Chicago, Hibbart Spencer & Barttell [Bartlett] & Co, Send me anything I want on 60 & 90 days time, and I have unlimited Credit in my own town McLeansboro, Ill. I am Also Gen agent for the Regina Music Box Co of New York, and have one of their 490.00 machines in my Store, With 100 Records at 60 Cts Each. I am also Gen Agent for the 19.00 Washer & Wringer Co of Binghamton New York and have Some of their goods in Stock. And Gen Agent for the Stewart

254

Iron Works of Cincinnati, Ohio fencing. And Agent for a number of other Specialities. I am Considered a Good, reliable buisness man. I Carry new & Second Hand Guns & revolvers, new & Second hand Bicicles & Sewing machines & Keep All Sundries for Some & repair them, Also Clocks & type Writers. I am getting Work from far & near. I have A Staunch friend here in a Mr John Lunn, A local Methodist Preacher & such. He And I use to work together years ago in Woolen mill at Piqua. O[hio], he was a Loom Boss. He is Very much interested in my Abstaining. He Knowed me in my balmy days. I use[d] to work here Years ago in a Woolen mill, wich is Still here but not running. I was Supt and made a good record as to my Abilities. The owner, Mr. Robert Meadows, Still lives here and owns the mill yet. He is Well to do and Comes in to See me often. He Says I made him more money With his Mill than any man he Ever had, and Says if he was Younger he Would back me up & Start the mill Again. He is about 80 yrs old.

You Can Write to Mr Lunn and ask him if I ain't doing Just as I tell you: he will back me financially for any amount, in reason. I often go to his house and dine with him.

I Am pleased, my dear friend, that you take Such an interest in My Success in Abstaining from Strong drink. I Am Proud to be Encouraged by Such Gentlemen of intelligence as you are. You Know better than any other person my faults, for I have made honest Confessions to you, wich I never done to any other person, not Even my Parents and near friends.

My dear friend, I promise you upon the honer of a man, that I Will forever hereafter Abstain from intoxicating drinks. You Can rest assured I mean Just what I Says. I thank you Kindly for your Excelent Advice And I Will Profit by it and heed it.

You will Understand by this letter why I came to McLeansboro. I Cam[e] here fixing Clocks & Sewing Machines, Walking with a Small Hand bag with Some tools & repairs, I did not have a Cent. I walked from Hoffman by the way of Centrailia and Mt Vernon Ill. I got my Pension Check at Hoofman & [Ed] Kelly Knowed it, so he insisted on going with me. I Knowed What he wanted, he wanted to Rob me or pick my pockets & probably would of murdered me to get that money, if he had of been man Enough. I was onto him and Kept my Eye on him at All times. We had it made up to beat our way from Centrailia [Centralia] Ill to Chicago, but I had no notion of going, I simply wanted to get Clear of him. And he Suspioned [suspected] me. We went down in the R.R. yards at Centrailia for the purpose of Jumping a freight for Chicago, in a lonely place, nothing but Strings of box Cars on

Side tracks. I noticed him Stoop down and pick up Something. It was a coupling pin. He ran up to me and Struck me with it along [the] Side of the head. The lick Stuned me butt I recoverd quickly, Clinched him and threw him between two Cars and pumeled him good and Strong. He begged like a baby. Finally I let him up and let loose of him and he ran like an Indian. And Soon got out of my sight amongst the Cars. He was a perfect Coward. He was young And Stout-built but was no ma[t]ch for me & I am 59 yrs old. He did not have the Sand; he no doubt would of murderd me if he could of got the Advantage of me. That was the last I saw of Kelly. I afterwards went into Centrailia and met the marshall. The Side of my head was Swolen and I was bleeding Considerable. My head was Sore for two weeks or more. The Officer Asked me my trouble, notieceing my head. I Explained it to him, not as Grafically [graphically] as I have to you. I gave him Kelly['s] discription. He telegraphed Ahead towards Chicago to the Officers in the different towns. I Stoped in a Hotel that night. About midnight the Officers Came and awoke me. They had a man they thought was Kelly. They thought he had Changed Cloths, but it was not the man. I left the next day and I have not heard of him Since.

The Japs Are Succeding Admireably. I believe they will Capture Port Arthur soon[221] & probably Kunapattein's[222] Army. They will at any rate give them a good drubing.

I believe Roosevelt will be Elected by a large majority this fall.[223] What is your Opinion? Teddy is my man. There is not much political Excitement here. I will send you a Cliping from a Centrailia paper describing partially my Adventure with Kelly. I am Under the impression I Sent you a Coppy of the paper at the time.

I will Close, it is late.

Sincerely Yours,

Wm. W. Aspinwall

Roving. Bill.

No. more

---

221 The Russian army at Port Arthur would surrender on 2nd January 1905, following a siege that had begun in April 1904.

222 Aleksey Nikolayevich Kuropatkin (1848–1925), Russian Minister of War.

223 Having become President following McKinley's assassination in September 1901, Roosevelt would win re-election and continue as President until 1909.

McLeansboro. Ill. 9-7-04

Profs Jno J McCook
Hartfort Ct
My Dear Friend.

I Am beginning to think you are forgetting me Gradually. I have not heard from you for over two months. You did not Awnswer my last but I Still think of you. I am well and living a Sober, Straight-forward life, and intend to so live from now on, to the End.

Intoxicating liquors does not temp[t] me any more, I am done with it.

There is a Merchant here by the name of F. H. Chapman, a friend of mine. A periodical drinker, he Came in to my place Under the influence of liquor with two pints of Whiskey And tried Very hard to induce me to drink with him. I told him 'No Sir', but thanked him Kindly.

After Seeing that his Arguments prevailed nothing, He Says 'I don't blame you.' He is a Sensible & a Smart Man And Sells more goods than any other two Stores in this Citty. He Says 'I am a friend of Yours, dad, and you Can have Any thing I got.'

I have Many offers of drinks but my awnswer is always 'No, Sir, I don't touch it' & [I] thank them for their Courtesies. I am done with the liqur habbit. I See my former follies. I am getting numerous friends here with the best People and my buisness is Growing rapidly.

I Enclose you one of my late Photographs. Don't you think I am improveing? I Should like one of your Photos. We have been Coresponding a long time And Are good friends And [yet] I have never Seen Your face. Good night.

Sincerely, Your Friend,
William. W. Aspinwall

Fig. 20

McLeansboro Illinois 11/25/04

Prof. Jno J McCook

Dear friend, I rec your last letter [and] was much pleased to hear from my old invisible friend. Once Again don't forget to Send me the Photograph, for I am awnxous to See your physoagmony [physiognomy, i.e., face].

Would it be posible for you to get me the magazines Containing 'The Diary of a Tramp'? The Series You sent me got wore out, lost & destroyed. I am in better Shape now to take Care of them. Will pay for them if I Can get them.

I am Still in the Temperance ranks and intend to remain so. Alcoholic beverages has no Charms for me any More, I am done with the Stuff.

I have an offer from the largest Publishing House in the World, Thomson & Hood of Chicago, to travel & collect for them and to represent them Generally. $25.00 per week and Expences. They Say they are well pleased with the information they posess of My Self.

The St Louis *Daily Star* will publish in their Sunday Edition my Photo & a partial History. I represent them here, and also their reporter.

I have a Horiscope of My Self from Profs Harris Edisonn,[224] Binghamton New York.

He Says I was born Under the Planet the Moon, wich Signifies the Gift of Hope, and the Zodiac Sign of Gemina [Gemini], Wich was Also the Sign of the Empress of Russi[a] and other famous people. My next lucky years [will be] 1905 & 1908.

He told me my disposition out & out. He Says I am Easily Suited & Can adapt My Self to the different Conditions of life. He Says I am amply Able

---

224 'Professor' Harris Edison (real name Edson) was an astrologer who advertised that he could foretell people's future. Calling himself a 'prophet,' Edison would conduct mail-order readings. A born grifter, Edson changed his name to Edison to associate himself with the credibility of the inventor Thomas Edison.

to manage my own Affairs and More Capable if I do not lean on others and he Says [I should] remember this. He Says I was not born for hard or dirty Work And should take life Easy, Everything Will Come My Way in due time.

He Says I will be Successful in any Calling where a Clever brain & quick fingers are required.

He Says I Should not depend on friends. I will always Stand by and defend them wright [right] or wrong.

He Says I am a natural lover of the opesite Sex[225] and to be Careful.

He Says I have A bad habbit of Seeking pleasure And fortune Without thought of the Consequences.[226]

Among Many good traits he finds me diligent, Kind-hearted, Sympathetic And [that I] have a quick Understanding.

He Says I Should be more Economical and Give away less, as I commonly Allow my Sympathies to overrule my Judgement, And that I Show Charity Where it is Undeserved.

This, he Says, Shows me to be well meaning and Kind but that I Should never Allow my Self to Carry it to Excess. Myne, he Says, is an Unusually important life in many respects. And that he Should like to go further in to the details if posible.[227]

Resp, Your Friend,

Wm W Aspinwall

[WRITTEN UPSIDE DOWN AT TOP OF PAGE]

Profs Edison Under Stands me, don't He?

---

225 This is not a particularly profound insight.

226 Nor is this.

227 Presumably, only if Aspinwall is willing to pay Edson a further fee for his services.

Bluffton Indiana; Dec 10 1905

Profs JnoJ McCook

Hartfort. Ct

   Dear friend, I left McLeansboro. Ill about Sept 1st last. I got me a plug [meaning old and worn out] Horse & Wagon And Started over the Country. When I got to within 30 miles of Indianapolis Ind, My horse died and I Sacrificed all my Stuff and Wagon.

   I am here now night Clerk in a Hotel. This is the town I went into the Army from. My old Capt and Comrades live here.

   I Should like Verry much to hear from You Again.

   There is not many Hoboes in this Country now, About all [of them have] gone to Work, or Some other Avocation.

   Write Soon. As Ever,

   Wm W Aspinwall

   C/o Commercial Hotel

   Bluffton

   Indiana

Nathinal Mil Home Marion Indiana; April 6 1906

Profs Jno J McCook

Hartfort

Ct

Dear Sir, I received your letter of Jan 4" 1906 at Bluffton. Ind.

I have been Around Considerable Since that time. I left Bluffton Soon after receiving your letter and went to Spence[r]ville & Lima Ohio, from there to Toledo. O. In Toledo I went broke and walked from Toledo to Delphos and Spencerville, About Eighty five miles, and landed back in this Home about two weeks ago. Quite a walk for a man 62 years old. I have got the nerve and Staying qualities left in me Yet.

The Surgeon of the Home, Dr Miller And his Assistant, Examined me. They was Surprised in the way I was preserved in manhood & health. They found I had heart trouble, Wounds & Dr Miller told me if I would take an oath and live up to it not to Use intoxicating drinks, he would insure me to live Until I was Eighty five or ninety years old. He Said one good drink would finish me, my heart would not Stand it.

I think I will take the Doctor's Advice, I think he is Correct.

I found A new Governor here. Gov Justin. H. Chapman of Connecticut is dead and buried in the Circle here.[228] George. W. Steel[229] of Marion Indiana And former Member of Congress from this district and former local Manager of this Home, is now governor of this Home. And the old Soldiers in the Home Are Verry much dissatisfied with his Administration here, with the Exception of a few Succors that hold petty offices.

Geo. W. Steel is a tyrant And devoid of humanity, And is not a fit person to govern Old Men. He has old decrepid Men, 80 yrs old And upwords, on the

228 At the Marion Home, the earliest graves were arranged in a concentric circle.

229 George Washington Steele (1839–1922), who had been an Indiana Congressman from 1881 to 1889 and then again from 1895 to 1903.

dump diging in di[t]ches, wheeling Ashes out of the Power House, and gives them 60 and 90 and 120 days. He Can't reform these old Men and he Should Know that Much. He is Simply making their lives miserable And driving them into lunacy. I Understand there is an imense petition being goten up here and will be Sent in to Congress protesting Against the Management. Gen McMahon is Considered no better than Steel and there is no Apeal to the bord of Managers.

Steel Keeps old Men locked up for 60 and 90 days and when they do go out they go Under Guard, the Same as Convicts. A great reward for patriotism and Gun Shot wounds.

Geo. W. Steel was Elected to Congress by Votes from this Home at one time but he Could not get more than 100 Votes in this Home now, and he Could not Carry one town Ship in his old district. Congressman Londis[230] Showed him lately that he was not in it now. I am affraid there will be another Gov. Smith Case of the Levenworth Home. Some of these old fellows will be driven to desperation if there is not a Change here.

I will Close for the preasant, Wishing that you are well and Enjoying good health.

I noticed that You was one of the favored few at the Langworth Weding at the White House.

I will Write Again as Soon as I Can get Some P Stamps. I have Something of more interest to tell you.

Respt Yours,

Wm. W. Aspinwall

---

230 Frederick Landis (1872–1934), who succeeded Steele as Indiana Congressman in 1903.

National. Military. Home. Marion. Indiana; June 4 1906

Profs JnoJ McCook
Hartfort. Ct.

My Dear Friend, About three months ago on my arrival here I wrote you but have not yet received any reply. I cannot conceive the trouble. You have heretofore been very prompt. It may be that I have ceased to be of any interest to you.

I enclose a cliping from the *Indianapolis Star*, wich I think will interest you. Maybe you can diagnose the disease the kid has got, if it is a disease.[231] I suffered under the same halucinations when I was a boy, runing away from a good home at different times, and as you know I have kept up the travel ever since. But I will never make a Robber or a highwayman or burgler or a drunkard, I don't take to the calling. I have often been insisted on by experts to join them but after mature deliberation have refused and taken a different direction. I never feared the Law but simply followed the dictates of my conscience. If I had of been a detective I could of made some important arests in my time. Just last winter on my trip from Toledo to Dalphas, I was in the company of a gang of cracksmen [robbers] overnigh[t] at the little town of Holgate, at the crosing of the B.O.R.R. [Baltimore and Ohio railroad] and Clover Leaf R.R. The next morning I eat breakfast with them and took a different direction from the way I knew they was going. I learnt what they was from their conversation to each other. I simply took items and kept my mouth shut and got away from them. I did not learn their names, only nic[k]

---

231 He encloses an article about an eleven-year-old British boy who ran away from home and traveled the world by stowing aboard a ship and later freight-hopping across Canada and the U.S. Several writers of this time period referred to such activities, including the wanderings of hobos, as being caused by a disease or mental fever that they termed 'wanderlust.'

names, they all had an alias. They was good-hearted fellows and treated me verry kindly. Two of them had been in the regular army. They took to me because I was an old soldier.

I will close by wishing this may find you in good health. Please don't neglect writing soon.

Verry Respectfully

William. W. Aspinwall

Nath Mil Home Marion Ind; July 22 1906

Profs JnoJ McCook

Dear friend, I received your letter yesterday. Was truly glad to hear from you once more. I was glad to hear of your good Work towards the purification of the ballot box in your locality, but that is not the only locality [where] Such work would be of benefit. It is high time All good Cittizens were getting Arroused on the Above Subject in this land of ours. That is, if they want to retain the blessings of a republic.

Yes, I Am yet in the Soldiers' Home and with all the privalege And good treatment I Could Ask for. Governor Geo. W. Steel and My Self have become fast friends. I Am all right if they will only Come at me in the right Way. I am a free born American, not a Russian, And will not Endure Rusian treatment [even] if the President of the United States so ordered.

No Sir. I never was Excluded from this home for drinking.[232] I left the Home on My own Ac[c]ord.[233] The then-Governor Chapman wanted me to do 75 days labor without pay for Chastising one of his Sucks [sycophants], a Captain of a barrack, A regular popinjay. I refused to do the Work at the time And ordered My papers and that At once, as an American Cittizen has the right to do. I have since done the Work, As that was a Condition of my readmittance, but you Can Just rest Easy that it was not much Work I done.

I have mailed you today A Hoosier democaic [democrat] Weekly [news-paper that was] recently Started in Indianapolis, And Some Clipings from

---

232 In 1898, McCook had received a letter from then-Governor Justin H. Chapman stating that Aspinwall had left the Marion Soldiers' Home while "under charges for being drunk at Sunday morning Inspection." Presumably McCook has asked Aspinwall about this incident.

233 This is technically true while also being disingenuous, since Aspinwall seems to have left in order to avoid charges of drunkenness.

the Marion *Leader*, my Compositions. I think there is going to be a political revolution in this State [in]the Comeing Election.

I take General Dan Sickels[234] View as he Expressed himself at one time here in Marion. He Said he had been a democrat All his life but he was not A democrat that year, That's my View of the Situation. I have been A Republican All my life but I Ain't one this year.

I will Close for the preasant as I have Considerable more Writing to do today. And I will give you Some time in the near future the acount of my leaveing McLeansboro and my horse dying on the road and my final Colapse Entirely.

The father of the young lady that I Saved from drowning Some years Ago near here Came to See me. Also the daughter, who is now married and got a family.

I Enclose you two letters that may interest you. Please return them Some time at your leasure.

Yours. Respectfully

William. W. Aspinwall

---

234 Daniel Edgar Sickles (1819–1914), soldier and diplomat.

Soldiers' Home Marion Indiana; May 7 1907.

My Kind Friend Jno J McCook

I received your letter and I Must Say I was pleased to hear from you, but I was Sorry to learn that you have not been in good health. I notice Very plainly by your Writing that you Must be failing. You are nearvous, are you not? I Sincerely hope you Will Soon recover from your indisposition. You are not advanced in years Sufficiently, if I remeber your Age Correctly to Ef[f]ect your nearves, or your health in General.

I Am not going away from the home June 1". [I am] to remain only on leave of Absence to Visit Some of my Grand Children in Ohio. I am getting along nicely here in the home. I have the good will of the Officers And my Comrades. I don't drink Any more Malt Vineous [i.e., wine] or Alcoholic beverages. I did not take no plege to Abstain. I had become disgusted with its Effects on my Self and others. In fact I never was in love with the taste or Smell of the Stuff. Nor do I have A hankering after it, as many Say they have. The canteen is closed And has been for Some time. I Use[d] to be in favor of A Canteen but have come to the Conclusion that a Soldiers' Home is better of[f] Without the Canteen. Of Course in Some respects it was a benefit, in others A neauasance [nuisance]. It Created more of a fund for Amusement And probably graft. Four-fifths of the members of this home Are Abstainers, or Use liquor in a moderate way. The remaining fifth never Got my pension, the Canteen got it all. And Some times they come out in debt to it. There is a number of Blind Tigers[235] near the home that sell Beer and rot gut to old Soldiers and Cittizens, Contrary to Stringent State laws, but they Seem to prosper. I think the detectives And Sheriffs notify the proprietors of the Tigers a few hours before they make the raids on them, to

---

235 According to the *OED*, "an establishment at which intoxicating drinks are surreptitiously sold." *OED, blind-tiger* (noun).

hide their Wet goods. Anyway there is never any Arests. If there is an Arest there is nothing [that] comes of it. Many old Soldiers get in trouble with the Athorities of the house by imbibeing to[o] freely at these Blind Tigers.

Your Work in preventing bribery in Elections I hope will prove of great benefit to your Citty, but Hartford is not the only place where Such Unfair work is practiced. We need Such Societies or Committees in Indiana. But the people are begining to get their Eyes open.

Sincerely Yours

Wm. W. Aspinwall

[WRITTEN ON THE NEXT PAGE]

The human Will that force Unseen
The offspring of a deathless Soul,
Can hew Away to Anny goal:
Though Walls of granite intervene.

Nathional Soldiers' Home; Johnson City. Tenn;
July 9 09

Profs John. J. McCook
Hartfort Ct
My Dear Friend

I have not heard from you for so long a time I am feeling awnxous about your health & [meaning etc.]

I have quit drinking intoxicating liquors. I have not touched Any for 14 months. I became Completely disgusted with the Stuff. I took no Pledge [n]or did I make Any promises to Any one, Simply made up my mind What I would do And done it. I am now Sergeant of D. Company Mountain Branch N.H.D.V.S [National Home for Disabled Volunteer Soldiers] And [am] considered the best Sergt in the Home. My Captain tells me that I will be the next appointed captain of a Company and I think he Knows, as he is in close touch with Head quarters And the Govenor. My Captain Says he is proud of his Sergeant. And I Know you will be when you Know all the particulars.

Please write Soon.

Sincerely, your friend,

William W. Aspinwall

Nathional Soldiers' Home Johnson City; July 16 1909 Tennessee

Profs Jno J McCook.

Hartfort Ct

My Dear Friend

Your wellcome letter arrived yesterday. I was truly glad to hear from you, I though[t] something might of hapened [to] you, I had not heard from you for so long a time. You Seem to think that I may break away and go to drinking again some time in the future but no, never, my dear friend, god helping me. I never had any particular likeing for Alcoholic liquors, it was the Company I was in and the state of mind I was in. I have fully made up my mind and you can rely on what I am telling you. I never felt as I do now on the liquor question. I am disgusted and Ashmaed that I was foolish for so long a time and wasted the best and most of my life. I never think about the Stuff any more, only when I have to deal with some poor Unfortunate drinker as a home oficial. Yes, I begin to Apreciate the Advice and pleadings of friends and men like you, along with my mother's pleadings that has passed to Eternity long ago.

I have the Confidence and respect of my superior Officers here. Our Governer is a Verry Staid Old gentleman. He is A Tennesseean and Was

Judge on the bench for a natural life time. His name is Colonel John. P. Smith. I send you a Bristol Tenn Paper and enclose some home views, wishing you well and to hear from you soon again. I have a fine room to my self on the 1ˢᵗ floor, shch [such] acomodations as I have there would Cost $3.00 per day in your City.

Verry Cordially Your Friend,

William Wesley Aspinwall.

nathional Military Home.

Johnson City.

Tennessee

Don't you think I am improveing in penmanship? I am studying the Palmer method.[236] But I am some nervous.

---

236 A method of handwriting developed by Austin Palmer in his book *Palmer's Guide to Business Writing* (1894). Aspinwall's handwriting improves noticeably during these years, although it deteriorates again towards the very end of his life.

William W. Aspinwall
Nathional Military. Home. Johnson City. Tennessee.;
Sept 13 1909

Profs J.J. McCook,

My Dear Friend, I write to tell you that I am going to leave Tennessee, The 1ˢᵗ of Oct, to go to Kiefer Oklahoma, to be employed by the Prairie Oil Co, I have been employed by them before. I have a Son out there in their employ for the last ten years.[237] I want to make some money. If I can stand the exposier [exposure], I will Succeed, I regret to leave bahmy [balmy] Tennessee, I have made numerous friends here, and after I leave I will have many pleasant recolections of this locality. Captain Milburn, our quartermaster, inspected my Company. D. on last Saturday.

After he was through, he placed an arm around me and Says, 'William, Your company and quarters are first Class', and says 'W[illia]m you ain't going to leave us, are you?'

I Says, 'Yes Captain, I am going.'

He pulled me Closer to him and Says, 'I do love a good man, you Come over to my House, and See my Self and family.'

He is an old Major in a Tennessee Regt that Served in front during the Civil war. I got a great Write-up in the *Bluffton Daily News*, Bluffton, Indiana by the Editor, an old *Chicago Tribune* Corespondent.

He Says, in part: 'no finer Student of literature or better News Paper writen ever Came out of the 47 Indiana, nor in fact no better Soldier was ever on its rolls than great hearted Billy Aspinwall and his old comrades will

---

237 This seems to be a reference to his son Ernest Mack Aspinwall (1875–1947), who in the 1920 census is listed as working as a 'driller' for an oil company in Tulsa, Oklahoma. My thanks to James Morgans for pointing this out to me.

be glad to learn that in the closeing days of cheerful Billy's life's campaign he is happy, Strong and thriveing. He has fought his old enemy whiskey to the last dich, not Touching a drop for more than two years. Handy with machinery and experienced in handling Engines he was recently offered employment With the Prairie Oil. Co. in Oklahoma, a place he held after leaveing Bluffton. His friends think he is getting to[o] old To Stand the exposier [exposure] of an Oil man's life, and would rather he would stay in the balmy clime of old Tennessee.'

I will send you a copy of the Paper if I can get it. They only sent me one, quite a send of[f] and I did not ask for it. Respt Yours, W.W. Aspinwall.

Soldiers' Home Danville Illinois; Dec 30 1910

Profs J.J. McCook
Hartford Ct

My Dear Profs, I have not heard from you for Some time. I was thinking this Morning over old times and you Came prominently before my Mind. I Sincerely hope you enjoyed a merry Christmas & will enjoy a Happy New Years'. I left Okla[homa] about three months ago. I got disgusted there with the dry Hot wether & poor Watter & the Prohibition Laws. There is as much whiskey Sold in Okla as any other State in the Union & no License to benefit the taverns or communities & Sold at double the price as it is in Licensed towns & Out Laws & Gamblers are running the Dives [here meaning drinking establishments]. Rotten Poisenous Booze at that. No Laws to Govern or Prohibit.

If there is Laws they are not

[August 1902]

William W. Aspinwall

As Officer of the day National military Home, Tenn. 4 yrs in front in Ciwel War. member Union Vetteran Legeon, and Junior Order American mechanics and Nathional Optqumistic League & Physcel success Club. And a terror to Bums and Transgressers.

Fig. 21

enforced. The Sheriff & marchalls Stand in with the Dives. Bottled Beer that Sells for 5Cts in St Louis, Sells for 25 Cts in Okla. You observe how the Prohibition Laws work in the much Heralded Prohibition State of

Oklahoma. It is all a Farce & a dettriment to the State. If Prohibition would only Prohibit I would Say "God Speed.' But it don't and is only a dettriment to the prosperity of towns in the State. I noticed the Same State of Afairs existed in Prohibition Tennessee while I was there. And I notice Local Option has the Same Dives & Bootlegers to Contend wi[t]h in Illinois & Indiana as they have in Oklahomo & Tennessee, besides Upseting Politicks & relegating Political Parties to the Scrap Heap. It is a Conceded fact that the abolishing of the Canteen in the Regular Army & Soldiers' Homes has been a Sad Afair.

I notice an acount of a man in Hot Springs Ark[ansas] who has lived thirty two days without eating, trying to Solve the hight Cost of living problem. "Bosh". He Should of turned Hobo – The Hobos have Solved the High-Cost-of-living problem many years ago. And now there is an army of about Half a Million in the U.S. If Capitalists Combine [then] the working Class Should Combine & Bum Hand Outs.

Wishing to hear from you Soon. Verry Respectfully Yours,
William. W. Aspinwall

Nath. Mil. Home Danville Ill.; March 30 1911

Profs J J McCook
Hartford. Ct.

My Dear Sir. I received a letter from you Some time Since. I notice from the trend of your letter that your opinion is that I have again gone to the Bow Wows [i.e., the dogs] through Strong drink; but you Are mistaken, I have no more Use for intoxicating liquors. The Stuff has no Charms for me any More, I have become disgusted with the taste, Smell and affects [effects] of the Stuff. It is very disgusting to me when I observe Old Soldiers making beasts of themselves through the Effects of the Stuff. But the old Soldiers Are to be congratulated, as the large majority of them are Sober, decent law-Abiding Old Gentlemen.

I often think that if I Could live my life over again, I migh[t] live it differently and better. I Spend much time looking backward over the multitude of mistakes that I have made and deviseing ways and means by wich I might of avoided them. I try to pick out the loose Ends I have droped And wipe out the blurs that I left on the walls of my memory. I really find enjoyment Sometimes in building Air-Castles out of the Wreck of my recolections and in going back and patching up the rents that I made in the Wet[238] of life.

But all of this is vexation of Spirit. The past is myne no longer and Shall never be returned to me. All that is left to me is the little Space of time that lies between today and eternity. I find it is useless to mourn over the past but I have the future in wich to make amends, With all the mistakes of the past to warn me.

I Shall make fewer mistakes in the future. Let the devil hang on to my past if I give it to him, but I won't let him get a mortgage on my future. I don't wish for the other fellows' Job nor for a return of wasted days. I will make

---

238 Aspinwall may mean 'tent' here.

the most of What is left. If I could dig a better post-hole than Any body else I might Some day dig a railroad Tunnel or a Panama Canal. Put a new Suit of Cloths on Some men and a pink neck-tie And you have elevated them beyond the Ken of man in greatness, while with others the advancement to a little position of trust over their fellows causes An enlargement of the Skull that Should be made [a] felony Owing to the extreme danger of the top pi[e]ce bursting And messing up their immediate territory.

Ancient history, with what it teaches us, is a very interesting Subject.

The rise And fall of nations, with the Cause and efect of Some together, with the attendant wars and blood Shed makes good reading. Many peopl do not Know as much about the Common bird that pe[r]ches on the house Top or faithfully Works away in the fields, exterminating the noxious weeds and the deadly insects, as they do about the Sphynx of Egypt or the Ancient languages. And [they] take no interest in this faithful insect and weed destroyer, unless if the person be a lady [and] the bird has been Slain, Skined And Stuffed and adorns her head gear. The featherd Tribe[239] Shall disappear beyond the distant hills and follow his best friend, though Savage he was, to the happy Hunting Grounds.

Faithfully Yours, With best wishes for Your health,

William. W. Aspinwall

Late H Co 47" Indiana Volls

Co I

Soldiers' Home

Danville Ill

---

239 i.e., Native Americans.

Fig. 22

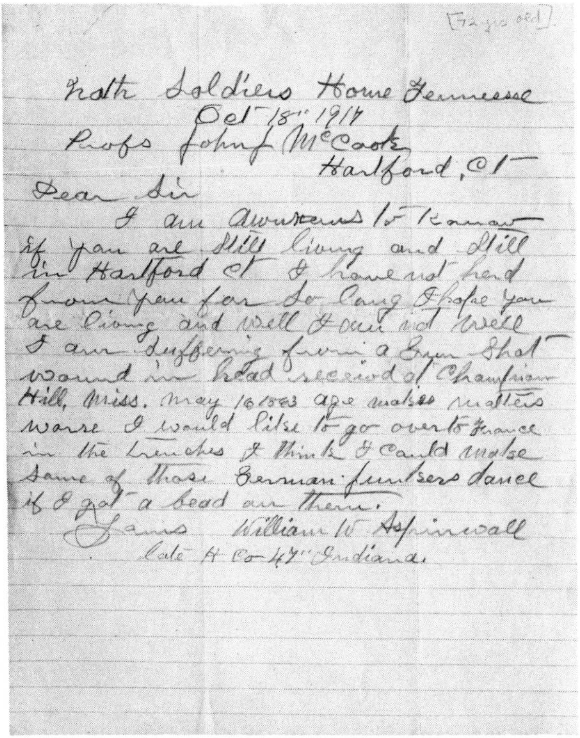
[72 yrs old]

Nath Soldiers Home Tennesse
Oct 18" 1917
Profs John J McCook
Hartford, Ct
Dear Sir
I am Awnxous to Know if you are Still living and Still in Hartford Ct I have not herd from you for So long I hope you are living and Well I am not Well I am Suffering from a Gun Shot wound in head receivd at Champion Hill, Miss. May 16 1863 age makes matters worse I would like to go over to France in the trenches I think I Could make Some of those German Junkers dance if I got a bead on them.
Yours William W Aspinwall
Late H Co 47" Indiana.

[72 yrs old][240]
Nath Soldiers'
Home Tennesse;
Oct 18 1917

Profs JohnJ McCook
Hartford. Ct
Dear Sir

I Am Awnxous to Know if You are Still living and Still in Hartford Ct. I have nor herd from You for So long, I hope you are living and Well. I Am not Well, I am Suffering from a Gun Shot Wound in head receivd at Champion Hill Miss. May 10 1863. Age makes matters Worse. I would like to go over to France in the trenches.[241] I think I Could make Some of those German Junkers[242] dance if I got a bead on them.

Yours William W Aspinwall
Late H Co 47" Indiana.

---

240 This note in square brackets, which appears on the original letter, may be by McCook.

241 i.e., the Western Front during World War I.

242 "A member of a class of aristocratic Prussian landholders, who dominated the Prussian military and later also the government of the German Empire." *OED, junker* (noun, 1).

STATE OF OHIO
BUREAU OF VITAL STATISTICS
CERTIFICATE OF DEATH

61589

District No. _34_ File No. _____

stration District No. _4154_ Registered No. _435_

_____ St., _____ Ward

(in a hospital or institution, give its NAME instead of street and number)

spinwall

_____ St., _____ Ward.

_____
(If nonresident give city or town and State)

_7_ ds.   How long in U. S., if of foreign birth?   yrs.   mos.   ds.

MEDICAL CERTIFICATE OF DEATH

16 DATE OF DEATH (month, day and year) _Nov. 14_ 19 _21_

17.
        I HEREBY CERTIFY, That I attended deceased from
Sept 25, 19 _21_, to _Nov 14_, _21_

that I last saw h _im_ alive on _Nov 14_, 19 _21_

and that death occurred, on the date stated above, at _9.30 p_ m.

The CAUSE OF DEATH* was as follows:

Chronic Myocarditis

_____ (duration) _____ yrs. _____ mos. _____ ds.

CONTRIBUTORY _____
(SECONDARY)

_____ (duration) _____ yrs. _____ mos. _____ ds.

18 Where was disease contracted
   if not at place of death? _____

Did an operation precede death? _____ Date of _____

Was there an autopsy? _____

What test confirmed diagnosis? _____

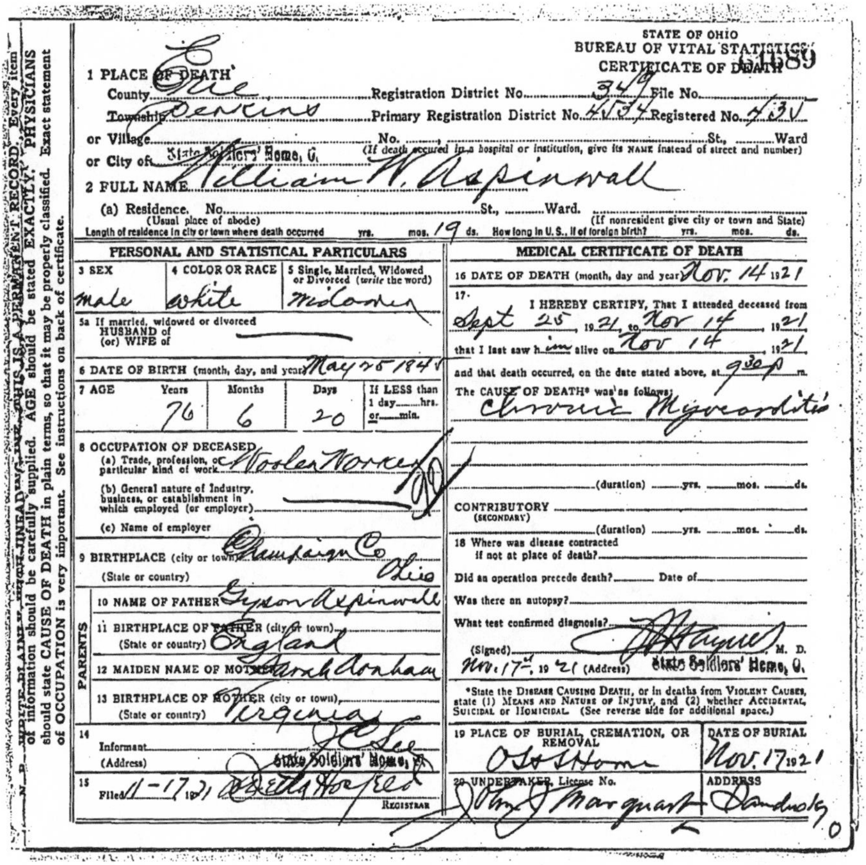

Fig. 23

Leaves from the Diary of a Tramp

I

FIRST ACQUAINTANCE

By Prof. John J. McCook

OF TRINITY COLLEGE

[No one in this country knows more about tramps than Professor McCook. It is with great pleasure that THE INDEPENDENT is able to announce to its readers that this article will be followed from time to time by several others—all making a pretty complete autobiography of a tramp —EDITOR.]

EARLY in May, 1893, on a bright, pleasant morning, I saw two men coming toward me whom I took to be tramps. One of them was white, the other black. I suffered them to pass; then, after convincing myself further by a rear view, caught up with them and broke the ice by the usual salutation:

"Out of work?"

To which the usual reply: "Yes."

Then followed other inquiries, as "Been on the road long?" "Where do you come from to-day?" and the like,

through which assurance was made doubly sure, and the foundation laid, as our legal friends say, for the somewhat delicate question, "Do you want to earn a quarter to-day?" "Yes? Well come up and have your picture taken for me." Both instantly and cheerfully consented. And it was not long before a white "hobo" and a youthful "shine" were added to my slowly increasing gallery.

After the sun had done his work upon the outward man I applied myself, after my customary fashion, to secure a vision of their inward make-up. This was soon over so far as the "shine" was concerned, for he was neither very learned in the ways of his calling nor very communicative. It was otherwise with "Connecticut Fatty." And the back passageway leading out of the protographer's room, if it had had ears, would have become the depository of some very curious facts—things that are so and that are not so, I dare say—for the conversation lasted not far from four hours.

At its close, having heard much of the

"Roving Bill"

traveling facilities and rapid flights of the genus jumper Tramp, I placed in the hands of "Connecticut Fatty" six postal cards, directed to me, which he faithfully promised to drop in the mail, with suitable memoranda, from time to time, on his way toward the far West.

In a few days one of these came back, much soiled and marked with spots suspiciously suggestive of housekeeping without napkins. It now lies before me and reads thus:

"JEWIT CITTY, CON., May 18, 1893.
"KIND SIR: I received this Postal Card from a gentleman of leisure I met on my Route; he said you was seeking information from the fraternity of Haut Beaus. I suppose you are writing some Book. Now if you want any points on this kind of a life I can give them to you. I went into the U. S. Army in 1861 when but 16 years old; served all through, have been on the Road ever since Discharged; been across the Pond to all European Ports to Calcutta and Bombay; in all Australian Ports, California. Just come from the South, was in Florida, West Indies and Mexico all this winter.
"You can write to me at Providence, Rhode Island. Gen. D(elivery.)
[" Signed] WILLIAM —— ——."

I preserve, and shall preserve, as near as may be, his spelling and capitalization, because I wish to let him make his own impression with as little editing as possible. His name is withheld. We shall call him "Roving Bill"—of which the first part at least can be vouched for as being his favorite road name. And in signing it he generally prefixes the formula, "Yours Fratulently."

My friend of the photographic gallery and the long colloquy had given a name very different from the one which this missive bore. Also he had professed to be headed West, while this was from a point east of Hartford. What did it all mean? I suspected a trick. Was it mere mystification for the pure fun of the thing? Or had the fellow thought it over and concluded that he had found a literary chap with whom a stroke of business could be successfully done? How was I to find out? I feel very proud of the scheme which, after long and painful weighing of pros and cons, I contrived to evolve from my inner consciousness.

I inclosed a copy of the photograph of "Connecticut Fatty" to the Providence postmaster, explaining my difficulty, stating that within twenty-four hours I should send a registered letter to "Roving Bill," and requesting the postmaster to direct his registry clerk to compare the person who should apply for it with the picture, of course, without letting the applicant become aware of the inspection, and detail the result to me.

In due time the obliging official informed me that the letter had been called for, that the person was obviously not identical with the original of the portrait, and that before receiving the letter he had shown papers which convinced them that he had given me his true name, that he was a pensioned soldier, &c.

This reply gave me a pang, for I had written very rudely to my wandering friend, on the supposition that he had been trying to deceive me, and now feared that a coldness would have been thrown over his spirits which would check all further disposition to epistolatory correspondence. But in this I reckoned very decidedly without my host, for I am now in possession of a parcel of let-

dence, had, as was to be expected, a business end. But I immediately replied that there was absolutely no money in the affair, and that the only compensation to be hoped for was the satisfaction and distinction which might result from possible mention of the writer and use of his facts in anything I might chance to print concerning tramp life. In a following letter he returned to the charge. Whereupon I appealed thus to him:

" If it were to become known—and it would

Connecticut Fatty's Shine

Connecticut Fatty

" There's just two kinds of people in the world that's really happy—the millionaire and the bum "

ters from his hand more than six inches through by actual measurement. They vary in length from a brief message on a postal card to fifty-one pages of closely written commercial notepaper.

Their author has revealed to me with excusable pride that he was once the correspondent of a rural weekly newspaper. And I cannot help reflecting with something like bitterness upon the blindness of fate which has diverted from fields of journalistic activity one capable of turning out such unlimited supply of " copy."

My first letter, which was from Provi-

—that I had been paying you in any way whatsoever there would not be lacking persons suspicious and ill-natured enough to say, ' There! One more greenhorn taken in by a tramp! Spinning yarns to order for pay! The old story! ' And you could not afford to expose yourself to this, any more than I."

This had the desired effect. And I am able to say that from that day to this not a hint has fallen from him in regard to compensation. And he has had neither pay nor reward. From time to time blocks of paper have been sent, of which

Water Works Men, West Hartford, Conn.

every scrap has come back; and postal cards and stamped envelopes have been furnished—always addressed, however; and they, too, have come back. And once ten cents' worth of tobacco was sent, which arrived after he had passed through the place addressed, and since, following his invariable custom, he had directed the postmaster to forward his entire mail, the poor fellow had fourteen cents postage to pay on that. As an off-

sonal friend. I wrote to all three and from the first learned that Bill had been a brave and faithful soldier during the Civil War, had been wounded three times, and was drawing a deserved pension. From the second it appeared that Bill had been taken from the road into the writer's factory, had been promoted to the charge of a room, and had at last taken to drinking and disappeared. From the friend I learned that Bill was

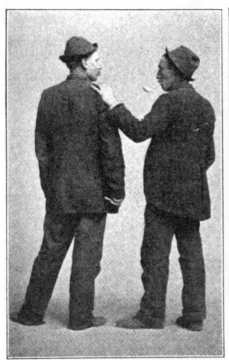

Sample " Water Works " Bums.—" A week's work won't kill you "

Sample " Water Works " Bums.—" Work didn't suit "

set to which I sent him at Christmastide a modest pipe, which I hope he is using now and will never pawn.

Whatever, therefore, may be said of the letters it cannot be alleged that they belong to that mercenary, or commercial, order of literature, which we are given to understand is driving out the old-fashioned ideals. " Roving Bill," at least, is in literature for the love of it.

Before quoting, it is proper that I should record one fact. In his first letter he gave the name and address of his captain, of a former employer and of a personal friend.

of a respectable family; had been a wanderer from his sixteenth year, and that his stories of travel were entirely credible.

Learning that one of his wounds was in the head, I further inquired whether any symptoms of brain disturbance had ever showed themselves, but was answered, from his captain, by an emphatic negative.

I take pains to make these things clear in advance, not because anything has been related by " Roving Bill " that is in the least improbable. On the contrary,

I have knowledge of more extraordinary doings and happenings from other tramps. But this is a sketch of experiences and feelings during a tolerably long itinerary, which possesses the advantage of being in the tramp's own words, written at the moment, on the spot; and it is important that its author's genuineness should be well established.

He shall speak for himself and I shall simply claim the privilege of weaving into his story from time to time what may occur to me from my own observations in confirmation or correction.

"I think," he remarks in his first formal letter, dated Boston, May 26, 1893,

"I think I can say without doubt that I have tramped and Roamed about more in my life than any man of my age in America, went through all the Vissisitudes and Hardships it is Posible for a Human to stand and live. At the same time I am Hale and Harty."

Hale and hearty after thirty-eight years of hardship and vicissitude! This is one of the mysteries of vagabond life. Go into the police station of a nasty night and you will see these people come in dripping and soaked. They pull off their shoes and jackets, lie down on oak plank or cement floor, and in a little while are sleeping as soundly and quietly as you contrive to do on your wire mattress. You may hear snoring, but rarely coughing. And they all but invariably admit that their health is good. This in spite of alcohol, in spite of licentiousness, in spite of scant clothing, in spite of seeming precariousness of living. The grip winter, about 1100 out of 1350 of them questioned by me admitted that their health was good, at the same time that three-fifths of them also admitted that they were intemperate, and divulged places of lodging ranging all the way from camping-out, barns and box-cars to shanties, boarding houses and hotels.

How explain it? Do all but the most robust die off? I doubt that. Can the explanation possibly be in this—that their life, as compared with the average, is free from worry and responsibility? "There are just two kinds of people in the world that are really happy," said one of them to me—it was "Connecticut Fatty"—"the millionaire and the bum." "The only time I ever feel worried," he added, "is when I am going into a bad city." He meant a city whose police officials are rude and inconsiderate in dealing with wanderers. This man attached prime importance to keeping the digestive organs in good working order, always carrying medicine with him for that purpose, and one of his most earnest objections to the Southern country was based upon the alleged indigestibleness of the meat and bread of that locality. "They give you nothing," he said with scorn, "but pork so fat it fairly shakes, and that coarse yellow bread," meaning corn bread, I suppose. From this criticism it is evident that he had not wholly mastered what may be a further element in the health of the vagrant—moderated desires.

It does, however, seem to be a serious fact that the parasite life, of which this is only one phase, is conducive to longevity, which means health. Life seems to be protracted beyond the average in our almshouses, and Paris pauperism shows similar phenomena. The curious will be interested in consulting the Hartford report on outdoor alms on this point.

But we must not be led away by our meditations. And, returning to "Roving Bill," we are called upon to note his protest:

"Now I want you to distinctly understand me. I am not a Bum. I would rather be kicked than go up to a House and ask for something to eat. I have went hungry a many a time almost starved before I would ask. I often wished I was more of a Bum when I was good and hungry, but I am constituted of to much Pride and Manhood."

How, then, has he been in the habit of supporting himself?

"I traveld all through the South and the West Indies and Mexico last summer, fall and winter fixing clocks and sewing M(achines). I have taken up Mush Faking or Umbrella mending since I left N. York and am traveling on that now. I go pretty hungry at times in this country, as there is to many of a kind."

And so he announces that he is "going up into N. Hampshire, Vermont, and Maine," "and then," he says, "I will strike West to the World's Fair."

"To the World's Fair!" You remember the Columbus naval fête in New York City, of course. One morning early I found an extremely seedy and rather unusually aged wanderer serenely washing off the patrol harness at the Hartford police station in courteous acknowledgment of his indebtedness to the city for a night's lodging. He had come from Meriden the day before, he said. And thereupon I remarked: "I suppose you took in the naval parade there?" "Of course I did," he replied, with a tone of gentle impatience at the superfluousness of the inquiry. "Why, you won't see such a thing as that again in the course of your whole life."

That was quite true and I felt it deeply,

A Common " Shovel " Bum

for I had not been able to go myself, and realized that my chance was now gone. He, however, had contrived to go, having given up a job to that end, and seemed in no wise downcast, albeit not particularly gay—even tho he was returning afoot. For he had become intoxicated and then, as he said, his companion, with whom the journey from Boston to New York had been made, had, in company with others, robbed him of all his money, and left him to shift as he might. This, by the way, is a common incident among these wretched folk.

The " butty," or " buddy," is by no means the ideal friend.

As for the Chicago trip. It was common at the time among philanthropists and others to speak of the great multitude of men attracted to the Western metropolis by the temporary work afforded by the colossal constructions of the fair and their equipment; and there is much in that. But there is also much, if not more, in that insatiable curiosity which impels the average tramp, as far as my observation goes, to flit about in search of every novelty, be it spectacular or industrial. Knowledge of a new piece of public work spreads among them with incredible rapidity, and they flock toward it from every quarter—partly, it is true, because such work is as easily laid down as taken up, and fixity in work is as little agreeable, to say the least, as fixity in any other condition of existence. But partly, also, I am persuaded, because they merely want to nose it over and feel of it, see whether they like it or not. Generally they do not like it. I have conversed with a considerable number of the men lately employed on the West Hartford water works reservoir, and with but one exception, as far as I now recollect, they criticised the food, the lodging and the character of the work. Several I met had run in on Saturday night and got two or three meals on a promise to begin on Monday, and had then retired. They had come a considerable distance merely to inspect, and the discovery that they were able to " beat " the contractor out of a square meal or so had evidently added zest to the enjoyment of refusing the work on the ground that " it didn't suit." One of the hands had heard of the job in Australia, so a fellow laborer told me, and had come all the way from thence to make trial of it. They rarely stayed longer than a week.

Lowell is our friend's next writing-place. " I did not fare well on Sunday," he says.

" I had one five cent loaf of Bread and 5 cts. worth of Bolona, all I had yesterday and it is 11 A.M. and no Breakfast yet. Slept in Box Car last night."

I had written for his photograph; so he says:

" I will try and get you a photograph just as soon as I Can raise the Stuff. I go from

PROF. JOHN J. McCOOK

here to Nashua and Manchester, N. H. Can write to either. Will write a letter in a few days.

"Respectfully, ROVING BILL."

This was a postal card. Quick upon its heels came the promised letter—thirty-two pages long, closely written. I had asked concerning his method of locomotion during his recent travels. He answers:

"My Present Business will not allow of me going by Rail. If I went so I would not get Mush-Faking or Umbrella mending to do. I have walked ever since I left N. Y. City. Came by the way of Bridgeport, New Haven, Hartford and all intermediate towns and then to Willimantic, Jewett City. I have asked no one for any alms since leaving New York. Have made enough to live by going hungry at times. I have slept most of the time in the Haut Beaus' 'Sweet Home,' the friendly Box Car; and nights that are too cold for the Box Car I look along the R. R. for a secluded nook and build a fire out of R. R. ties and sleep as comfortable as I would in a king's palace; and when it rains I find a box Car or some Barn. The day before I arrived at Jewett City I stoped one day and two nights in a Barn; it rained all the time.

"You wanted to know if I ever Rode trains. I have rode on the Baggage Car, just in rear of the Engine and on the Engine under the Head Light. in Box Cars and between Cars, but never under Cars, as that way of getting along always looked to dangerous for me and I preferred to walk; but still there is many a one rides the trucks and rods. I have seen them on."

How they ride will appear in my next.

HARTFORD, CONN.

Leaves from the Diary of a Tramp

TRAIN JUMPING—A DIGRESSION ; NATURE ; THE SOUTH

By Professor John J. McCook

OF TRINITY COLLEGE

PERHAPS I shall be permitted to be led by this last remark of our friend into a brief digression on the subject of " train jumping," which is the most characteristic feature of American tramping.

Our friend has been walking a good deal of late, because his business required it. But he, too, has " ridden " not a little. And it may be stated as a general proposition that the Ho-Bo only walks when walking will better answer his purpose.

For shorter distances and ordinary occasions the freight train is employed. A place is selected where the up-hill grade compels a slackening of speed, and then with a quick run and spring the train is boarded—nearly always successfully, but occasionally there is an accident ; the railroad returns suggest that there may be an aggregate mounting into the thousands annually. A man who recognized me at the door of St. Bartholomew's Mission in East Forty-second Street on " sandwich-night," told me that while on the way down from Hartford he saw a tramp run over by one train as he was making ready to jump another. And it was a gruesome reflection that one of them made : " When we fall off there is a fight between the towns as to which shall furnish the box ! " To stay on a train thus boarded, whether it is made up of box cars or open ones—" gondólies " they call these latter—requires, of course, some sort of consent on the part of the hands. They may be able to

evade apprehension for a while, by running about over the cars, but observation they can hardly hope to escape. It

" Dublin."—" I'm too old to jump any more "

follows that the brakemen must be actively or passively consenting parties— considering especially that the general

The Feast.—" Jerry " Leads Off.—" What happy times if we was all in the woods together "

rules of all the companies are against the practice.

A young student friend of mine, finding that he had lost the last passenger train of a Saturday night, brought into requisition skill acquired as a boy in "stumping" other boys of the town in

A Hopper Gondola.—" Providence Bob " and " Philadelphia Shorty "

jumping on and off passing trains, and "jumped" a freight. Great was his amazement when the brakeman, instead of rebuking or threatening him, began, from his throne on the brake-wheel, to give him pointers as to the best way of hanging on. The mystery was explained when on approaching a grade the real brakeman roused himself from his reclining position, a car's length away, and directed the man at the wheel to let off the brake and later to put it on again. The wheelman was, in fact, a tramp who was working his way, under tacit contract with the brakeman, and he had taken my friend, who was all in summer white, for some sort of a fantastic, dude-greenhorn apprentice Ho-Bo!

Not infrequently the brakeman demands compensation of other sort for

winking at the violation of orders. On which account I have more than once heard it said by tramps that with tobacco, or a pint bottle, they can go anywhere. This is not mathematically accurate, I dare say, but there is no doubt something in it. One man has told me that in default of these creature comforts inquiry is sometimes made after personal property, as knife or razor, and on one occasion his necktie was demanded.

There are, of course, all kinds of brakemen: and they even vary greatly with the road. But the life of freight brakemen is a rough and dangerous one, neither inviting nor fostering gentleness of character. Many of them have passed to and fro from life on the road to life along the road. And this naturally gives them sympathy with wanderers.

The safer and more common methods

Striking Gravel

of riding have been alluded to. When comparative concealment is desired the "blind-baggage"—i. e., the end of the baggage car toward the tender—is a favorite, because not much visited by the "Con," who is always dreaded above any of the crew. The "bumpers" come next—the man stands on one, with his back braced against the end of the car— I have counted a dozen this way on as many trains, successive evenings; less frequently the man straddles the two, steadying himself by his hands.

The box car is often entered by springing the door off its iron way at the side opposite the seal. A party going one way will do this for a party going the opposite direction and then, when all are in, spring the door back again. Since

feels a longing to be off again whenever spring comes.

A railway accident, whether by water or fire, is a very serious affair to passengers of this sort. You have doubtless read more than once, as I have, of tramps drowned like rats, or burned or crushed to death, while stealing rides in this fashion.

Riding the trucks is done in various ways. A locomotive engineer of my acquaintance has shown me the precise spot from which he had taken out two men

Corrupting the "Shack."—"Have a Chew"

everything externally is in the best of order long trips may be made in this manner without disturbance or interruption.

Now and then the prisoner is exposed to danger of starvation. A case of this kind has been related to me—where only the accidental visit of a train hand saved a man from death. The brakeman inspected the intruder's papers, and, finding that they showed him to be in good standing in his union, took him out, fed him up and then replaced him—to finish his journey in peace. The hero of the incident is a printer, who has been leading a settled life now for thirteen or fourteen years. But he says he still

at one time. It was on the rear truck of the tender. They were resting face downward on the truck beam, with just eleven inches of vertical space for their bodies, by actual measurement. He also showed me the little cage under the "cow-catcher" of his rather old-style engine, whence he had once extracted two tramps. And it so happened that the week following this relation, as his engine drew up close to another train, a man crept out from the same spot and started calmly off for the neighboring station, simply remarking: "Seems to me you run up pretty nigh!" "Yes, and what if we'd happened to hit?" was the rejoiner. To which the tramp replied: "Oh, I'm used to that. I'm not afraid."

And when you come to think of it, a place inside the cow-catcher is not much less safe than one anywhere else on the train. Still, it must be a little billowy and a trifle airy withal.

The same engineer showed me another place from which he had seen tramps issue forth—the old fashioned tool-box, still occasionally found under some of the cars. It is about three feet wide and two and a half high, and has a convenient is roughly grooved to allow the rods to fit in and catch. As my correspondent suggests, this sort of riding is too hazardous to be much used. And the same is true, tho in less measure, of truck-riding.

A poor fellow, whom I have met several times, each time further down the hill, while standing at a saloon corner in "the ward" the last time I encountered him, looking wistfully up and down the street, dead-broke, remarked to me that he had ridden the trucks years ago—

On the Pilot.—" Philadelphia Shorty " and " Providence Bob "

flat-door at the end. It is always very greasy and dirty, and must be excessively dark. Otherwise, it ought to be commodious enough.

The rods, referred to in the formula "riding the rods," are the truss rods which, after the fashion of bridge trusses, support the middle stretch of the car between trucks. They are generally in pairs, from one to four feet apart, and the body may be supported upon the pair crosswise, resting commonly upon a plank, and I have heard of one case of slinging a hammock from the rods. The plank, called by some a " ticket," is liable to work off and let the body down—a fatal lapse. To prevent this the plank

" But I'm too much broken up now to do it any more," he concluded in a way that was really pathetic.

I have a very curious collection of photographs illustrating this phase of tramp experience, in which actual tramps and actual train hands figure.

But I am neglecting " Roving Bill." In the letter which I began to quote a little while ago, he goes on gossiping as follows:

" I was stealing a ride down in Florida on the J. T. & R. W. R. R. from Enterprise to Titusville. The conductor caught me and wanted to know whither I was going. I told him. He says: ' Are you a glass blower?' I told him no. He says: ' You fellows come down here in winter to blow glass and go up North in summer to pick oranges. Get off!' I took him at his word."

The conductor, by the way, touched upon one of the humors of the road in Germany. Tramps call themselves by the most preposterously impossible avocations—" Highway-ditch upholsterers;" " Gilders of dome-peaks; " " Removers of mountain and valley "—in a word, what nobody does do, or can do, that is their trade!

In spite of this conductor our friend

man; had been a Southern soldier, but was now a good union man.

" The colored people in the South," he says, " are very good and hospitable; but the most of them are very poor and have nothing much to give, but they will generally divide with you when asked." He stopped in their houses a good many times, paying for his entertainment by fixing their clocks or sewing machines. Corn bread, molasses and fat meat was the " Fair."

Another Ho-Bo has spoken to me in

In the " Tool Box."—" Providence Bob " and " Philadelphia Shorty "

pronounces the Southern people in the South very charitable—more so than

" the people that has emigrated there from Northern States." " I stayed at a place," he goes on to say, " one day near Lake City, Fla., on the G. S. F. R. R., a farm house. He was an old Reble soldier; he gave me my dinner and treated me kindly. He said there was an Irish Ho-Bo stopped there one morning and knocked. He went to the door. The son of Erin says: ' I don't want anything to eat but I just want to borrow your looking glass. I want to see how an Irishman looks starving to death.' He told him to come in and he got his feed."

He says he stayed about a week with an old planter between Savannah and Augusta, who was a good whole-souled

the same way of the blacks, but not of the whites, in the South. He says the latter were wont to refuse him rudely, exclaiming: " You came down here and took away our slaves and now you want to come down and live off us." Both may be telling the truth.

Let us go back now to the letter, which is a long one, starting at Boston and ending at Manchester, N. H.:

" *On the Road Between Nashua and Manchester, N. H.*—I arrived at Nashua last night. Met a fellow H. B. yesterday. He did not know where he was going. Had no particular point of view. We took in an empty box car. The air was chilly. I slept very comfortable; my feet got a little cold towards morning. My partner got very cold. I could hear him shivering and shaking every time I was awake during the night. He left me this morning. He said he was going to bum some Priest for a quarter as he wanted to get a shave and get something to eat. I bid him good-bye. He told me he used to keep saloon somewhere near New Britain, Ct. He had been on the bum for six weeks this time. I met an old Irishman last Sunday on the Rail Road between Lowell and Boston. He stopped and asked me for a match. I accommodated him. He said he had worked in Lowell ever since last Christmas and now he was walking out of the town. He said the drink was the cause. To-day being Decoration Day I did not do

Think of it! This battle scarred union soldier receiving hospitality of that last named kind. There is reunion and fraternity with a vengeance!

He had helped guard convicts in the South, he once wrote me. A later installment expands the incident:

"There were four other guards besides myself and they were all old Reble soldiers. The Sergeant of the Guard was an old Captain in Lee's army."

He was "never treated better in his life than he was by these men." They

Jumping a " Boxer," " Pullman Side Door."—The " Shack " Objects.

much faking. I had a part of a loaf of Bread. I done on that for Breakfast and dinner and then I made fifteen cents fixing an umbrella. I got some crackers and cheese for supper.

"You wanted to know if I ever stopped at an Alms house or Soldiers' Home. I stopped at the National Military Home at Dayton, Ohio, about eight years ago for about six weeks; and again last winter one year ago over night. I stopped in the Soldiers' Home at Marion, Indiana, about three days, this spring one year ago. I stopped over night at the Soldiers' Home at Bath, N. Y., two years ago. I stopped at the Soldiers' Home in Chelsea, Mass., near Boston, when I came through last Friday night. And I stopped o-er night at the Confederate Soldiers' Home at Richmond, Va., last winter."

would, in a joking way, call him a "——Yankee," and "I would return the compliment," he says, "and call them ——Johnny Rebs, and it would all pass off with a laugh." But he adds:

"It was horrible the way the poor convicts was treated when we was picking cotton. They had a task of 200 lbs. and if they did not get this done they would make them lay down on the ground, and then a big, stout negro convict that weighed about 200, chose for his size, with an inch hemp rope twisted and looped around his Hand, would beat those convicts over the bare hide until the Sergeant would say enough. The poor fellows would scream and hollor. Sometimes one would say 'Sergeant, oh! Sergenat, I will get my task.' The Sergeant would answer: 'A h—l of a time to get it now. Hit him harder, or I will have all the men whip ploughing take a trace chain and put it around the convict's neck and chain him to the round

On the Rods, "Ticket" Riding.—"Providence Bob" and "Philadelphia Shorty"

Riding the Brake Beam

you.' It was outrageaous the way they was treated. I have seen them when they was of the plow. I saw a mule run away with a Plow and a convict chained to it. That Convict done some tall running and pulling with his hands on the lines, and his head and neck on the chains—the Sergeant and guards sitting on the fence laughing. I went to him afterwards and the chain had cut deep gashes in his neck. Most of the convicts," he explains, " were colored men. There was several white convicts but they was never treated as cruelly as the negroes."

Hounds were used to reclaim runaways.

The penal system has improved in some of the States since then; but there is still room for improvement.

After he quit guarding he and a professor of sleight-of-hand, by the name of Jeff Tate, went into the show business.

" I was a Professor of Phrenology. We would have our shows in the school houses. The Planters would aid us all they could, as the most of them liked fun. I would feel the Darkies' heads—give a lecture at times. It must have been laughable,"

he thinks, " for I did not know but little about it—an invaluable qualification, no doubt." He " only staid in the profession until spring and then struck out for New Orleans."

" But I must be moving on, or I won't get to Manchester to-day," he suddenly ejaculates, and evidently moves; for his next begins. " I am now in sight of the city of Manchester, N. H." Later he accounts for mistakes, bad spelling and writing on the plea of the numerous " inconveniences " under which he has been writing. " The muskeetoes is very troublesome to-day," he half apologetically remarks. Furthermore: " As I sit on the ground, my Back against a pine tree, my knee for a desk, it is not as comfortable as it is in an easy chair in library or office."

But from these minor drawbacks he turns again to Nature and her calm beauty :

" The Country looks Beautiful in its spring suit, and the Birds sing sweetly and Nature seems to have taken life anew. I often in daytime, nice days, get into the woods in some secluded spot, lay down in the shade of some friendly tree and sleep from two to three hours, sometimes longer. And oh! such sweet sleep, such nice dreams. If I were where I dream I was sometimes, I would be happy! I often think God intended man to live as the Indians use to—all the Land common property. What happy times if we was all in the woods together! "

Sure enough!

HARTFORD, CONN.

Leaves from the Diary of a Tramp
III

By Prof. John J. McCook
OF TRINITY COLLEGE

I HAVE noticed that Chesapeake Bay oystering is one of the last resorts of the vagrant in search of temporary work. Curiously enough, as if by contrast, Roving Bill's mind strays off from these tranquil idyllic scenes, over which he rhapsodizes in our last, to the stormy billows and the rough experiences of a voyage oystering. I will not qoute his description, but only say that it corresponds so entirely with descriptions that have come to me orally that I am disposed to believe them all, in the main, and to conclude that Baltimore oysters ought to be very good, indeed, to justify so much discomfort and so little profit in their quest. He says his crew were "treated well to what some crews were." But, nevertheless, once was enough for him.

On May 31 he writes:

"I stopped last night in a shanty alongside the Railroad. It had a stove in it: built a fire, was Comfortable. Was out before sun up, met a Frenchman that wanted his Umberella Mended, went with him to his home, done the job, got my Breakfast and fifteen cents before five A. M. I am now eight miles from Manchester. Will arrive there about 12 M."

I fear he reckoned, in this, without his host, for he keeps on chatting about his past until the sun must have been high in the heavens.

"I have made two trips through the Southern States. Eight years ago I went all through the Southwest, Illinois, Missouri, Mississippi, Arkansas, Louisiana, Texas, Alabama. I guarded Convicts on a plantation near Greenwood on the Yazoo River, Miss. Was there three months. Was Superintendent of a Cotton mill [he was brought up in one] near Carrolton, Miss., was there the time of the yellow fever. I run a grist mill at Cumberland, Miss., near West Point. I heard Jeff Davis make a speech in a grove near Tupelo, Miss. I have been in New Orleans and Mobile a number of times, been hunting in the wilds of the Yazoo, Tallahatchie and Yellow Bash Swamps. I have been on almost all the Battle fields of the Civel War East and West. Been in the famous Brandywine and Delaware River of Revolutionary times, seen Bunker Hill, Boston Common, also Washington Monument at Washington City; been in all the Capitals of the States of the Union and seen the White House and Capitol at Washington, was in U. S. Pension Office, Treasury Building and other places too numerous to mention; seen Pulaski's Monument, also Confederate monuments in several cities of the South."

The following remark was quite superfluous:

"I take a great interest and visit all these Places of Note in my travels. I made a trip to Leadville, Colorado, the time of the first gold excitement—was going to make a fortune there, but got through in three days; went back to Denver, from there to Salt Lake, thence to Sacramento, San Francisco. Signed as a sailor, sailed across to Melbourne, and Sidney; done the same coming back. Was over there about three months. Came back to 'Frisco. Beat my way Back. Went down into New Mexico and Arizona. On my way back was out in the Indian Territory among the Indians two months—Comanchees and Cherikees. Fixed Clocks and Sewing Machines all through Southwest Missouri that winter; came out in the spring Fat and Raged. I could tell you many a laughable incident.

"I went over to London on a Cattle Steamer near six years ago." [I have met several who have duplicated this experience; that and oystering in the Chesapeake seem to be final resorts.—J. J. McC.] "Worked my way over. After I got over there my employer gave me five lbs. for being a good Hand. I traveled through England. I have some relatives living in Yorkshire, on my Father's side; went to Scotland, Dublin and Cork; back to Liverpool and signed on a vessel as ordinary seaman to Calcutta and Bombay; came back on the same ship, had enough money to pay my way steerage to New York and some left when I arrived, but soon had to strike out on the Tramp."

Bill is heard from next at **Keene, N. H.,** under date of June 5:

"I have just arrived here to-day. I am going from here to Brattleborough, Vt. Write me at Brattleboro. Will go from there to Bennington, Vt. I have not money to get photograph. Yrs of 31st came to hand to-day. Rough times in this Country. But still I live. Yours,

"WILLIAM."

The photograph business is again alluded to here. I had greatly desired to have my friend's portrait, but since I remained true to my first resolve to have no question of dollars and cents cloud or

The Prize-Fight, Street Corner Fake

complicate our relations, it was a matter of some difficulty to know how to get it and be sure of its genuineness. At length I wrote to him to go to the best artist in Bennington and tell him that if he would take his picture and send me one copy, with the negative, I would forward my check for a dollar and a half, and that my letter might be exhibited as evidence of my good faith. It was further stipulated that there must be no fixing up, no shaving or polishing, but that everything must be taken as if on the road. Would any photographer assume the risk?

The answer came in the shape of a fresh negative,* with excellent cabinet impression, bearing the imprint of a Bennington photographer; and much rejoiced at the success of the venture, I with great alacrity returned the stipulated fee.

* This was published in THE INDEPENDENT of Nov. 21, p. 2761.

With true artistic feeling the operator has arranged a hillside background, with attractive cottage in the distance, embowered in trees, and in the foreground rocks, weeds and wild flowers. Against this stands a man rather under the middle size with mustache and stubby beard, smallish eyes, and nose slightly *retroussé,* a long, straight mouth, with lips braced to sustain the weight of a long-stemmed corncob pipe. The chin is not strong, nor notably weak. The throat is bare, save for a little patch of dark woolen shirt with white cording. Jacket, waistcoat and trousers are of dark check, of uniform pattern. The trousers are turned up, and the shoes, an important item in

Portrait of the Prize-Fight Fake.—A " Gauger "

the diagnosis of these cases, are muddy and worn. The hat is a derby and looks in fair condition.

Photographs, however, are exceedingly unsatisfactory in matters of this kind. There is apt to be an indefinable tint to garment and hat and complexion, the resultant of various forces—dust, sun, rain, wind, contact with mother earth under varying conditions of comfort and discomfort, ebriety and inebriety—which it would be worthy of the highest ambition of the most aspiring artist to secure, but which has thus far eluded the science of the most scientific.

One circumstance, however, is conclusive as to one point. The photograph

PROF. JOHN J. McCOOK

reveals the garments as being fairly neat
and tidy. And this shows that " Roving
Bill " is no vulgar shovel or city bum.
They are prone to be very ragged and
slatternly—tho even they never look like
the comic newspaper type. It also exhibits the parts as belonging to the same
original suit. This is fair evidence that
the owner has been reasonably sober and
well to do during his immediate past.
Otherwise the pawn shop would have introduced variety.

Our friend has described himself as
being for the time engaged in " mush-
faking "—in plain English, umbrella
mending. He is here pictured with a
wooden box hanging by a strap from his
left shoulder, and to the top of the box is
strapped a bundle of umbrella sticks and
frames. The box is labeled on end and
side " Pepper Sauce." It looks about ten
inches high and twelve or fourteen long.
He will himself tell us later what is in it.

Meanwhile there is a letter from Bennington, dated June 9, that offers some
passages of interest:

" I am hungry now and have not a cent to
get anything to eat, but may strike something
before long. I won't beg if I can Help it. I

slept last night in a vacant house between
here and Wilmington, Vt., five miles up on
the mountains. There was no other house
within a mile of it. I went up stairs, got into
a little bedroom, shut the Door, Pulled of
my shoes and coat and made a pillow of my
umberellas and slept sound. Got up at day
break and came here. I had quite an eventful
trip since I left Manchester. I had many a
weary step climbing of those mountains, and
the muskeetoes, knats and other insects made
me miserable. I slept in box cars and once
in the woods. It was dark and I was verry
tiard and the muskeetoes were nearly eating
me up. I filed to the right up the side of the
mountain and Built a Fire. Stumbled around
in the dark and found Some wood, pulled off
shoes and coat and turned in. I left Manchester on June 1st, slept in a Barn that night.

" I came down Hill ten miles yesterday afternoon. Part of the way it is a surging
river Running alongside of the Road, the
Watter trying to pass itself to get down Hill.
At first there would be little lakes connected
by a little stream, and further down it turned
in to a Roaling tumbling River. Here and
there a Saw mill and when I arrived at Bennington I found it Propeling numerous Factories. Nature is great to Behold in its Beauties and Might."

This is a fair sample of my friend's elo-
quence when face to face with " Nature."

Raiding the Bull Barn

302

Tramps often call themselves "gentlemen tourists." Here is one who writes down his feelings. One may criticise the manner of expression, but the emotion appears to be correct.

I had asked him to give his classification of the genus Ho-Bo, in order to compare it with other systems. Here it is:

"There is several clases of tramps or Haut Beaus. I can make about three out of them with occasionally a woman. There is 1st the Harmless Tramp that tramps because he has no home, no Friends and got on the road from Drink and then No. 2 is Fakers and Mush Fakers, Mechanics and others on the Tramp hunting work, and some of the finest mechanicks in the country, comprising all

Guardian Angels of the Bull Barn, Kelly, "Tip" and "Sport"

trades, get on the road by spending their money too liberal and Partly from drink and get down and ashamed to ask for a Job, and good fellows they are, will divide the last nickel with you or the last Biscuit. There appears to be a kind of Brotherly feeling amongst this Class, but they have no use for Class No. 3 as they are composed of ex Convicts, Jail Birds and Regular Dead Beats. There is some mean Haut Beaus that will venture to do anything—insult Women, steal and fire Barns, Can't be trusted. This makes it bad for an Honest man as the Public thinks they are all Chips of the same block, but far from it. Just as much difference in the Classes as there is in the Classes of societies in a Citty, or a Vilage.

"It is the last Class that has all the signs and Camps and patronizes the Poor Houses, Jails, &c. They manage to get some money by stealing or Begging and Buy Alcohall, dilute it in Watter and drink that. They call it Alca', or Booze and other names.

"I have seen several women on the tramp, but generally very low down creatures. The boys call them Bags, old Bags. A man along with a Bag don't stand very high in Haut Beau society. Farmers are called Rubes. When a Bum goes to a house and gets a lunch they call it Hand out, Lump, Soup, Slop, &c."

Four day later, June 13, our pilgrim is at Troy, N. Y., where he acknowledges receipt of a letter and says he is bound for Schenectady, Fort Plain and Utica, and that I may write to any of the three. Twenty-five days have now elapsed since we first heard from him at Jewett City. He has crossed part of Connecticut, and traversed Rhode Island, Massachusetts, New Hampshire and Vermont. The distance from point to point, in a straight line, is 248 miles, and leaving out three Sundays, when he generally rests, we have an average of eleven and a third miles a day, as the crow flies. If we allow a third more for crooked roads and indirect routes, we have not far from fifteen miles a day—certainly not extremely rapid marching, but not discreditable, either, for a long stretch like this—the pedestrian practicing a trade, too, meanwhile! Sherman's "Bums" were considerably less fleet of foot.

Our friend is a "loner." They are not common. Where there is one you will generally find two, if you look closely enough. If number one is at your door trying to "strike" you, his "buddy"— brother, I suppose—will be at some lamppost or corner that commands a view of the house, with his back turned, but casting quick glances from time to time over his shoulder to see what has happened. I have more than once watched the operation, following the pair in and out to the end of their pilgrimage, invariably a saloon. But "Roving Bill" generally prefers his own company.

"I most always travel by myself unless I can strike a good civel partner. I don't take up with every one. Sometimes I get with a good fellow and we stay together for some time until he wants to go one way and me another, or we get lost from each other. I had a Partner when I left N. Y. City but he had to Return to N. Y. as his folks wrote for him.

He was a good, straight fellow. I was sorry to part with him."

And again, under date of June 10th, he writes from a barn:

"This is a pleasant Place—cool and the smell of the hay is fragrant. I like to be to myself: no one to interrupt my meditations."

The advantage of having a "good, straight fellow" for a partner is not far to seek. It is regard for health that makes the tramp remove his shoes before retiring for the night. But it is from quite a different motive that he uses them for a pillow, first carefully stowing away in them the most precious of his personal belongings!

HARTFORD, CONN.

Leaves from the Diary of a Tramp
IV.
By Prof. John J. McCook
OF TRINITY COLLEGE

TO me there is something very interesting in Bill's "meditations." He begins one letter thus:

"I do not know where I will Roost to-night yet. But I did not know where I would get anything to eat to-day—but I got it and all I wanted. I am a great Believer in a God and nothing will convince me but that there is a Supreme Ruler for I have tested his mercy too often to believe otherwise—but still I am no fanatic."

The basis of his belief on this occasion was having met an old friend on the road who recognized him and gave him a dollar, which he "accepted gracefully and went and got a good dinner and" —the tramp's luxury—"a shave."

The result that night justified his confidence in Providence, for he begins his next thus:

"Well I came out all Right as far as sleeping was Concerned. I found a barn about half full of Nice Hay; I crawled into it long before dark slept well, had a good rest and now it must be 9 A.M."

—for him an unusually late hour to be stirring; but it was Saturday and he didn't want to get to Troy before Monday.

That the day was not passed in complete idleness is evidenced by the fact that he wrote me thirty-five pages, containing about 6,000 words, besides attending to his household cares. He here tells me something about himself in a very naïve way.

Thus, for his tastes:

"I am not a glutton, I am easily satisfied as far as my stomache is concerned. Give me good plain food."

So he breakfasted well on "crackers and dried Herron" (herring).

And again, for his habits:

"I have been intoxicated a number of times but am not an inveterate drinker. I don't

His Trousers were Troublesome

fancy whiskey much but like good pure wines, ale and beer."

I used to think that "bad whisky" was the customary drink of this sort of people, and held it and its "badness" especially responsible for their deterioration and their misdoings. But careful experimentation has convinced me that whiskies are "much of a muchness" and observation has shown me that anyhow "Bill's" taste represents fairly that of the average wanderer. They get more alcohol for the money in ale and beer, and therefore prefer it.

But, if not drink, what is our friend's chief temptation? Hear him:

"Women has done more to keep me down in life Financially than any other evil. Fast and designing women I have Refference to."

Respecting this *faiblesse* he and others have given me details which would not bear transcribing. And advancing years effect no change; for only the other day, eight full years since the above confession, he writes from Tahlequah, Indian Territory, whither he had suddenly jumped, out of a snug berth in a Soldiers' Home:

"I am going into Oklahoma and the Comanche nation may marry and get some land."

He has not yet divulged the genesis of this particular exodus; but on other occasions, and there have been several of them, it has been drink and its usual concomitants:

"I have had numerous chances to become a good citizen and have been regarded as such, but I get down in the world and am ashamed of myself and lose courage, get disheartened and take the Road."

—A not uncommon history.

He is sensitive to the remarks, and even to the suspicious glances, of those whom he passes. "Children sometimes run and then look back to see if I am coming—as if I was some dangerous Beast." On such occasions, he says, "I stop and take out my pocket-glass and look at myself, but see nothing new, only more wrinkles." And then he expresses his mind about the people of the East, who "as a general rule are not so hospitable and kind as they are in the South and West," but more "narrow minded" and "pattern more after the nobility of the old world"—their "tramp laws show that a poor unfortunate man has no chance!"

William is unjust to us in this, I think; but in another matter he touches upon what I fear is a real point the country over:

"There is lots of crimes committed by people that are residents of the community that is laid at the feet of the unfortunate Tramp. If a barn is burnt the first theory is some tramp set it on fire, when it was some of the drunken careless hoodlums of the community gambling smoking and lighting matches more careless than a tramp ever thought of being."

Careful inquiry satisfies me that tramps are extremely intolerant of the slightest carelessness in the use of fire in their sleeping places. They have no fancy for being roasted alive. And I have in my possession a letter from an ex-tramp who, looking back at the past through several years of orderly life, still complains bitterly of the discrimination against his kind exhibited, as he

"Drunk and Assault," Hartford Police Station, 8.30 a.m.

contends, even in prisons, where he found himself subjected to indignities to which the worst felons were not exposed. And his complaint is made in no spirit of apology for his old ways, which he plainly condemns.

If this be true, and I fear it is in part, it is a pity. Tramping is at worst only felony, and an Anglo-Saxon contempt of idleness should not lead us to assume it to be the mother of unproven vices. The laws of some of our States have, indeed, gone so far in this direction as to make their enforcement practically impossible, with the unfortunate result that tramping escapes all penalty and increases without restraint.

Here is a statement which is worth pondering—I fear there is much truth in it; at all events, my statistical inquiries show that the average tramp is a young fellow:

"I know the ones that are the most daring and the ones that does the most depredations on the Road are young fellows that runs away from home. I have seen lots of boys not out

of their teens on the road and young men of good sense and learning."

Then he gives instances: A Michigan boy of seventeen, the son of a rich farmer, who had stolen his mother's gold watch and was now adrift in company with a Boston hoodlum of twenty.

"I advised him to go back home and ask his mother's forgiveness; but he said he was ashamed to. What become of him I don't know."

Our rising sympathy for the lad is chilled by the ensuing remark: "I know he would not starve, for he had the cheek of a mule!"

Another was the son of wealthy parents of Joliet, Illinois. "He had layed by fires until he had burnt nearly all his clothes off, and bare footed and wreaking with vermin." Another was from Atlanta, Ga. It was in the middle of winter; he had

"a straw hat on, no coat, just a cotton shirt

"For God's Sake Get Me Sent to Jail, Governor"

and an old pair of overhauls; no undercloths, no suspenders, and you see the naked Hide every time he made a step, through the Holes in his overhauls burnt by fires."

Here again our kindly emotions are checked, for "Still he was in good spirits" follows remorselessly from the pen of our historian. And I have myself been astonished to find how much exposure could be endured by these people without inconvenience.

One midwinter day, when dampness added special chill to the air and I was shivering in a thick overcoat, I found one of my young tramp friends in a thin summer suit, a cotton shirt and no underclothes—of which latter fact I convinced myself by opening his shirt front—and he scorned the very suggestion that he might be cold. His only anxiety was for a supply of alcohol: the flow of external spirits was entirely adequate.

And I recall another occasion when I took two veterans out with me to pose for train-jumping photographs. An early snow storm had covered everything, and after several hours of wading, uncomfortable enough to myself with Arctic shoes and great coat, they, with their ragged shoes, made no complaint of wet feet; and on my offering, at parting, to take them to a restaurant for a square meal, they preferred to "take its price in money and get supper at their own boarding house." I deferred to their wishes and then followed them at a discreet distance to their "boarding house"—which turned out to be a saloon, where, as the friendly bartender told me next morning, they had two rounds of ale apiece.

Both these men had been drunk first when mere children, both had run away from home, both had fallen into licentiousness early, and had paid the penalty in disease, both had been often the wards of the community in jail and hospital, both had not only sold their votes but repeated—they recounted all these incidents circumstantially, even to the kind of drink on which they first became intoxicated; and there was no boast-

fulness about the avowals, nor even flippancy—rather an air of seriousness and regret, as for something past hope of retrieving.

One of them is dead now—died in an apoplectic fit. He was a confirmed tramp, if there ever was one, a sorry liar and a desperate drunkard; but I think one of the last things he ever said to me was really the sincere expression of that which corresponded in him with

A Quintet of Lodgers

what we call "resolution"—"Oh! Yes, I mean to brace some time."

And while we are at it we may as well make an end of the religious side of our friend's diary by a couple of brief quotations:

"People should bear in mind that it is not the coat or the outside appearance that makes the man. If it was so we would of had no Christ, no Saviour, for He was considered in those days what now days is called a Tramp —but I am just illustrating, don't think I am comparing; far from it, I am not worthy."

And again:

"Sunday, June 11. To-day is the Lord's day and I will not desecrate it any more than circumstances will admit of."

This is charming! He had retired as usual with his shoes for a pillow and his coat over his chest, had "awoke but once," when, feeling "a little chilly," he had "spread some hay over his lower limbs and soon was again in the land of morpheus," had wakened in the morning—I quote him—"to find myself in an old barn all alone except birds flitting over my head—they was all the friends I appeared to have." And when he arose it was, he tells us, "Rather late, old Saul being far up in the Horizon: but it being Sunday I was in no hurry."

Really, for all the essentials of Sunday observance this might have been just an ordinary Christian and no Tramp!

And the illusion is hardly dissipated by what follows; for, tho there is mention of fire and breakfast and pipe and newspaper, "for we must have our newspaper, too," there is nothing said about going to church!

Love of nature is here again in the saddle:

"It was in a secluded nook—a Beautiful spot about two yards from the road along a Babling Brook, the watter as clear as crystal and cool. Most any monarch would envy my Position. But alas: There is always something to mar your pleasure; the musketoes were just as thick as they could be without flying against each other; also there are innumerable ants of all species, spiders large and small and they all appear to be crawling towards you and to see what you are doing and to see what Business you have intruding on their Homestead. They will crawl over your paper while you are writing: musquitoes and bugs will bite you on the Hands and fingers, crawl over your face and neck, get into your eyes and ears and even try to get into your mouth—the impudent creatures! Crows will fly over your head and squak, a woodchuck will come galloping out of the bushes towards you and stop and look at you as if to wonder what Business that fellow had on these premises; spiders will stop and look at you as if wondering—I have had before now nice plumaged Birds to come and sit on my shoulder."

That is not at all bad, as a description of what everybody has noticed in the woods.

He explains that he is a great lover

of birds and "when people harm such helpless creatures" he thinks: "It shows the animal in them and I always chastise them for it."

These universal backsets to unalloyed pleasure are dismissed with the philosophical remark: "I think it was so intended or else your Pleasure might be incomplete." If Emerson had said that his commentators would have felt it to

A Youthful Rounder

be "deep," "stimulating," and I know not what else.

I threatened, while describing William's photograph, to tell what was in his box. He here, while describing his breakfast, reveals the secret: "This box is my tool box and commissary, also contains my cooking utensils and camp equipage." The culinary apparatus is simple enough: "My coffee pot is an old tomato can I cleaned out and put in a wire bail. My cup is a potted ham can."

When the importunity of insect life compels the return of washing day the shirt is boiled down, as he elsewhere describes, in "a big tin-bucket from a dump." A "Lord's day" is chosen for this, too; and when the garment is dried and replaced and the week's beard removed through the help of razor and hand glass, or the mirroring brook, and the pipe has been lighted and the newspaper or writing material spread out, he more than once gives vent to his quiet delight in the holy day with a fervor that recalls George Herbert's rhapsody:

"O day so calm, so cool, so bright,"

to which there is not always lacking the pathetic ending:

"The dew shall weep for thee to-night,
For thou must die."

Tobacco! Carlyle and "Roaving Bill" join hands: "I smoke and chew a great deal of tobacco," he tells us in one place. And how great his love is appears from the following:

"Sometimes I have no money to buy tobacco. I haft to go around depots and Public Places and gather up Stumps of Cigars—or Short 'Snipes,' H. Bo's call it."

He is not alone in this practice, as we know—and as he also tells us; for he relates circumstantially how he had once seen a lawyer interrupted in a curbstone talk with a "Please stand a little to one side," from a gentleman of the road who had discovered "a good big snipe" under the toe of the legal shoe, and who, on securing compliance with his request, gravely picked up the precious piece of flotsam and jetsam and walked off—creating thereby "quite a laugh."

That a lawyer should have been so readily induced to give up a thing he had his foot on seems to have powerfully affected our historian's imagination, for he relates that the picking up and walking off were both done "in an unconcerned business way," and adds: "Some of the Ho-B's has all the cheek imaginable," and he is led thereupon into an excursus upon the evil habits of the

"Professional H. B's—Those that make a Profession of Begging and stealing and won't work, never did work, visit all charitable institutions, Priests, Preachers, Alms houses—'Pogies' they name them—Police stations; not so much the latter as they are generally afraid of the Police. They get their under-

wear and shirts off from somebody's cloths line—the H. B's call it 'picking a gooseberry bush;' you will hear them talk about such and such a town being a 'good' town or 'no good.' as the case may be. This class never walk, or 'drille' as they call it: they will wait at a water tank, or the end of a division, two or three days, sometimes a week to get a train—don't generally haft to wait that long; but some of them will go into a city or town and stay there 'holding down the town' H. B's call it, until the Police or 'Bulls,' as they call them, get on to them and either arrest them or Run them out of town."

"These are the fellows that you see loafing in the Parks and other public places with a white shirt collar, shoes blacked, coat or pants to big or to small, shoes to large, that has been begged or got some other way, standing on the street corner at night begging for a night's lodging in some cheap lodging house or to buy 'alkca' to get drunk on."

"These are the fellows that does most of the riding on trucks and rods, mostly young fellows from ten to thirty, and are the ones that have most of the Phrazes, slang and signs; and they will tell you of good houses to bum—'sure to get a sit down, or a hand out any way:' 'Such a house is good for money, or such a Priest, Doctor or whoever it may be.' They will get arrested Purpose in the winter where there is no workhouse to pass the winter in."

And he promises a description some time of "cheap lodging houses, woodyards, missions," adding significantly, "I have had my experience."

"You will see these fellows' names in old houses, depot water closets, water tanks—such as 'Philly-Shorty arrived such a time, bound west or east, north or south;' 'New York Slim,' 'the Brooklyn Kid,' 'Boston Jack' and a thousand other apelations. These are the fellows that receive most of the charities and generally never go Hungry because they have indomitable cheek; won't eat Bread, or Punk as they call it, must have cake or pie or dainties; and the ones that are sassy to women; won't saw wood or work of any kind. This class is composed of Jail Birds, escaped convicts young fellows that have done something where they lived that they dare not go back. Some of Highly respected families, others have no Homes, probably never had any."

This is a fairly comprehensive description of the Professional Tramp. How numerous is he?

Γ HARTFORD, CONN.

Leaves from the Diary of a Tramp

V.

By Prof. John J. McCook

OF TRINITY COLLEGE

OF the more than thirteen hundred tramps examined by me nine or ten years ago, only two in every hundred avowed that they "never" meant to work, eighteen said they "didn't know," and fifty-five had not tried to get work that particular day. Here are all the elements for a guess that I know of. Downright professionals, in the strictest sense, are very rare. Tho on the road for thirty years or more our friend could not rank with them; for he works a good part of the time. Indeed, there are times when he wholly refuses to be called a tramp of any kind. The very large majority, I am sure, do not exhibit all the characteristics of the professional set down by him.

Take the one single incident of directions for rendezvous, memoranda, etc., on water tanks and in stations. I have looked for such with but very small success, considering the bulk of the legends about them, tho I have found them. And altho very striking cases of selection among houses for begging purposes have come under my notice, I have never yet found a perfectly authentic instance of designating mark. When, therefore, the residence of my friend, A. L., was visited regularly, and that of his next door neighbor, P. B., a lawyer, neglected, and that of his opposite neighbor, Sheriff A. M., shunned, I am confident it is all due to oral communication. And it shows what was possible in the days before the telegraph and newspaper that when my friend Judge S.'s patience finally broke down, and from being the defender of tramps in court and their feeder at home he told one of them to let it be known from Hartford to Boston that he "would arrest the next one that came to his door," inside of forty-eight hours the plague had ceased!

There is exaggeration, of course, in the statement that the professionals get all the alms and monopolize the missions. But it would be well if the whole picture were to be studied by everybody connected with the administration of charity and justice and by every householder.

"You hardly ever see any foreigners with this class," he thinks, "once in a while a London or a Liverpool bum." Foreign born he means, doubtless.

Speaking of that, you rarely find a Jew tramp; and Jews are very scarce in almshouses, jails and prisons here. But a careful examination of a printed vocabulary of German tramp slang shows a considerable percentage of Hebrew words, whether brought in by Jew tramps or gleaned by native tramps from the second-hand clothing shops in the slums, I cannot say.

I shrink from quoting the closing passage of his description, but it should be given:

"I have seen these kind of fellows traveling with young boys, the boys doing the begging, and I am allmost ashamed to tell it—not fit to be written, that Human Beings will become so low, but I will tell the truth, they use these boys as . . ."

The rest must be imagined. "I have saw them at it in Box cars," he says; and exclaims: " Disgusting, lower than Brutes."

Details of a similar character have come to me over and over again, and in general facts relating to licentiousness of incredible horror and impossible of belief but for the concurrence of evidence. I do not know that anything can be done about it among tramps any more than among people of settled life. Now and then it forces its way out in both cases

Whisling Joe—Brooklyn.
Yankee Slim, Whiskey Pete, Yonkers Pete.
Jack the Ripper, London, Eng.
Montana Bill, May 21, '91.
Missouri Kid, B. W. 10—90.
Allentown White, B. W. 10—91."

" Some of these," he adds, "had signs or marks under their names, such as Maltese cross or a star; some a figure or a letter;" and " I see thousands of these

" Just a Common Drunk." Station House, New York City

and compels attention. For the most part it festers and spreads, equally in both instances, in secret.

I have said that written memoranda and signs are not much used. They are used, however, and by the kindness of a locomotive engineer friend I have a number in my possession, in addition to the few I have found myself. And here is a list which Roving Bill sends me—from the door of a hand-car house:

" Yonkers and Slim and Boots; 1—5, 92 B. W.

Troy Whitey; Tunnel 4—2—69.

names of all kinds on all buildings along the R. R." But they are pretty plainly only signatures and contain but little designed or adapted to give definite information for meeting or begging.

The religious tone which occasionally crops out in this diary and the specific allusions to " Priests, Preachers and Missions," tempt me to a word about this question of religion among tramps. It may, perhaps, be recalled that 113 out of 1,329 examined in my " Tramp Census " had no religion and that I guessed this to be about fifty per cent. in excess of the proportion in our entire adult population.

It may be profitable to give here the religious preferences in numerical order: " Roman Catholic, Lutheran, Methodist, Congregationalist, Presbyterian, Episcopalian, Baptist and Dutch Reformed;" and some of these were found in numbers considerably beyond what their strength in the country entitled them to have. The Episcopalian, for instance, my own Church, was much distinguished in this regard. But plainly there is no real dependence to be placed upon this in the way of generalization because the facts had to be gathered where they could and not, as should have been, uniformly from every part of the country.

Still, I am convinced that Episcopal clergymen are apt to be worked more assiduously than any other; partly, I suspect, because it has come to be known that there is a " poor fund " in every parish and that the clergyman is the official almoner of that fund. But, from the nomadic bum to the accomplished ecclesiastical confidence man, or dead beat, I conclude by numerous private communications that the Episcopal clergyman is commonly thought to be " always good for something any way."

I once put the question in its reverse form to an avowed " professional: " " Which is the worst kind of a clergyman for you people? "

" Well, I think the Methodists," he replied, after a pause for reflection.

" Why, are they not as kind and charitable as the rest? " I again queried.

" Oh, not that. They'll always give you a good meal! "

" What's the matter with them, then? " I insisted.

" Why, don't you know, they'll always sit down by you and preach you a long sermon, while you're eatin','' so that you can't rightly enjoy your food." And his face was perfectly serious; in fact, the admission had the air of being forced from him!

The poor " sisters " have to suffer more than the clergymen, I fear. They are not safe early or late. It is true, they have

Fourth Floor, Seven-Cent Lodging House, East Side, New York City

312

themselves to thank, for where there is no supply there will be no demand.

Still, this whole matter of giving food is one of acknowledged difficulty. If all were professionals—or even like the majority—the thing would be simple enough. Or if there were in every town, as there are in so many German communities, private houses, or inns, or refuges to which every applicant might be referred, one's duty would be plain. But one does not like to refuse when one

plicant for help, sent him, as, alas! so often happens, by a person of abundant means and leisure on the same street. He received his visitor at a side door of the church leading into his study, over which stood out, carved in the stone, the pious scripture legend, "A Door of Hope," and, on hearing the case, broke out with: "You go back to Mrs. —— and tell her with Dr. ——'s compliments that he thinks she might take care of her own tramps without sending them to

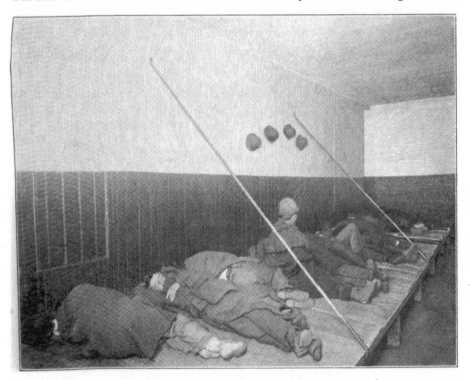

Police Lodging House, New York City. Men's Side

knows that the applicant may be an honest man in that hardest of all hard predicaments, beaten in life and obliged to confess it. The average conscience would probably feel less inconvenience from feeding ninety-nine professionals than from sending one such away starving and despairing.

This word despair recalls an interesting story illustrative of the not infrequent cleverness of these wayfaring men. A very busy clergyman in Philadelphia was interrupted one morning by an ap-

him "—and retired. Presently some one shoved under the door of the parsonage a bit of soiled paper, on which was written the following:

"The person whom you denounced so unceremoniously this morning would suggest that a more fitting motto above your study door would be, 'All hope abandon, ye who enter here.'

"(Signed) The man you called a Tramp."

As I turn over the leaves of these fat letters from my roving friend I am embarrassed by the difficulty of making

313

choice. While in the country the dominant note is joy at freedom, the earth,
air, sky,—with, however, a constant re-
version to the minor chords of " musketoes," " knats," flies, insects. Once
" bees," and these last, too, when he was
in a peculiarly defenseless condition in a
hay-mow, his clothes being out for wash
and repair, so to speak!

In town he tells of Memorial Day cele-
brations, of saloons, of lodging-houses,
of companions "snoring, rolling, scratch-

In spite of a not unnatural desire to
avoid it, drink figures prominently, if
not conspicuously. Once he with three
others contrived to accomplish the remarkable feat of " taping " and empty-
ing a keg of beer, which two of them
had presumably " sneaked from some
brewery." The wonder was not so much
in that alone, I hasten to say, for these
folk are mighty drinkers on occasions, as
I can testify from actual observation;
but in this, that the thing was done be-

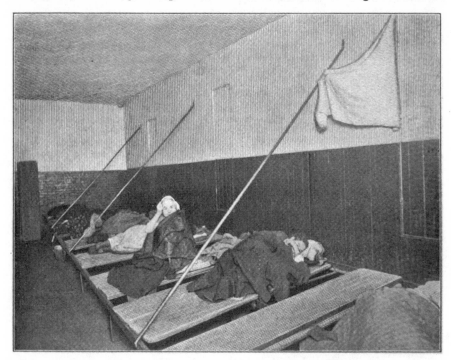

Police Station Lodging House, New York City. Women's Side

ing, singing, drinking, vomiting; " of
evil smells, of sleeplessness—" a man in
your position can have no idea how low
and depraved Human beings can become."

On the road he tells of long " jumps "
on the blind baggage. He even conducts
me through the companionship of those
frail ladies to whom he earlier attributed
the chiefest of his misfortunes in life.
Some of these things would richly pay for
transcription if there were space. Some,
as I have said, would not bear transcription.

tween cars on a train, while jumping,
between Chicago and Valparaiso, Ind. " It
was near all drank up by the time he was
put of," he says, with honest determination to be accurate. And he well adds:
" I would not of believed it myself if I
had not of seen it and of Helped drink
the Beer."

But it will not do to neglect the economical and political side of his writings.
We have already heard him express his
leaning toward " common property in
land," with life in the woods, but evi-
dences are not lacking that community

314

of property in other things is not regarded with entire disfavor. Under date of July 2d he writes:

"This morning, as I was comeing along I came across a fine Patch of Strawberries; as the Farmer was still in Bed I climbed the Fence and Had a fine Bait of lucius Berries fresh from the vines. I don't think it is much Harm in taking a few Berries to eat, as a great many of them will go to waste any way before they are Picked."

Realizing, however, that the social order had not yet fully adapted itself to his code, he adds:

"However I would cast and eye over towards the Farmer's House to ascertain if the Cost was clear and that the old Rube, as H. B's call them, was not coming with Bull-Dog and Gun to disturb my pleasure."

He did not come and there was no disturbance, for only an hour or two later our friend was able to write:

"How well I enjoy this lovely Sabbath morning and how Happy I feel with Nature adorned in her lovely Summer Robes all around me; everything so quite except the Rusling of the Breeze through the Butiful foliage and the sweet singing and the warbling of Birds."

Having begun, as was fitting, with fruit, he had

"a quart of good, strong Coffee, Bred, Cheese and some cooked Beef & Onions; and there I sat on the grass with an umberella cover for a Table-Cloth my Blue Handkerchief for a napkin, a lard can for a Coffee Pot, a small Potted Ham Can serving for both cup and saucer and I eat a harty Breakfast and I enjoyed it."

And thereupon, what? As on these holy occasions in general:

"I filled my Pipe with tobacco and Set it on fire and am now enjoying a smoke and writing. . . . I would rather sit close to this Butiful sheet of watter and write than to be in the most luxurious drawing Room in this land."

And when the writing was done there was still something to look forward to, for:

"I have yesterday's Papers and will spend

Wayfarers' Lodge, Charity Organization Society

315

some time in Reading, as I like to keep posted on what is transpiring in the world."

Can we wonder that he bursts out: "Surely God has blessed me!"

Other fruits of the earth, in their season, go the way of the strawberries. September 8th, he tells us:

"I had to cook Potatoes and green corn several times to fill up on, and to drive Hunger from the door. I procured the Corn and Potatoes in Fields as I passed by, borrowed them you know."

This, however, is easily explained:

"I had had quite a trying experience in that country as I could make no money: everybody was out of work and had no money and was giving it to the present Democratic Administration!"

There is, besides, occasional mention of the use of unoccupied houses, while railroad cars of all kinds, shanties and barns are appropriated as a matter of course.

But this mild heterodoxy in respect to the *tuum* is, as usual, altogether consistent with strict orthodoxy as to the *meum*. We have seen how he used his shoes for a pillow. On one other occasion he has just been buying a new pair, and here are the precautions he takes against having them stolen:

"I placed my Bundel of Umberella-Handles and Ribs for a Pillow, took of my coat and shoes, tied my shoes to Bundel for fear a H. B. might come along and want them; if he did he would haft to wake me before he got them and then it would be a Question of Manhood; my combativeness would come to the front."

These measures, conspiring with the "downy grass" and an extra "bundle of umberella covers" on top of the handles and ribs, procured undisturbed repose; and as "the clock in the church tower was tolling five o'clock" the shoes were carrying him five miles along upon his next day's journey.

HARTFORD, CONN.

Leaves from the Diary of a Tramp
VI.
By Prof. John J. McCook
OF TRINITY COLLEGE

WITH all his love of nature and the solitary life in the open, Roving Bill does not despise or avoid the habitations of men. Two or three of his letters are from hotels, with the name of the hostelry printed at the head of the sheets. He had once before written me with great satisfaction:

"I have got one Dollar in the Treasury this morning, after paying all expences. Gaining! I want to get the Treasury sollid Financially and surplus Capital."

But at the time of the hotel episode he was reveling in opulence. For he had left the road for a few weeks—first for a farm and then for a factory. At the former, he says, "I earned fifteen dollars; my tobacco and some working cloths came out leaveing about $12;" at the latter, "I made $10." So, with $22 or more in the treasury, a hotel was the proper thing, of course; and he paid for hotel bills and railroad fares "about $6," and for "Bord and Washing" in the factory town about $5.50. "And I bought," he furthermore states, "a suit of cloths, some underweare, socks, white shirt collars, Buttons, socks and other necessarys, a new felt hat, a valise."

I hope he never slept in his hat. But it is at least a suspicious circumstance that, only a short month before, he had had a gift of a nearly new straw hat, and was in general so well provided with clothes by his patriotic friends in connection with Fourth of July festivities that he sent me his portrait, taken at his own expense, "to give you some Idea of my appearance when in private life." In that portrait the straw hat was needlessly conspicuous, I thought, and the picture as a whole did not please me as well as the one taken just as he came from the road. I should add his own verdict, however: "It does not do me Justice."

He shows throughout the earlier stage of our correspondence a sturdy feeling of self-respect. Indeed, he takes almost too much pains to vindicate the dignity of his then calling. Coupled with his subsequent insistence that he "looked like a gentleman now," when the only real difference was in his make-up, it arouses suspicion, in spite of one's self, that his praise of umbrella mending was, like much that other authors have written in praise of poverty and old age, a special

me the manufacturing towns," he exclaims, "where everything goes free; those are the people to patronize my business or any other Business;—not the narrow minded fanatics. I don't care anything about saloons, but I notice where they are you will find the Best and most liberal People."

Not always inside the saloons, however; witness the following, only a week later, written from Niagara's "Mighty Falls:"

Group of Lodgers Before Wayfarer's Lodge, Boston

plea for the inevitable. Only two days before this pride in his newly wrought gentility I find him breaking out: "Why can't a gentleman just as well fix umbrellas as practice law; it is not the business that makes the man." And again: "A man may mend umberellas if he has brains to do it;" and again, "It is not the cloths that makes the man."

Similarly his enthusiasm for the country has its metes and bounds. The people are apt to be "very penurious and superstitious," and "Self-esteem is verry prominent in their craneums." "Give

"Last night after coming from my camp I droped into a saloon on the outskirts. It proved to be an Italian joint and there was a conglomerated mass of Human beings from all Nations. The negro was very prominent, all drunk and getting drunker. I just took a seat and took in the show, it beat any variety I ever saw, Polocks, Italians and Negroes kissing and Huging, fighting, shooting crap. You can judge the sights for Sunday."

Possibly he may have done something more than merely "look on." At all events, only a week earlier and in the very letter in which his personal indifference to saloons is avowed, after giving a detailed account of his receipts and expenditures, wherein it appears that he had made $3.25 in three days and spent $2.96 in two, he utters the following complaint: " Some way I can't save any. I made a quarter this morning as I came along—fixed a Parisol for an Italian lady—or else I would only have 4 cts. in my Pocket; " and then, with an attack of introspectiveness and candor not unworthy of Jean Jacques, comes the naïve confession, " I will haft to let up. I am drinking too much Beer. I don't drink anything else but I can spend a great deal of money on Beer."

Indeed, his only recorded collision with the majesty of the law is in this connection:

" As I was comeing along last night on the sidewalk," he adds, " I Run into a Bull. I had my arms full of Bundles, a tin Bucket, my tool Box, Bundle of Umberellas—I could not carry any more and I had about all the Beer I could well carry. I run my bundle of umberellas into the Bull's abdomen. He jumped to one side and says, ' What! Are you moveing? ' I told him yes, I was going out in the suburbs to rent a house."

This pacified the representative of the law, for " he laughed and said I would do to travel." He adds the assurance, which I can abundantly corroborate from many witnesses, " I can spend a great deal of money on Beer."

In another letter he tells of a street fakir whose acquaintance he made at Oswego, who, besides making him a " Preasant of a $5.00 Bill for my kindness," together with " different lots of his goods," " told me that he had Blowed fifty Bills last night "—denomination not stated—and " said if he made one thousand dollars per day he would Blow it."

No doubt! And I have numberless instances in my notebooks of the most surprising prodigality on the part of members of the tramp class, of which I have personally witnessed enough easily to believe anything they say, or that barkeepers and others have said to me about

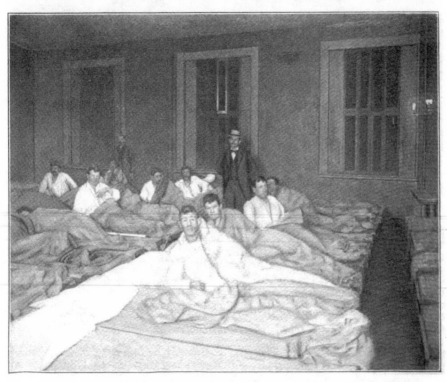

Rising, 5.30 A.M.—Wayfarer's Lodge, Boston

them in this respect. Here are a few of the entries: $180 spent in five days, $644 in five weeks, $200 in three or four weeks, $27 in three days, $40 or $50 in a week, $760 inside a week, $28 in a single evening; $125 in a night—$120 by the same person the next day, of which $100 to take a " friend's " earrings out of pawn and $20 for her sick mother. Here I find, reported from an institution, nearly $6,000 (back pension) within a month; $3,500 same source, same time—and cases of $500 or less, from the same institution—a Soldiers' Home—so common as to be labeled " small sums," and to excite no special remark.

Gambling, licentiousness and robbery account for the larger part of these expenditures, of course; but they also include a prodigious amount of drink. Of the above, for example, one item represents 125 quarts consumed by a party of six in an all night's carouse. Another of $28, represents a single evening's treating by a " bum," as related by the bartender. " Money is no consideration with them," he said. Forty glasses of beer has been frequently given as the approximate limit of their daily consumption on occasions, while it was once put as high as a hundred, " or may be two hundred." Absolute accuracy in the count was for the most part carefully repudiated, but understatement in such things is quite as common as the reverse.

My friend is intensely interested in all the political and economical questions of the day and writes out his views with great fullness. One day, in the summer of 1893, he " Met several H. B.'s—all of them was going East and all said times was verry Dull out West." Thereupon I wrote him: " What do you think of the rumors in the papers of the West and South seceding from the East?" To which he promptly replies:

" The money Barrons work to much to the interest of Europe. I don't blame the South and West: they are bound to have their Rights; the day has gone by that these two great Powers the South and West to be governed financially by the East. There is any amount of idle men through this country not more than one out of ten working."

He does not quite despair, however. " It is my opinion Congress will Remonetize silver and make every satisfactory Law for all parts of the U. S."

One night he found a barn, where he had previously been alone, occupied by " about twelve H. B.'s " and was not unnaturally " greeted with the Remark," when he " climbed up into the Mow," " Say, don't step on me! Be careful, I am over here," and so on. In fact he had " been at the free Theater;" it was "near twelve, midnight," and he had to pay the penalty by taking such accommodation as he could find. But there was compensation in the discussion he was privileged to hear:

" They got into quite a Political argument. Some of them were Democrats and some were Republicans; but the Democrats seemed to outnumber the Republicans. One advanced the Idea that the moneyed men and manufacturers of the country were all Republicans, and—he emphasized with an oath—they were so mad that Cleveland was elected and Democratic Congress that they shut down all the mills and closed all the Banks and took the money out of circulation to spite working men that voted the Dem. ticket; and the argument got warm at times. Some of them are very ignorant and it makes me tiard to hear them talk; others again are farely well informed on these subjects."

" My Ideas about the silver question are the same as Congressman Bland's of Mo. He spoke to the point last week in Congress. And my views on the Tarriff question is to let the Tarriff alone as it is; if it must be changed at all they should do so gradually not to throw the Country into a Panic By sudden changes of the Tarriff-laws. Of course the Democrats has made no laws as yet, but it is their threats and what their Platform purports to do that Has caused this presant stringency and Hard times." " It is all as plain as the Nose on a man's face,"

etc., etc.—much as we remember to have read in the eloquent speeches and able editorials of the period.

In December he writes about the tramp laws, condemning them as " an outrage on Humanity, worse than Barbarous; the chief fault being that they make no discrimination."

" There is a great deal of difference in Ho Bos—just as much difference as there is in Saciety in natural life. I am a H. B. but I don't Rob or Burglarize or murder. I am a gentleman when it is Necessary, and can make just as good an appearance in Society as any and a great deal better than some."

And to myself comes this improving admonition:

" Theory will do but Practice makes perfect.

I have had the Practical Knowledge but I know you have had nothing but a theoretical knowledge. Of course we differ. Can't Help it. I refer you to the Gov. of Kansas once a H. B. and (he) don't deny the fact. I am proud of what I have been through because I know there is know ordinary man could endure what I have. Our Reffermation is coming slowly and will come. I want the Wilson Tarriff Bill Passed. I think it is the best for the H. B.'s to get them something to eat and get somebody to work and down the Syndicates and Monopolies. They are worse than the H. B.'s."

His views at this time seem to have been tinged with a gloom not entirely of the season. For, having wearied of roaming three months before, he had established himself in a little repair shop in a Western city, sending me his printed card and advertisement, and the venture had not been a success. And he closes, accordingly, with the desperate cry:

"Let us all live, and we must live at all Hazards. I am going to bust up my shop. Can't stand the times. My landlord is a Presbyterian Preacher and his terms don't suit me, these times. Write soon to Gen. Deliv., Pittsburgh."

I think there was an inaccuracy as to the profession of the landlord, and I fear —in fact, I know—that something besides the tariff and the times had to do with his insuccess. Just what, my readers will conjecture.

"My opinion," he had once written me, "is the Government should be so managed as to have good times always;" and he here amplifies the precept, giving it, as he loves to do, Biblical sanction:

"You know my position. I am not a Radical. I want all to have their just dues, Rich, Poor and Ho Bos of all denominations; there is none Perfect, not one says Paul."

Two years later he develops this thought at considerable length in special reference to the tramp question. I wish there were room for the whole letter, but brief excerpts must suffice:

"I think and am of the opinion (I may be mistaken, I hope I am, but barely possible) that this country, loved America, is nearing a

Steaming Clothes, Wayfarer's Lodge, Boston

crisis in her history. If all the manufacturing plants in America and the mines and all improvements were Running full blast still there would be thousands of Idle people that could not get work. You say what is the cause?"

He states it to be (1) machinery; (2) immigration. The latter could and should be stopped. "I believe in the doctrine America for Americans." But "Machinery" is different; it "has come to stay and we will still have more machinery that will take the place of men or human Musel." He admits, it is true, that there are thousands of the unemployed that are worthless, that "won't work, and live from Begging or some criminal act." But, then, there are also "thousands that would work and lead an honorable life if they had the opertunity;" and the "crisis of our beloved America" will come in making laws to "seperate the honerable unemployed from the dishonerable unemployed."

"This is a problem in the 2d century of this U. S. existence for our Philosophers to Study out. They can fence in half a dozen Tramp farms in every state in this Union and it will avail nothing."

Because, through such undiscriminating treatment,

"Numbers of inocent will suffer with the guilty; and Holy Writ says that ninety-nine guilty should go free where one inocent man should be punished. I think the Holy Scriptures is the true foundation for all Laws of man."

And now for the remedy:

"My opinion is, the only way to solve the Problem is to Create a demand for mechanics and labor in this country and the Problem will solve itself and then all men found Beging and out of work the authorities can find them a job and the great Tramp and Ho Bo nuisance of the U. S. will be settled!"

Is not that simple?

In this letter he sets the number of the unemployed at two millions, and thinks:

"A large portion of America's population is drifting back to a nomadic life far worse than the native Red men of our Country, for they had a home of some kind but our present nomads have no place they call Home only a Friendly Box Car or the shade of a tree, and in winter Jails, Calibooses and Camp Fires."

This pessimistic view of Hoboism is, however, shaded off a bit on the very first page of the letter, where he tells me that, in spite of a long stretch of circus and "mush-fake" experience since his last, he "came into this city healthy."

"I think this nomadic life is a healthy life. I think if some of you Proffessors, students, etc., would live more of a nomadic life and feel the enjoyment of the fresh air more and take more good wholesome outdoor exercise and live more of a rough and tumble life you would enjoy better health and live longer."

In short, fewer of us "great, smart men" would die in the prime of life, and "mankind would enjoy your usefulness a much longer period."

"I was fifty years old last May, he déclares (1895) "and I feel as well as I did 20 years of age, with the exception of my wounds."

HARTFORD, CONN.

321

Increase of Tramping: Cause and Cure

VII

By Prof. John J. McCook

OF TRINITY COLLEGE

THERE seems little reason to doubt that vagabondage is increasing in the United States, and beyond the population rate.

My tramp correspondent for the past eight years, whose literary name is "Roaving Bill," thought there were 30,-000 tramps in Chicago alone at the time of the World's Fair in 1893, and I have no doubt that nearly all of them who could got there some time before it was over, for their curiosity is insatiable and they travel light. There were probably sixty-six or seven thousand on the road two years ago, and there are over fifty-six thousand now.

The only basis for an estimate of which I have any knowledge is the daily average of lodgers in the public lodging houses of Massachusetts, which, by the way, is in substantial agreement, during a course of twenty-three years, with the average shown by the census taken in these same houses on the nights of January and July first. By multiplying this by 3.58, which is the proportion between the public lodging places and all lodging methods given by the 1,349 tramps whom I studied statistically the winter of 1890-91, a guess can be made at the number in Massachusetts; and this, multiplied by the proportion between the population of Massachusetts and that of the United States, will give another guess at the total in the whole country.—Guess, you will observe!

In 1870 the daily average of lodgers in Massachusetts was 179.1, which means, at a rough guess, 641 tramps in Massachusetts and 26.5 times as many, or 16,001 in the United States. In 1880 the daily average was 461, indicating 1,650 in Massachusetts and 46,376 in the United States—an increase of 172.94 per cent., while the population increase was only 30.08 per cent., or not much more than a sixth as great.

The year 1890 showed a falling off from 1880 to 42,687 tramps, but the increase from 1870 was still two and two-tenths times as rapid as that of population.

The figures for 1899 have just been given me by the obliging deputy inspector of institutions in Massachusetts, Dr. Prentiss. They indicate 56,896 tramps in the United States now, which is a gain, since 1870, of 235.4 per cent.—three and four-fifths times that of population.

How account for this increase? My tramp friend, Roving Bill, is constantly urging in his letters that the greater proportion of the tramp population are not "professionals"—that most of them are men "out of work;" and thereto agree the representatives of those examined by me statistically seven years ago. Can there be anything in this? I must confess my earlier impressions were against the theory of any connection whatsoever between tramping and trade. But after getting together in tabular form the Massachusetts figures from 1870 I am inclined to a different view.

The most noticeable advances are in 1874 and 1894, where there was an increase, in a single year, of 75.1 and 63.9 per cent., respectively; and it will occur to every one that those were the years following the remarkable business panics of 1873 and 1893. In the former year the tramp army had swelled from seventeen to forty thousand, growing 136 per cent. in four years, or more than eleven times as fast as population; in the latter it had grown to 62,026, nearly four times as rapidly as population. Again in 1895, to speak of a period fresh in all memories, there was a further increase of 107 per cent., and it will be recalled that the business depression continued with increased severity that year. In 1896 there was a fall to about the point of 1894; and it will be remembered that in April, 1895, the tide in business turned. The improvement was short lived, however,

company had nearly a score of tramps. One of the officers, I will remark in passing, told me they made better soldiers than their non-tramp associates. "Know how to take care of themselves better out of doors, and more used to being ordered around," was his explanation. They "lighted out," he said, nearly all of them, after the first pay day. "But it was just to spend their money;" and they nearly all came back or were easily found, when the money was gone!

The rise of 40 per cent. observed in Massachusetts in 1878 and the fall of 77 per cent. in 1881 seem independent of

The Feast—Solids

and in 1897 there is a gain in tramps of about seven per cent., the change showing itself chiefly in the summer census, and being, therefore, synchronous with the reaction in business consequent upon the failure to realize that immediate improvement which had been predicted from a change in administration. From 1897 to 1898 there is a fall of four per cent., and 1899 shows a further fall of 11 per cent. Here again there is a period of business revival, marked in the first year and strongly accentuated the second. There is a war, too, which has offered attractions to a considerable number. I have knowledge of one company in a New England regiment largely recruited from this element. And another

industrial causes, but they may be accounted for, perhaps—the former by the great strikes associated with the well-remembered railroad riots; the latter by the rigorous tramp laws then newly adopted in that commonwealth.

But why should the tramp be especially liable to be affected by business depression? Probably most persons would reply: Because he is below the average in skill and intelligence. That does not seem to be the case, however. I have seen a great deal of many of them and can vouch for their average intelligence. And out of twelve of our chief employers of labor in Hartford, hiring in 1895 4,750 persons, mostly skilled hands, eight have, or have had drinking men and known tramps on their rolls, and three of the eight, representing 1,200 hands, assure me this class of men are at least up to the average in skill and brightness; and five, representing 2,800, say they are among their best men.

But the invariable habit of all these employers, so they tell me, is, when they have to reduce force, to drop first the drinker, second the indifferent or negligent workman, third good single men and last of all sober, industrious married men. The tramp, therefore, has a double chance to go, since he is almost never married and almost always a drunkard;

1870 and 1899 nearly four times as great as that of population.

I suppose it must be because a considerable proportion are all the time discovering that they like tramping better than the sedentary life. My correspondent, Roving Bill, after more than thirty years of it, has described himself at various times as " hale and hearty," " sassy," " healthier and stronger than he was at the beginning;" and it is plain that his settled view, in spite of occasional sentimental longings in the other direction, is in favor of the superior advantages of the nomad life. Most of us are kept

The Feast—Liquids

and inasmuch as thriftlessness is apt to go with his estate and his habits, the road is his prompt and only recourse. How prompt it is appears from the answers given, in the statistical inquiry above alluded to, to the detached questions: " How long since you had a job? " and " When did you take to the road? " which showed that the end of the job and the beginning of the tramp were virtually simultaneous in most cases.

But why does not the number of tramps shrink back to its former size on the return of prosperity? For it is a fact that, altho there are losses in eleven years out of the twenty-nine, in all the rest there is gain; and the whole series shows, as stated, an increase between

domestic because tradition, precept, religion, above all habit, persuade us that therein lies our only chance for virtue and happiness. Apparently when the charm is broken and one discovers that virtue can be dispensed with and that contentment can be had some other way, there are a great many who resign domesticity permanently.

Just so a horse is spoiled for the harness when he has once or twice successfully run away.

And this would suggest an obvious reflection that one way to abate the tramp nuisance would be to keep men from running away, or if we cannot do that, to whip them back into the traces just as speedily as possible. How? By interfering with their becoming drunkards; by encouraging or compelling thrift; by breaking up train-jumping; by stopping indiscriminate charity; by applying something like scientific principles to their reformation.

Thus far we have scarcely got beyond an impatient "Move on!"—for our tramp laws in the several States have been for the most part so fierce and panicky that after a year or two they have everywhere ceased to be enforced. What we need now is "Stop!"—all along the line and in sober earnest. These 50,000 men are costing us at least eleven millions a year and producing nothing—to say nothing of the disease and crime of which many of them are active centers. If reformatories are effective, as it appears they are, in seventy-five out of every hundred cases of ordinary felons, there is assuredly no reason why they should not be tried upon at least the younger among our tramp population.

Do methods distinctively religious deserve to be reckoned among the "scientific?" I think they do. At all events they show results that can be tabulated and estimated and where there is a plain connection, as of cause and effect, between instrumentality and outcome. Things are not altogether left dangling in the mid air of uncertainty here, or

relegated to the vagueness of an eternal hereafter, as some seem to think.

Thus, I have an authentic report from one institution which exhibits the following results in 206 cases:

24	have kept straight for 5 years and over.				
22	"	"	"	from 4½ to 5	years.
15	"	"	"	" 4 to 4½	years.
22	"	"	"	" 3½ to 4	years.
26	"	"	"	" 3 to 3½	years.
18	"	"	"	" 2½ to 3	years.
21	"	"	"	" 2 to 2½	years.
26	"	"	"	" 1½ to 2	years.
32	"	"	"	" 1 to 1½	years.

It is true that this is but a small percentage of the total number under treatment and that the confessed failures have been appallingly numerous; and it may be conceded that better results might have been secured by the use of different methods—there are always possibilities of this kind; but here are tangible results, and it is only necessary to multiply 206 by $200, the ascertained annual cost of this sort of people for arrest and maintenance, to see how important they are from the standpoint of dollars and cents.

A number of these men have found employment in the place and some of them have been traced by me with the following result:

One establishment has had seven for permanent places as salesmen, porters, clerks, etc.—four of whom were what I should call downright "bums"—and six more for temporary jobs. "None

The Feast—Solids and Liquids

have ever disappointed me," the proprietor says; and he always sends there when he wants a man. Another establishment has found them part good and part bad. A third has had a number and none of them have gone back. A fourth establishment has had one—it keeps him, tho he is not satisfactory. On the other hand, two other employers have tried in all from eighteen to twenty-seven of them and found them "thoroughly unsatisfactory."

This testimony is on the whole corroborative of the modest claims of the institution—much failure, much uncertainty, but definite success sufficient to pay for the effort and cost.

In the German labor-colony system much dependence is placed upon the religious element, and not in vain, tho I have been able to secure no claim of results from persons associated with the management more definite than the "hope" or "belief" that their effort had not been thrown away.

It would certainly surprise any merely "scientific" observer to visit any institution conducted on these lines. He would find appeal made to the immaterial parts almost exclusively—supernatural causes and appliances and precepts and results as much taken for granted as education, and drill and mechanical trades, and promotion and marks and punishment are in our institutions of the other sort.

I do not think either class of institution ignores the value of the other kind. And I am sure that there are multitudes of cases where the secular treatment is indispensable in order to secure that absolute segregation for a year or more which is required for the displacement of the old alcoholic nerve tissue and the enforcement of habits of industry, and which institutions purely religious are unable to enforce.

Might not the two methods, both justly entitled to the name scientific, be more thoroughly combined than heretofore? The mixed character of our population religiously is, perhaps, the greatest obstacle in the way, and we have here an additional motive for wishing its speedy disappearance.

"Roving Bill" has more than once addressed himself to the solution of the tramp problem. In March, 1896, he wrote me, after one of his customary blasts at the

"professionals, who have the indomitable cheek, dress so well that it is hard to distinguish them, commit all the low dastardly crimes, and for whom a reformatory is too good. There is another class of Hoboe that are getting very numerous in this country, in which a reformatory would be very useful; but they are like Black Birds—you could fill a reformatory and you would not miss the number: these are the boys from ten to twenty years old, and some of them are from respectable families; all such should be most emphatically be kept off the road and discouraged from such work. They drift into criminals of different kinds and professional Hoboes. They are the only kind it would be worth while to work with. As it would be a great undertaking to try to learn old Dogs new tricks."

In another place he speaks in a very uncomplimentary way of my friend Brockway, recently superintendent of Elmira, and on the whole, it seems to me, shows an aversion to anything like a general application of institutional treatment.

Another correspondent, a confirmed drunkard and vagabond and a thoroughbred of the young tough species, with whom I have had some very curious and interesting experiences, writes thus at Uintah, Utah, on his way back from a little trip to California:

"When you get your Reformatory finished I will either stop tramping, or fight shy of Connecticut, because you might get me in there and throw the key away."

I consider their avowals a valuable contribution to the settlement of that much debated question whether the State should try chiefly to punish its criminals, or to make them better. It should do both, and it can. For the thing most likely to cure is apt to be the thing most likely to hurt.

There are two broad planks in that part of "Roaving Bill's" platform which relates to the cure of vagabondage. I bring them together from different letters

"1. My opinion is the Government should be so managed as to have good times always."

"2. I think the General Government should furnish all idle men work of some kind, and compel all to work, or leave the country—transport them to some portion of Africa, or make them take the Whipping Post."

A striking program, certainly!

Leaves from the Diary of a Tramp
VIII
By Prof. John J. McCook
OF TRINITY COLLEGE.

THIS mention of Government interposition, for the cure of tramping, fairly introduces the subject of our friend's patriotism.

He is everywhere, and through everything a lover of his country. He pauses on his journey, for the Fourth of July, and records with great particularity the festivities in which he shared on that day sacred to memory. In a supplementary note dated O——, July 4th, 5 P.M., he writes, in a spirit of satiety, but not of disgust, I am sure:

"At Presant I am Sitting in my Room (in a hotel); can Hear Bands of music, but lend a deef ear as it Has become to familiar in the last few days."

Greater things than these had been his share. There had been processions, speeches, excursions, and, the crown of all,

"A Lady Pinned on to my Coat lapel a Boughka of Celuloid Rose and a Bough of the national Flag in Small sizes just under it, and I step around as Proud as any millionair. Why Not! I am no menial, I have made several friends amongst the Ladies!"

One in particular, of course.

And in his present abode he breaks out into this eloquent denunciation of drunkenness in uniform:

"I do abhor to see a man with the national uniform of this Republic on making a Hog of himself in plain view of the hordes of visitors. If they want to do so they should adorn themselves with the garb of Bums, not the Blue."

It only remains to show how this patriotism took a practical turn, and how he who had served his country as a soldier in 1861 stood ready to serve her in other capacities in 1897.

He was a life long Republican; had voted in Mississippi when his ballot " was the only Republican ballot in the box," and " I never sold my vote but once," he says, " and that was in the city of Chicago where some of the politicians offered me ten dollars to vote for —— " (the Democratic candidate). And for this momentary lapse there was abundant explanation;

"Now I did not care who was the Mayor of Chicago; it was of no importance to me, and the ten dollars was. I accepted the money and voted with them—and thousands of others done the same in Chicago on that day."

Still he had always drawn the line at Presidents:

"I would not sell my vote at the Polls of a Presidential election; I think to much of the Principles I fought four long years for, and spilt some of my Blood on Southern Battle fields."

And accordingly the recent campaign (1896) found him in line, with all previous leanings toward Mr. Bland, and Mr. Wilson, and the Kansas statesman and the silver-men thrown to the winds—a Republican, a Gold man and a McKinley man to the backbone. He writes to Mr. McKinley—and gets a polite answer. As the battle waxes hot he even appeals to me with the exhortation: " Give us a rousing majority in grand old Connecticut." " What all thinking and loyal people now want for the next four years is confidence and prosperity;" and he predicts that " Comrade McKinley will be elected by the largest majority that ever a President of this United States received."

The prediction was verified, and shortly after came the following:

"Nothing new here—the same old rotine. We are having winter now. I want spring to come, I want to get away from here. I think President elect M'Kinley will apoint me to some position; he writes verry favorable to me. By the way could you not help me some with him. I think I am worthy of something. I done considerable in last campaign and have done my part to maintain the government; don't you think so?"

I did think so, and hoped that his vacillation on the gold question and his occasional lack of perfect orthodoxy on the tariff issue might be overlooked, as in the case of many another statesman. Nevertheless I feared he would not get even a consulship, and tried to prepare him as well as I could for the probable result.

To turn from politics to the soil, here

is a description of a well known annual event by a participant therein:

"I was in this country two years ago during Hop picking. A great many Hoboes come here from all parts to pick hops and also all the town Bums from surrounding citties and some from New York Citty, Philadelphia; and all this country, or the hop country, is full of Bums and H. B's of all descriptions two and three weeks before hop picking begins, camping, sleeping in barns and all conceivable ways. Petticoat Bums or Bags are numerous as they can pick hops as well as anybody, some of them being experts, and the farmers' potato patches, Cornfields and orchards suffer, as all class of H. B's carry Cans and Kettles and Cook out of doors. The potatoes, apples, corn and other truck is in good condition for plucking, as hop picking takes place in September, and lots of prostitutes from surrounding citties; and every one that is idle, when hop-picking begins, the farmers take their teams and haul them out to their farms by wagon loads and pay their way out on the cars. They have to be harvested as quick as possible for some Reason and the more Hands the better; and a great many operatives in mills in surrounding towns and citties go out more for a holiday or recreation, in other words a Spree, during Hop picking; and every body has a good time, whiskey being one of the Principle ingredients and there is lots of it Punished during this time.

"Hop Dances are all the go every night, sometimes Sunday included. Some dances are Respectable; others are free and easy. One of the main pastimes on Sundays is carousing and drinking, as the numerous surrounding villages are full of saloons. I have seen drunken men and women scattered all over the fields, along Roads, in fence corners. Fighting is a pastime: Black eyes are numerous in both sexes.

"Hop picking generally lasts about three or four weeks and a great many leave Broke and get arrested on their way out in some of the towns. The farmers pay so much a box for picking. They feed the hands and furnish a sleeping place in their Barns, outhouses, wherever they can put up a bed. A great many sleep in the hay.

"From Hop picking I went to Albany, there got rid of all the money made in the hop country; then made my way to —— N. Y. and picked Grapes. This is simply a repetition of Hop picking: also Berry picking in Jersey and Southern Illinois. All the H. B's flock to these parts, both male and female, and have a good time. All the money earned goes for Bug juice, or whiskey, or 'Alka.' There is lots of H. B's follow these Pickings up every year and Has done it for years—both sexes.

"A great many H. B's gets a wife very sudenly about these times and build a shantie in the woods—keep house at times; the Union breaks up in a row, all House Hold goods are destroyed: Black eyes, sore Heads and may be an arest of both, three months in jail or work house. A number of these Clandestine Unions end in this way. After these Pickings are over All Hobos disapear. Nobody knows where the Haut Beau goes."

This testimony, both as to the participation of large numbers of tramps in these harvest festivals, and the temporary unions established on these and other occasions, has been abundantly confirmed by other wanderers. I wish it were possible to publish certain details given me by more than one of their number. Tho not exactly unacquainted with what goes on in "the world which amuses itself," I confess that I have been convicted thereby of practical ignorance. And I am sure more people will have to learn the same lesson before the requisite number can be stirred up to doing something in real earnest toward getting at two or three of the festering sores in our present social arrangements. If the most unchaste of all the brutes could speak I feel confident they would make no such revelation of deliberate, conscious, grossness, covering every age and both sexes, as have come to me from the lips of human beings, graduates from the school of vagabondage.

I now recall one fellow, blear-eyed, scrawny, shambling, unkempt, about as unattractive, one would say, as well could be, who somewhat sheepishly but firmly avowed that, however low in funds, he never lacked opportunity for *affaires du cœur*. And on my expressing by my manner my astonishment at his apparent attractiveness and my curiosity to know the source of it, he answered by the simple word, pronounced with a smile which intensified his ugliness—"Love!"

My friend, Roving Bill, too, in his vivid account of how he and a casual "silver fake" acquaintance captured Troy, remarks apropos to his conquest of some fair Helen there. "I am quite an Adonois." And he, too, is capable of a devout allusion: "I could have had a quarter this morning if it had not of been for yesterday's carousal. But I will trust in Providence for the future."

HARTFORD, CONN.

Leaves from the Diary of a Tramp

IX

By Prof. John J. McCook

OF TRINITY COLLEGE

TRAMPS are like travelers in general. Some recall only the pleasant things, some only the unpleasant; some forget nothing. To the first the life is all gay. A German tramp, recalling in a conversation with me his two or three "wanderjahre" in the Rhine valley, fairly drew in his breath with delight at the recollection of the delicious odor of the grape blossoms, and plainly regretted nothing. But a friend of his who had tried the same route, listening to his enthusiasm, shook his head doubtfully and expressed his complete satisfaction at being done with it all; and I have the written verdict of an American ex-tramp: " For genuine 18-carat misery commend me to tramping."

Roving Bill has moods corresponding with his experiences, which are highly contrasted. We have been witnesses of his all but ecstatic joy in the calm, sylvan retreat on a quiet Sunday morning in June, and of his unaffected content on the road when creature comforts abounded; but he is not insensible to the frequent miseries of his life, and now and then the " disease of longing " crops out.

After his New England tour, the mere sight of a Pennsylvania oil derrick delights him, and in the midst of old familiar surroundings he makes that heroic attempt at a settled business life the speedy and dramatic ending of which has already been recorded. " I am tiard of the road," he had said, " and am going to make a bold stand to hold out. I am sure that intemperance will not hold me back; " and again,

" I am getting tiard of Roaming around and I would be Happy indeed if I only had a permanent Home. I am satisfied I could apreciate a Regular Home, but will haft to do what God intends for me to do."

It is midwinter when he makes the new plunge back to trampdom, and no mere extracts can give the picture as it stands—to us pretty nearly all shadow— and to him plainly not all sunshine, in spite of his manifest contentment at his newly recovered liberty.

His first bulletin is dated January 15, 1894: " I am stoping by a camp fire to-day; to cold to travel." But he has " lots of company, and it is as good as a circus to hear the conversation ! "

February 2d he has: " Walked twenty miles through rain to F——; got there about 8 P.M., very cold, found the police station, got lodging that night. There was 32 bums in that station, and one night's stay was the limit." I wonder whether it smelled as some police stations do, and was as full of predatory insects, and the shouts and songs of drunkards as some that I know.

He had written me a long letter, but the rain of that tramp had soaked through everything and ruined the manuscript. But with patient industry he repairs the loss and hammers out eight closely written pages.

Then follows an itinerary of five days, aggregating 420 miles by rail and 96 afoot—one unbroken line of " blustering days; " herds of bums shivering by camp fires, marched to police stations, marched out to the corporate limits, fed sometimes —once in a hotel—sometimes going hungry; floundering through snowy roads, making long " jumps " in open freight cars; sleeping in brick yards, smoke houses, vacant dwellings, station houses.

Nevertheless, " most every house gave them something," the hobos told him, for " the people are very charitable." And even the law itself could abate its customary rigors, for in one place where two hours of stone breaking was customarily required for a night's lodging at the station, " I mended," he says, " an umbrella for a policeman and got relieved of my task."

And, finally, at the end of his pilgrimage was his old home, where he has a " brother and a married sister and a niece. You see I am at home there," he exclaims. " My dear mother lies buried here in Elm Grove Cemetery." His numerous relatives give him all their work. He seems likely to take root once more in his native soil.

But no. Before the letter is ended, he exclaims: " I don't know how long I will stay here—I don't think I will remain more than a month more." The boom was out of the town, business was dull— in fact, one reads it between the lines, life itself was stale and flat. The bird that had tasted freedom was not tolerant of the cage. And that very spring, so he tells me a year later, he was " with a circus for three months " and " had a great experience; " and then graduated into a woolen mill where he remained a while; then off to another similar job in another place, where he was " overseer of carding."

But he had had " a very bad cough during the winter," and " had done no tramping since leaving the circus." Moreover, this last venture had left him, he ruefully remarks: " As wealthy when I quit as when I commenced; " he had " got enough; " it was " about time to settle down somewheres." " Don't you think it will be a wise conclusion? " he asks. And then he straightway proceeds to tell me that he is negotiating for another job. " Superintendent of a woolen mill in C——, Tennessee ! "

For eighteen months, in fact, he left me in doubt whether he were in the old job or the new—whether I should hear from him next, if ever, as a smug capitalist, or a hobo; and only in September, 1895, was the suspense removed. Then came a letter from a city in Indiana inclosing a card, with gorgeous red, white and blue edge, whereon was inscribed his name, street and number. Concerning the happenings of the long interval of silence not a word was said. He was working in a canning establishment at $1.25 a day, but was to leave that the next day for a job on the iron work of a new building, where he said: " I think I will get better pay if I can do the work." And once more he tells me:

" I am getting tiard of romeing around. I have seen about all the Country it is possible to see and it would only be a repetition of scenery to go over the ground again; but if I should get out of work and Hard up I may go South. When I get out of work and financially Busted I think there is no other alternative only to take to the Road."

I fully expected from his very protest that the winter birds would have him for a companion on their yearly trip; I recalled his own happy words of earlier days, " The sun is just coming up; I will soon go down into the town, and they will hear my baritone voice in all the streets and in every nook and corner, ' Umbrellas and Parisols to mend, to mend ! ' "—and I pictured my friend once more in contact with nature, enjoying quiet industry with intervals of abundant repose in the midst of the trees and the flowers and the genial hospitality of the sunny South.

It was not so to be. He was next heard from in a comfortable home provided by the gratitude of a nation, where again, as usual, everything delighted at first, but soon palled, compelling at least two separate flights, for minor jaunts of a few hundred miles, followed by willing returns. From thence I have had frequent letters—the most recent dated October 17th. In many ways they are not as interesting as the ones from the road. He has established relations once more with a newspaper, and, according to his own testimony, is " getting considerable notoriety as a writer and a humorist." He even has " a free pass on the city street car lines."

But, in spite of all these bourgeois symptoms, the bird is again plainly beating against the bars, and how long they will hold him I cannot say.

But one of his letters has an inclosure which exhibits the old pathos of the road in such touching and striking fashion that I transcribe it almost entire. He has sent me other verses, but I cannot find

the slightest merit in them. Portions of this seem almost too good, but I have not been able to trace them to other authorship.

THE TRAMP'S SOLILOQUY.

And men are housed and in their place,
    In snug and happy rest,
Save the tramp, who walks with weary pace
    The highway's frozen breast.

His limbs that tremble with the cold,
    Shrink from the Comeing Storm;
But underneath his rugged fold
    His heart beats quick and warm.

He hears the laugh of those who sit
    In home's contented air,
He sees the busy Shadows flit
    Across the window's glare.

His heart is full of love unspent,
    His eyes are wet and dim;
For in those circles of content
    There is no room for him.

He clasps his hands and looks above,
    He makes the bitter cry:
" All are happy in their love,
    All are beloved but I ! "

Across the threshold streams the light
    Expectant o'er his track;
No door is opened in the night,
    To bid him welcome back.

Our frames are worn and little worth,
    And hard our rugged hands;
We struggle for our hold on earth
    With the storms of many lands.

Say that we curse if you will,
    That the tavern and harlot possess our gains,
On the surface floats what we do of ill,
    At the bottom the manhood remains.

I wash my hands, I bathe my brow;
    I see the sun on hill and plain.
The old allegiance claims me now,
    The old content returns again.

One of his poems is entitled an " Ode to Soldier's Beer." Acknowledging a printed paper of mine on " Pauperism and Whisky," he is good enough to say that " the facts cannot be denied; " and then he adds: " I myself am not much of a whisky drinker. My favorite drink is ale or beer." But, " I no longer partake so much of any kind of drink as I use to in former years," and " sometimes, I think, I will make up my mind to let it alone entirely,"—which he is sure he could easily do—" It would be no trouble or discomode me in the least."

However, he makes this admission: " It has in my life and experience caused me a great deal of trouble and bitter experiences; " and then he gives the following bit of biography: " My first experience in drinking was after my enlistment in the army. My mother was a great temperance advocate. and said many a time she would rather follow one of her boys to his grave than to see him come home drunk ; but she saw it before she died, and it nearly broke her heart. I often think of her and her teachings in my lonely hours."

Let no one be surprised at these tender reminiscences. Men rarely break entirely loose from them. Listen to any mission speaker in the slums and you will find that " home " and " mother " are his *pièces de résistance:* when he wishes to be sure of making a hit he falls back upon them. And the favorite songs and hymns of these nomadic folk look the same way. I once heard a drunken tramp in the Hartford police station singing at the top of his voice: " Where is My Wandering Boy To-night? " And he paused for a moment at the close of the refrain, lowered his head, and soliloquized: " In jail; " then started again with what sounded like a little quaver in his voice, tho it may have been only a fancy of my own:

" Once he was pure as the morning ‹ ew
As he sat on his mother's knee."

. But three years earlier our friend was more explicit in his admissions. Just after the Fourth of July celebration I had written him as follows:

" Your postal card of July 6th leads me to suppose that you may have met with one of those sudden vicissitudes incident to the life which you are following and I have guessed that experiences similar to those of Troy, some time ago described by you, may have been at the bottom of it. In a word, that you may have been celebrating the Fourth of July and your prosperity by drinking more than was good for you—with all that that usually implies. I am curious to know whether my conjecture is correct."

And, four days after, he replied:

" Yes, sir! Your conjectures were correct to a certain extent. I was exceedingly prosperous on the 3d and 4th inst. I met and

made many good friends through my Patriotism and devotion to my Native Land. And in other ways I no doubt partook to freely of the flowing Bowl. Yet at the same time keeping my equalibraum. . . . I am verry quite and gentlemanly in such a state."

And in this connection it is comforting to be reminded how rich and poor may meet together with one only law for all, spite of what we sometimes hear : " I always make friends with police officers," says " Roaveing Bill ; " " I have had them when I got a little too much, to take me to my hotel." And we shall not question his further statement: " One cause of my misfortune and poverty at times is my liberality and Big Heart ! "

A few weeks later he is still more explicit and sweeping: " As you say all that are Hard up now have been intemperate, or to lavish in some way.'"

And I have before me the written opinion of another, younger than Bill and less widely traveled, albeit no mean authority in matters of the road. It was given one Sunday afternoon when he had called with the apparent purpose of displaying his prowess at begging. He entered my library, reeling under the double weight of alcohol and a bundle of clothes. He threw the latter down on the floor before me much as a cat lays a mouse at the feet of its mistress, with a " See there ! " and a look of pleased but embarrassed pride: " What the —— I'll do with them *I* don't know," he exclaimed.

And sure enough ! There were two pairs of flannel shirts, three of drawers, four of socks, one vest, five neckties, and an excellent pair of patent leather shoes, all " bummed " from a " mechanic " who had given them to him in order that he might have " a front " wherewith to apply for work in a factory. And only the day before he had brought another parcel, secured in the same way, and containing: One black suit, complete ; one black coat and vest ; one pair light trousers; one black derby hat : one brown hat ; one pair russet colored shoes ; two suits of underclothes ; three shirts ; two pairs of socks ; four handkerchiefs, and one roll of neckties—all second hand but in good condition.

His load of alcohol, according to his own statement, was: Ales, six ; whiskies, two ; gin, one pint.

As he sat blinking and talking in his

bright, drunken way—he has an excellent mind—I suddenly asked him: "When are you going to brace up. N——?"

He looked at me steadily, and then replied in a fashion that seemed to me so striking that I presently asked him to write it down. And here it is, the steadiness and clearness of the chirography testifying at once to his business training and to the persistency with which acquired gifts assert themselves:

" WHERE THERE IS HONEY THERE ARE BEES
" WHERE THERE IS BEER THERE IS BUMS.
" N. E.
" Hartford, March 22nd, 1896."

With which, and an aphorism from our peripatetic philosopher, in whom I at least have come to see much that is to be pitied and to be loved, as well as condemned, I will close:

" But such is Human nature and it is Hard to remedy."

SEQUEL.

Since the last of these words were written my foreboding has proved true. The bird left the cage; tried the road once more; again and still again sought the quiet of one of those retreats to which his wounds entitle him—and again left it.

Then came a long period of commonplace industry—so long that letters became rare, brief and dull; so long that I once more said, and this time with all but conviction: "He is cured of it!"—followed, must I confess it? with a half sigh for what had disappeared from his life—and mine!

Then, one bright summer day, came a postal card, in pencil, in the well-known hand:

" TAHLAQUAH, INDIAN
" TERRITORY, July 1, 1901.
" You will no doubt be surprised, this is a good country, good crops, plenty of everything, fine spring watter. I am going into Oklahoma and the Comanche nation. May marry and get some land Can't tell, hope you are well, I am fat and hearty. Yours
" R. W."

This has been followed by letters dated July 29 and August 20. The first gives an account of his attempt to " get a slice from Uncle Sam's domains."

" As there is only thirteen thousand chances and some of them verry poor and there was over 160,000 registered, I am of the opinion that the chances would of ben better if the money had been bet on some crap game or country horse race instead of being invested in Uncle Sams' lottery scheme."

Moreover, the thermometer had been standing 108 in the shade and, although it was the Fourth of July, he " had been drinking excessive quantities of the alkali water they was selling at 25 cents per bell," and " took the fever;" " I think," he says, from said " drinking." Furthermore, extended experience had taught him that the Indian Territory was not up to his first impressions: " It is one hundred years behind the States in improvements and civilization generally."

But, notwithstanding all these painful disillusions, an air of cheerful philosophy pervades this Neosho, Newton County, Mo., letter, that is sadly lacking in the next, which is headed " On the Road Walking," and written " Sunday, near Boston, Mo." He had been passing a week at " a soldiers' reunion in Jasper County," along with old Union comrades, " an old Confed, with one leg, spoke "— and he had " had a good time."

I am told that reaction is not altogether unknown, after times called " good," and that one symptom of this reaction is political gloom. However that may be, there is the suddenest kind of an explosion in this instance: " And you folks wonder why there is Tramps," he snarls. " You are not educated up to the causes of all these social plagues. You will be in time." And to the very last word he sustains this high standard of pessimism. He disapproves of legal measures for regulating strikes and strikers and, alluding to the Tampa episode, cries out: " Ye gods! What a picture for an intelligent nation to stand and view with calmness. A nation which bosts of being the freest and most democratic of any nation on Earth. All now is dead calm. But in the words of McCullough, the tragedian, in his great character, Virginius, It is calmness born of sullen determination. For years a steady undercurrent of Unrest has been flowing through all those that are not millionares or hundreds of thousand people through the tyranny of the aforesaid class. Labor and all the common people are now so strong as to be almost

PROF. JOHN J. McCOOK

uncontrolable and threatens to burst forth and engulf the world in Chaos.

" The storm is upon us."

Then he reverts with bitterness to the Oklahoma lottery, quotes Mr. Bookwalter, of Ohio, in behalf of the prediction that a " World wide war is comeing between the centres of wealth and the common people and that it is comeing first in the U. S." Then he gives us this picture on his own account:

" There is a half million Nomadic helthy tough Ho-Bos in America. If I had them organized equiped and disciplined they would make the grandest army that ever shouldered a gun and would be invincible. I would have no trouble in getting them transportation they would beat their way and subsist at the back doors of towns they passed through."

Then he deals a blow at the property clause in the new Virginia constitution, and another at the editor of an " Arkansaw paper," for a patriotico-optimistic utterance about what he himself has not scrupled elsewhere to call " our beloved America."

" His paper shows that it is not equiped for decent printing and if he does not know his own buis it is not likely that he knows much of social philosophy. But he does verry well to back up the Capitalists. They do not need to know much."

And with that contemptuous remark and these views tinged with a melancholy so foreign to his average nature he closes, promising " more anon."

I have written to him, as he requests, to Sedalia, Mo., and asked him whether it has occurred to him what would happen to his Army of Tramps if a train of wagons laden with free beer were to be sent to meet them.

And I shall hear from him promptly, I have no doubt, and confidently expect to find him once more in his earlier and more cheerful mood.

THE END.

HARTFORD, CONN.

List of Illustrations

Unless stated, all illustrations are used (with permission) from Connecticut Landmarks.

Acknowledgments

First of all, thank you to Jessica Parfrey (and everyone at Feral House) for believing in this project, for being willing to field my many questions, and for always saying 'yes' when I asked for yet more images. It has been a pleasure and a privilege to work with you.

My thanks to Landmarks, especially Erin Farley and Jocelyn Weaver, for letting me use this material and for providing the high-quality photographs that appear in this book. I must also thank Yale University whose microfilm copy of the letters provided the basis for this transcription. Bill Landis was especially helpful.

I am deeply grateful to Jenny Adamthwaite for her excellent work transcribing these letters. Roving Bill's handwriting is appalling, so the job was much harder than a normal transcription assignment. Thank you for your diligence, good humor and friendship.

Thank you to James Morgans and family for your willingness to provide me with biographical information about your ancestor, William Aspinwall. James also read and provided useful corrections to my Introduction, for which I am very grateful. It has been a huge pleasure to correspond with you from across the pond.

Finally, my thanks to Katie Dorr for putting up with me blathering on about a nineteenth-century hobo that almost no one had heard of, and for being willing to read drafts of the Introduction. You have my warmest and deepest love.

ISBN: 9781627311229

Transcription by Jenny Adamthwaite

Roving Bill Aspinwall is part of the Tramp Lit Series
for Feral House. For further information on these
titles, see www.feralhouse.com

Feral House
1240 W Sims Way #124
Port Townsend WA 98368

Designed by Unflown | Jacob Covey

Printed in the USA